GREENWOOD
G U I D E S

THE GREENWOOD GUIDE TO
NEW ZEALAND

hand-picked accommodation

We have aimed this book specifically at those travellers who want independence of movement, but also a measure of reassurance that they will get the best out of their holiday and be well looked after wherever they choose to go.

We have spent now some 7 years in New Zealand and published 5 previous editions. The 6th comes out in September 2009. During that time we have whittled down the myriad of possible places to stay until finally we were left with just those that we deemed truly exciting, fun, unusual, interesting, rewarding etc. Anything humdrum or half-hearted we have left out.

We have personally visited and chosen each place to stay for its exceptional character and genuine friendliness. These are the places that we ourselves would choose to return to on holiday.

To order a copy

If you would like to order any books, please fill in the coupon and send it with payment to Greenwood Guides, 12 Avalon Rd, London SW6 2EX. Payment can be made by UK cheque made out to 'Greenwood Guides Ltd', or by Visa/Mastercard. We will not process payments until the book is sent out.

THE GREENWOOD GUIDE TO
NEW ZEALAND
Fifth Edition 2008/9

hand-picked accommodation
things to do and places to eat

Order form

	copy(ies)	price (each)	subtotal
THE GREENWOOD GUIDE TO SOUTH AFRICA **Hand-picked accommodation** (latest edition)			
THE GREENWOOD GUIDE TO NEW ZEALAND **Hand-picked accommodation,** (latest edition)			
post and packing costs			
£2 per order in the UK or South Africa			
£3 per order within Europe			
£4 per order elsewhere		**Total**	

Name ....

Address to send the book to ....

....

....

....

Payment is by UK sterling cheque made out to 'Greenwood Guides'

or by VISA/Mastercard (only)

Card number

Expiry date

CCV number

Please send this coupon to
12 Avalon Rd, Fulham, London, SW6 2EX, UK

simon@greenwoodguides.com

First published in 2000 by Greenwood Guides,
12 Avalon Rd, London SW6 2EX, UK.

Eighth edition

Copyright (c) June 2009 Greenwood Guides

Simon Greenwood has asserted his right to be identified as the author of this work.

ISBN 978-0-9551160-4-9

Printed in China through Colorcraft Ltd., Hong Kong.

THE GREENWOOD GUIDE TO
SOUTH AFRICA
AND NAMIBIA
hand-picked accommodation

Including Phophonyane Lodge in Swaziland
and Malealea Lodge in Lesotho

eighth edition

www.greenwoodguides.com

Acknowledgements

Series Editor: Simon Greenwood

Writing collaboration and inspections: Phil McGee, Emily Elgar, Giles Milburn (South Africa), Lily Yousry-Jouve (Namibia).

Map data provided by Collins Bartholomew Ltd.

Production, DTP and Design: Tory Gordon-Harris and Jo Ekin

Printing: Colorcraft, Hong Kong

UK Distribution: Portfolio, London

SA Distribution: Quartet Sales and Marketing, Johannesburg

Cover photo courtesy of Whalers Way at Churchaven, entry number 60. Photo by Mark Williams. Cover design and digital manipulation by Tory Gordon-Harris.

Back cover photos from left to right courtesy of Dusk to Dawn (entry number 261), Lukimbi Safari Lodge (entry number 317) and Naries Namakwa Retreat (entry number 290).

Title page courtesy Whalers Way at Churchaven, entry number 60, photo by Mark Williams

Province intro images as follows:

Western Cape, Cape Town Side Dishes, KwaZulu Natal, Free State & Lesotho, North-West Province, Swaziland, Limpopo Province and Namibia by Jamie Crawford; Eastern Cape (Black Oystercatchers) by Peter Chadwick; Northern Cape courtesy Naries Namakwa Retreat, entry number 290; Gauteng and Soweto by Tina Hillier; Mpumalanga courtesy Lukimbi Safari Lodge, entry number 317.

The Team

Simon Greenwood on
Stiffkey Marsh

Phil Mcgee at Lake Atitlan

Mike Munro

Emily Elgar in Fish Hoek

Giles Milburn in Fish Hoek

Contents

Symbols
and what they mean

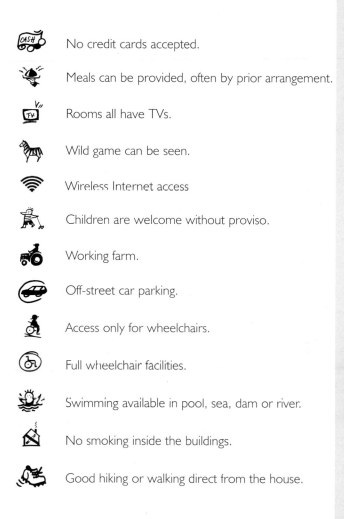

No credit cards accepted.

Meals can be provided, often by prior arrangement.

Rooms all have TVs.

Wild game can be seen.

Wireless Internet access

Children are welcome without proviso.

Working farm.

Off-street car parking.

Access only for wheelchairs.

Full wheelchair facilities.

Swimming available in pool, sea, dam or river.

No smoking inside the buildings.

Good hiking or walking direct from the house.

Introduction

This year marks the Greenwood Guides' tenth anniversary. Already! South Africa was our first country and we started hunting for great places to stay in the dying days of the last millennium. I cannot actually remember now why, since we were based in London, we picked South Africa as our first country, but I am very glad we did. It was then - and still is - a wonderfully positive place for a brand-new business to cut its teeth and it was the start of a great relationship with the country for me personally. The South Africans are an incredibly hospitable and supportive bunch... of each other, of their guests (those of you who have been before may well be returning for this very reason), and also of new enterprise. And it is truly a pleasure, when I look down the list of this year's entries, to see so many who have been with us since that first edition.

I receive a great deal of mail from travellers, which I encourage. It gives us a good idea of how our choices are being received out there in the field. And since we live or die on the happiometer of our travellers, i.e. you, then this info is vital.

We have made genuine human hospitality our common denominator rather than the sterile but safe judgement of a place's worth according to its facilities. We do not therefore distribute stars or tiaras. A place is either right for the guide or it isn't. Beyond that each traveller will need to look at location, rates and exactly what sort of place it is and make their own decisions.

First and foremost we assess the people running the accommodation and choose only those for whom looking after others, whether they be friends, family or paying guests, is a natural pleasure. Taste, furnishings, facilities, views, food, beds, bathrooms... all these things are important too, but only if they are provided by friendly people.

Thank you for choosing our guide. We do put in an enormous amount of effort each year, revisiting each place each edition, weeding out places that have lost their energy - as often happens in the world of accommodation - and sounding out all the new great, good and ordinary places that open each year. The standard rises continually in South Africa and this does mean that new places emerge at the top and old places drop off the bottom too. We seriously recommend therefore that you make sure that this is a latest edition of the guide. It is published annually in June.

As I always say, we would be delighted to hear from you when you get back from your travels.

NEW THINGS: SIDE DISHES

This year we have decided to publish a diverse collection of extra non-accommodation recommendations for you, steering clear of anything large and obvious that you would find in any major guide-book to South Africa (such as Kirstenbosch or Table Mountain). Instead, the restaurants, maverick shops, activity organisers, festivals and markets that we have included are almost all small, owner-run and perhaps not hugely well advertised, especially if you are coming to South Africa from overseas. We have called them Side Dishes for good or ill. Not every area of South Africa is well represented and clearly these recommendations are just a drop in the ocean. But we saw no reason to keep them from you....

All come highly and personally recommended by Mike Munro (resident South African and ex-GG guesthouse owner) who is the editor of this section of the book... and is also the GG lifestyle guru. Above all, we have selected according to the people in charge of each establishment. Owners should be professional and charming in equal measure. Most of these people spend too much time cooking or surfing or searching for meerkats to concern themselves too much with the marketing of their businesses.

We would be very interested to hear what you thought of any of these recommendations if you get a chance to try them out? Or if you want to recommend to us any other restaurants or activity organisers that you think would fit the bill (small, very friendly, a bit different, fab food but great atmosphere too, a great day out, not well known etc), do please drop me or Mike an email when you get home, if you can muster the energy.

You will find the Side Dishes at the beginning of each geographical area.

simon@greenwoodguides.com
mike@greenwoodguides.com

SOME INFO ON TRAVELLING WITH THIS BOOK IN SOUTH AFRICA
(There is a separate introduction for Namibia before the start of the Namibian section.)

ARRIVAL
Make sure that you have two clear pages left in your passport. I am told that they are very strict about this and it would be a crazy way to be refused entry.

DRIVING
There is nowhere in South Africa that would make a 4-wheel drive a necessity. However make sure you confirm this issue if booking into Namibian places.

CAR HIRE
Make sure that you have considered the amount of daily mileage your car hire company gives you. 100km or even 200km a day is virtually nothing and the final cost can be far higher than you estimated. Try and work out roughly what distances you will be covering and ask for the correct daily allowance. Or ask for unlimited mileage. There is usually a surcharge for taking your car across the border from SA into other countries.

N.B. Also make sure you are insured to drive the car on dirt roads.

We highly recommend Allen's Car Hire, 417 Main Rd, Kirstenhof, Cape Town for local trips to and from Cape Town on 021-701-8844, abradley@mweb.co.za, www. allenscarhire.co.za. They are very friendly and helpful and we use them ourselves. Airport pick-ups and drop-offs no problem.

MOBILE/CELL PHONES
Airports all have shops that provide mobile phones. They are invaluable and we recommend that you get one. You can buy a cheap handset or just rent one for the duration of your stay and then pay for calls as you go with recharge cards.

TELEPHONE NUMBERS
The numbers printed for entries in SA or Namibia in the book are all from within South Africa or Namibia.
To call South Africa from the UK dial 0027 then drop the 0 from the local code.
To call Namibia from the UK dial 00264 then drop the 0 from the local code.
To call the UK from South Africa you now dial 0044 - it used to be 0944 but this changed recently.
Another change is when dialing a local number you now always have to dial the full number including the area code.

TORTOISES
Look out for tortoises. They are slow, but seem to spend a lot of time, completely against the tide of advice put forward for their benefit, crossing roads.

TIPPING
• In restaurants we tend to give 15%.
• At a petrol station my policy is to give no tip for just filling up, 3 rand for cleaning the windows, and 5 rand for cleaning the windows and checking oil and water. If you really don't want the attendant to clean your windows you need to make this a statement when you ask for the petrol… or they will often do it anyway.
• At a guest-house I would typically give R30 per person staying for up to two nights. If you are staying longer than two nights then you might feel like adding more. If there is obviously one maid to whom the tip will go then give it to her direct. If there are many staff members who will be sharing the tip then give it to your host.

THE GARDEN ROUTE
Many people imagine, not unreasonably, that the Garden Route is a bit like a wine route where you can go from garden to garden, smelling roses and admiring pergolas and rockeries. Not so. The Garden Route is so named for its lushness and greenery.

The area is covered in forests and rivers, which spill into the sea. And, although many people there surely do have lovely gardens, the name is a little misleading. A fantastic area for walking though.

TIME OF YEAR

I got in a bit of a tangle in the first edition trying neatly to package up what is really quite complicated. So I will limit myself to one observation. It seems to me that most Europeans come to South Africa in January, February and March to avoid their own miserable weather and write taunting postcards home from a sunny Cape.

However, the very best time of year to visit the Northern Cape, Mpumalanga, Limpopo, North West Province, KwaZulu Natal and the Karoo, i.e. the whole country except the southern Cape, is from May to October. The air is dry and warm, game viewing is at its best and there are fewer tourists keeping the prices higher.

PAY FOR ENTRY

We could not afford to research and publish this guide in the way we do without the financial support of those we feature. Each place that we have chosen has paid an entry fee for which we make no apology. It has not influenced our decision-making about who is right or wrong for the guide and we turn down many more than we accept. The proof of this is in the proverbial pudding. Use the book and see for yourself. It is also very hard for us to write up a place that we are not enthusiastic about.

THE MAPS SECTION

The maps at the front of the book are designed to show you where in the country each place is positioned and should not be used as a road map. There are many minor and dirt roads missing and we recommend that you buy a proper companion road atlas.

Each place is flagged with a number that corresponds to the entry number below each entry.

Some have complained that it is hard to find detailed road maps of South Africa in the UK, so I suggest you buy one at the airport when you arrive in SA. Or try Stanfords in London on Long Acre in Covent Garden, 020-7836-1321.

CANCELLATION

Most places have some form of cancellation charge. Do make sure that you are aware what this is if you book in advance. Owners need to protect themselves against no-shows and will often demand a deposit for advance booking.

PRICES

The prices quoted are per person sharing per night, unless specifically stated otherwise. Every now and then complications have meant we quote the full room rate. Single rates are also given.

We have usually put in a range within which the actual price will fall. This may be because of fluctuating prices at different times of year, but also we have tried to predict the anticipated rise in prices over the book's shelf life. Obviously we cannot know what will happen to the value of the rand and prices might fall outside the quoted range.

Most game lodges quote an all-in package including meals and game activities.

Although South Africa has become substantially more expensive since the first edition of this guide came out 10 years ago, it is still great value on the whole. The value-for-money increases significantly the more off-the-beaten-track you wander.

CHILDREN
We have only given the child-friendly symbol to those places that are unconditionally accepting of the little fellows. This does not necessarily mean that if there is no symbol children are barred. But it may mean chatting with your hosts about their ages, their temperaments and how suitable a time and place it will be. Most owners are concerned about how their other guests will take to kids running wild when they are trying to relax on a long-anticipated holiday… from their own children. Places that are fully child-friendly are listed in the activities index at the back of the book.

DISCLAIMER
We make no claims to god-like objectivity in assessing what is or is not special about the places we feature. They are there because we like them. Our opinions and tastes are mortal and ours alone. We have done our utmost to get the facts right, but apologize for any mistakes that may have slipped through the net. Some things change which are outside our control: people sell up, prices increase, exchange rates fluctuate, unfortunate extensions are added, marriages break up and even acts of God can rain down destruction. We would be grateful to be told about any errors or changes, however great or small. We can always make these edits on the web version of this book.

DON'T TRY AND DO TOO MUCH. PLEASE.
It is the most common way to spoil your own holiday. South Africa and Namibia are huge countries and you cannot expect to see too much of them on one trip. Don't over-extend yourself. Stay everywhere for at least two nights and make sure that you aren't spending your hard-earned holiday fiddling with the radio and admiring the dashboard of your hire car.

PLEASE WRITE TO US
Our email address is simon@greenwoodguides.com for all comments. Although we visit each place each edition many of the places featured here are small, personal and owner-run. This means that their enjoyability depends largely on the happiness, health and energy of the hosts. This can evaporate in double-quick time for any number of reasons and standards plummet before we have had a chance to re-evaluate the place. So we are also very grateful to travellers who keep us up to date with how things are going. We are always most concerned to hear that the hosting has been inattentive.

OTHER GREENWOOD GUIDES
We also have a guide to New Zealand, which is available in bookshops or by emailing us direct or mailing us the order form at the front of this book. The Greenwood

Guides to Canada and Australia are available at www.greenwoodguides.com only.

THANKS
So that's about it for another year. My great thanks this time to Phil, Emily and Giles for all their efforts in researching and updating this 8th edition of the guide. And a huge thank-you to Mike Munro who wears so many hats in the GG colours!

I hope that this book will be seen as the main reason why you enjoyed your holiday as much as you did. Please feel free to write to me with praise or criticism for individual places that you visit at simon@greenwoodguides.com. And have a look at www.greenwoodguides.com before you set off.

Simon.

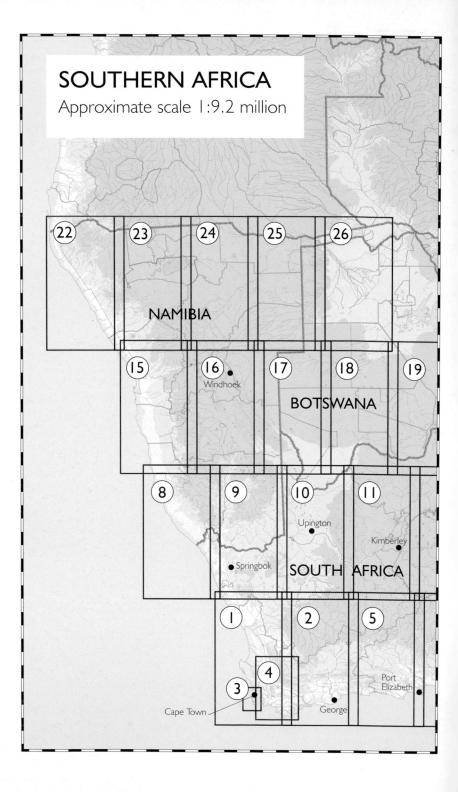

SOUTHERN AFRICA

Approximate scale 1:9.2 million

22

23

24

25

26

NAMIBIA

15

16
Windhoek

17

18

19

BOTSWANA

8

9

10
Upington

11
Kimberley

Springbok

SOUTH AFRICA

1

2

5

Port
Elizabeth

4

3
Cape Town

George

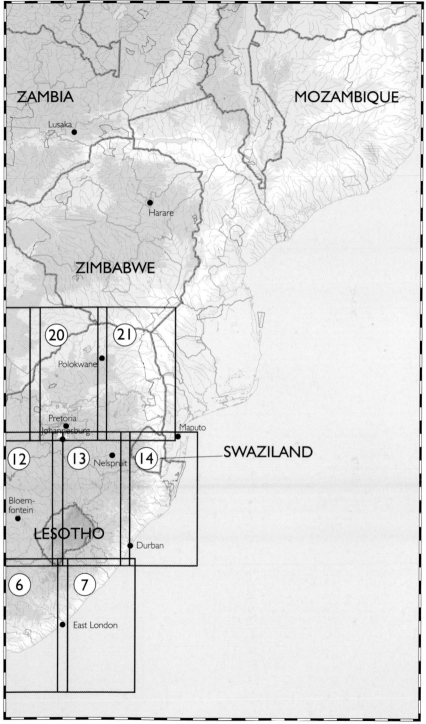

ZAMBIA

Lusaka

MOZAMBIQUE

Harare

ZIMBABWE

20   21

Polokwane

Pretoria
Johannesburg

Maputo

SWAZILAND

12   13   Nelspruit   14

Bloem-
fontein

LESOTHO

Durban

6   7

East London

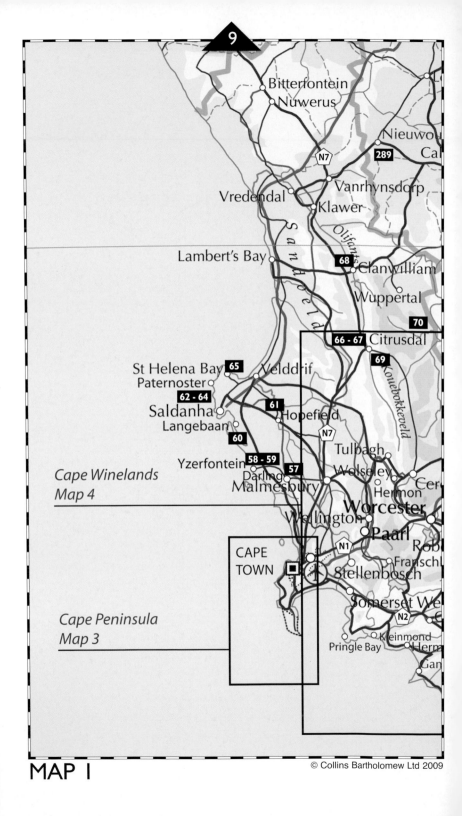

MAP I

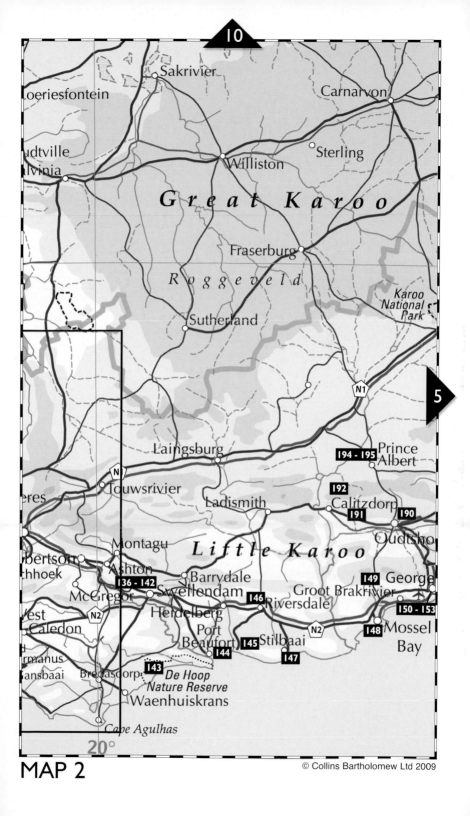

Loeriesfontein

Sakrivier

Carnarvon

udtville
lvinia

Sterling

Williston

Great Karoo

Fraserburg

Roggeveld

Karoo
National
Park

Sutherland

N1

Laingsburg

Prince
Albert

194 - 195

192

Touwsrivier

Ladismith

Calitzdorp

191

190

eres

Montagu

Little Karoo

Oudtsho

bertson
hhoek

Ashton

136 - 142

Barrydale

Swellendam

146

Riversdale

Groot Brakrivier

149

George

McGregor

150 - 153

est
Caledon

N2

Heidelberg

Port

Stilbaai

148

Mossel
Bay

rmanus
ansbaai

Beaufort

144

145

N2

147

Bredasdorp

143

*De Hoop
Nature Reserve*

Waenhuiskrans

Cape Agulhas

20°

MAP 2

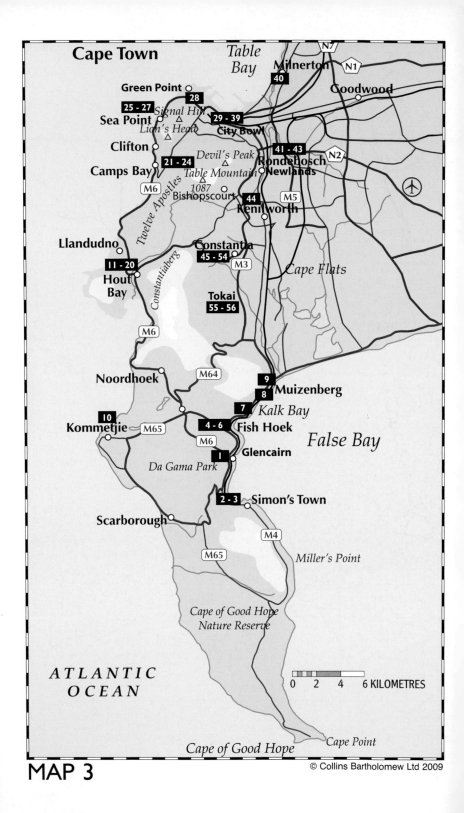

MAP 3
© Collins Bartholomew Ltd 2009

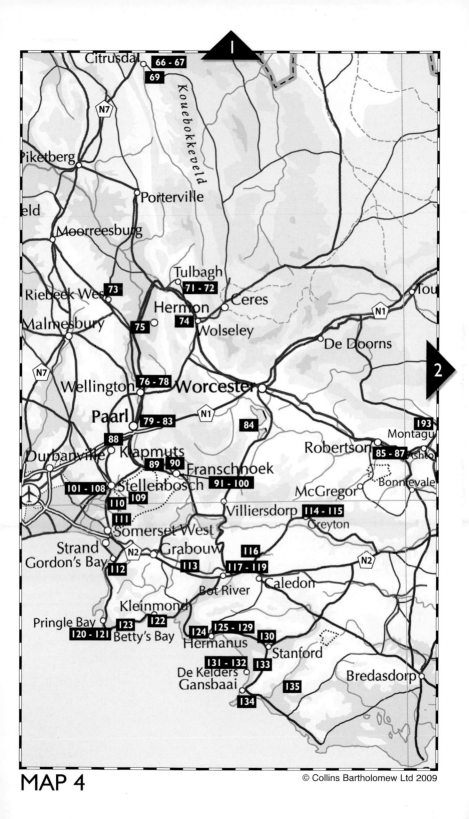

MAP 4

© Collins Bartholomew Ltd 2009

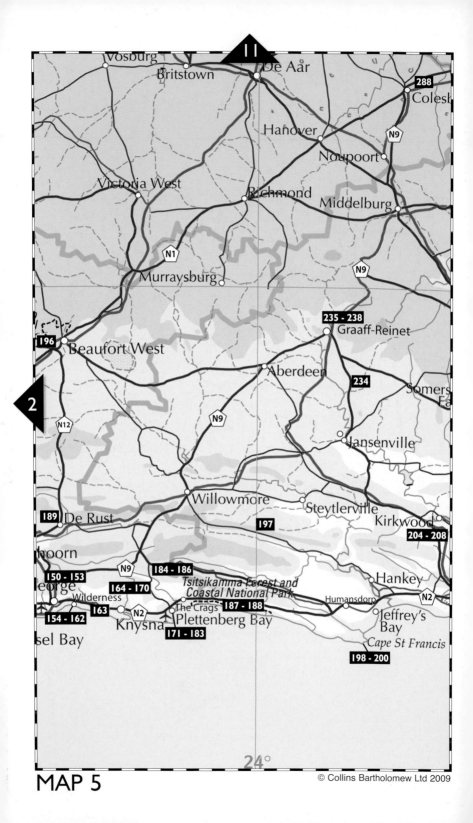

MAP 5

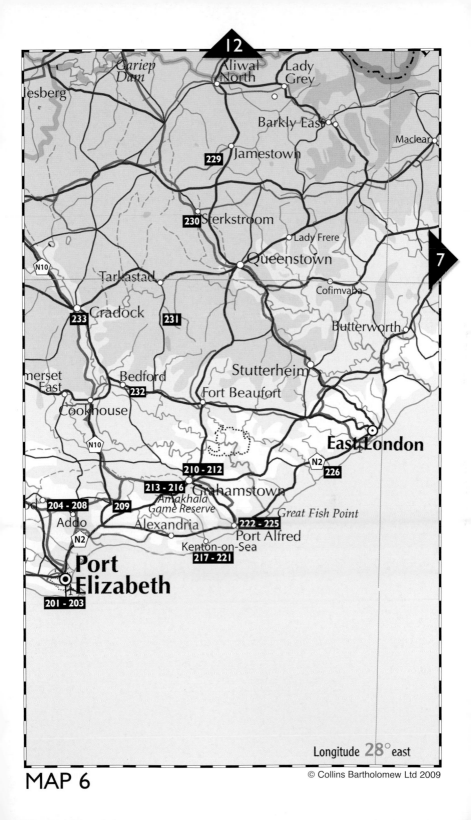

MAP 6

Longitude 28° east

© Collins Bartholomew Ltd 2009

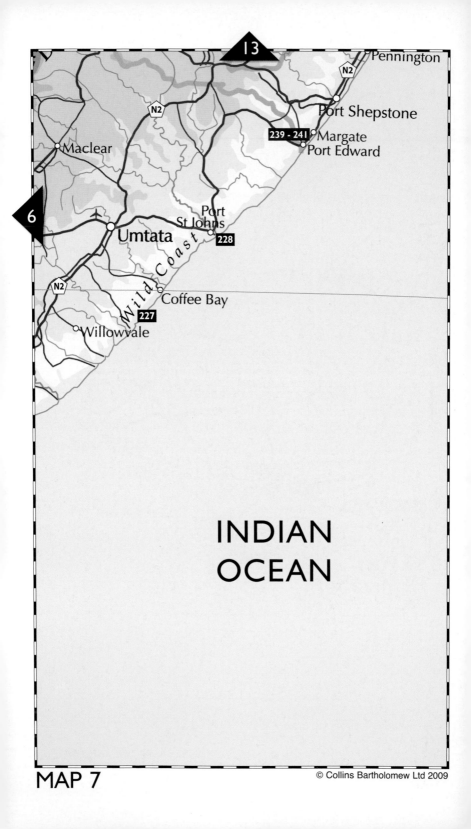

INDIAN
OCEAN

MAP 7

© Collins Bartholomew Ltd 2009

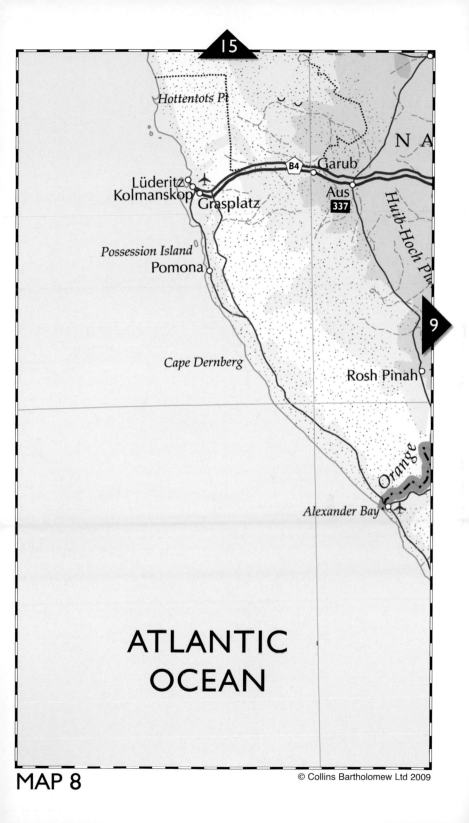

ATLANTIC
OCEAN

MAP 8

© Collins Bartholomew Ltd 2009

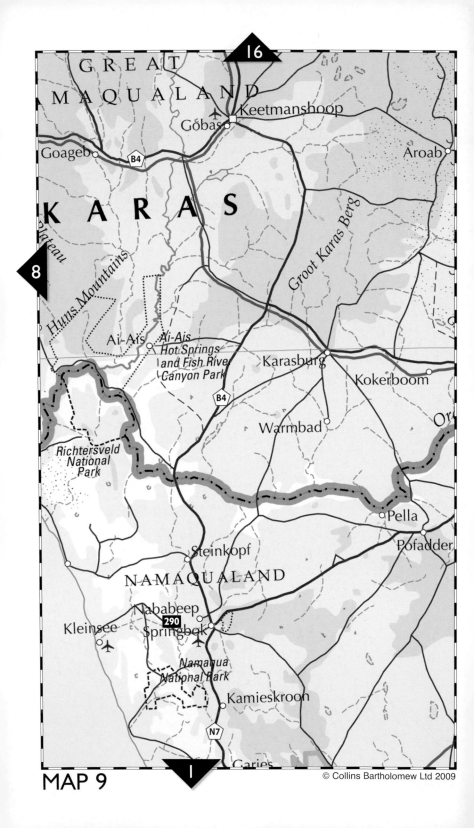

MAP 9

© Collins Bartholomew Ltd 2009

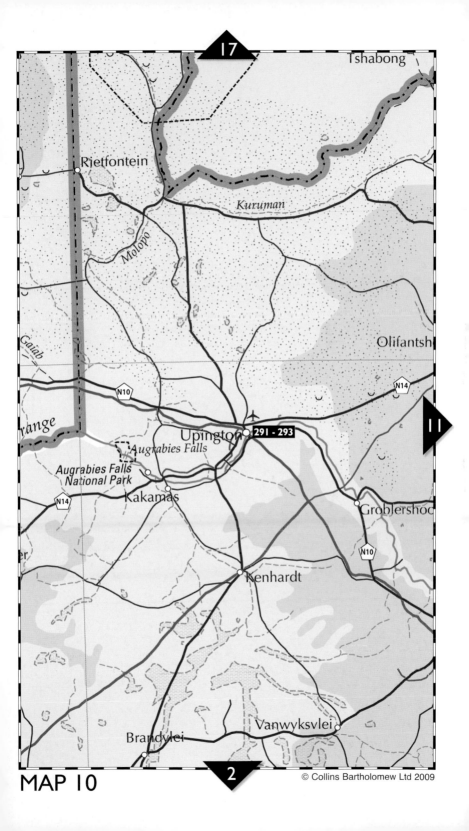

MAP 10

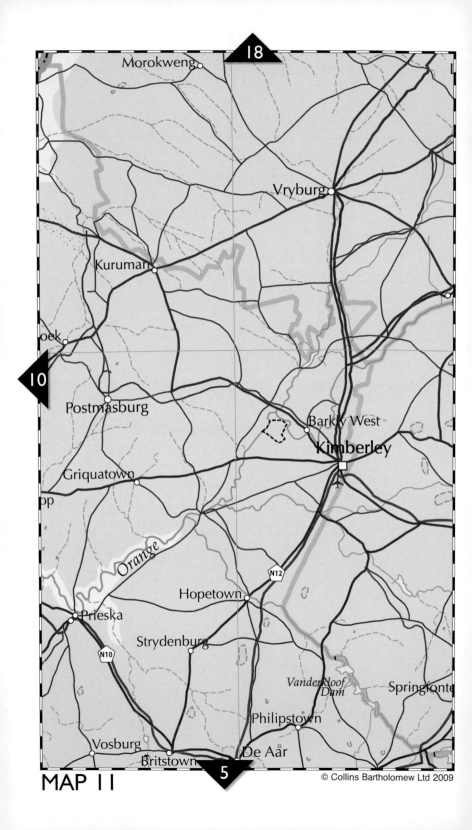

MAP 11

© Collins Bartholomew Ltd 2009

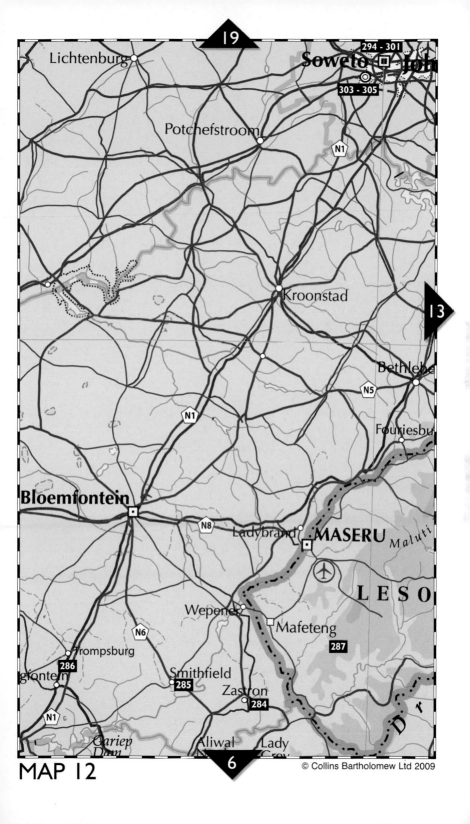

MAP 12   © Collins Bartholomew Ltd 2009

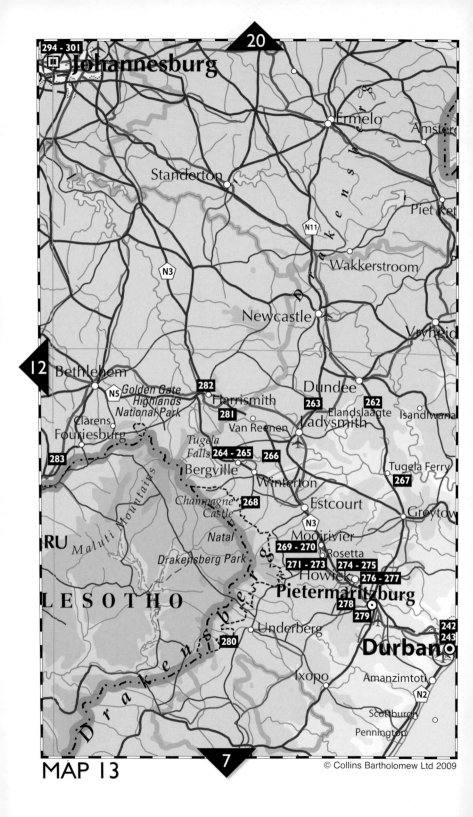

294 - 301
Johannesburg

Ermelo

Amster

Standerton

Piet Ret

N11

N3

Wakkerstroom

P

Newcastle

Vryheid

12

Bethlehem

Golden Gate Highlands National Park

N5

282

Harrismith

Dundee

263

262

281

Elandslaagte

Isandlwana

Van Reenen

Ladysmith

Clarens

Fouriesburg

Tugela Falls

264 - 265

266

Tugela Ferry

267

283

Bergville

Winterton

Champagne Castle

268

Estcourt

Greytow

RU

Maluti Mountains

N3

Mooirivier

269 - 270

Rosetta

Natal

271 - 273

274 - 275

Drakensberg Park

Howick

276 - 277

LESOTHO

Pietermaritzburg

278

279

242

243

Underberg

280

Durban

Ixopo

Amanzimtoti

N2

Scottburgh

MAP 13

7

Pennington

© Collins Bartholomew Ltd 2009

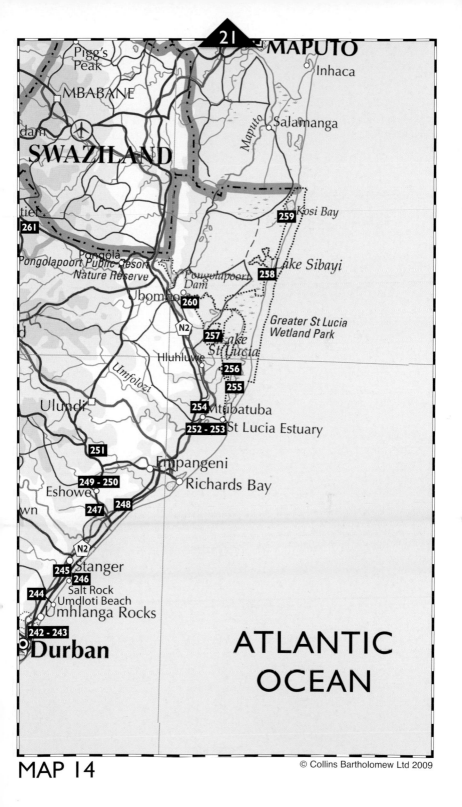

MAPUTO

Inhaca

Pigg's Peak

☐ MBABANE

Salamanga

SWAZILAND

dam

tier

261

Kiosi Bay

259

Pongolapoort Public Resort
Nature Reserve

Pongolá

Lake Sibayi

Pongolapoort
Dam

258

Ubombo

260

N2

Greater St Lucia
Wetland Park

257

Lake
St Lucia

Hluhluwe

256

255

Umfolozi

Ulundi ☐

254 Mtubatuba

252 - 253 St Lucia Estuary

251

Empangeni

249 - 250

Richards Bay

Eshowe

247 **248**

wn

N2

245 Stanger

246

Salt Rock

244

Umdloti Beach

Umhlanga Rocks

242 - 243

Durban

ATLANTIC

OCEAN

MAP 14

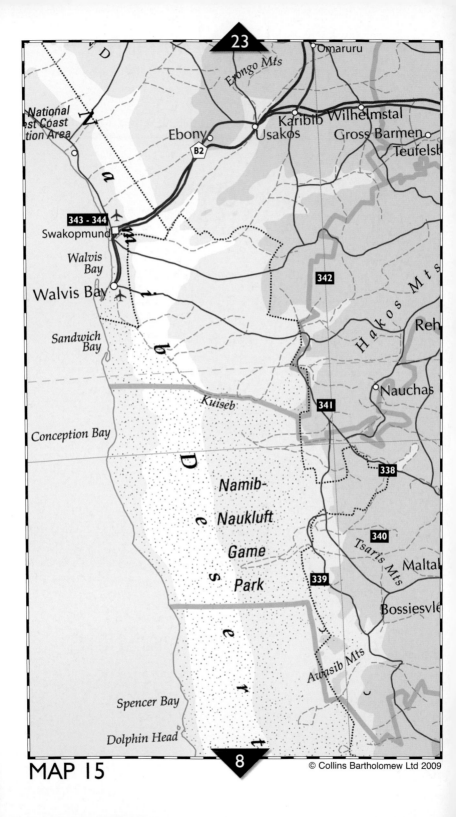

MAP 15

© Collins Bartholomew Ltd 2009

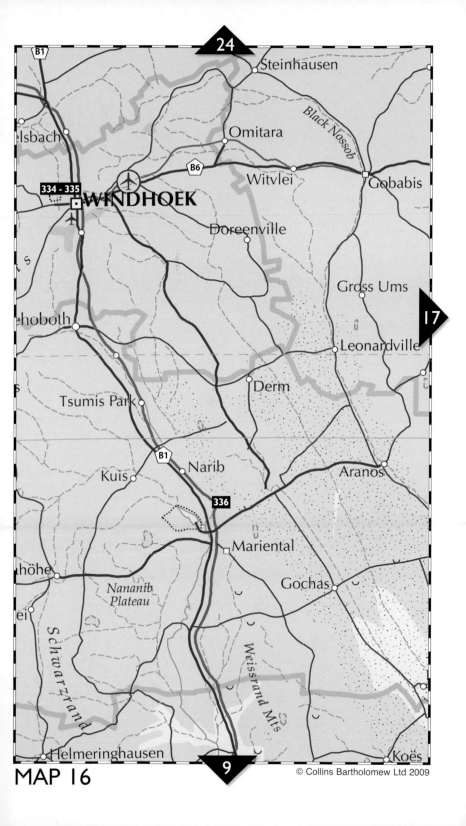

MAP 16

© Collins Bartholomew Ltd 2009

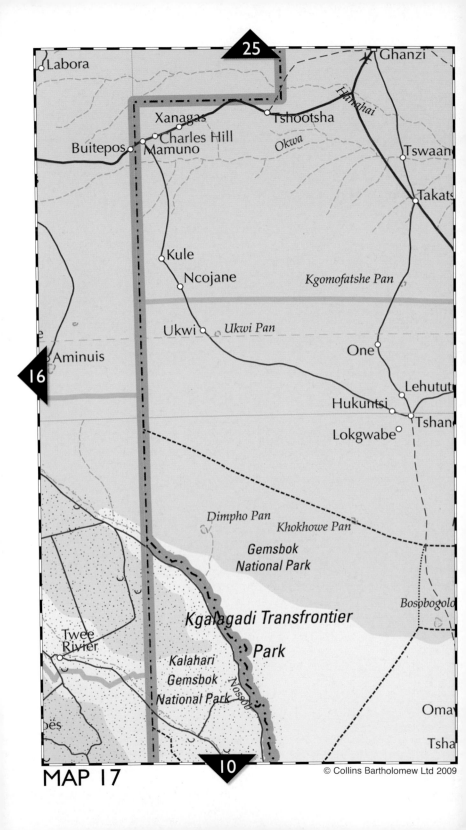

MAP 17

© Collins Bartholomew Ltd 2009

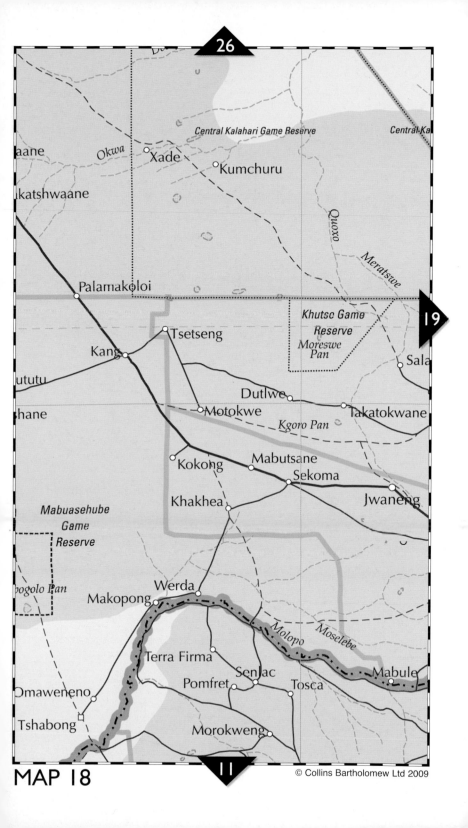

Central Kalahari Game Reserve

Central-Ka

aane
Okwa
Xade

katshwaane

Kumchuru

Qxoxo

Meratswe

Palamakoloi

Khutse Game
Reserve
Moreswe
Pan

Tsetseng

Kang

Sala

ututu

Dutlwe

hane

Motokwe

Takatokwane

Kgoro Pan

Kokong

Mabutsane

Sekoma

Khakhea

Jwaneng

Mabuasehube
Game
Reserve

ogolo Pan

Werda

Makopong

Molopo

Moselebe

Terra Firma

Senlac

Mabule

Pomfret

Tosca

Omaweneno

Tshabong

Morokweng

MAP 18

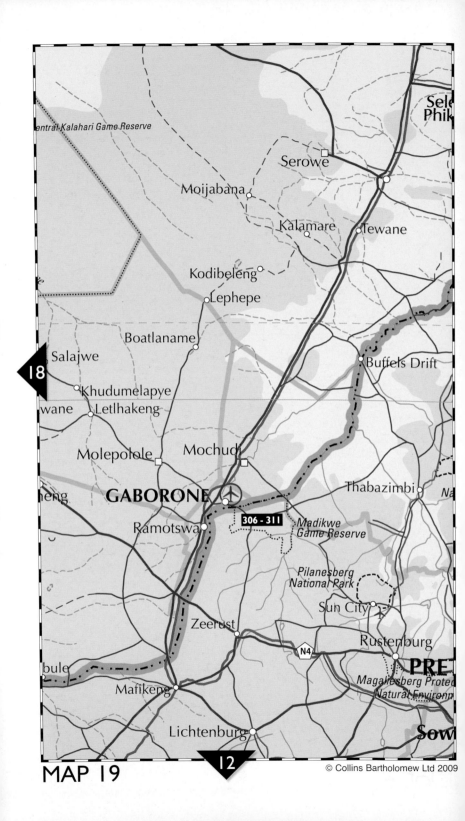

MAP 19

© Collins Bartholomew Ltd 2009

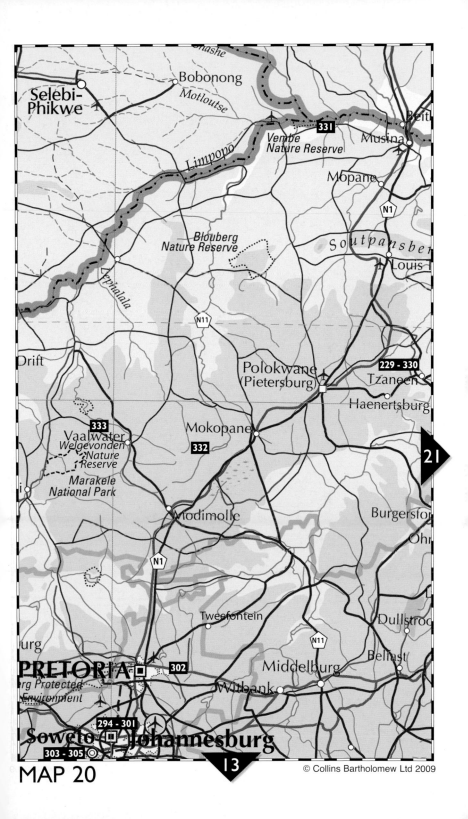

MAP 20

© Collins Bartholomew Ltd 2009

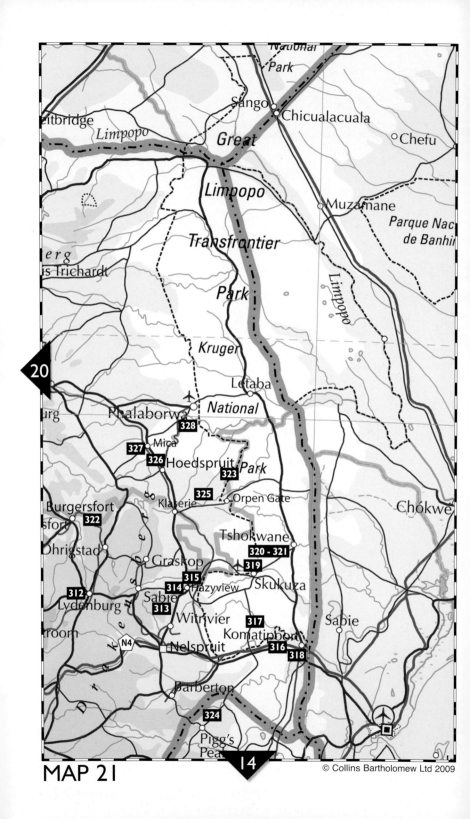

MAP 21

© Collins Bartholomew Ltd 2009

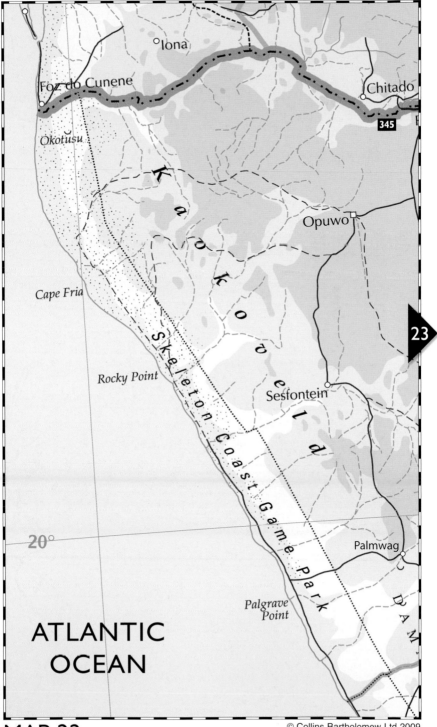

Iona

Foz do Cunene

Chitado

Okotusu

345

Kaokoveld

Cape Fria

Skeleton Coast Game Park

Opuwo

23

Rocky Point

Sesfontein

20°

Palmwag

Palgrave
Point

DAM

ATLANTIC
OCEAN

MAP 22

© Collins Bartholomew Ltd 2009

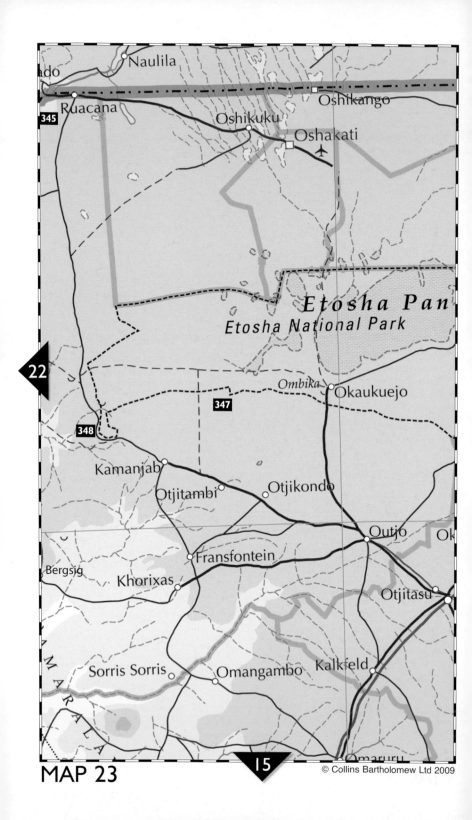

MAP 23

© Collins Bartholomew Ltd 2009

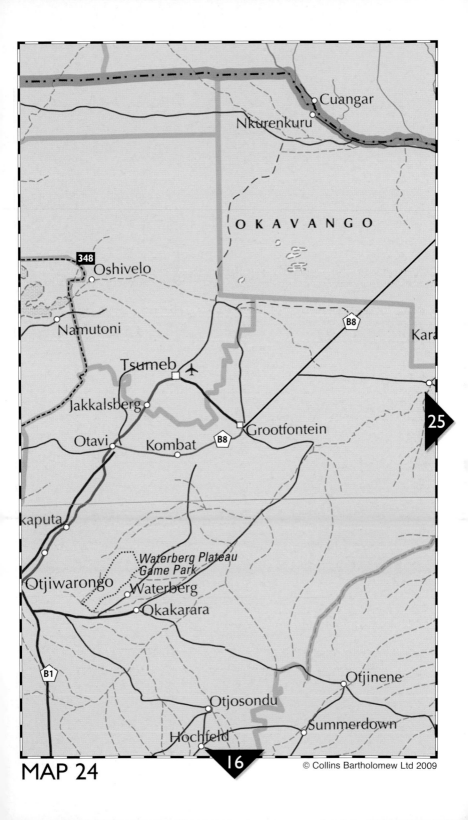

MAP 24

© Collins Bartholomew Ltd 2009

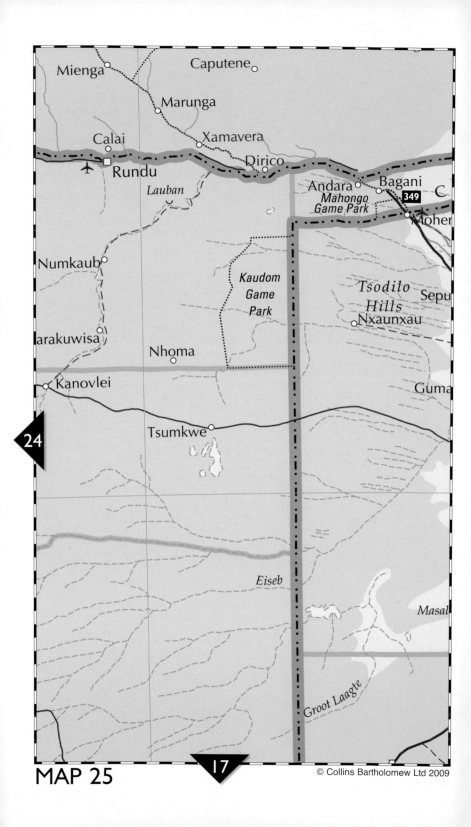

Mienga

Caputene

Marunga

Xamavera

Calai

Dirico

Rundu

Lauban

Andara

Bagani

Mahongo Game Park

349

C

Moher

Numkaub

Kaudom Game Park

Tsodilo Hills

Sepu

Nxaunxau

arakuwisa

Nhoma

Kanovlei

Guma

Tsumkwe

24

Eiseb

Masal

Groot Laagte

MAP 25

17

© Collins Bartholomew Ltd 2009

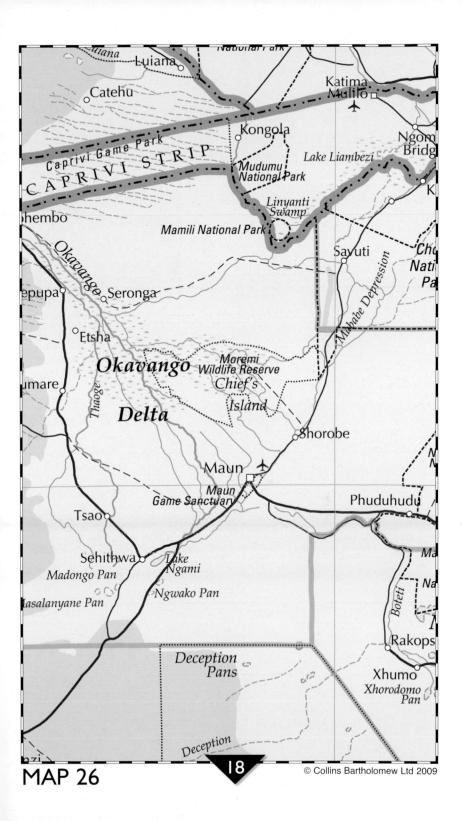

MAP 26

Western Cape

Cape Town Side Dishes

A handful of highly-recommended things to do and places to eat in the Cape Town area...

Uthando South Africa
It's not a township tour, a trip down guilt lane, nor a begging bowl route... it's a cultural field trip to discover, learn, understand, experience and be inspired by amazing human stories written in the face of almost insurmountable adversity. Uthando ("Love") South Africa is a registered non-profit organisation supporting a broad range of projects in the poorest and most marginalized communities in South Africa.
*Contact: James Fernie, Uthando South Africa, Cape Town; **Tel:** 021-683-8523; **Email:** jamesfernie@uthandosa.org*

Daily Deli
Tucked away in Tamboerskloof, the diminutive and super-friendly Daily Deli is a great pavement café favoured by locals who meet there for the best cappuccino in town, lasagna, moussaka, lentil bobotie, pizzas, muffins, pastries, croissant-based bread and butter pudding... if they're feeling hungry. They are open from 8am until 10pm and all meals are available to order if you feel like eating in.
*Contact: Paul and Theresa Daly, 13 Brownlow Road, Tamboerskloof; **Prices:** Mains with a side salad: R48; pizzas from R33, cakes from R15 and breakfast from R20; **Tel:** 021-426-0250; 021-426-0249; **Email:** dailydeli@vodamail.co.za*

Addis in Cape Ethiopian Restaurant
Thankfully no touristy bells and whistles, just an authentic Ethiopian dining experience prepared by talented Ethiopian chefs. Ethiopian cuisine is famous for its rich aromas and generous use of herbs and spices; it's served on a communal pancake-like 'Injera' which is used to scoop the delightful mosaic of traditional saucy favourites. Addis in Cape is a must-do opportunity to experience another African culture while in South Africa.
*Contact: Senait Mekonnen, 41 Church Street, Cape Town; **Prices:** Mains: R75 - R90; lunch: R40 - R50; **Tel:** 021-424-5722; 021-424-5053; **Email:** celebrate@addisincape.co.za; **Web:** www.addisincape.co.za*

Extreme Scene
For those wanting to take advantage of the Cape's natural splendour and outdoor opportunities. Whether it's learning to surf, tandem skydiving or watching a Great White breaching in False Bay, Gavin (and Extreme Scene) will sort you out. An ex pro rugby star, Gavin deals with all his guests personally, leaving nothing to chance. Extreme Scene will plan just about any adrenaline-inducing activity for you without a hitch, and will even pick you up and drop you back home.
*Contact: Gavin Pfister, 1st Floor, 297 Long Street - above Long Street Liquors, Cape Town; **Tel:** 079-666-9789; **Cell:** 086-603-1574; **Email:** info@extremescene.co.za; **Web:** www.extremescene.co.za*

Vaughan Johnson's Wine and Cigar Shop

Browse, taste and choose from an incredible collection of South Africa's finest wines. Vaughan has an uncanny knack of having in stock 'that wine' that no-one else can get their hands on. He takes the time to talk you through his favourites and points you in the best direction for your palate. Throw in his selection of Cuban cigars and you may be here for a while. Prices are very reasonable too.

Contact: *Vaughan Johnson, Dock Road, V&A Waterfront;*
Tel: *021-419-2121;* **Cell**: *086-509-6401;*
Email: *vjohnson@mweb.co.za;* **Web**: *www.vaughanjohnson.com*

The Olde English Shaving Shop

Gentlemen pay attention! Don't have your hair cut before your holiday. You are going to need something to pass the time while your better half hits the V&A Waterfront. Wave her off and sit back in an original barber's chair for a gent's cut followed by a hot towel shave. This is the real deal with leather chairs, copper taps, cut-throat razors, badger brushes and their own brand of balms, soaps and colognes. It's a man thing. The Olde English Shaving Shop is at Shop 6252 while Mr Cobbs the Barber is at Shop 279. Both are owned by Bob and Vandah.

Contact: *Bob and Vandah Lansdowne, Shop 6252, V & A Waterfront;* **Prices**: *Gents cut: R120. Hot Towel Shave: R150;* **Tel**: *021-418-8068; 021-592-5286;* **Email**: *mcraft@mweb.co.za;*
Web: *www.englishshavingshop.com*

Rust-en-Vrede Gallery

A listed Cape Dutch monument in the heart of Durbanville with art galleries showing monthly exhibitions of S.A. artists and a much-praised ceramics museum. The Gallery Café serves light Mediterranean meals best eaten in the courtyard in summer or scoffed around the log fire in winter.

Contact: *Monica Ross, 10 Wellington Road, Durbanville;* **Tel**: *021-976-4691*
Email: *rustenvrede@telkomsa.net;* **Web**: *www.rust-en-vrede.com*

Brian's Birding

There are more than 900 bird species in South Africa, so best to have someone on hand to put a name to a face. Brian leads birding trips from Cape Town as far afield as the Kalahari National Park, the Karoo and Garden Route. Trips can be geared for everyone and anyone, using his own vehicle for up to seven clients, and a hired one thereafter.

Contact: *Brian Vanderwalt, 133 Mauritius Crescent, Stellenberg;*
Prices: *Rates depend on trip. Cape Peninsula day trip for min 2 people from R850;* **Tel**: *021-919-2192;* **Email**: *info@brians-birding.co.za;*
Web: *www.brians-birding.co.za*

The Old Biscuit Mill

The Old Biscuit Mill is a vibrant, warm-hearted little village in the heart of Woodstock where talented people come together to share, collaborate and show off their heart-felt passion. Experience an incredibly different shopping experience and artistic journey at The Mill, home to day and night markets, a range of workshops and designer stores, a decadent restaurant and an inspiring line-up of festivals and productions.
*Contact: 373 - 375 Albert Rd, Woodstock; **Tel**: 021-462-6361;*
*Cell: 086-669-0797; **Email**: info@theoldbiscuitmill.co.za;*
Web: www.theoldbiscuitmill.co.za

Stardust Restaurant

All the staff are students of the performing arts or studying other vocations and have a passion for fun and performing. Our waiter, a 5th-year medical student, literally let loose with a Freddie Mercury number that made us all want to break free too. These guys put on a dinner party like no other with ongoing performances including tap-dancing dance-offs and plenty more. The Mediterranean food is great and no-one leaves before 1am.
*Contact: Yuda, 165 Main Rd, Rondebosch. **Prices**: Starters: R45 - R55;*
*Mains: R70 - R150; **Tel**: 021-686-6280; **Fax**: 021-686-0674;*
Email: admin@stardustcapetown.com or stardustrestaurant@yahoo.com;
Web: www.stardustcapetown.com

Café Roux

Paul, Bern and Lindi are all about good times and fantastic food. As they themselves put it: "we wanted to create a special place where we could sit outside with our family and friends, eating great food, drinking our favourite wine, simply enjoying life..." This mission has been accomplished... and in spades.
*Contact: Paul, Lindi, Bern Le Roux, Noordhoek Farm Village; **Prices**: Breakfast: R18 - R54; Lunch: R38 - R98; **Tel**: 021-789-2538; 021-789-2577;*
*Email: info@caferoux.co.za; **Web**: www.caferoux.co.za*

Salty Sea Dog Restaurant

Head here for the absolute best fish 'n' chips. The building is the old fish market on the wharf and you can eat in or take away freshly-grilled or -fried fish, calamari, squid, prawns and all sorts of other marine delicacies. Friendly service and packed with locals - just what we like.
*Contact: André and Debbie Duraan, Wharf St, Simon's Town; **Prices**: R40 - R68; **Tel**: 021-786-1918; 021-786-1918;*
Email: saltydog@telkomsa.net

Aquatrails

If you are looking for a way to do something about all the delicious Cape Town food you are unable to say no to, then head straight down to Aquatrails. They will sort you out. This family-owned and -run company do things the way we like it: small, personal, safe and bucket-loads of fun. They hire a range of craft including kayaks, wave-skis, surf- and body-boards for a day of action in False Bay. Alternatively book onto one of their fantastic Breede, Orange or Doring River trips.

Contact: *Hugh Tucker, Shop 2, 150 Main Rd, Fish Hoek;*
Prices: *R100 - R200 per day for hire of craft.* **Tel:** *021-782-7982;*
Email: *aquatrails@mweb.co.za;* **Web:** *www.aquatrails.co.za*

Moonglow Guest House

Gillian O'Leary

7 Bennett Close, Cairnside, Glencairn, Simon's Town
Tel: 021-786-5902 Fax: 021-786-5903
Email: seaview@moonglow.co.za Web: www.moonglow.co.za
Cell: 082-565-6568

"We've been here seven and a half years now but I still get goose-bumps every time I see the moon hanging over it," Gillian confides in me as we stare out over the smooth expanse of False Bay. I challenge you to find a better view of the bay than this one and unsurprisingly most of the rooms at Moonglow take full advantage - even the ones that don't still get their own private seating areas round at the front. With Jess the dog staring lovingly at the succulent blueberry muffin that was supplied with my tea, I could have happily stayed for an eternity ensconced on the sofa of the bar-lounge... but an ever-enthusiastic Gillian was keen to show me more and I had a job to do. Throughout this house you'll find original artworks everywhere, including a stunning leopard print and four-foot-high figurines honed from solid granite. If it catches Gillian's eye she's got to have it. Vibrant oil paintings add a splash of colour to creamy rooms, all drenched in sunlight from large picture windows or glass doors. Beds and tables have been individually designed, and a multitude of mohair blankets and the finest quality linens have had Gillian's hand-embroiderers busy detailing them with intricate dragonflies and bumblebees "... just so the colours match." Moonglow shines.

Rooms: 6: 4 queens all with shower only; 2 twins with bath and shower over.
Price: R375 - R495 pp sharing. Singles on request.
Meals: Full breakfast included. Lots of restaurants nearby.
Directions: Map on website or directions can be emailed on booking.

Albatross House

Leon and Sandy Strydom

37 Victory Way, Simon's Kloof, Simon's Town
Tel: 021-786-5906 Fax: 021-786-4297
Email: albatrosshouse@absamail.co.za Web: www.albatrosshouse.co.za
Cell: 082-363-6449

You can see the sea from every room in Albatross House. Despite this, you'll probably want to spend most of your time outside on the terraces overlooking the whole of False Bay and keeping an eye on the movement of the navy ships below. The terraces, dotted with deep wooden chairs, are the perfect spot for sundowners. Inside, décor is fresh and summery throughout with wooden panelling in the bathrooms that lends them a boathouse feel. With private sitting rooms and connectable terraces (lightly screened off if privacy is preferred) this is a perfect place to come with friends. Indeed I was quite envious of three English ladies who, as Sandy explained, had been chatting, laughing and playing (three-handed) bridge on the balcony into the early hours. A highlight of any stay is, of course, to indulge in Sandy's breakfasts out on the balcony or in the dining room if the weather insists. Each breakfast is tailored to your wishes, from a personal fruit platter and cereals to a hot breakfast of your choice. While Sandy is in the kitchen, Leon chats to guests and gives them tips on making their day more productive and enjoyable. As a member of a weekly hiking group, Leon knows the hiking trails, birds, fauna and flora well and can give good tips on where to go, during what times of year and weather. There are stunning jaunts just minutes from the house. If you'd rather soak up some history in Simon's Town take the path below the house, especially constructed by Leon and Sandy, through the fynbos and down into the village and beyond.

Rooms: 4: 1 king with en-suite bath; 1 queen with en-suite bath and shower, plus option of honeymoon suite; 2 twin/doubles with en-s shower.
Price: Doubles: R800 - R900. Suites: R900 - R1,000 for two, or R1,600 - R1,800 for four. Studio: R700 - R800. Single supplement: R550 - R650.
Meals: Full breakfast included.
Directions: From Simon's Town station on your L go past Admiralty House on L. Move to R lane. Cross to R over oncoming traffic, turn immediately L up Soldiers Way. R into Arsenal, L into Cornwall. Cornwall becomes Runciman. Continue past 3-way stop, turn R into Simon's Kloof & follow signs.

Map Number: 3

Entry Number: 2

Fort Vic

Dr Lance Tooke

14 Victory Way, Simon's Town
Tel: Lance in UK: +44 (0)7986-557652
Email: simonstown@btinternet.com Web: www.simonstown.net

I didn't get the pleasure of meeting Dr Lance who's based in London, but his friendly voice beaming down the phone was a reassuring start. And sure enough Fort Vic in Simon's Town, his second home, did not disappoint. The house was built by his neighbours and is entirely made of wood and stone dug from the mountain it sits upon. Inside is a forest of dense wood beams, bamboo ceilings, red stone walls and open-plan wooden staircases making it feel a bit like a bush lodge. The real drawcard here, however, is the view. You don't - can't! - get much more of a sea view than this and the best place to absorb it from is the huge master bedroom upstairs, although big sliding glass doors run throughout the house. Actually there are many places to enjoy the view from: the plunge pool, the sitting room or the smart kitchen lined with yellowwood cupboards and fitted with a central island, complete with gas cooker and fancy oven. The motto here is keep it simple with cream sheets, stylish free-standing showers and soft natural furnishings like basket lamps, wicker chairs and red cushions. The black cloth hanging in the kitchen covered in badges from all over the world is testament to Lance's travelling days prior to finding his favourite destination, Fort Vic. Although this is definitely a self-catering arrangement, the house manager is available at all times to troubleshoot any problems, arrange trips or make bookings. Whales can be viewed (July - October) from the master bedroom and the pool.

Rooms: 1 self-catering house, 1 double room with victorian bath and shower in the room, 2 twins with showers in the rooms. Full kitchen and lounge area.
Price: R1,400 - R3,000 per day for the house, depending on season. Discounts of up to 50% for long stays.
Meals: Self-catering.
Directions: Detailed directions available on booking.

Bed & Breakfast Inn Between

Cees van Rijk and Inge Luyten
49 Herschel Road, Fish Hoek
Tel: 021-782-2844 Fax: 021-782-2844
Email: innbetween@telkomsa.net Web: www.innbetween.co.za
Cell: 082-696-3324

The consistency of the weather here may not be guaranteed, but the hospitality on offer is. Together, Cees and Inge have clocked up over twenty years of experience in the service industry whilst working for KLM. The multitude of places they've seen has clearly left its mark and not just in terms of aesthetics. As I arrived, horribly late and without warning, Cees showed genuine understanding and rustled up a hearty plate of pasta, knowing full well this late arriver had already missed last orders. Meanwhile two young, polite and utterly soppy members of the household befriended me: Bugsy and Lola, sandy Boxer and black Great Dane respectively. Lola, it turned out, had just been rescued from a post and chain on an abandoned farm after Inge spotted her woeful tale in a news snippet. No doubt Lola can't believe her luck as she pads out on deck nowadays: the views stretch out across the residential valley of Fish Hoek to Clovelly, which sits in the nook of the mountain range directly to the north. There's fantastic, extensive hiking all around here, with spectacular views possible of the Atlantic Ocean to the west and Indian Ocean to the east. You can definitely expect to see whales up and down the bay between August and November, and if you want to get more involved, Cees can point you in the right direction for kayaks, canoes and all things beachable. Inside they have had the place gutted and revamped to an impeccable finish. But it was the obvious kindness, warmth and enthusiasm of Cees and Inge that will stay with me longest.

Rooms: 4: 3 king/twins and 1 queen, all with en-suite showers.
Price: R360 - R500 pp sharing. Singles R450.
Meals: Continental breakfast included, with eggs to order. Excellent restaurants in nearby Kalk Bay for lunch and dinner.
Directions: See owners' website for detailed directions from Cape Town International Airport (allow about 45 minutes).

Blue Yonder

Sally and Bruce Elliott

14 Hillside Rd, Fish Hoek
Tel: 021-782-0500 Fax: 021-782-0500
Email: info@blueyondercape.co.za Web: www.blueyondercape.co.za
Cell: 082-441-9589

For those of you on the self-catering trail this is a must. A three-storey house converted into flats, Blue Yonder is a luxury ocean liner of a place. When Sally opened the door to an invading GG team the sun was blasting through the wall-to-wall windows. She was keen to show me around, but I spent the first ten minutes standing out on the enormous silver-railed balcony, transfixed by the view. From all three apartments here you can watch the full arc of the sun, rising over a glittering False Bay, and finally sinking behind the red-tiled roofs of the Fish Hoek bungalows below. Excellent for whale-watching. Once the trance wears off (which it won't) head inside and polish off your complimentary drinks or make the most of the stainless steel and cream kitchens, complete with all mod cons (including my personal favourite: the dishwasher). Sally grew up in this house, but after a huge conversion job the Rhodesian teak floors are the only reminder of her family home. Now, gloriously indulgent queen-sized beds look out on the bay and cool, beige armchairs are just waiting to be lounged in. Once you summon the energy for a dip in the ocean, your own private steps lead down to the beach, just a stone's throw away. My advice? Bring the whole family, light up a braai on the balcony and settle in for at least a month. *5 mins to food shops. All apartments have braais.*

Rooms: 3 self-catering apartments: Upper: 1 queen with en-suite shower & 1 twin with en-suite bath & shower; Middle: 1 queen en-s b & sh, 2 twins en-s b & sh; Lower: 1 queen en-s sh only. Serviced every week day.
Price: R240 - R400 pp sharing.
Meals: In fridge on arrival: fruit juice, wine, tea, coffee, milk, sugar. Full kitchen.
Directions: Head to Muizenberg from Cape Town, continue south along main road through Fish Hoek. At roundabout at the end of Fish Hoek main rd turn L towards Simon's Town. 1 km further take 1st R at traffic lights up Hillside Rd. Blue Yonder about 300m up on the R.

Echo Terrace

Brian Dreyer and Renée Parker

3 Echo Road, Fish Hoek
Tel: 021-782-3313 Fax: 021-782-3313
Email: renee@echoterrace.co.za Web: www.echoterrace.co.za
Cell: 083-646-8348

I defy anyone not to be dazzled by Renée's verdant and plentiful garden. While I swooned at the clivia, bougainvillea and protea, Renée patiently named all the plants and chatted about how important privacy is for her guests. Which leads me to the next remarkable thing about Echo Terrace. From each apartment's private entrance and cleverly concealed balcony, you'd never know this was a guesthouse. In fact, all five of the alabaster cottages feel like their own perfectly-contained little home; but with Renée and Brian's house next door, there's always someone from whom to glean restaurant tips or who will donate some sugar. The cottages are delightful – immaculate but not prim – and each has their own small garden and plunge pool or huge balcony. With open-plan kitchen, dining and sitting area the apartments are roomy-yet-cosy and decorated with old family furniture. "Everything's from way back when," said Renée as I inspected an ancient sewing-machine and admired the local seascapes on the walls. The windows that stretch the length of the sitting room and the dazzling white walls throughout make each apartment so light I almost had to pop my sunglasses back on. I was pleased I refrained however, as immersing oneself in the staggering sea view (that's all there is... sea) and tuning into the soporific roar of the waves is a treat worth experiencing with all senses fully switched on.

Rooms: 5 self catering apartments: all 1 queen and 2 twins. 4 have 2 bathrooms all with bath and shower and 1 with 1 bathroom with bath and shower.

Price: R300 - R450 pp sharing. Singles R500 - R600.

Meals: Fully self-catered.

Directions: N2 from airport to Cape Town. Take M3 to Muizenberg. Turn off to Muizenberg and turn right at traffic lights to Muizenberg. Continue through Kalk Bay and Fish Hoek. At circle turn left and at traffic light right. Take first sharp left to Echo Road. Driveway is first on left.

Kimberley House

Marsha Sanders

7 Kimberley Road,
Kalk Bay
Tel: (UK) +44-208-348-5797; (SA) +27-72-769-3164
Email: marshasanders@blueyonder.co.uk
Web: www.kimberley-house.co.za
Cell: (UK) +44-790-430-3569; (SA) +27-82-793-4223

As soon as I had reached the top of the winding stair that began at the cobbled street below, I imagined this place buzzing with families and friends. Picture the scene. You make yourself at home in one of the bedrooms, all sea-light breezy and creaky on timber floors, before settling into a day on the stoep where the braai is stacked with fresh yellowtail from the Kalk Bay harbour market, slowly cooking with a dozen or so periperi prawns. Gradually you take in the fabulous view. Colourful St James houses descend to sea level, where False Bay begins and ripples along lines of perfect corduroy into the wild blue yonder. On the other side, faraway, the Hottentots Holland mountains seem weightless in the sea haze. Moving back indoors, the kitchen should be alive with activity and conversation that spills into the dining area and through concertina doors into a laid-back sitting room with a welcome fireplace. For a bit of quiet, try the patio out back. Tell-tale signs of 1875 origins include high ceilings and tall sash windows, but most of all in the very bones of the house, in the cellar, where the rocks of the mountainside itself form the foundations. It's also a great place to store the surf-boards. Unusual for the area, the house also keeps a surprisingly large walled garden with a lawn and vibrant flowerbeds, as well as a pleasantly-shaded bench and table. Kalk Bay is home to GG when we're in South Africa. We love the walks into the hills, the toothless fisherwomen and, of course, the peerless Olympia Café.

Rooms: 1 house with 3 bedrooms, all double and shower en-suite. There is a separate bathroom plus a TV room with sleeper couch.
Price: R2,000 - R2,800 for the house per night.
Meals: Self-catering.
Directions: Coming along the coast road from Muizenberg, as you approach Kalk Bay, 0.5 miles further on from St James railway station, turn right into Kimberley Road, a narrow cobbled street (easily missed). The house is half-way up the hill.

Rodwell House

Robin von Holdt

Rodwell Road, St James
Tel: 021-787-9880 Fax: 021-787-9898
Email: info@rodwellhouse.co.za Web: www.rodwellhouse.co.za

This is the kind of boutique hotel that would make Gatsby weak at the knees. And Rodwell's owner Robin - a bit of a Gatsby himself - has refused to cut a single corner. Whether it's the thrillingly expensive teak panelling on the walls, the team of 60 he employed to make it perfect, or the 15,000-bottle refrigerated wine cellar, he has made it his mission that everything at Rodwell should be as exclusive, stylish and luxurious as possible. From the trimmed lawns and vine-covered walkways of the front garden you can admire the classic Cape Town view of the St James tidal pool and multi-coloured beach huts out front, and the looming Kalk Bay mountains out back. Behind the façade of the house lies an intricately-tiled Moroccan courtyard with terracotta walls offering welcome shade, and a tinkling fountain to get you into siesta mode. Robin used to work in finance, but as an art collector and enthusiastic fan of good food and wine, designing Rodwell has been serious fun. His extensive Masters art collection can be seen all over the house, including original pieces in all the rooms. All eight rooms have been positioned so that you can see the sea, either from your windows or private balcony. And modern, open-plan bathrooms are separated from the bedroom only by a risqué waist-high wall. But my favourite part has to be the tasting room, with a sweeping bar, whose curve is continued by lights in the floor, and whose stock of wine would rival the top restaurants of NY or London. *2 mins to coffee shops, restaurants and wine bars; 15 mins to Simon's Town and Constantia vineyards; 20 mins to Kirstenbosch Gardens.*

Rooms: 9 suites: 7 doubles with full en-suite bathrooms; 2 doubles with en-suite showers. All have balconies or gardens.
Price: R2,000 - R7,000 per room per night.
Meals: Full breakfast included, with fresh pastries baked daily. Picnic hampers, lunches and fine dining facilities. 1000-choice award-winning wine list; wine tastings by arrangement.
Directions: Directions on website or can be faxed or emailed.

Bella Ev Guesthouse

Kerime and Ursula Sinclair

Bella Ev, 8 Camp Road, Muizenberg
Tel: 021-788-1293 Fax: 021-788-1293
Email: info@bellaev.co.za Web: www.bellaev.co.za
Cell: 082-547-3568

Kerime had promised she'd make a Russian cake for my arrival, but I found myself feasting not only on cake, but also fresh Kolböregi – Turkish cheese and spinach pastry, hot from the oven – and silver-coated, almond-shaped chocolates washed down with Turkish coffee and ginger tea. And this wasn't even an official mealtime! Afterwards, Ursula (Kerime's well-read and very charming daughter) graciously shed some light on the Middle-Eastern connection at Bella Ev: 'my great-grandfather moved here from the Ottoman Empire to teach theology and marry Captain Cook's niece,' she explained. Thus the well-thumbed collection of 'The Treasured Writings of Khalil Gibran' in the hall library; and the twelve colourful pairs of Turkish slippers queuing at the foot of the stairs. And all that yummy food. Muizenberg was always the place to have a summerhouse and, though much has of course changed around it, the character of this century-old house remains fully intact from the Escher-esque wooden floor downstairs to the Napoleonic king upstairs. There are original John Muafangejo linocuts and eccentricities like the obsolete servants' bell call box… but every nook and cranny demands investigation. The eclectic surroundings are due to the family's exotic roots and natural interest in the wider world around them. Kerime delights in getting to know her guests, which in turn feeds her own creativity. Not content with dishing up Armenian lamb or Algerian soup, she's also a couturier, often called on by guests with commissions.

Rooms: 4: 1 king with en/s bath (optional child bed available); 2 doubles with en/s baths; family room has 1 king with en/s shower leading to separate single (which shares en/s).
Price: R450 - R500 pp sharing.
Meals: Full breakfast included. Other meals on request (price dependent), including packed lunches.
Directions: From airport take N2 towards Cape Town. Turn off onto M3 to Muizenberg. Follow this road to Muizenberg, then take a left onto Simon van der Stel Road. Turn right at the junction with Main Road. Follow this until a set of traffic lights with Shoprite to your left; turn right into Camp Road.

Sunset Beach Guest House

Charlotte and Dave Lombaard

73 Wireless Rd, Kommetjie
Tel: 021-783-4283 Fax: 021-783-4286
Email: info@sunsetbeach.co.za Web: www.sunsetbeach.co.za
Cell: 083-325-8321

I arrived at Sunset Beach in a thunderstorm, but even with wind and rain buffeting the windows, the house puts you in the mood for lazy summer days. The design is seaside inspired, but don't expect any cheap bucket and spade murals here: bleached wooden floorboards, plump furniture and white drapes make this a truly sophisticated coastal spot. Under the thatched eaves upstairs, the soft chairs and bookcase looked like the perfect place to spend a rainy day. And if home-made cookies in each room weren't enough to entice children in from outside, a toy box and bunk beds in the family room should do the job. There's a back garden with a swimming pool, but it's what's out the front that I got excited about. The house is so close to the sea that there is nothing between its large windows and the ocean but unspoilt beach. And the beach at Kommetjie really is unspoilt. With miles of white sand making me wish the rain would go away so I could explore, it's hard to believe you're just a short drive from Cape Town centre. But if you don't fancy moving (and there's a high chance you won't) the city will come to your table. A mouth-watering menu boasts fresh seafood dishes such as prawn and peach kebabs and mussels with sundried tomato sauce. This barefoot haven is perfect for young families and honeymooners alike, who come in droves for the guest house's relaxed philosophy that sandy footprints are welcome reminders that guests are at home. They also specialise in small, intimate weddings with the ceremony taking place on the beach.

Rooms: 5: 2 queens, 1 twin; 1 queen with bunk beds & 1 4 poster queen; all rooms with en-s bath.
Price: R360 - R800 pp. Rates are seasonal. Singles plus R200 per night. Whole house R3,000 - R8,000.
Meals: Full breakfast incl'. Personal chef on site for lunches, gourmet picnics & dinners from R120 pp.
Directions: Take N2 from Cape Town or the airport. Join M3 towards Muizenberg and continue till road ends. Turn right at lights and take Ou Kaapse Weg over mountain to Noordhoek. Turn R into M64 towards Kommetjie then turn R again onto Wireless Road as soon as you enter town. 700m on LHS.

Frogg's Leap

Jôke Glauser and Stewart McLaren
15 Baviaanskloof Rd, Hout Bay
Tel: 021-790-2590 Fax: 021-790-2590
Email: info@froggsleap.co.za Web: www.froggsleap.co.za
Cell: 082-493-4403

The huge Frogg's Leap verandah, with its impressive views of the Hout Bay mountains and sea seems to be the focal point of life here. At breakfast the house springs to life with Jôke (pronounced *yokie*) and Stewart engaging in easy banter with all who emerge, and chiding guests for sitting at the long wooden table inside when the parasol-shaded tables outside are so enticing. Then, in the evening, with the sea breeze swinging the hammocks and a sundowner in your hand, it is not hard to get to grips with being lazy and on holiday. I can't remember a place where guests made themselves so at home. Jôke and Stewart used to run charter boats in the West Indies and Frogg's Leap has a breezy Caribbean feel with many open French doors and windows. Bedrooms are cool ensembles of natural materials: painted floors, seagrass matting, palms, natural stone in bathrooms, lazy wicker chairs, reed ceilings, thick cotton percale linen and old wooden furniture. Hout Bay itself is a fishing harbour enclosed by mountains and is within minutes of beaches and hiking trails. Jôke and Stewart keep a 26ft catamaran there and, when the spirit moves them and weather permits, will take guests cray-fishing, or whale-watching when whales are in town. This is a place that has been consistently recommended both before and since the first edition and it is a continued pleasure to recommend it myself. *Guest phone 021-790-6260.*

Rooms: 6: 5 doubles/twins and 1 double, all with en-suite bathrooms; 2 with shower, 4 with bath and shower. Plus extra single room.
Price: R350 - R490 pp sharing. Single supplement: +50%.
Meals: Full breakfast included and served until 10am. There are 20 restaurants nearby for other meals.
Directions: A map will be faxed to you on confirmation of booking.

Makuti Lodge

Doreen and Peter Wright

Farriers Way, Tarragona Estate, Hout Bay
Tel: 021-790-1414 Fax: 021-790-1414/1227
Email: doreen@makutilodge.co.za Web: www.makutilodge.co.za
Cell: 083-457-5231

Forget Kirstenbosch, head for Makuti Lodge! (Well, almost….) Gardeners will find plenty of common ground with Peter and Doreen who are hugely welcoming. It's not that the grounds of Makuti Lodge are especially large; but they are just so full. From the patios, the lawns, the flower beds and the 'forest' area, to the hidden bark paths that twist between the cottages, you could spend hours wandering around contemplating life (or joining in a game of pétanque, if you've the stomach for it). Even if you do manage to exhaust the riches of the garden, just minutes from the driveway you'll find yourself at the foot of Myburg Peak, with walks to waterfalls in winter and red orchids (disas) in the summer. Doreen and Peter insist on leaving 2 bottles of wine out for guests and, if you play your cards right, you may be invited to a wine-tasting session in the stone depths of the cellar! Here, among the animal carvings and hanging swords, you can sample vinous treats from all over the southern hemisphere. In the summer, because they just can't help entertaining, they put on alfresco dinners on invitation. Just another opportunity to sit in the garden and watch the birds as the sun goes down. The cottages themselves are quaint (Peter is responsible for construction, Doreen for the finishing touches) with local art on the walls and wood-burning fires. And I haven't even mentioned the dogs, the pool, the hot tub or the breakfasts.

Rooms: 4 cottages: 1 x 1-bed cottages; 2 x 2-bed with 2 bathrooms; 1 x 3-bed with 2 bathrooms.
Price: R250 - R100 pp sharing. Or in winter: R450 - R1,100 per cottage; summer: R600 - R2,000 per cottage.
Meals: Full or Continental breakfast an extra R60 - R75 pp.
Directions: M63 to Hout Bay. Turn R at Disa River Rd, L at end. First R into Garron Ave. Then R into Connemara Drive. Then L into Hunter's Way. R into Farrier's Way. Makuti on R.

Paddington's

Di and Don Lilford
3 Lindevista Lane, Hout Bay
Tel: 021-790-1955 Fax: 021-790-1955
Email: dlilford@telkomsa.net Web: www.paddington.co.za
Cell: 083-259-6025

Standing in Di's garden, I sighed with relaxed satisfaction, gazing across a valley and beach bathed in late-afternoon sunshine. Well away from the hustle and bustle of Cape Town proper, Hout Bay runs at a pace of its own, and Paddington's and the Lilfords are right in step. After years on their valley-floor farm, they have moved up onto the hillside accompanied by a gaggle of visiting guinea fowl (impatiently tapping on the French doors for their tea when I arrived), Rollo the dog and their steady stream of guests. There's a relaxed feel of country living here and while the building itself may be new and square, it's full of old prints, family furniture and well-trodden rugs. Visitors have the run of the tiled ground floor, with both bedrooms just two yawns and a stagger from breakfast, tacked onto the drawing room and kitchen. One room gets the morning sun, the other the afternoon rays and both are blessed with gigantic beds. If you feel up to it, Don and Di will point you in the direction of the best golf courses and the beach, while for the lethargic loungers among you there's pétanque on the gravel patch or a book on the verandah. Oh and there's always the heated pool behind the house! Choices, choices....

Rooms: 2 king/twins, 1 with bath, 1 with shower.
Price: R400 per person per night. Singles on request.
Meals: Full breakfast included.
Directions: Faxed or emailed on request.

Dreamhouse

Ivanka Beyer
53 Mount Rhodes Drive, Hout Bay
Tel: 021-790-1773 Fax: 021-790-4864
Email: dreamhouse@yebo.co.za Web: www.dreamhouse.de
Cell: 082-547-7328

You cannot fail to be inspired by Dreamhouse and its mountainous harbour-view setting. The staggered garden contains many intimate leafy places that envelope both you and the landscape in the foliage. This is an artist's oasis and, if the mood takes you, Ivanka will dish out brushes, watercolours, canvas and frame so you can paint your own memories and take them home. The house and rooms reflect your host's own creative flair in colour, texture and line, with sweeping-armed suede sofas (it's always handy when your other half deals in furniture), a heavy wooden-beamed fireplace and high ceilings. The rooms are all different and named after their predominant colour, my favourite being the red luxury suite at the heart of the house where I imagined star-gazing from bed or rocking in the balcony-bound hammock for two. Hand-made mirrors, draped sarongs from Pakistan and an abundance of shells adorn the daily-different table décor. "Everything has its own story," according to Ivanka. Devoted to her guests, she applies attention to detail and impeccable yet unobtrusive service at all times. Whether it's a picnic basket you need, a cocktail at the pool lounge or directions for a sunrise walk up Little Lion's Head, she'll be there. Also trained in reiki, aromatherapy, reflexology and various massages there are a multitude of blissful experiences available at her hands. As we used to say at university (for some reason), "live the dream!" Bikes available for guests to use.

Rooms: 7: 6 king/twin with en-suite bath/shower, 2 with en-suite kitchenette, 1 queen with en-suite shower.
Price: R450 - R850 pp sharing. Singles on request.
Meals: Full breakfast included. Dinner and light lunches on request (preferably with 24-hours notice as only fresh produce used).
Directions: Emailed or faxed on request.

The Tarragon

Mark and Julia Fleming
21 Hunters Way, Tarragona, Hout Bay
Tel: 021-791-4155 Fax: 021-791-4156
Email: info@thetarragon.com Web: www.thetarragon.com
Cell: 076-191-7755

These globe-trotting Brits have retired their backpacks and settled at the opposite, luxury end of the accommodation world. Seduced by South Africa's charm and sunshine, Mark and Julia permanently unpacked, kids and all, building a new life and some very stylish self-catering cottages on the wooded southern slopes of Hout Bay's leafy valley. When I arrived a fruitless effort to find a pen sent Mark dashing for a replacement and I was able to enjoy a purple moment inspired by the towering evergreens and the incredible stillness. A koi pond plinked occasionally with frogs or fish exploring the sun-freckled surface. Other visitors to the Flemings' subtly-crafted garden include peacocks, Egyptian geese, cormorants, butterflies and dragonflies. From the pool-side sun-loungers and braai area your eye will be drawn across the lawn and rocky peaks before sweeping, like the garden, into an area of dense wood. All units have private outdoor areas dappled by vine-wound frames. Marble-topped kitchens are fully kitted out with everything from top-of-the-range toasters to dishwashers, and laundering is available with the lady who does the daily servicing. Living areas, bedrooms and bathrooms are kept simple with clean-cut lines and contrasting tones; high-quality white linens gleam against dark leather headboards, fresh-cut sunflowers pose upon polished tables and square silver-tapped sinks rest against natural slate or travertine tiling. The Tarragon offers a finely-tuned mix of character and luxury.

Rooms: 5 fully-contained serviced self-catering units: 2 x 3-bedroom units, 1 x 2-bedroom unit and 2 x 1-bedroom units. All with full kitchen, living area and en-suite bathrooms.
Price: R700 - R2,300 per cottage per night.
Meals: Fully self-catering.
Directions: Faxed or emailed on request.

Manor Cottage & Tranquility Base

Christopher Grinton

50 Baviaanskloof Road, Hout Bay
Tel: 021-791-0212 Fax: 086-558-9420
Email: info@themanorcottage.co.za Web: www.themanorcottage.co.za
Cell: 072-211-7725

Christopher is one of those lucky people who just love what they do. Wonderfully friendly and ultra-efficient, his pride and joy are his three delightful self-catering cottages. Pacing around in his crocs, Christopher led me through breezy open-plan layouts, the sun pouring in across the wooden decking. I felt immediately at home and felt the urge to kick off my shoes and start moving my things in. Everything is white and fresh with blue bedding, deep creamy sofas and white-painted panelling. Tranquility Base feels the biggest with its huge white and granite kitchen, antique dining table and grandfather clock. It also houses Christopher's glass bottle collection, some of which he found himself on nearby beaches - my favourites are the decorated wooden shoes from the Greyton Arts Festival. This cottage also gets priority over the swimming pool, a real bonus in summer. Manor Cottage is the really homely one and can actually sleep more people; and Marmalade Sky (so named after a Beatles-inspired kaleidoscope from Christopher's childhood) is a cosy nest for two with great views over the valley. They all have lots of outside decking and individual gas or charcoal braai facilities. Christopher thinks of everything – an optional gate at the pool for kids, night lighting along the paths, free wireless internet and even a computer in case you forget your own. He also knows about a leafy glade with a waterfall only 3km away, so don't forget to ask him or he might just keep it to himself!

Rooms: 2 houses: Tranquility Base: king with en/s bath & shower, queen & twin with shared bath & shower, king with en/s shower; Manor Cottage: queen and king with shared shower, queen & twin with shared bath & shower.
Price: Tranquility Base R1,200 - R2,400 per night, Manor Cottage R800 - R1,600. All prices are for whole house up to the maximum it sleeps. Tranquility Base sleeps 8; Manor Cottage sleeps 8.
Meals: Self-catering, but coffee/tea tray provided.
Directions: Please refer to directions on the website or contact Christopher.

6 in the Circle

Nikki and Paul Barker

6 Scottsville Circle, Hout Bay
Tel: 021-790-7962 Fax: 086-554-7658
Email: nikki@6inthecircle.co.za Web: www.6inthecircle.co.za
Cell: 082-824-2218

England was their launch pad, but the travel instinct propelled Nikki and Paul to various parts of the globe before they finally landed in South Africa; "when my feet touched the tarmac, I just knew this is where I wanted to stay." And so they did, cutting themselves a generous slice of tranquility pie at 6 in the Circle. There are two luxurious rooms available here and comfort is king: big beds, gigantic pillows and large bathrooms with underfloor heating and natural therapy toiletries. If you want to get nearer to nature ask for the room with the outdoor shower - some, and I am one, love an outdoor shower! Each suite also has its own fully-equipped fitted kitchen, so if you're not in the mood you don't have to slog out to a local restaurant at dinner time. Instead wrought-iron chairs and a table placed outside on your private stoep make an ideal dining venue. There's even a herb garden so you can sprinkle on the freshest mint or thyme and the nearby harbour will provide you with the catch of the day to cook on your braai. It's only an 8-minute walk to the beach, or a short step to the solar-heated pool in the garden... but all we really wanted to do was slouch in the plump armchairs and enjoy a sundowner with our hosts.

Rooms: 2: 1 with shower, 1 with bath and shower. Both have full kitchens.
Price: R750 - R950 per suite, per night.
Meals: Self-catering. A choice of 25 restaurants in Hout Bay.
Directions: M63 to Hout Bay. L into Baviaanskloof Road. Then L into Darling Street. R into Pinedene. L into Scottsville.

Le Marais

Denis Correas and Patrice Boyer

2 Harold Close, Oakhurst
Estate, Hout Bay
Tel: 021-790-9562
Email: patrice@le-marais.co.za
Web: www.le-marais.co.za
Cell: 079-173-4353

Cape Town, Western Cape

Rethink impressions you have of 18th-century Cape Dutch homes flaunting white interiors and possibly the odd frill. Two years ago, Denis and Patrice went home with drawings of just this type of property. But after serious brainstorming, Le Marais (named after a popular quarter of Paris) conforms to no such traditions. Apéritifs may still be served at six, but as you lean over the bar your reflection will now be cast in an inky granite worktop that has ousted the yellowwood table. Outside, uninterrupted views of the back of Table Mountain remain, as does a sun-drenched courtyard, enclosing an azure pool. It's within its whitewashed, tightly-thatched exterior that this building flies so mischievously and capriciously in the face of convention. A bath stands proud as an armchair in one suite's reception, a bed usurping the gallery overhead; an open shower in another suite rains onto rippled, lava like, two-tone screed underfoot. Throughout its H-shaped plan, colour and form once thought too risqué are embraced. Five suites (Red, Rooi, Rouge, Rojo and Rosso) are given various treatments, ranging from a Spanish pop art theme to the über-chic, with an ultra-modern finish. Patrice's cuisine is also peppy (bobotie, gazpacho or Spanish omelette breakfasts and variations of Babette de Rozières' specialities for dinner), but "I am not a cook", he insists, "I am a civil engineer". I recalled the precision screed I'd just seen, and the fact that he designed a 65km concrete tunnel for Lesotho. A lot of both, I thought, but I kept it under my hat.

Rooms: 5: 4 king/twins with en-suite showers or baths and showers; 1 apartment with en-suite bath and shower (sleeps 4, with option of self-catering).
Price: R450 - R600 pp sharing. R800 for singles.
Meals: Full breakfast included. Dinners on request with 24hrs notice: R250 for 3 courses (including wine, coffee and aperitifs).
Directions: From Hout Bay Road (M63), 3km after circle with Constantia Main Road (M41) look out for the Oakhurst Farm sign on your left. Take the left immediately before this farm, which is marked Dorman Way. Continue up this, straight over Oakhurst Avenue and into Harold Close.

Platinum Guesthouse

Nina Trost
4 Little Lions Head Road, Hout Bay
Tel: 021-790-6470
Email: theplatinum@me.com Web: www.platinum-guesthouse.com
Cell: 072-877-3899

My initial reaction on arrival was 'you have got to be joking!'… and I hadn't seen the building yet. I was faced with a 40-metre, 80° mountainside driveway to negotiate; but even if you need to take a run-up, the excitement of the driveway is perfectly in keeping with the dramatic guesthouse I found at the top! Mother and daughter team Ute and Nina have moved over from Hamburg and if it's modern, innovative, European style and decor you want, well the bar has just been raised even higher. The lofty position gave me the feeling of being suspended on stilts; look left onto the last of the Twelve Apostles, straight ahead over Hout Bay village or right onto Chapman's Peak and the sea! My favourites are the three upper-level rooms whose sliding doors open onto a 20m lap pool, lawn and 'that' view. Everything is chic and functional with stone-chip concrete flooring, concrete double basins and crete-stone bathroom walls. Unusual use of materials, but they work a treat. Breakfast is taken, well, wherever you would like it: in the pool-room perhaps, or on the pool deck or in your room? If you prefer to prepare your own meals then the lower-level self-catering apartment provides you with high-tech appliances, space and comfort. You will leave Platinum not only full of memories, but also inspired by new ideas and techniques for those home improvements you've been contemplating. Check your brakes before you leave.

Rooms: 5: 4 kings with en-suite shower. 1 self-catering apartment with en-suite bath.
Price: R300 - R800 pp sharing. Self-catering apartment R1,800 - R2,200. Prices include beverages except wine and spirits.
Meals: Full breakfast included.
Directions: Faxed or emailed on request.

Bayview Lodge

Hermina Friess

19 Luisa Way, Hout Bay
Tel: 021-790-6868 Fax: 021-790-6867
Email: info@bvlodge.co.za Web: www.bvlodge.co.za
Cell: 073-116-3446

Hermina is one of those people who embodies everything that the Greenwood Guides hold most dear. She is nothing short of a bubbling delight and has an uncanny ability to make her guests feel like friends. Her enthusiasm is so engaging I immediately felt right at home. Basically she is in the right job! During her seventh holiday visit she came across Bayview, bought it, gave up her job and life in Germany, moved here, began renovating, decorating and running her guesthouse... all within just a single three-week period. The upstairs rooms allow you better views of the harbour, especially since the new wooden decks have been added, and this is where two rooms and the self-catering apartment are. She renovated the apartment to accommodate families needing a little more space and a there's a fold-out sleeper-couch for kids. Downstairs is the communal lounge and four further rooms, which are homely with pieces of locally-sourced art reminding you of where you are. Solid brass taps and mixers complement chequered tile bathrooms. Open your sliding doors to the sunny breakfast terrace, onto the pool and braai area further down the garden. Hermina is still in the process of upgrading the property (at the time of writing), but I got a pretty clear idea of how things work here by paging through the visitors book. Bayview is all about a happy team led by an inspired owner for whom caring and looking after their guests is a natural pleasure.

Rooms: 7: 1 queen with en suite shower, 1 twin with en-suite bath and shower, 2 twins with en-suite shower, 2 kings with en-suite shower, 1 king with en-suite bath and shower; 1 self-catering apartment with king and en-suite bath and shower.
Price: R295 - R375 pp sharing. Singles R490 - R550. Self-catering apartment R890 – R1,090 for unit sleeping 1 - 4.
Meals: Full English breakfast included.
Directions: See website for directions.

Ambiente Guest House

Marion Baden and Peter Forsthövel

58 Hely Hutchinson Ave, Camps Bay
Tel: 021-438-4060 Fax: 021-438-4060
Email: info@ambiente-guesthouse.com Web: www.ambiente-guesthouse.com Cell: 072-460-1953

Marion and Peter's affair with Ambiente Guest House began with a holiday. An initial joke to buy from the previous owners became a reality that ended in signatures on more than one dotted line: they not only bought the place, but also got married here. Seven years later and they're still going strong. So what does Ambiente have to sustain such marital harmony? A base of sturdy functionality is hidden beneath a layer of exciting features and continual surprises. Original native masks, chairs and colour schemes are fused with a Mediterranean feel to produce an effect of African-themed modernity. Choose from beds suspended by chains or with wavy topless posts. Immerse yourself in the big luxurious bathrooms where showers are powerful, sinks are exciting (trust me, sinks can be exciting, you'll see) and baths cry out for a glass of champagne. Amidst these mirror-filled havens things aren't always what they seem. Is that an African spear disguised as a towel rail? A boulder in the shower? This place has playful passion. It has the drama of half the mountain in the breakfast room, the shock of sand beneath your feet in the loo. If that's not enough to keep you amused, the views of mountain and ocean will make you gawp, the pool and garden will refresh and the paintings, if you look long and hard enough, will make you blush.

Rooms: 4: 3 king suites, all with en-suite bath and shower; and 1 double room with en-suite bath/shower.
Price: R490 - R780 pp sharing.
Meals: Full breakfast included. BBQs possible by arrangement.
Directions: Take the N1 or N2 to Cape Town and follow signs to Cableway/Camps Bay. Remain on M62, Camps Bay Drive, with the 12 Apostles to your left and Camps Bay down to your right. Turn Left into Ravensteyn Ave then first right into Hely Hutchinson Ave. Ambiente is number 58.

Sundowner Guest House

Cherry Crowden and Michael Kohla

41 Geneva Drive, Camps Bay
Tel: 021-438-2622 Fax: 021-438-2633
Email: stay@sundowner-guesthouse.com
Web: www.sundowner-guesthouse.com Cell: 083-690-5683

Cherry and Michael insist on superlative quality and at Sundowner Guesthouse the freshly-ground coffee is even praised by Italians. It is Cherry's hobby to gather authentic ingredients and transform them into a specifically-tailored, innovative feast. As she spoke of locally-sourced seasonal fruits, cold meats and cheeses, home-made preserves, croissants, muesli and crispy-baked loaves, I wished I had coincided my visit with breakfast. This Anglo-Austrian duo have built up a remarkable knowledge of their locality which they enthusiastically share with guests (I also gleaned my fair share of advice). Cherry's unique flair, originating in her design background, permeates the guest-house where a wholesome base of whites, creams and dark chocolate browns are spiced up with flashes of tangy oranges and lime greens. In the Penthouse Suite strips of window frame sections of Table Mountain, which appear to hang like pictures on the wall, a peep show of the Camps Bay view. Vibrant décor, quiet reading corners and a quirky, cube-seated TV area gather to form a living space accommodating of every holiday pursuit; or you could just take it easy by the pool. I pitched up for a grapetizer at Michael's watering-hole, but there are far heftier drinks on offer for those not driving and wishing to toast the sunset. A fantastic place that will keep everyone happy. *Not suitable for children under 12.*

Rooms: 4: 3 double bedrooms with en-suite bath and shower and 1 king-size bedroom suite with en-suite bath and shower.
Price: R550 – R800 pp sharing. Singles plus 50%.
Meals: Full breakfast included and light meals available on request.
Directions: Faxed or emailed on request.

Cramond House Camps Bay

Gail Voigt
Camps Bay
Tel: 083-457-1947 Fax: 021-438-1167
Email: gailvoigt@mweb.co.za
Cell: 083-457-1947

Easily stylish enough to keep the smart crowd calm, Cramond House is yet as walk-in-and-make-yourself-at-home as you'll find anywhere. Set high up, dandled on the knees of the Twelve Apostles, wall-to-wall windows along the ocean-facing front look down over Camps Bay's palm-fringed crescent of white sand. The glorious view is unavoidable, from the bedrooms, from the pool, from the wide sundeck. Will you get out of the house at all, I wonder! This is a dreamy place, the epitome of understated easy living, big on simplicity, space and light and small on clutter. My suite was huge and super-swish, with a cavernous walk-in wardrobe, deep spa and a sun deck… but all the rooms are special, particularly the fabulous new queen-bedded suite. The pool and stunning garden are also for guests, whether occupying the bed and breakfast rooms, or the complete house in peak season. Delicious things to eat and drink spill from the fridge, the bar and cupboards. Gail will be there to settle you in and introduce you to the permanent house staff (Gerald, Jan, Beauty and Miriam). Luxury at Cramond House is only half the story.

Rooms: 4: 1 queen with en-suite spa bath & shower; 1 twin en-s bath & shower; 1 double en-s sh'r & adjacent area with sleeper couch; 1 queen en-s bath & sh'r plus kitchenette. Cot, high chair etc available.
Price: R750 to R1,500 per room per night. Or complete house available in peak season R4,000 - R5,000 per day.
Meals: Refrigerator filled on arrival with everything you could possibly need, but meals can be provided.
Directions: Call or email for directions.

Ocean View House

Katrin Ludik

33 Victoria Road, Bakoven
Tel: 021-438-1982 Fax: 021-438-2287
Email: oceanv@mweb.co.za Web: www.oceanview-house.com

There's no end to Ocean View's eccentric delights with its Russian marble and award-winning gardens. Everyone has either a balcony or a terrace with fabulous views of sea, pool deck or garden. It is a hotel, but such a personal one with huge wooden giraffes hiding behind every corner and elephant print tablecloths and cushions. There's also a great pool and how many hotels run an honesty bar? To cap it all, Ocean View has its own nature reserve, a tropical garden that ushers an idyllic river from the mountains to the sea. They have placed tables and sun-loungers on the grassy river banks, a sort of exotic Wind in the Willows scenario with rocks, ferns, trees, tropical birds and butterflies. If you ever feel like leaving Ocean View, Camps Bay is a stroll away with its string of outdoor restaurants and zesty atmosphere. It's a good place to watch trendy Capetonians at play. Tired out long before they were, I walked back to the hotel. The nightwatchman was expecting me and escorted me to my room, which was also expecting me, tomorrow's weather report by my bed.

Rooms: 14: 7 suites (1 Presidential, 1 Milkwood, 4 Royal, 1 Garden); 5 Luxury Rooms (2 sea-facing, 3 garden views) & 2 Pool Deck rooms. 13 have showers, 1 Royal has bath & shower.
Price: R500 – R1,700 pp sharing. Single rates available all year.
Meals: Full breakfast is included and served until 10am.
Directions: On the coast road a mile out of Camps Bay towards Hout Bay.

Huijs Haerlem

Johan du Preez and Kees Burgers

25 Main Drive, Sea Point
Tel: 021-434-6434 Fax: 021-439-2506
Email: haerlem@iafrica.com Web: www.huijshaerlem.co.za

Don't even try and pronounce it! Imagine, it used to be called 't Huijs Haerlem, so small thanks for small mercies! But what a great place: a secret garden, perched high on the hill above Sea Point, enclosed behind walls and gates, abloom with tropical flowers in beds and earthenware pots, with suntrap lawns, a pool (salt-water, solar-heated) and views over Table Bay. The verandah frame is snaked about with a vine and small trees provide the shade. Johan and Kees have a lovely, caring approach to their guests and look after you royally. There's no formal reception area, the bar is based on honesty, all their fine Dutch and South African antiques are not hidden away for fear of breakage. In fact both of them suffer from magpie-itis and walls and surfaces teem with eye-arresting objects: a tailor's mannequin, cabinet-making tools, old linen presses. Of course breakfast is enormous with fresh breads, rolls and croissants, fruits, cheeses, cold meats and the full cooked bonanza. This is Johan's domain, a chance for him to banter with guests and make a few suggestions. All the bedrooms are different, but all have their advantage, some with private terraces, some great views, one a four-poster. Whichever room you are in you will feel part of the whole.

Rooms: 8: 5 twins and 3 doubles; all en-suite, 2 with separate bath and shower, the rest with shower over bath.
Price: R700 – R900 pp sharing. Singles plus 25%.
Meals: Full breakfast included.
Directions: Faxed or emailed on booking.

The Villa Rosa

Lynn Stacey and Heather John
277 High Level Rd, Sea Point
Tel: 021-431-2768 Fax. 021-434-3526
Email: villaros@mweb.co.za Web: www.villa-rosa.com
Cell: 082-785-3238

How I managed to drive straight past the Villa Rosa I'll never know. With dramatic red- and white-tinged walls the villa is hardly a shrinking violet. But I did anyway…. I wandered up the front path through mingled scents of wild jasmine, chives and roses and was met at the stained-glass door by Lynn, who emits the same bright warmth as her villa walls. As we chatted over juice in the kitchen we were interrupted by Buttons, a newly-adopted and very vocal cat - a happy addition to the family. The villa continues its rosy persona within. Soft rose pinks are set off with hints of contrasting greens and dark wooden furniture. Most rooms are lit by enormous bay windows and intricate chandeliers, each one unique in its delicate hanging flowers, gems and metalwork. I soon discovered that Lynn had had a chandelier 'binge' at some point. And that chandeliers were just one of many such undeniable urges; the 'bathroom binge' resulted in a complete bathroom overhaul producing the fresh stone-floored en-suite beauties now in place. The metal leaf-chairs in one room (literally chairs that look like giant leaves) were "so wacky we just bought them," says Lynn. The art binge is ongoing and the walls continue to fill up with local talent. Looking at Buttons, I wondered if Lynn would ever consider an 'adoption binge'. If so I'll be volunteering myself as the next eligible stray.

Rooms: 8: all doubles, 4 with en-suite bath and shower, 4 with en-suite shower. Possibility of joining two rooms to form a family suite. 1 self-catering unit.
Price: R290 R450 pp sharing. Singles R400 - R590.
Meals: Full breakfast included.
Directions: Emailed or faxed on request. Also on Villa Rosa website.

Blackheath Lodge

Antony Trop and John Stewart
6 Blackheath Road, Sea Point
Tel: 021-439-2541 Fax: 021-439-9776
Email: info@blackheathlodge.co.za Web: www.blackheathlodge.co.za
Cell: 076-130-6888

Another GG accommodation inspector heard about Antony, Blackheath Lodge's owner, when her brother tried to make a booking. There was no room at the inn, but instead of turning him away, Antony located a beautiful, sea-view apartment for him and charged the same price. This sort of beyond-the-call-of-duty kindness is typical of him. When I visited on a busy morning, the patio was buzzing with the happy murmur of breakfasting guests, some sitting at tables and some lolling by the solar-heated pool. Antony, meanwhile, was helping guests with the day's 'to do' list. A short walk from Cape Town central, he and his partner John decorated the house with beautiful touches. Rooms have high, corniced ceilings, pine floors, embroidered lampshades and super-soft, super-white linen. Each has its own quirk: red pattern chaises-longues, chandeliers, leopard-print armchairs, antique clocks and original cast-iron fireplaces that will warm even the coldest heart during (what can be) an icy Cape winter: "they work, let me tell you, they work!" says Antony with feeling. Most importantly guests can tuck into complimentary biscuits, and the fridge is in the bathroom so no annoying electrical hum. Lion's Head beckons for the energetic and Sea Point beach promenade, Cape Town's answer to Beverly Hills where lycra and biceps are de rigueur, is close by. If you're visiting at Christmas and New Year make sure you ask for the swish new apartment that the pair have lovingly renovated next door. *Children over 12 are welcome.*

Rooms: 10: all air-conditioned doubles/twins with en-suite bathrooms; 9 have showers and 1 has both bath and shower.
Price: R500 - R825 pp sharing. Singles on request.
Meals: Breakfast included. Specials include quiche, French toast, cinnamon pancakes & full English. Evening meals on request from about R150.
Directions: Follow signs on N1 or N2 to Cape Town then Sea Point. At end of Table Bay Boulevard turn R at second lights onto Western Boulevard. At ocean merge L, then turn L at traffic lights into Three Anchor Bay Rd, continue over lights into Glengariff Rd, then turn R into Blackheath Rd – No. 6 is on R.

De Waterkant Cottages

Tobin Shackleford and Richard Gush

40 Napier Street, De Waterkant
Tel: 021-421-2300 Fax: 021-421-2399
Email: book@dewaterkantcottages.com
Web: www.dewaterkantcottages.com Cell: 072-157-4387

Now here is something a little bit different, the chance to have your own home (albeit only for the period of your stay), right in the centre of one of Cape Town's trendiest neighbourhoods. De Waterkant Cottages is a constantly-evolving array of brightly-painted former slave cottages (some dating from the 18th century) and more modern, but sympathetically-styled, homes in the National Preservation site that is De Waterkant Village. Each is individually owned, but all are run on a day-to-day basis by Tobin, Richard and their team. Only the best are selected, assuring you of high-quality fixtures, fittings and furnishings. All have standardised luxury linen, plates, knives, forks etc, in fact everything you could ever want or need to make your stay here a pleasure. The concept is all about choice (which, trust me, will be no easy thing). First you'll have to choose between traditional and contemporary, but then you'll need to choose your exact cottage. Tobin and Richard used to live in one – could there be a higher recommendation? This particular home has furniture made from car parts, speakers are embedded in the walls and the shower has a glass roof, allowing you to gaze up at the stars while you wash. There are too many to go through them all, but I also witnessed roof decks galore, exposed wooden floors, luxury leather sofas, private gardens, roof-top jacuzzis, rain-head showers, flat-screen TVs, real fires, amazing views, plunge pools… the list goes on. (See, I said it wouldn't be an easy choice). *All accommodation serviced daily. Massages, pre-stocked fridges and airport pick-ups available. Ask for details.*

Rooms: 18 fully-serviced cottages, with one, two or three bedrooms (queen, king & twin). All main bedrooms with en-suite bathrooms, showers and air-conditioning. Online bookings and availability.
Price: R750 - R2,000 two persons per night per cottage. Additional persons R200 - R400, under 2s stay free.
Meals: All meals can be provided on request.
Directions: See website for map and instructions.

Dunkley House

Sharon Scudamore
3b Gordon St, Gardens
Tel: 021-462-7650 Fax: 021-462-7649
Email: info@dunkleyhouse.com Web: www.dunkleyhouse.com

Tucked into a quiet street in central Gardens this compact boutique hotel is a mosaic-floored, chic-Mediterranean-villa of a place. Chic maybe, but delightfully relaxed with it. This really is a place you are encouraged to feel at home in, no small feat for a hotel, however small and 'boutique'. You want to lounge under palms by the pool?… lounge; you want to help Eunice in the kitchen?… go for it. She's a fantastic cook and aside from endless breakfast delights (don't miss the fluffy omelettes), she has been known to rustle up a feast for those who want to eat in of an evening. The long dining table is neatly arranged next to a pot-bellied wood-burner for winter nights and framed by black-and-white prints of Dar es Salaam. Thankfully the bedrooms - bay-windowed, whitest linen on beds and flashes of colour in the cushions - are just a stagger away. Completed last year, Dunkley House 2 is something else. It has four ultra-modern rooms with black-and-white stucco and stained-pine flooring, an outdoor plunge pool and cubic bathrooms with angular fittings and a remote controlled, state-of-the-art lighting and air-con system. And just to add to the style, there are top-of-the-range Tivoli radios in each room. They went for the 'wow' factor... and they got it!

Rooms: 11: 6 kings, 3 queens, 1 with bath, 3 with bath and shower, all others with shower only. One apartment with 1 double and 1 twin sharing shower.
Price: From R675 – R725 pp sharing. Singles R900 – R1,100. Apartment R1,450 per night.
Meals: Full breakfast included. Other meals by arrangement.
Directions: Faxed or emailed on booking, also on website.

Acorn House

Bernd Schlieper and Beate Lietz

1 Montrose Avenue, Oranjezicht
Tel: 021 461-1782 Fax. 021-461-1768
Email: welcome@acornhouse.co.za Web: www.acornhouse.co.za

Bernd and Beate can barely contain the happiness they derive from Acorn House, and their enthusiasm rubs off quickly on all but the stoniest of their visitors. I was a pushover. The listed building, designed by busy Sir Herbert Baker in 1904, sits on the sunny, sea-facing slopes of Table Mountain with tip-top views to Table Bay. The house is typical Sir Herbert, timber colonnade, broad verandah et al, but despite the age of the house there is no sense of mustiness at Acorn, which is always kept fresh-feeling - and fresh-smelling - with its wooden floors and modern fabrics. And there is an immaculate garden with black-slate swimming pool and a sun-lounging lawn, cleanly demarcated by agapanthus and lavender bushes. Breakfast, often served by the pool ("until the last guest comes down", i.e. you can sleep in), is a no-holds-barred display of meats, cheeses, eggs and freshly-squeezed fruit juices; "probably the second best breakfast in Cape Town" is Beate's carefully-worded claim! Upstairs, in your bedroom you will find notes of welcome or farewell, chocolates and sprigs of lavender. Wine-lovers are also well served: Bernd is pazzo for the stuff, and regularly visits local vineyards to ensure that his house wines are up-to-the-moment (just for his guests' benefit, of course). Having lived in South Africa for several years now, Bernd and Beate are still awash with excitement about their surroundings; a stay in Acorn House will leave you feeling much the same.

Rooms: 9: 1 king, 3 twins and 3 doubles all with en-suite bath; 1 family suite with twin; 1 private family cottage with king.
Price: R500 - R620 pp sharing. Singles R600 - R850. Family suite and private family cottage as double R1,000 - R1,240 + R200 for up to 2 kids.
Meals: Full breakfast included.
Directions: See website or ask for fax.

Lézard Bleu Guest House

Chris and Niki Neumann
30 Upper Orange St, Oranjezicht
Tel: 021-461-4601 Fax: 021-461-4657
Email: welcome@lezardbleu.co.za Web: www.lezardbleu.co.za
Cell: 072-234-4448

It's going to be hard to book the treehouse, particularly when word gets round, but you have got to try! Surely the most wonderful bedroom in Cape Town. The trunks of two giant palm trees spear through a wooden deck at vertiginous heights and a tiny balcony is in among the topmost fronds and spikes. Lézard Bleu was just about the best guest house in Cape Town anyway, so this latest extravagant addition represents one great big cherry on a mouthwatering cake. Niki is an actress and Chris is a chef, although he has hung up his hat now… no, don't even ask! They are still young and humorous and the house remains sleek and modern with solid maplewood bedframes, white pure cotton, sandy shades and tones, bright splashes of local and modern art on the walls. Breakfast is the best beanfeast in Cape Town (and that's the opinion of other guest house owners). The Blue Lizard snakes pleasingly from area to area, each room with its own doors out to a patio and to the large pool, where deck loungers take it easy on a surrounding timber deck. There are real fires in winter, an honesty bar, free ADSL Internet access - mere details, but typical. Individual, creative, very comfortable, but most importantly this is somewhere really natural and friendly.

Rooms: 7: 1 family room; 5 doubles/twins; 4 with en/s bath and shower; 1 with en/s shr; 1 tree-house double en/s bath and shower.
Price: R440 - R660 pp sharing. Single occupancy: R650 - R1,000 pp.
Meals: Full (enormous!) breakfast included and served till 10.30am.
Directions: Ask for directions when booking.

Redbourne Hilldrop

Jonny and Sharon Levin
12 Roseberry Avenue, Oranjezicht
Tel: 021-461-1394 Fax: 021-465-1006
Email: info@redbourne.co.za Web: www.redbourne.co.za

One of the happiest and most humorous guest houses in Cape Town, so it always seems to me. Many of Jonny and Sharon's guests refuse to stay elsewhere and gifts arrive daily from overseas… well almost. It's a small, intimate place and you are spoiled: free-standing baths, fluffy duvets, big white pillows, unflowery good taste in mirrors and wood floors, magazines, African artefacts, great showers. One room has a spiral staircase down to its bathroom. You eat breakfast at a diner-style bar stretched along a wall of pretty windows with incredible city views. Guests are treated as far as possible as friends and each time I visit I notice the easy rapport that Jonny and Sharon have generated with them – probably overnight. After a mere five minutes in their company I felt all the formality of my visit slipping away like a coat in hot weather. The wall-enclosed pool comes complete with a mini-waterfall spanning the length of it and Table Mountain looming above. From here you can see if the cable car is working and for the more adventurous you're not far from the start of one of several routes to the top. Otherwise it's an easy ride down to the city bustle, the Waterfront and the Atlantic beaches. Perfect location, great hosts, GSOH!

Rooms: 4: 2 doubles with en/s showers; 1 twin with en/s bath and shower and 1 twin family room with en/s bath and shower plus a sunroom (can fit 4/5 beds).
Price: R395 - R495 pp sharing. Singles on request.
Meals: Full breakfast included. Dinners by prior arrangement. Restaurants nearby.
Directions: On website.

An African Villa

Jimmy van Tonder and Louis Nel & Keith and Cindy Whitfield

19 Carstens St, Tamboerskloof
Email: villa@capetowncity.co.za Web: www.capetowncity.co.za/villa
Tel: 021-423-2162 Fax: 021-423-2274 Cell: 082-920-5508

Louis ditched the interior design world to focus his full creative zeal on this magnificent house – or rather houses – and when I pitched up he was hard at work, pen in mouth, bent over plans for the next step. He and Jimmy have converted three entire houses into a den of 'African Zen'. The structure may be classically Victorian, but the décor is anything but, with bold, tribal colours offsetting black-painted floorboards and neutral carpets. Jimmy gave me the grand tour – trailed as ever by dachshunds Zip and Button – pointing out Louis' designer eye in every detail, from the lacquered ostrich eggs and porcupine quills (please don't pinch them, he pleads) to the hanging Zulu spears and African wedding hats. The bathrooms are compact but perfectly formed, the bedrooms are wonderfully roomy, and when you finally and reluctantly slide from between the percale cotton sheets, breakfast is a communal affair in the large airy kitchen or out on the terrace. This house is a haven, a cool retreat and while others may be sweating their way up Table Mountain just minutes away, you can be thumbing through a book in the shade of an orange tree or cooling off in the plunge pool. Go on… treat yourself. Jimmy and Louis have recently taken on two new partners in Keith and Cindy Whitfield… well three if you include their golden retriever, name of Brandi. *Library and Internet available to all guests.*

Rooms: 12 king/twins all with a/c: 5 'Superior' with bath & shower; 5 'Classic', 3 with shower, 2 with bath & shower; 2 'Standard' (street-facing).
Price: R495 - R710 pp sharing. Singles on request.
Meals: Full breakfast included.
Directions: From central Cape Town follow signs to the Cableway. At the bottom of Kloofnek Rd double back and turn left into Carstens St. Look for the second block on the left with a yellowwood tree outside.

Bayview Guesthouse

Christine Matti
10 De Hoop Avenue
Tel: 021-424-2033
Fax: 021-424-2705
Email: baychris@iafrica.com
Web: www.baychris.com
Cell: 082-414-2052

Christine and her partner Corinne are passionate about their wine and, well, passionate about just about everything. When not buzzing around the house, Swiss-born Christine is usually out cranking up Cape Town kilometres on her racing bike or working on her annoyingly low golf handicap. She arrived in South Africa a wide-eyed whippersnapper some twenty years ago, and has never quite got around to leaving. When I arrived a few renovations were reaching completion. With Christine at the helm, this is a constantly evolving place with new works of modern art from large abstract copper sculptures to paintings of women splashed in colour. But whatever changes take place the fundamental theme of the guest house as an airy haven of healthy living thankfully remains constant. White-washed walls, floor-to-ceiling tinted windows and tiled floors make this a perfect mountain-side retreat from the city centre's summer heat. Breakfasts are an Alpine feast of German breads, selected cheeses and cold meats and guests are encouraged to help themselves to a bottomless bowl of fresh fruit. Take a dip in the pool, head off for a massage at any number of nearby wellness centres, read a book on your decking balcony, and - once you've done all that - lie back on the sofa and gaze at a perfectly-framed Table Mountain through the sitting room skylight. My only disappointment? I didn't have time to stay the night. *Personal computer for guests.*

Rooms: 5: 2 queens, 1 with en-suite shower and bath, 1 with en-suite shower; 1 double with en/s shower, 1 twin with en-suite shower. 1 self-catering unit.
Price: R280 - R650 pp sharing.
Meals: Healthy breakfasts included. Cooked breakfast on request.
Directions: Follow signs from the city centre to the Cableway. From Kloofnek Rd turn R into St. Michael's Rd and then third L into Varsity St. At the T-junction turn R into De Hoop Avenue and Bayview is the second on the right.

Hillcrest Manor

Gerda and Gerhard Swanepoel
18 Brownlow Rd,
Tamboerskloof
Tel: 021-423-7459
Fax: 021-426-1260
Email:
hilcres@mweb.co.za
Web:
www.hillcrestmanor.co.za
Cell: 082-700-5760

Step inside my fantasy world for a moment: the real state of real estate doesn't exist and you can choose anywhere in Cape Town to build your new home. You'd probably end up precisely where I am now. Sadly, you're a hundred years too late and Gerda and Gerhard already live here. Happily, however, they've opened their home to guests and you'll be assured a warm welcome. Situated at the foot of Lion's Head in a leafy hillside suburb, their Victorian town house looms above the street and faces the most stunning view of Cape Town. From pool, balcony or bed you can see all the detail of the city and waterfront and Table Mountain's acclaimed acclivity clearly. This elegant house, its tall windows and wooden shutters set atop an elevated blue-stone foundation, is where Gerhard grew up. Nowadays the whitewashed steps lead up past a sunny lawn, patio and pool to a sitting room with original pressed-metal ceiling and a bright breakfast room, where the local artwork is for sale. Upstairs the bedrooms are designed to give respite from the long hot summer. Floors are a mix of polished timber and seagrass, beds are pine, furniture wicker. Ceiling-fans loll lazily and curtains billow in the breeze. One bedroom is pure C.S.Lewis, though here the wardrobe leads not to Narnia, but to your own claw-foot bath.

Rooms: 6: all doubles with en-suite shower, one with bath too.
Price: R380 – R450 pp sharing. Singles R680.
Meals: Full breakfast included.
Directions: Faxed or emailed on booking.

Jardin d'Ebène

Pascale Lauber and Ulrike Bauschke
21 Warren Road, Tamboerskloof
Tel: 021-426 1011 Fax: 021-422-2423
Email: info@jardindebene.co.za Web: www.jardindebene.co.za

I wonder if the neighbours are aware that sandwiched between them is a tropical paradise and surely one of the most exquisite places to stay in Cape Town? Perhaps not, as this Old Cape Dutch (1900) townhouse is well sequestered behind gates, walls and giant bamboo. But on entering you will be transported by Le Jardin d'Ebène (almost pronounced day-ben). I'm not exactly sure where to, such is the eclectic nature of the decor and the originality of the design… but somewhere exotic anyway… and somewhere rather wonderful too! Every area of the house provides a powerful atmospheric 'kick'. I was served tea on the verandah, a cool place looking through billowing white drapes over a black-slate plunge pool, where gorgeous pygmy beds from central Africa are arranged on decking. Inside, much of the furniture is locally made to Pascale and Ulrike's specifications. And ALL (capitals intended) of the antiques, modern paintings and artefacts have been picked out and creatively arrayed with impeccable good taste. I loved the carved double doors from India, for example, but there are so many fascinating things to catch the eye that my tour around the house was slow and envious. Each of the five bedrooms has an African feel, but this theme is so idiosyncratic that you can put away any naff notions of zebra print or spears on the wall. On top of the gorgeous looks of this place, Pascale and Ulrike pay incredible attention to detail in caring for their guests and I have a feeling this is going to become a big favourite among GG guests. *Children over 14 are welcome.*

Rooms: 5: 1 king/twin with en-suite open-plan double shower; 1 queen with en-suite bath/shower; 1 queen with en-suite double shower; 1 luxury king with separate bath/shower; 1 luxury king with open plan bath in room.
Price: R375 - R600 pp. Singles on request. Airport transfer available.
Meals: Full breakfast included. Freshly-squeezed orange juice and great coffee.
Directions: See website.

Map Number: 3

Entry Number: 36

Alta Bay

Ariel Glownia
12 Invermark Crescent, Cape Town
Tel: 021-487-8800 Fax: 021-487-8822
Email: info@altabay.com Web: www.altabay.com

Alta Bay is perched high up on the last bit of Table Mountain that still slopes and above me I watched the cable car disappear into the 'tablecloth', a stream of white cloud pouring off the plateau. Behind the house walls, thick purple wisteria clambers everywhere, hiding the house from view and creating any number of private corners. I stepped across what felt like a small bridge and was met by Ariel, my urbane and very friendly host, who led me onto the first-floor balcony and a wonderful branch-framed vista of the city and harbour below. Ariel's penchant is for the modern and artworks throughout the house are always gorgeous and often unexpected; one New York artist has, for example, cleverly adapted the words of various presidential inaugural speeches. Sometimes the style resonates with Ariel's Portuguese roots, but everywhere there is coolness and space. Furnishings are all of a very high 'urban chic' standard with extra-length beds with slatted, wooden headboards, percale cotton sheets and a range of mod cons such as flat-screen TVs, phones, DVD/CD players etc. For a little more privacy, the separate apartment with its mezzanine bedroom is the obvious choice. On a lower level you'll find a breakfast room of coloured-glass tables and jaunty bulb-shaped vases. Here, too, there is a living room that opens onto a gorgeous terrace, with sun-beds and a pool. From Alta Bay you can look down on not just the city and harbour, but also on all those that have foolishly booked in elsewhere!

Rooms: 7: 4 king/twin, 3 king; all en-suite - 3 with bath and shower, 4 with shower only.
Price: May - August incl. R1,300 - R1,700 per room per night. Sept - April incl. R2,500 - R3,000. Prices include all beverages.
Meals: Full breakfast included. Lunch and dinner snack menu.
Directions: Near Orangezicht area. See website for details.

Gap Lodge

Linda and Le Roi Steenkamp
13 Newport Street, Tamboerskloof
Tel: 021-424-6564 Fax: 086-6424-674
Email: book@gaplodge.co.za Web: www.gaplodge.co.za
Cell: 082-896-8165

From the foundations to the stylish interior every inch of Gap Lodge has been primped and preened to Linda and Le Roi's exacting standards. With just three double rooms Gap Lodge is a small and ideal pocket of calm in the most vibrant part of the Mother City, within 5 minutes' drive of Table Mountain and within walking distance of the restaurants of Kloof and Long Streets. Each bedroom is practical and stylish with an antique hanger here and a vase of fresh lilies there, crisp white linen and towels offset by bold orange or blue bedheads. Linda's artistry decorates the earth-coloured walls with bold and beautiful paintings. After a deep sleep on "the best mattress in Cape Town" – thus spake a previous guest but I had a go too and it is magically giving yet supportive! - Linda conjures up an exceptional full breakfast. Le Roi personally tailors day trips or tours for guests. Having worked as a tour guide since 2002 with his own company (Gap Tours), Le Roi is a fountain of knowledge and will whisk guests away in the house mini-bus. For anyone who has spent a morning queuing, sweating and possibly even swearing in a tourist information office, going on your own personalised tour with Le Roi is like being upgraded from the luggage hold to first class. From 'Flora, Fauna and Vino' day trips to golf tours he will take all the hassle out of holiday-making. 'Beyond the call of duty' is an unfamiliar phrase to this couple: Linda has even been known to raid her own wardrobe on behalf of those guests who forget to pack essential items of clothing!

Rooms: 3 kings with en-suite shower.
Price: R450 - R600 pp sharing. Singles R700.
Meals: Full breakfast included.
Directions: From the airport take N2 to City. Follow signs from City Centre to Cableway. Once in Kloofnek Road look out for convenience store 'Kloofnek Superette' on left. Turn left into Newport Street immediately afterwards and Gap Lodge will be on your right.

Gilmour Hill B&B

Maureen Marshall
7 Gilmour Hill Road, Tamboerskloof
Tel: 021-422-5111 Fax: 021-422-5111
Email: mhmarshall@telkomsa.net Web: www.gilmourhill.co.za
Cell: 083-459-5377

Everyone from puppeteers to film crews comes to stay with Maureen in her picture-postcard 1892 Victorian townhouse. Original features that you would want retained have been retained... large open fireplaces and snug window-seats etc. And original features that you would prefer to see replaced over the last hundred years have been replaced!... the very modern wet room, for example, is brand spanking new. Rooms are peppered with artefacts from Tibet, India and Nepal as well as Africa. The Blue Room is particularly special with views of Table Mountain and Lion's Head from the bath and the Atlantic from the bed. The family photos on display are a clear invitation to guests to make themselves at home – an intimacy rarely encouraged, perhaps, in one of the city's trendiest central areas and an indication of why repeat visitors to Cape Town choose to stay with Maureen. Who is, by the way, as vibrant as the home she's created. Whilst pouring tea (from her family's antique silver tea pot, naturally) on the suntrap terrace, she spoke self-deprecatingly in her Scottish lilt of her own travels. On further grilling it transpired that Maureen is something of a local celebrity. When not making Knickerbocker Glories or eggs Benedict for her guests ("I like a culinary challenge"), she's probably being interviewed about the shop she runs with her daughter or fund-raising for various social projects. She is sure to become a Greenwood celebrity as well. *Children by arrangement only.*

Rooms: 4: 1 luxury queen suite with bath and shower; 1 king/ twin with shower; 2 twins, 1 with bath and shower and 1 with shower.
Price: From R450 - R650 pp sharing. Singles from R700 - R900.
Meals: Continental breakfast included. Full breakfast on request (NB - Knickerbocker Glories!).
Directions: From CT airport, take N2 to CT/ Waterfront.

Cotswold House and Lagoon Lodge

Nick and Bettina Wiesmann

6 Cotswold Drive, Milnerton
Tel: 021-551-3637 Fax: 021-552-4228
Email: cotswoldhouse@gmail.com Web: www.cotswoldguesthouse.com
Cell: 076-112-7796

I was touched by three wide-smiling welcomes before Bettina knew I'd arrived. The beaming gardener ushered me through the gates, taking a momentary break from his sterling work on these immaculate grounds, followed by the upbeat assistant manager, Zintle, and her equally chirpy colleague at the main door. There's certainly a buzz in the air at this c.1930s historic house, which stands proud with six ornate, gabled facades. This was the private retirement residence of Mr Van Zyl, the last governor of the province, which much wall-space pays tribute to. From the Governor's Bar (with plenty of chocolates, dates and other nibbles to hand), guests are welcome to tinkle on the 1920s Allison baby grand from London, or take stock of framed, turn-of-the-century photos (starting with Muizenberg Railway Station and Cape Town Harbour, before working their way along the corridors, staircases and landings beyond). The energy emanating from the breakfast room is part gastro and part solar: the ubiquitous window-panels draw in a sun-saturated terrace, palm, lapa, fountain and pool (which is one to be proud of). Table Mountain dominates the view from the vine-topped patio, and from the upstairs rooms Robben Island begins to creep in. In addition to views of Lion's Head, Signal Hill and the sea, you overlook the only true links golf course in South Africa. Just across the road lurk Lagoon Lodge and more resident rooms with further perks: massive outdoor braai facilities, pillared verandahs, ducks, ponds and pools.

Rooms: 18. 7 in Cotswold House: 5 king/twins w en/s bath & shower; 1 queen with en/s shower, 1 queen with private bath & sh'r. 11 further B&B & self-catering options available, just call Bettina.
Price: R400 - R700 pp sharing. Singles on request. American Express cards not accepted.
Meals: Full breakfast included. Plenty of restaurants nearby, and braai facilities if you want them.
Directions: Emailed or faxed on request. Directions are also available on the website.

Medindi Manor

Kyle Bowman and Lynda Bomyer

4 Thicket Road, Rosebank
Tel: 021-686-3563 Fax: 021-686-3565
Email: reservations@medindimanor.com Web: www.medindimanor.com
Cell: 082-857-9735

Medindi is a secluded Edwardian manor of grand dimensions, banded by ground and first-floor verandahs with a garden and swimming pool tucked away behind tall hedges and bushes. Some of the rooms have their own doors out onto the verandah and the main building has been renovated with panache and a sensitive feel for the period. Although well stocked with bar fridges, telephones, TVs etc, Medindi avoids like the plague any h(ot)ellish homogeneity in its décor and design. The Oregon pine floors, bay windows, intricate ceilings and marble fireplaces are original and there are unique, antique touches everywhere, such as Edwardian designs for stately marble and slate floors. Bathrooms have free-standing baths, Victorian 'plate' showerheads, brass fittings and a small antique cabinet has been found for each. There is modernity too, in bright wall colours (yellows and blues), and splashes of modern art – from the turn of one century to the turn of the next. Music is an important ingredient for Medindi's owner, and classical music and a bit of smooth jazz wafts through reception. A freewheeling, relaxed and youthful place. Kyle and Sharon share the day-to-day management of Medindi and six new rooms have been created from a converted outbuilding – the smaller rooms are cheaper.

Rooms: 15: 7 in the manor house: 6 dbles & 1 twin, 4 with en-s bath + shower, 3 with en-s shower; 3 garden rooms & 3 large garden suites in converted outbuilding, all en-s shower; 2 self-catering cottages.
Price: R385 - R855 pp sharing. Singles R685 - R1,455.
Meals: Continental buffet breakfast included. Full cooked breakfast extra R55. Many restaurants nearby for dinner or take-out.
Directions: See map on website or phone ahead.

3 Pear Lane

Vo Pollard
3 Pear Lane, Newlands
Tel: 021-689 1184 Fax: 021-689-1184
Email: pollards@iafrica.com Web: www.pearlane.co.za
Cell: 082-926-3080

At the foot of Devil's Peak mountain, deep within the lush greenery of Newlands and within one decently hooked six from the cricket ground, there lies a distinctly English garden idyll. The hugest oak I've seen marks the spot and the place in question is Vo's picture-perfect pad. A food stylist by trade, it's good to see that she employs her craft after hours too. Everything here is just as you'd like it; the huge sash windows breathe beams of light into the rooms, the king-sized bed is dressed up in the best percale linen and embroidered cotton throws and the bathroom comes with storage space aplenty, two big stone basins and a mighty-looking, pebble-floored shower. With its French wrought-iron table, silk-cushioned chairs and vase of delicate daisies, the view out to the garden could be straight from one of Vo's shoots; home-baked scones, strawberry jam and clotted cream, naturally, would be the scene's edible accompaniment. There's a nice collection of guide-books and yes, foodie mags for you to devour, perhaps whilst lounging by the salt-water pool. Lavender, moonflowers, roses and azaleas, to name but a few, adorn the patio and lawn. Manicured but never overdone, sniffable but not overwhelming, this is exactly the way gardens... well, dainty English ones anyway... should be. Should you want to stretch your legs, Newlands Forest, my favourite Cape Town walking haunt, is right next door. Vo is also now an authorized tour guide. In her own words: "I now have the knowledge of the Cape Province to pass onto visitors who wish to go on day tours out of Cape Town."

Rooms: 1 garden suite with king/twin bed, en-suite shower and well-equipped kitchen.
Price: R350 - R420 pp sharing. Singles on request.
Meals: By prior arrangement, menu on request.
Directions: Take M3 from Cape Town towards Muizenberg. Take the Newlands feed-off and then turn right into Newlands Avenue. Go over one set of lights, then turn first left into Palmboom Rd. Pear Lane is half-way down on the right.

Hedge House

Judy and Graham Goble

12 Argyle Road, Newlands
Tel: 021-689-6431 Fax: 021-689-1286
Email: hedge@mweb.co.za Web: www.hedgehouse.co.za
Cell: 083-324-0888

The Gobles are an intriguing mixture of Doctor Doolittle and the Swiss Family Robinson, for Hedge House is home to all creatures great and small. It even has its own tree platform and a pirate-boat swing, not to mention prime views of Cape Town's highest mountain, Devil's Peak. Judy was once a veterinary nurse, and the family owns three dogs, two cats, an elusive chameleon and an assortment of avian oddities, including Doris the parrot who insisted on calling my name throughout the whole visit! She (Judy not Doris!) showed me the family home, accompanied by the glorious smell of wild jasmine. I climbed the outdoor spiral stairs to a deck perforated by a camphor tree, where I beheld the setting sun pouring into a large guest room, making the splendid wardrobe glow an even deeper red. A guest recovering from a knee operation was staying in the room facing onto the vegetable garden, where onions, broccoli, red cabbage and lavender poked out from behind a miniature hand-made fence. The gardens are nourished by Judy's own earthworm farms. All the rooms have private entrances, so guests can stroll to the pool or wander around the garden. The pathways, winding their way from the new deck through tree ferns and indigenous plants, is a mini botanical adventure, although there is treasure to be found inside too. Don't miss Graham's private collection of paintings in the 'Loo-uvre', found near the huge refectory table where guests eat breakfast. What a perfect place to be refreshed!

Rooms: 4: 2 twin/king, 1 king & 1 queen with en-suite bath and shower. Families accommodated with single beds on request.

Price: R550 pp sharing. R800 singles.

Meals: Fruit salad and yoghurt come every day, plus a variety of home-made croissants and crumpets. Full English breakfast served daily.

Directions: From the airport travel on the N2 towards the city. Take Exit 8 – Liesbeek Parkway. At bottom of off-ramp turn left to Rondebosch. Travel 3.5km. When you see the traffic lights, one road before Keurboom Rd, turn left into Argyle Road. Hedge House is No. 12 on the RHS.

Highlands Country House

Carole Armstrong-Hooper
36 Tennant Road, Upper Kenilworth
Tel: 021-797-8810 Fax: 021-761 0017
Email: info@highlands.co.za Web: www.highlands.co.za

Highlands Country House, sitting splendidly on Wynberg Hill beneath Devil's Peak, is one of the Cape's most majestic homes. In front, a formal garden runs along avenues of fig trees down to trim lawns and flowerbeds - picked daily for fresh bouquets - and I went for a wander, ambling past a fountain and various Grecian urns before reaching one of two swimming pools. Here there is a spa where they will pamper you to within an inch of your life. Up at the house, meanwhile, all was efficient bustle, with smartly-dressed maids busily clearing away breakfast, leaving only the faint but delicious smell of bacon and eggs lingering on the terrace. I passed a magnificent, carved foot-throne in the foyer and a dining room all dressed up in starched white linen on my way to meet Carole in the library for a chat… and a delectable strawberry smoothie. She fell in love with the place when she once came here for tea, which is a special time of day at Highlands, honoured with freshly-baked cakes. Meanwhile, gourmet dinners are best served by candlelight in the conservatory. Separate from the house, large European style rooms are elegant in neutral tones, while England prevails inside a rush-carpeted warren of staircases and wings. Styles vary subtly in traditional rooms from African flourishes, to Cupid-guarded loft rooms, to Brosely-tiled bathrooms, to shades of blue in St Leger silk curtains. Part the shutters or step onto your balcony and look onto woods, sports fields, mountains and sea... and be very content with your choice.

Rooms: 14: 6 twin/king, 3 king, 4 queen and 1 honeymoon suite with king. All are fully en-suite, with the exception of one shower en-suite.
Price: R575 - R1,500 pp sharing. Singles: R975 - R1,800.
Meals: Full breakfast included. Lunch and dinner on request.
Directions: Tennant Road is a continuation of Newlands Road, reached either by the Constantia or Rondebosch exits on the M3. See website for more detailed directions.

Dendron

Shaun and Jill McMahon
21 Ou Wingerd Pad, Constantia
Tel: 021-794-6010 Fax: 021-794-2532
Email: stay@dendron.co.za Web: www.dendron.co.za
Cell: 082-4911-647 or 082-296-0691

(Quite) A few years ago, Shaun bought a Land Rover in Taunton (UK) and drove it here. Hardly odd when you see the place, now replete with relaxed family atmosphere, collie dogs and cricket pegs (or whatever they're called) on the front lawn. You get all the benefits of living the South African good life by default here. Green-fingered Jill genuinely loves having guests and her enthusiasm for life is evident in everything. The cottages are private in leafy, jasmine-scented gardens and have fully-equipped kitchens stocked with basics, a braai and stunning views to the mountains on the right and False Bay in the distance. Two cottages have terracotta-tiled or wooden floors and beds with Indian cotton throws - perfect for families. The other two are newly-renovated cottages with kilims, safari prints and plump sofas. All are fully serviced. Evening pool-side views at sunset and moonrise, helped along by wine from over-the-hedge Groot Constantia vineyard, will make you want to throw away the car keys and stay (which is exactly what Shaun did when he first clapped eyes on the place). When you are hungry, Jill will send you off there through the back gate and across the vineyards to the Simons restaurant for dinner. Return by torch- and moonlight. Dendron (GK=tree) is a small slice of heaven.

Rooms: 4: 2 cottages with 1 double and 1 twin with bath and shower; 2 cottages with twin, 1 with bath & shower, 1 with shower only. Serviced daily Mon - Sat.
Price: From R350 - R500 pp sharing. Singles on request.
Meals: Breakfast for first morning provided and afterwards if requested (R50 pp).
Directions: Fax on request.

Klein Bosheuwel and Southdown

Nicki and Tim Scarborough
51a Klaassens Rd, Constantia
Tel: 021-762-2323 Fax: 021-762-2323
Email: kleinbosheuwel@iafrica.com Web: www.kleinbosheuwel.co.za
Cell: 083-227-0700

Who needs Kirstenbosch? Nicki has manipulated the paths and lawns of her own garden (which is pretty well an extension of the Botanical Gardens anyway - less than a minute's walk away) so that the views are not dished out in one vulgar dollop! Instead you are subtly led into them, with glimpses through mature trees (flowering gums, yellowwoods and camellias) and lush flower-beds. And finally your stroll leads you down to umbrellas on a ridge with Table Mountain and the Constantiaberg laid out magnificently before you and the sea distantly below. "Keep it plain" is Nicki's motto, so the upstairs bedrooms are simply white and all naturally endowed with garden views. The salt-water swimming pool is hidden deep in the garden and Klein Bosheuwel is the sort of place where you could just hang out for a few days. I was introduced to one English guest who had clearly no intention of going anywhere that day - the cat that got the cream! Or you can stay next-door at Southdown. With a small-scale Lost Gardens of Heligan on her hands, Nicki peeled back the jungle to find pathways, walls and, best of all, enormous stone-paved circles just in the right spot between the house and pool. Today the house is filled with surprises: zebra skins, porcupine-quill lamps, onyx lamp stands, a whole stuffed eagle, a wildebeest's head, a piano, two tortoises, deep carpets and couches, marble bathrooms and terraces off most rooms.

Rooms: 8: 1 twin en/s bath; 2 queens with en/s bath & sep' shower; 1 queen en/s large bath; 1 king with corner bath & separate shower; 1 twin & 1 king with en-s bath & shower. 1 self-catering cottage (2 bedrooms, 2 bathrooms, open-plan kitchen & lounge area).
Price: R620 - R695 pp sharing. Singles R915 - R1,025.
Meals: Full breakfast included. Other meals can be provided by prior arrangement.
Directions: Fax or website.

Kaapse Draai

Annelie Posthumus
19 Glen Avenue, Constantia
Tel: 021-794-6291 Fax: 021-794-6291
Email: info@kaapsedraaibb.co.za Web: www.kaapsedraaibb.co.za
Cell: 082-923-9869

Annelie has been charming Greenwood Guide travellers since the very first edition and should be in the running for some sort of award for B&B brilliance. Relaxed, simple and beautiful seems to be the rule here. Her daughter is an interior designer and their talents combine to make the house a peaceful temple to uncluttered Cape Cod-style living. Neutral furnishings and white cottons are frisked up with pretty floral bolsters and country checks. Sunny window-seats are perfect for reading guide-books on the area and there are posies of fresh flowers in each room. I was lucky enough to stay with Annelie and once installed in my room, she invited me down for a soup later. She is a prolific gardener and you can walk (perhaps with Annelie's dogs) from the tropical greenery of Kaapse Draai, with its mountain stream, huge ferns and palms, into lovely Bel-Ombre meadow and the forest next door. From there it is a three-hour walk to the Table Mountain cable station. Porcupines come into the garden at night from the mountain (they love arum lilies apparently) and there are many birds too, including the noisy (and palindromic) hadedah. A grand old willow tree is what you'll park your car under. Delicious breakfasts are taken outside in the sunshine whenever possible. All I can say is – do. *Wine estates and Constantia shopping village nearby.*

Rooms: 3: 1 double and 2 twins with en-suite shower.
Price: R350 pp sharing. Singles R450. Between Nov 1st and March 31st there is a supplementary charge of R50 per room for 1-night stays.
Meals: Full breakfast included. Annelie sometimes cooks if the mood is upon her. But do not expect this....
Directions: Ask for fax or email when booking.

Constantia Stables

Lola and Rick Bartlett

8 Chantecler Lane, off Willow Rd, Constantia
Tel: 021-794 3653 Fax: 021-794-3653
Email: tstables@mweb.co.za Web: www.constantiastables.co.za
Cell: 082-569-4135

I loved The Constantia Stables and would be as happy as a pig in clover to be among Lola and Rick's regular visitors. Not only is it a stunning spot of shaded indigenous gardens and beautifully renovated stable buildings (ask for the hayloft room!), but there's a genuine family feel to the place that is immediately relaxing. The Bartlett children are actors and their photos are plastered across the drawing room and bar. This is the heart of the Stables, a congenial snug of heavy armchairs, low beams and earth-red walls where guests are encouraged to tap into a well-stocked bar. I liked the breakfast room too with its red-brick fireplace. My mouth watered as Lola reeled off her gargantuan breakfast menu: fresh fruit salad with home-grown guava, quince and peaches, hams, salamis, a giant cheese board, yoghurts, cereals and croissants and that's before you even think about cooked delights. She and Rick have done a fantastic job converting the original stables into bedrooms with old, olive-green stable doors opening onto an ivy-fringed courtyard. This year they have also added a self-catering studio accessed via an outside staircase onto a sundeck overlooking the vineyards and mountains. The garden suite overlooks the pool and, like Lily's cottage, seamlessly blends into the mass of plants that spread out beneath two enormous plane trees. And once you're suitably chilled there's a whole bunch of vineyards and restaurants to explore just next door.

Rooms: 7: all en-suite with either king, queen or twin beds with bath or shower or both; 1 self-catering cottage with 2 bedrooms, 2 showers, lounge & kitchenette; 1 self-catering studio with bath and shower.
Price: From R495 pp sharing. Singles on request.
Meals: Full breakfast included.
Directions: Follow M3 towards Muizenberg. Take Ladies Mile off-ramp. Turn L at traffic lights onto Ladies Mile and L at next lights onto Spaanschemat River Rd. Keep L at fork then L into Willow Rd and L into Chantecler Lane. The Stables is at end on L.

Cape Witogie

Rosemary and Bob Child

9 Van Zyl Rd, Kreupelbosch, Constantia
Tel: 021-712-9935 Fax: 021-712-9935
Email: capewitogie@netactive.co.za Web: www.capestay.co.za/capewitogie
Cell: 082-537-6059 or 082-852-9084

Even if you're not a dog lover you'll soon find yourself falling for the charming Miss Poppy, Cape Witogie's desperately friendly Boston Terrier. In fact, such is her popularity that guests come back year after year to see her. Then again that could also be because of her equally charming owners, Rosemary and Bob. When I visited, Rosemary was frantically packing for a trip to the UK, but she happily showed me round their red-bricked home with its two guest bedrooms. Both rooms are whitewashed, tile-floored self-catering units, one with an airy conservatory/sitting room. They open on to a compact garden full of ferns and firs, lavender pots, lemon trees and citrus-smelling verbena. Hot-plates, a small oven and microwaves give ample scope for knocking up your own meals, though Rosemary enjoys making occasional breakfasts. I'd recommend coming with some pals and taking both rooms as a base from which to explore the Cape Town area. From the City Bowl and beaches to Table Mountain, the botanical gardens and nearby winelands there is just so much to do in the Cape that a full week with Bob and Rosemary flies by in the blink of an eye. These are great people (with a great dog) running a great-value get-away.

Rooms: 2 units: both consist of 1 twin room (1 extra single bed can be added to each if required) with en-suite showers and small kitchens.
Price: R260 - R285 pp sharing per night self-catering. R50 pp supplement for one night booking.
Meals: Self-catering.
Directions: Faxed or emailed on booking.

Beluga of Constantia

Daphne Hough
5 Connor Place, Constantia, Cape Town
Tel: 021-794-4594
Email: info@belugaguesthouse.com Web: www.belugaguesthouse.com
Cell: 076-477-0395

Was it the fact that we had both lived in Dorset that made me feel so at home with Daphne? Or was it the sense of serenity that welled up in me even as I passed through the gates of Beluga? I reckon a bit of both, and even if for you Dorset is a wild place in a far-flung corner of the globe, you'll be sure to feel it too. Daphne and I drank tea and ate biscuits on the terrace under the baleful eye of a wooden giraffe, and I relaxed and luxuriated in the colourful vibrancy of the garden and the radiance of the sun. The walk back from brilliant sunshine into the traditional dining room, with its forest of family photos on dark furniture surfaces and sonorous grandfather clock, is a brief journey of delightful sensory contrasts. The bedrooms are all painted a different shade of eggshell. Daphne's lightness of touch is visible in all of them. Fine brass bedsteads and red-and-white chequered stools lend a Provençal charm to the rooms, and little wooden birds peek shyly out from under the bedside tables, their feet warmed by the underfloor heating. On re-emergence, my ears took time to re-adjust to the hustle and bustle of Cape Town after the calm of Beluga. Its traditional and cosy interiors and colourful exteriors, along with Daphne's easy hospitality, are an unbeatable formula. People who are after a thoroughly relaxing stay in a charming guest house will be hooked.

Rooms: 3: 1 king and 1 single with en-suite shower; 1 king with en/s shower; 1 king with en/s bath and shower.
Price: R350 - R495 pp sharing.
Meals: Full breakfast included.
Directions: From the airport on the N2 turn left onto M3 signed Constantia/Kirstenbosch. Left Junction 14 signed Constantia/Hout Bay. Then Left onto M41, then right onto Brommersvlei Rd. First left after Southern Cross Drive into Connor Close.

Majini

Suzy Digby-Smith

4 Broadacres, Colyn Road, Constantia Hills
Tel: 021-715-0155 Fax: 021-715-0155
Email: suzyds@kingsley.co.za
Cell: 082-439-9490

'Majini' is Swahili for 'by the water' but it wasn't apparent to me why the name was appropriate until I had strolled past vivid flowerbeds to the bottom of the velvety garden. A large wooden deck awaited, laden with a huge braai, one side opening to the pool and the other to a small dam and stream with views of the lesser-known Elephants' Eye Peak and Suzy's chickens and ducks squabbling in the foreground. This little farmyard neighbours a flourishing, organic veg patch and Suzy's guests are encouraged to help themselves to eggs and any potatoes, passion fruit or greenery that they like the look of. The garden offerings don't end there either – the path to the cottage winds its way through a herb garden and there are beautifully-tended lilies and colourful daises which parade themselves in the open-plan kitchen and sitting room as well as the bedrooms. A self-confessed auction-addict, Kenyan-born Suzy has decorated both the cottage and salon simply, but with great care. Touches like well-thumbed paperbacks make the house familiar while luxuries like a Krupps coffee-machine ensures that all comfort bases are covered. Suzy easily high-jumps the hospitality bar set by most self-catering owners, happily stocking the fridge for guests, loaning her garden for small parties or creating a romantic haven by the pool for couples. A sign in the loo reads, 'Always Give Thanks'. At Majini this is an unnecessary reminder.

Rooms: 2 units. 1 cottage with 1 king/ twin and 1 queen. 1 en-suite with shower and 1 bathroom with bath and shower separate. 1 salon with 1 double and en-suite shower room.
Price: Cottage R1,000 - R1,750. Salon R750 - R1,000.
Meals: Fully self-catering.
Directions: On the N2 from the airport, take the N3 towards Muizenberg. Exit 16 for Ladies Mile. Turn right at traffic light and take 3rd exit at roundabout. Take second left onto Soetvlei Avenue. After 0.9km left onto Colyn Road and first right into Broadacres.

Bishopsgrace

Katrina Weixelbaumer and Clare Black
5 Upper Hillwood Avenue, Bishopscourt
Tel: 021 762-2250 Fax: 021-762 0249
Email: info@bishopsgrace.com Web: www.bishopsgrace.com
Cell: 082-713-5683

As I was waved out of Bishopsgrace with a smile on my face, a tummy full of chocolate biscotti and an armful of Cape Town recommendations, I tried to put my finger on what puts it in a league of its own. Bishopsgrace synthesises the lavish comforts of somewhere rather starry with the personable, slightly eccentric feel of an outstanding homestay. Let me explain. Starting at the huge outside area where a worn leather sofa presides over a view of Kirstenbosch Gardens and Devil's Peak, Clare led me on a tour of the house, chatting to me all the while, but also finding time to exchange quips and pleasantries with smiling members of staff and equally smiling guests as we went. Classical figures printed on opulent curtains and bedspreads are typical of the grand style throughout the house, while Kathrin's inventiveness means that there are many little creative marvels to be discovered. My favourites were a hand-painted tree on an antique dresser and a pair of brass bedside lamps that were once spray-cans in a local vineyard. The smaller rooms each have four-posters, while a double bed on the balcony awaits residents of Room 3. Genius ideas are de rigueur. Each guest, for example, is loaned a local mobile phone full of credit and useful restaurant numbers. You may not need it though. With two pools, a floodlit tennis court, endless walks and even a gym kit, you can prepare for your goose-feather mattress without leaving the grounds. Well deserving of the glowing accolades that jostle for prominence in the guest book.

Rooms: 8: 5 king/twin, 3 x 4-poster kings. 7 with bath and separate shower and 1 with shower.
Price: R625 - R2,025 pp sharing. Singles R810 - R2,790.
Meals: Full breakfast included. Other meals can be provided only by prior arrangement.
Directions: From Cape Town take the M3 to Muizenberg, pass the university, through 4 traffic lights. Up Edinburgh Drive, take right-hand exit to Bishopscourt, first left into Forest Avenue, first right into Hillwood Avenue.

Number 8

Lesley Arnot
Avenue Beauvais, Constantia
Tel: 021-794-6150 Fax: 021-794-0975
Email: lesarnot@iafrica.com Web:
Cell: 082-412-6220

The Arnots used to live at number 9 and decided they had to move. That much was certain. But where to? They couldn't bear to leave Avenue Beauvais, one of Constantia's prettiest roads. In the end they upped sticks and moved lock, stock and barrel... to number 8. Which I have to admit is a serious pile. The interiors have been sensationally made over by Lesley, who is an interior decorator by profession, and would pose perfectly on the front page of any lifestyle magazine on any coffee table. Walking through the front door, past an exquisite rosewood piano and a vase overflowing with lilies, I stopped and gawped. I am a stopper and gawper by nature! The modern kitchen, dining area, sitting room, outdoor (and indoor) braai, garden and swimming pool all morph into one cathedral-like space with the help of some vast folding glass doors. Lesley's got it pitch perfect because, although the space is baronial and ideal for liquid dinner parties, I could also well imagine kicking off my shoes and curling up in front of the fire. Upstairs, modern décor continues to mingle spicily with antique furnishings. Walls and fabrics are various shades of bronze, pewter and chrome and the bathrooms are open-plan with globe-sized shower heads (one of the showers opens safari-style for a full-body airing). The more modest cottage juxtaposes earthy colours and stripy antique rugs with modern walls and is a delightful little retreat with its own private patio, which opens to the pool, which opens to the tennis court and finally looks towards the Stellenbosch mountains.

Rooms: 5: 4 in main house with 1 luxury, 1 superior with separate bath & shower & 2 standard with shower. Cottage: king/twin en-s sh'r. Fully serviced.
Price: Whole house with cottage and staff R9,000 - R11,000. Cottage R1,200 - R1,500. Luxury suite R1,200 - R1,400 pp. Superior room R900 - R1,400 pp. Standard R500 - R700 pp.
Meals: B&B on request. Chef also on request.
Directions: From Cape Town take M3 to Muizenberg. Take Constantia turn-off & turn L at stop onto Constantia main road. At 2nd lights turn R onto Brommersvlei Rd. Take L onto Klaassenbosch & at end of road turn L into Beauvais.

White Cottage

Jane and Derrick Verster-Cohen

12 Upper Primrose Avenue,
Bishopscourt
Tel: 021-762-1047
Fax: 021-762-4992
Email:
info@cape-townbb.co.za
Web:
www.cape-townbb.co.za
Cell: 082-492-2281

Jane's jolliness and eccentricity are in perfect equilibrium and I knew as soon as I met her - and her bouncing canine companions - that she had the Greenwood *je ne sais quoi* in abundance. Whisking me through her sprawling, beautiful, lived-in home we arrived in a wisteria-draped courtyard where two rotund cherubs splash in a central fountain and French doors open to the larger cottage. Here, rose-patterned bedspreads and large blue-and-white porcelain pieces betoken Jane and Derrick's European tastes and passion for antiques. Huge modern showers and a small kitchenette show an appreciation for modernity in its rightful place, but the joy here is really in the used and beloved. Pretty with sweet peas in a vase, the upstairs cottage (I can't bring myself to call it a 'unit') is atticky with sloping ceilings. With its double and single beds, sitting area, walk-in wardrobe and huge bathroom (with free-standing bath) it's cheerful and roomy. Before Jane and I sat to a three-course breakfast feast, served from the family silver and prepared by grinning Phyllius (described by Jane as "the best thing about White Cottage"), we took a turn around the garden, busy with bougainvillea and butterflies. After energetic conversations about beehives, wormeries and Jane's post-op nursing, I propped myself up against a well-positioned tree, to soak up the colours, smells and feels of this hideaway. *The White Cottage is 100% chemical-free.*

Rooms: 2 self-catering units: 1 with double & twin room & 2 bathrooms 1 with bath & 1 with shower; 1 with 1 double and 1 twin bed & bath & shower.
Price: R375 - R450 pp sharing. Singles R500 - R600.
Meals: Full breakfast included.
Directions: From airport take the N2 to Cape Town then M3 to Muizenberg. After the 4th traffic light follow sign to Bishopscourt - Upper Torquay Ave. Cross over highway in Torquay. First left into Forest Ave. Over Hillwood. Left into Upper Primrose, house is last on left with big green gate.

Forest View

Pat Gardiner
20 Dalmore Road, Tokai
Tel: 021-715-1310 Fax: 021-712-6729
Email: forestview20@gmail.com
Cell: 082-745-4858

Such a pretty place that TV crews come to film here and newly-weds have their photos taken in front of the agapanthus. It's intimate too, this sweet little studio that sits just apart from the house and overlooks an abundant garden. Pat reeled out the names: hydrangeas, indigenous geraniums, drooping willows, spectacular cannas, the remains of arum lilies after the porcupines had finished with them (see her collection of quills)... and I took it all in hoping to improve my off-the-cuff horticultural knowledge. She leafs through her guest book and remembers every visitor individually, beginning with her first eight years ago. It's one of the reasons why guests tend to come back. They also love the simplicity of having just what they need. The kitchenette is well stocked, there's a writing table for postcards, wicker chairs for reading, a crisp white duvet to slink under and a sleeper-couch for any extras. We took tea on the little private balcony draped in shrub and flower, enjoying the bird-life and a splendidly trimmed lawn that dropped, by levels, past a once-in-vogue trompe l'oeil and a contemplative little pond to the garden gate below. Here, beneath a lushly-grassed and shaded arbour (shared with the neighbours), the Princess Kasteel stream trickles down from the golf and wine estates of Groot Constantia. There's no better breakfast seat this side of Table Mountain and you should choose at least one evening to braai by the large salt-water pool. Lanterns hang and the whole garden is lit by night.

Rooms: 1 studio flat with a queen double and shower en-suite.
Price: R350 - R400 pp sharing. R350 singles.
Meals: Self-catering.
Directions: Take the Tokai exit (21) on the M3 heading toward Muizenberg, connecting with Tokai Road. Take the 2nd right into Lismore Avenue and then left into Dalmore Road.

Morningside Cottage

Ursula Edwards

3 Thatch Close, Tokai
Tel: 021-712 0141 Fax: 021-712 4054
Email: info@morningside-cottage.co.za
Web: www.morningside-cottage.co.za

Tucked away in a sleepy cul-de-sac, Morningside Cottage provides its guests with a quiet central base from which to explore the Cape Peninsula. Within a ten-minute radius you have beaches, golf courses, mountain and forest walks, wine farms and many of Cape Town's favourite eateries. Originally a farmhouse, Morningside is full of Cape cottage charm with its thatched roof, whitewashed wooden ceilings and cottage pane windows. Days start with a generous full English breakfast on the poolside patio where a symphony of birdsong is conducted by tree squirrels searching for acorns in the lush garden. On cold winter days breakfast is taken indoors, a much cosier affair next to the log fireplace. On returning to your room you are greeted by fresh St Joseph's lilies, a little touch typical of Ursula who also trains local women to become registered guesthouse housekeepers. Each room has its own patio or small private courtyard where you can enjoy a glass of local wine while you tally up the day's birdies and bogeys. A rejuvenating dip is an almost compulsory afternoon ritual to soak weary feet and sunburnt skin, and a good time to get your orders in for dinner reservations, tee-off times and any other arrangements that the English-, French- and German-speaking team are happy to help with. If it's local Cape charm you're after, look no further. Morningside has oodles.

Rooms: 7: 3 with en-suite bath and shower; 4 with en-suite shower.
Price: R275 (low season) - R450 (high season) per person sharing. Singles R490 (low season) - R540 (high season).
Meals: Full breakfast included.
Directions: From N2 take M3 towards Muizenberg, take exit 21 Tokai and turn right, then take left into Forest Road then first right into Mountain View and left into Thatch Close.

West Coast Side Dishes

A handful of highly-recommended things to do and places to eat in the West Coast area...

Voorkamerfest

Buy a ticket and get taken by a local taxi on a mystery "live theatre in the lounge" route through Darling. The people of Darling open their homes to host professional local and international artists. The best part is, you don't know who or what you might see. This is a one-of-a-kind theatrical adventure that I doubt exists anywhere else in the world. The Voorkamerfest is held annually the first weekend in September, the start of the Spring Flower festivities. Online and telephone bookings open 1st July.
*Contact: Tasha St John-Reid, Darling; **Prices**: R100; **Tel**: 022-492-3427; **Email**: bookings@voorkamerfest-darling.co.za; **Web**: www.voorkamerfest-darling.co.za*

The Marmalade Cat

On my first visit to the Marmalade Cat, Sandi wasn't in. She had popped out to show a British couple her secret wild-flower spot. With the real 'Marmalade' at my feet I browsed through the kaleidocope of gifts and collectables while aromas of my bacon and feta omelette filled the shop. Don't miss Friday night pizzas and don't leave without a memento off the shelf. I settled for a jar of home-made sun-dried tomato mustard.
*Contact: Sandi Collins, 19 Main Rd, Darling; **Prices**: Breakfast: R16 - R40. Lunch and Dinner: R35 - R65. **Tel**: 022-492-2515; **Web**: blands@mweb.co.za*

The Noisy Oyster

The crew is a close-knit group of misfits dedicated to food, wine and good times... sounds perfect to me. Chef Brian changes the menu daily, with the usual seafood suspects of fresh oysters, mussels, calamari, prawns and line fish being the obvious focus. If you are in the area it's a must; if not, it's well worth a day trip from Cape Town.

*Contact: St Augustine Rd, Paternoster; **Prices**: Starters: R40 - R50. Mains: R65 - R140. Deserts: R35 - R40; **Tel**: 022-752-2196.*

Darling Lodge

Mathe Hettasch and Suzie Venter

22 Pastorie Street, Darling
Tel: 022-492-3062
Fax: 022-492-3665
Email: info@darlinglodge.co.za
Web: www.darlinglodge.co.za
Cell: 083-656-6670

Mathe, who is specifically a European (she's says she has lived in too many places to hail from just one country), came here by chance in 2004 and instantly fell in love with the house. This emotion is manifest even at the front door, where a thick wired heart hangs around the knocker. The main house, whose oak floors were originally laid in 1832, is flooded with life and colour by an abundance of flowers brought down from Mathe's protea farm in nearby Hopefield. All the bedrooms are rich in light and colour too, with inviting canopies hanging over the beds and crisp white linens lying on top of them. Each room is named after a different local artist, whose work adorns the walls and is, by the bye, for sale. I would personally opt for Nicolas Maritz with its deep Victorian clawfoot bath. But it was the garden that finally stole the laurels, with its ancient pepper trees, fountain spraying water over blossoming roses and mass of lavender. Sadly I wasn't staying the night, for I could think of nothing better than sitting under a tree with a glass of wine from one of the five nearby vineyards and digging into a good book or, simply watching the industrious weaver birds, amongst others, as they built their nests. And Mathe's description of her breakfast extravaganza was also a matter of deep regret! A darling lodge indeed.

Rooms: 6: 2 queens, one with en-suite bath, 1 with en-suite bath and separate shower; 1 king with en-suite shower; 2 twin/doubles, one with en-suite shower and one with en-suite bath.
Price: R350 - R400 pp sharing. Singles on request.
Meals: Full breakfast included. Supper on request.
Directions: Enquire on booking.

Map Number: 1

Harbour View B&B

Marlene and Koot de Kock
8 Arum Crescent, Yzerfontein
Tel: 022-451-2615 Fax: 086-616-1363
Email: info@harbourviewbb.co.za Web: www.harbourviewbb.co.za
Cell: 082-770-3885

Protruding out on a fynbos-covered promontory, the sea seems to fill every window at Harbour View. The north-facing aspect means a continual influx of sunlight that brightens the fresh blues or oatmeal hues in each bedroom. "You can whale-watch from any bed in the house," Marlene tells me proudly and, as she is a keen birder, that's not the only watching to be had. There's an active fishing harbour alongside the property and personally I'd be content just gazing out all day at the boats as they come and go. Most mornings start with patches of mist bought up from the ocean and is the perfect time to place the day's first footprints on the 16-mile stretch of beach that runs by outside. Breakfast is a different event every day, the table decoration as changeable as the seascape it looks out on. I wondered if the ever-growing collection of wooden cats, an ongoing fad started and continued by guests, would ever make a table-top debut. "We grow crayfish in the garden," Marlene nodded and I followed her gaze. The 'lawn' at Harbour View is blue and white-crested and, if you want to pick some crayfish you just take your fishing net down to the pier. *Crayfish permits available at the local post office. The West Coast National Park is just 15 minutes away. Wind- and kite-surfing available in the area.*

Rooms: 7: 2 suites with own lounge area kitchenette and en-suite shower; 1 luxury/honeymoon suite with en-s shower and bath; 4 doubles, all with en-suite shower and shared lounge & kitchenette facility.
Price: R395 - R515 pp sharing for standard rooms. R475 - R620 pp sharing for suites.
Luxury/honeymoon suite R595 - R750 pp sharing. Single supplement R300 - R400.
Meals: Full breakfast included. Kitchenette facilities in rooms for limited self-catering. Meals by prior arrangement.
Directions: On the R27 heading north from Cape Town take the left signed Yzerfontein. When arrive in village follow 'Harbour View' signs to front door.

La Villa a L'Ouest

Robert and Florence Masson

La Villa a L'Ouest, 16 Se Sauerman Street, Yzerfontein
Tel: 022 451 2095 Fax: 022-451-2099
Email: info@lavilla.co.za Web: www.lavilla.co.za
Cell: 078-648-1222 (manageress: Maretha Roux)

On the day I visited La Villa, rivers of sunlight were flooding in through large windows onto whitewashed walls, and I wished I could rest for a week at this beautiful, fresh-feeling apartment. With a (tastefully-handled) nautical theme throughout - blue-and-white colour scheme, black-and-white photos of sea-going yachts and lighthouses on the walls - Robert and his interior designer wife, Florence, have created the perfect self-catering haven, surrounded by a natural garden of sandveld fynbos and just three minutes' walk from the sea. Offsetting the 21st-century comforts of the bedrooms, bathrooms and an open-plan kitchen (very modern, very well kitted out, big squashy sofas), they have made inventive use of simple beach-treasure - driftwood, buckets of locally-gathered shells and more shells as drawer handles - which bring the beach into the house. Bedrooms are beautifully done, with low-slung beds draped at the four corners, huge showers, huge chairs and floor-to-ceiling windows for the view. The apartment is serviced six days a week. Yzerfontein has a 16km beach and nature reserve and with the Darling wine route, the wonderful West Coast National Park and the Buffelsfontein Game Reserve within easy reach there's much exploring to be done. For me, the most appealing spot at la Villa was the expansive patio on top of the apartment, with its stone table, looking out over the fynbos to the scintillating Atlantic in the distance. At time of writing Robert is converting the downstairs into a 1 queen bed studio with separate entrance and patio to be rented separately (for 2 people) or together with La Villa (then up to 8 people).

Rooms: 3: 2 queens, 1 twin, all with en-suite showers (+ 1 studio with 1 queen and en-suite shower).
Price: R1,300 - R2,250 per night.
Meals: Fully self-catering.
Directions: Directions will be emailed on booking.

Whalers Way at Churchaven

David and Helen Untiedt
West Coast National Park, Churchaven
Tel: 021-790-0972
Email: stay@perfecthideaways.co.za Web: www.perfecthideaways.co.za
Cell: 082-775-7797

As you may well imagine, in this job booking one's own holiday becomes an issue of professional pride. But for me, a minute at Whaler's Way saw a quick resolution to this tricky decision and I am now drumming my thumbs in anticipation of holidaying there. I'll try my best not to get too carried away. West Coast National Park, one of the world's most important wetlands, represents mother nature in her Sunday-go-to-meeting best. To find any place to stay within the park would have been exceptional enough. Thrice I stopped on my drive – once to rescue a tortoise and twice to gawp unashamedly at the jade lagoon that stretches out to the roaring Atlantic. The cottage with its white walls and driftwood awnings blends beautifully with the surrounding fynbos. I was pleased to be on my own, so that I could take in fully all that was around me (old-fashioned kettles, slipper baths, gnarled beams) and appreciate all that was not (noise, distraction, tourists). The cottage is unfussy with sticks of furniture sitting together comfortably like old friends – there's a reclaimed chest, sun-bleached rugs, a paint-dappled ladder leading to a tiny attic and a robust fireplace which takes centre stage. Floors are off-white cement giving a sea-sandy feel, especially where walls are inlaid with white beach pebbles. Seaside simplicity continues in the bedrooms with quilt bedspreads and shell garlands giving texture to light walls and windows open to the waters of the lagoon where flamingos wade. Here you can stroll for hours, skinny dip solo and buy fish straight from the boat and *I really can't wait*.

Rooms: 3: 1 double with ensuite shower room. 1 queen and twin sharing bath and separate shower.
Price: Week rate: R2,000 - R3,000 per night. Weekend rate: R2,200 - R3,000 per night. Min stay 2 nights.
Meals: Fully self-catering.
Directions: Please see website.

Kersefontein

Julian Melck
between Hopefield and Velddrif, Hopefield
Tel: 022-783-0850 Fax: 022-783-0850
Email: info@kersefontein.co.za Web: www.kersefontein.co.za
Cell: 083-454 1025

Nothing has changed at Kersefontein since the last edition. Julian's convivial dinner parties are still a reason to book in on their own. And Julian himself remains a Renaissance man, described on his business card as 'Farmer, Pig-killer, Aviator and Advocate of the High Court of S.A.' He farms cows, sheep and horses on the surrounding fields, and wild boar appear deliciously at dinner. He also hires and pilots a six-seater plane and a flight round the Cape or along the coast is a must. He modestly leaves out his virtuosity as a pianist and organist and some of us trooped off one Sunday morning, braving a 40-minute sermon in Afrikaans, to hear him play toccatas by Bach, Giguot and Widor at the local church. When not eating, riding or flying, guests lounge on the pontoon, swim in the river or read books from Kersefontein's many libraries. Or they use the house as a base to visit the coast or the Swartland wineries, which are really taking off. The homestead is seventh generation and the rooms either Victorian or African in temperament, with antiques handed down by previous Melcks. You are fed like a king, but treated as a friend and I am always recommending people to go here. Julian is currently restoring a 6th room which will be ready by the time we go to print.

Rooms: 5: 2 doubles, 2 twins and 1 separate 2 bedroom cottage.
Price: R420 - R540 pp sharing. No single supplements. Aircraft hire prices depend on the trip. Julian will also do fly/picnic trips out to various destinations.
Meals: Full breakfast included. Dinners by arrangement: R190 - R230 excluding wine.
Directions: From Cape Town take N7 off N1. Bypass Malmesbury, 5km later turn left towards Hopefield. After 50km bypass Hopefield, turn right signed Velddrif. After 16km farm signed on right just before grain silos. Cross bridge and gates on the left.

The Oystercatcher's Haven at Paternoster

Sandy and Wayne Attrill

48 Sonkwasweg, Paternoster
Tel: 022-752-2193 Fax: 022-752-2192
Email: info@oystercatchershaven.com Web: www.oystercatchershaven.com
Cell: 082-414-6705 or 083-267-7051

Sandy and Wayne, ex film and advertising people, do things in style and their guest house is a knock-out! The Cape Dutch house sits on the fringes of the Cape Columbine Nature Reserve, a spectacular, fynbos-covered, hand-shaped headland, bearing its lighthouse aloft like a nine-million-watt jewel. All along the coast and a mere 40 metres in front of the house knobbly fingers of grey and black granite merge into the sea and around the rocks there are secret white sandy coves where the dolphins come throughout the year. It is quite simply beautiful and I can assure you that the Oystercatcher is a haven by anyone's standards. Heave yourself out of that plunge-pool, off the rocks and away from the view (available from your bed) and head inside the house. The interior, with its white walls, untreated timbers and reed-and-pole ceilings, is intentionally blank-yet-rustic to showcase some exquisite pieces, such as a four-foot-high Angolan drum, some Malinese sinaba paintings (you'll have to come and see them if you don't know what they are), Persian rugs, art-deco couches, courtyards…. Just about everything is a hook for an eager eye. Beds and bedrooms too are bliss - trust me, I'm a professional. Although they do not do dinners any more (there is no need with so many good eateries in Paternoster) they do offer fresh-out-of-the-bay crayfish dinners in season on demand.

Rooms: 3: 1 queen with en-suite bath and shower; 1 queen and 1 twin, both with en-suite showers. All rooms have private entrances.
Price: R625 - R680 pp per night.
Meals: Full breakfast included.
Directions: From Cape Town take the N1 and then the R27 north following signs to Vredenburg. Follow signs straight through Vredenburg to Paternoster (15km). At crossroads turn left and travel a full 1km towards the Columbine Reserve. Turn right into Sonkwas Rd. It is No.48.

Farr Out B&B

Marion Lubitz and Deon van Schalkwyk

17 Seemeeusingel, Paternoster
Tel: 022 752-2222 Fax: 08022-752-2222
Email: marion@farrout.co.za Web: www.farrout.co.za
Cell: 083-410-4090

The five-minute drive from Paternoster to Farr Out was not what I would exactly call far. But when you arrive in this sandy bushveld wilderness, you do feel pleasingly remote. Crunching up the glinting shell pathway came a very cheerful-looking Marion, who sat me down with an Englishman's best friend (an excellent cup of tea, of course). From the kitchen you can see across their indigenous garden and right out to sea. Earlier risers than me may catch some of the wildlife that comes by when it thinks no-one's looking. Deon showed me a picture he'd taken at five that morning of a duiker drinking right from their koi pond. After 26 years in the air force, Farr Out is now his playground, and the excitement has definitely not worn off. I would recommend joining him on a beach buggy excursion. I only had time for a little loop, but with a little wind in my hair, I really wished I could have packed the coolbox and gone out over the dunes. Rainy days are also covered, with a host of board games, including a much-loved, thirty-year-old, German edition of Monopoly. Rooms are modern, with televisions, stereos and some of the most exciting loo seats I have ever seen. Make sure you get a chance to spend a few minutes in the garden basket chair before you leave. Specially imported from Germany, it shelters brilliantly from the wind, allowing you to sit in peace, looking out over the dunes for an hour or ten. Oh yes, I'd recommend a lunch- or dinner-time braai. It's not often you'll get to eat one in a teepee. *German, English and Afrikaans spoken.*

Rooms: 3: 1 king, 1 queen and 1 family suite with 1 queen and 1 twin room. All with en-suite showers.
Price: R275 - R375 pp sharing. Singles on request.
Meals: Full breakfast included. Dinner and picnic baskets on request.
Directions: From Cape Town, take the R27 approx 125km to the R45, which passes through Vredenburg and continues 15km in the direction of Paternoster. Farr Out is situated at the far end of Pelgrimsrust - small holdings just before Paternoster on the left-hand side.

Paternoster Dunes Guest House

Gavin Sproule and Deon Van Rooyen

18 Sonkwas Street, Paternoster
Tel: 022-752-2217 Fax: 022-752-2214
Email: reservations@paternosterdunes.co.za
Web: www.paternosterdunes.co.za Cell: 083-560-5600

When I told GG guest houses in the area that I was staying at Paternoster Dunes for the night, the collective response was, "Oh, that's LOVELY." But 'lovely' simply doesn't do it justice. I was met by Gavin and escorted past the open-air courtyard with its tempting pool and daybed and shown to my room (named Vanilla). Gavin and Deon worked in interior design for ten years before swapping the big smoke for the salt breeze. If Vanilla was anything to go by – open-plan, huge bath with its own sea-facing window, equally huge stone-floored shower and king-size bed with plump pillows and Egyptian cotton - they were surely at the top of their game. But the best treat of all was my verandah, accessed through French doors. The ocean is less than ten yards away between grassy dunes and it was here that I decided to settle down and finish off my book of the moment. Clapping the covers together an hour later, I took my satisfaction up to the communal bar/lounge, with its panoramic ocean views, for a sundowner. The design throughout the house never jars and always excites. The walls are adorned with original artwork, from contemporary pastoral scenes to palette nudes, the lamp-shades are made from oryx antlers and the leather armchairs could have been found in a London gentleman's club. My egg and pastrami soufflé at breakfast was clear proof of fine cooking (dinners are also available). But by that time you would hardly expect anything less. More 'wow!' than 'lovely'!

Rooms: 5: 2 queen with en-suite bath/shower; 1 king/twin with en-suite shower, 2 queen with en-suite shower.
Price: R550 - R900 pp sharing. Singles on request.
Meals: Including breakfast. Light lunch and dinner on request.
Directions: From Cape Town take the N1 and then the R27 north following signs to Vredenburg to Paternoster (15km). At crossroads turn left then travel a full 1 km to the Columbine Reserve. Turn right into Sonkwas Street. It is No.18.

Oystercatcher Lodge

Luc and Sue Christen
1st Avenue, Shelley Point St, St Helena Bay
Tel: 022-742-1202 Fax: 022-742-1201
Email: info@oystercatcherlodge.co.za Web: www.oystercatcherlodge.co.za
Cell: 082-903-9668

You can't miss Oystercatcher Lodge. If you do, you'll end up in the sea. It's set right on the tip of Shelley Point, overlooking the full curve of Britannia Bay with its flocks of cormorants, pods of passing dolphins and wallowing whales (in season). Luc (smiley and Swiss) and Sue (home-grown, but equally smiley) are both from the hotel trade. After years doing a great job for other people deep in the Mpumalanga bushveld, they decided to work for themselves and made the move. Quite a change. Here on the West Coast the sea air has a salty freshness unlike anywhere else, the sun shines brilliantly on arcing white beaches and the crunching waves are a bottomless blue. A special spot indeed where the Christens' newly-built house juts out towards the ocean like the prow of a ship, a large pointy pool in its bows. Each of the six rooms, painted in calming sandy colours, looks across grassy dunes and beach to the sea. All have extra-large bathrooms. Breakfast feasts are served in the bar. If you're lucky Luc might summon some whales for you to view by blowing on his 'kelperoo' (a whale horn made out of seaweed!) as you munch on the Christens' 'special Swiss recipe' bread. For other meals there are restaurants nearby and, if you ask in advance, the ex-restaurateurs will do their best to cook up something scrumptious. New self-catering apartments were in the pipeline when I visited and will be finished by the time this goes to print.

Rooms: 6: 4 kings, 2 with bath and shower, 2 with shower only; 2 twins with shower only.
Price: R460 - R700 pp sharing sharing.
Meals: Full breakfast included.
Directions: Head north on R27. Turn L into Vredenburg. At lights turn R. After 10km turn L towards St.Helena Bay. Just before Stompneus Bay turn L. After 200m turn R. At the S/Point entrance sign in. Pass Country Club on your L. Continue on until fountain. Half circle fountain, thatch cottages on your L, Oystercatcher will be on your R.

Petersfield Farm Cottages

Hedley Peter
Petersfield Guest Farm, Citrusdal
Tel: 022-921-3316 Fax: 022-921-3316
Email: info@petersfieldfarm.co.za Web: www.petersfieldfarm.co.za
Cell: 083-626-5145

Hedley is an instantly likeable and funny host and Petersfield, his family farm (citrus and rooibos tea), ranges over the back of the mountain behind the main house, forming a huge private wilderness reserve. De Kom, an idyllic, simple-but-stylish stone cottage perched high in sandstone mountains will appeal to your inner romantic. This charming electricity-free cottage is lit by hurricane lamps and flares with gas for the stove, fridge and hot water. A private plunge pool with river stones at the bottom overlooks this secret valley with the Olifants River and purpling Cederberg peaks as a backdrop. And what a setting, guarded to the front by a citrus orchard, to the rear by craggy sandstone and looking deep and far from the stoep down the mountain. There is a secluded farm dam nearby (300 metres) to swim in or picnic by while watching nesting eagles. Or, 2km away, there is (electrified) Dassieklip Cottage, a sweet wooden mountain cabin secreted in its own kloof and reached down an avenue of oaks. It too has a plunge pool to cool off in and other mod cons such as fridge, air-conditioning, TV and CD player. And there's Die Veepos, the latest and most luxurious addition to the Petersfield stable. Built in the 'sandveld' style, the high bamboo-reed ceilings and cretestone walls will keep the house at perfect temperature and, along with the customary plunge pool and mod cons you can expect from Hedley's cottages, there is also an open-air bush bathroom looking out across the Cederberg mountains. Bring your own food, although breakfast materials for you to cook can be provided. *Wood is supplied at no extra charge and pets are also welcome.*

Rooms: 3 cottages: two with 2 bedrooms and one with 3.
Price: Week-nights: R500 for 2 up to R700 for 5/6. Weekends, public holidays, flower season (10 Aug - 10 Sept): R800 for up to 6 people. Prices are per night for whole cottage.
Meals: Self-catering, but breakfast materials provided in the fridge by prior arrangement.
Directions: From Cape Town 4km after Citrusdal on your left on the N7 travelling towards Clanwilliam.

Rockwood Cottage

Brent and Nikki Mills
Rockwood Farm, Citrusdal
Tel: 022-921-3517 Fax: 086-607-5851
Email: info@rockwoodfarm.co.za Web: www.rockwoodfarm.co.za
Cell: 084-209-7150

Rockwood is an extremely beautiful protea farm in the Cederberg highlands 800 metres above sea level. I discovered, over a delectable soup and cheese lunch, that Brent and his wife Nikki have seamlessly taken over from Brent's parents in running the cottage and farm and it was clear to see why they both grinned as they told me. Both the main house and their large and lovely guest cottage have front stoeps that overlook a succession of dams, the hinterland channelled away for miles and miles by rugged sandstone mountains. The highest peaks of the Sneeuberg Conservancy are often covered with snow in winter. The guest cottage is cradled among giant rocks with the eponymous rockwood trees growing from beneath. And to the front, a story-book stream burbles past the stoep and oak trees there. A wide expanse of lawn leads to more treasure; two natural rock swimming pools are filled all year round by the river with fresh, drinkable water that cascades gently over the rocks. A sundowner in either of the pools allows you time to digest the magnificent view and feel properly smug. Behind this there is a deep gorge and waterfall, an idyllic world of water and rock (I couldn't resist a skinny-dip in the sweltering November sun!), full of wildflowers in season with many bush trails cut through natural gardens with ancient rock art waiting to be discovered. Brent and Nikki will happily show their guests all there is to do on the property and in the region, still so unspoiled by tourism.

Rooms: 1 cottage with two bedrooms: 1 double and 1 twin sharing 1 bath/shower. Outside bedroom with 2 twin beds and en-suite shower.
Price: R550 - R700 for 2 people. R100 per additional person.
Meals: Self-catering. Restaurants are five minutes away.
Directions: From N7 into Citrusdal. At four-way intersection in centre of village straight over and up mountain for 7km. Second white gates on the left.

Oudrif

Bill and Jeanine Mitchell
Clanwilliam
Tel: 027-482-2397
Email: oudrif@telkomsa.net
Web: www.oudrif.co.za

Fifty kilometres of fabulous sandstone formations, dams and flower-covered passes lead you deep into the Cederberg Mountains and eventually to Oudrif, the perfect hideaway-getaway on the banks of the clear, clean, cool Doring River. I was met by my hosts Bill and Jeanine, who provided me with iced tea, before escorting me to my environmentally-friendly lodge where walls and roofs are straw bales and power is solar and views spectacular. Bill and Janine met whilst Janine was working as a goatherd (absolutely true) and their shared passion for wildlife is palpable. Together they're a veritable encyclopaedia of life in the wild from eco building to bird rescues to taming their half-Siamese, half-wild pet cat Barry. My room was light-filled, with sofas to snooze on, but it was a hot day, so I donned my trunks and ran to the river for a dip. The main house is the meeting point, library and supper room and I was quickly introduced to the other guests. Oudrif holds ten at full capacity, with a rare atmosphere whereby guests know they are sharing a unique experience, evenings around the communal table can be very entertaining. After a laughter-filled evening and too much home-made bread (both Bill and Jeanine are master bakers), I headed off to bed. Well, in fact… eschewing the comforts of a lovely king-size double bed, I actually decided to sleep outside under an amazing starlit sky. This is a truly special spot. *Guided excursions also included.*

Rooms: 5: All twin/double with en-suite shower.
Price: R660 - R720 pp sharing. Singles on request.
Meals: 3 meals a day and all drinks (wine, beer, soft drinks) included.
Directions: Enquire on booking.

Wolfkop Nature Reserve Cottages

Werner Rontgen

Wolfkop Nature Reserve, Citrusdal
Tel: 071-191-6511 Fax: 086-617-5868
Email: info@wolfkopnaturereserve.co.za
Web: www.wolfkopnaturereserve.co.za Cell: 083-775-0144

What better way to wind down after a long day's drive than sitting in your own jacuzzi, chilled beer in hand, looking across a valley full of citrus orchards and rooibos fields, watching the sun sink behind the Cederberg mountains? And that was where I found myself on a hot spring evening while Werner, my convivial host, busied himself at the braai. I would have been just as happy, mind you, in one of the hammocks strung across the stoep, or singing happily and tunelessly to myself in the gorgeous outside hot shower. The two red-brick cottages are homely and simple. The main sitting room has a high, wood-beamed ceiling with deep, cushioned sofas and a big open fire, while the adjoining kitchen has all the mod cons you will need for a weekend away, including freshly-ground coffee. Both cottages even have their own small herb gardens on hand to help when you cook. Meanwhile, the two bedrooms are cool and welcoming with plump pillows, soft cotton sheets and spectacular views across the reserve. There are over 150 species of birds in the Wolfkop Nature Reserve and as Werner and I sat on the stoep, munching our perfectly-seasoned lamb chops, their various calls rang out of the dusk, eventually giving way to the sounds of the night and a sky full of stars. Waking early, I looked out across to the mountains and wished I had more time to head up and explore, but sadly the road was calling. I only hoped it would come full circle.

Rooms: 3 cottages: each with 2 twin/doubles with a shared bathroom and outside shower.
Price: R225 - R375 pp.
Meals: Fully self-catering.
Directions: Enquire on booking.

Mount Ceder

André and Jaen Marais & Thomas and Rachelle Marriott-Dodington

Grootrivier Farm, Cederberg, Koue Bokkeveld
Tel: 023-317-0848 Fax: 023-317-0543
Email: mountceder@lando.co.za Web: www.mountceder.co.za

Do not lose confidence as you rumble along the dirt roads that lead through the Koue Bokkeveld Nature Conservancy to this secluded valley - it's always a couple more turns. Finally you will arrive in the very heart of the Cederberg, dry sandstone mountains rising all around you in impressive dimensions. You will be given the key to your new home and drive off along half a kilometre of sand track to one of three fantastic rustic stone cottages. The river flows past the reeds and rock right by the cottages, clear, deep and wide all year round. You can swim and lie around drying on flat rocks. Birds love it here too. I imagine sitting out on that stoep, on those wooden chairs, looking at that view, beer or wine in hand… a piece of heaven, as they say. You can either self-cater or you can eat at André and Jaen's restaurant back at the lodge. There are a few other cottages nearer the lodge, which are fine, but you must ask for the stone cottages, which are in a league of their own. A pristine slice of unspoiled nature, cherished by a very knowledgeable Marais family who will help with Bushman rock art, horse-riding and fauna and flora. Do not reach for your red pen by the way… that is how you spell ceder (in Afrikaans) and that is how you spell Jaen! *Serious hiking is possible from here. Daughter Rachelle will happily take you horse-riding.*

Rooms: 3 river cottages with 3 bedrooms each.
Price: R1,560 – R2,470 per cottage per night self-catering (cottage sleeps 6).
Meals: Meals on request, breakfast R50, dinner R110 (extra for wine).
Directions: From Ceres follow signs to Prince Alfred's Hamlet/Op-die-Berg, up Gydo Pass past Op-die-Berg. First right signed Cederberge - follow tar for 17km then straight on on dirt road for another 34km into a green valley.

Cape Winelands Side Dishes

A handful of highly-recommended things to do and places to eat in the Cape Winelands area...

Bastille Festival

Franschhoek, being the French Corner of South Africa, celebrates Bastille Day with reckless abandon. In fact, they like to commemorate their forefathers by celebrating for the entire weekend closest to July 14th. Expect music and merriment - plus, of course, good food and wines galore. These are possibly the only days in the year that you can get away with wearing a beret! Other Bastille highlights include a French Film Festival, a Chefs and Waiters Race, a pétanque tournament, a barrel-rolling competition and lots more.

Contact: Franschhoek Tourism Information Centre, 28a Huguenot Road, Franschhoek; **Tel:** *021-876-3603; 021-876-2768;* **Email:** *info@franschhoek.org.za;* **Web:** *www.franschhoek.org.za*

Topsi and Co

"I cook and we care about our guests," Topsi tells me - summing up her much-loved eatery in a nutshell. She is a culinary legend in these parts and her restaurant an eclectic and hectic spot. Watch her cooking from your table before devouring heaped salads, fantastic fish and cracking crumbles. Ask about the parrot.

Contact: Topsi, 7 Reservoir St West, Franschhoek; **Tel:** *021-876-2952; 021-876-2952;* **Email:** *alodieorr@gmail.com*

Paradise Stables

Wine-tasting on horseback... the only way to travel. Pieter Hugo leads you on a four-hour trail via two wineries on pure-bred Arabian horses, stopping for half an hour or so at each. Other horse trails are also available and we'd suggest taking a picnic too to really make a trip of it.

Contact: Pieter Hugo, Robertsvlei Rd, Franschhoek; **Prices:** *R450 pp for wine tasting trip or R150 per hour for riding;* **Tel:** *021-876-2160; 021-876-2160;* **Web:** *www.paradisestables.co.za*

Cabriere

It was a dark, stormy Cape winter morning when I first visited Cabriere, and within three minutes I was wrapped up next to a log fire with three options of ""something to warm you up"" being poured into glasses with my name on them. The Cabriere team look after you like long-lost family. Enjoy a Saturday morning with Achim von Arnim for entertaining, informative tastings and cellar tours. Chances are he may even demonstrate the noble art of sabrage (removing a champagne cork with a sabre)!

Contact: Franschhoek; **Prices:** *Bubbles: R75 - R120. Wines: R40 - R125;* **Tel:** *021-876-8500; 021-876-8501;* **Email:** *cabriereinfo@mweb.co.za;* **Web:** *www.cabriere.co.za*

Joostenberg Bistro

Hearty, country breakfasts and delectable lunches are served in this open-hearted, roomy, friendly bistro. Fresh local produce and the seasons dictate the menu, with their own farm-reared pork and hand-crafted wines always a feature. In winter snuggle in next to the huge log fire and in summer watch the kids playing on the lawns from the shaded stoep. Be sure to pick up a few speciality delights from the adjoining deli on your way out.
Contact: Susan Dehosse, Klein Joostenberg Farm, R304, Muldersvlei;
Tel: 021-8844-208; 021-8844-135; **Email:** bistro@joostenberg.co.za;
Web: www.joostenberg.co.za

The Olive Boutique

What do you do when you reach Riebeek Kasteel, the olive capital of the Cape? Answer: head straight for the ultimate olive experience to taste a fantastic range of olives, oils, pastes and mustards. My favourite is the kalamata olives roasted with a mixture of lavender and white truffle oil. Make a point of attending Juliana's hand massage demonstrations with frangranced massage olive oils. They even make an olive shampoo.
Contact: Juliana Meredith, 49 Church Street, Riebeek Kasteel;
Prices: Entrance and tasting free of charge; **Tel:** 022-448-1368; 022-448-1628;
Email: olives@riebeeck-kasteel.co.za; **Web:** www.olive-boutique.co.za

Bar Bar Black Sheep

What a find! From the moment you walk through the doors you can feel Mynhardt's passion for what he is doing here, i.e. serving mouth-watering dishes, using the freshest of local ingredients. Sit inside or out in the garden and try the Waterblommetjie Bredie, Courgette Flowers, Harissa Seafood Pan or Fillet au Poivre. Better get there soon before Bar Bar Black Sheep becomes too famous.
Contact: Mynhardt Joubert, Bar Bar Black Sheep, Unit 7, Short St, Main Rd, Riebeek Kasteel; **Prices** Starters: R28 to R45. Mains: R65 to R95. Desserts: R25 to R35; **Tel:** 022-448-1031; **Email:** bbbs@telkomsa.net

Lafayette Wine Bar and Restaurant

Sit inside, on the pavement, or in the courtyard and feast on continental and traditional fare at this local Stellenbosch favourite. Combining great food and wine is Marie and Guido's passion and they have twenty wines served by the glass. The menu changes regularly with specials posted on a blackboard. Their interactive fire-food night where Chefs Guido and Marie cook a small a la carte menu on the fire in the courtyard is a must. Relaxed and bustling... make sure you book.
Contact: Guido Righard and Marié Steyn, 1 Andringa Street, Stellenbosch; **Prices:** Starters: R30 - R55; mains: R60 - R130; **Tel:** 021-886-6777; **Email:** marie.lafayette@gmail.com; **Web:** www.lafayette.co.za

Waterford Estate

Famed for its classic reds and wine and chocolate tastings. Belgian delights from chocolatier Richard von Gesau are intimately matched to the wines. Try Waterford Estate Cabernet with Rock Salt Chocolate... it's to die for. Free tours on an ad hoc basis.
Contact: Blaauwklippen Rd, Helderberg; Stellenbosch; **Tel:** 021-880-5316; 021-880-1007; **Email:** info@waterfordestate.co.za; **Web:** www.waterfordestate.co.za

Villa Tarentaal

Graham and Brandi Hunter
Tulbagh
Tel: 023-230-0868
Email: grahamjhb@gmail.com Web: www.villatarentaal.com
Cell: 074-194-8202

Graham is Mike and Christine's son and, having had an ample sufficiency of life as a highway patrolman in America (put away your Hollywood movie stereotypes, Graham is charming!), he and his wife Brandi (also charming) have returned home to take over the family business. Over a rich and spicy Cape Malay lunch, I was reassured that the feeling of the place will stay just the same, despite the change of hands. "People come here for the comfort and view," smiles Graham, "we just like to think of it as an upgrade." This being the renovation of the two original cottages and the building of a third. All the cottages now have open fireplaces, the bathrooms have been stylishly modernized with new tiling and top-of-the-range showers and new ceiling fans have been installed for those hot summer nights. But fans of Mike and Christine needn't worry. Christine will still be there to offer her therapeutic massages and Mike, known locally as the 'Man of the Mountain', will still be there to enchant you with his passion for his pristine garden: wisteria and grapevines spider up the mustard-coloured house; an orgy of colour is provided by the roses; and the lawn is so well-kept it would make the green-keepers of Augusta, well… green with envy. Guests are not the only ones flocking here. You'll also witness an abundance of bird life here including Egyptian geese, fish eagles and probably a brace of mating blue crane. I really enjoyed the breakfast here, by the way. The French toast is sinful but delicious!

Rooms: 3 cottages: Blue Crane: 2 singles and 1 queen in separate rooms with en-suite shower and bath. Fish Eagle: 1 queen, 1 single bed, en-suite shower. Egyptian Goose: 1 queen, en-suite shower. All have aircon, fireplace and full DSTV.
Price: R325 - R380 pp sharing B&B. R325 pp sharing self-catering. Single supplement plus R100.
Meals: Full breakfast included served in the privacy of your own cottage or on private verandah.
Directions: N1 from Cape Town to exit 47 Wellington/Franschhoek/Klapmuts turn-off, left onto R44 via Wellington. Follow for approx 1 hour to Tulbagh. Straight through town, 1.2km on left.

De Oude Herberg Guest House

Leslie and Jane Ingham
6 Church St, Tulbagh
Tel: 023-230-0260 Fax: 023-230-0260
Email: ingham@mweb.co.za Web: www.deoudeherberg.co.za
Cell: 072-241-4214

Leslie was a pilot in his former life and his last foray skywards saw him flying aid missions for the UN throughout Africa. Thankfully for a man who has lived with his head in the clouds, Jane's always been there to bring him back down to earth, and now she has brought him (luckily for us) to Tulbagh, to run a guest house. But this is not just any old Tulbagh guest house. Church Street is the town's - and indeed one of the Wineland's - most historic streets and De Oude Herberg is a jewel in the crown. Beautiful on the outside in a thatched-roof and gable-fronted kind of way; venerably ancient on the inside in an everything-wobbles-when-you-walk-through-the-room kind of way. From the resplendent, flower-filled, basket-carrying bicycle, to the ribbon-tied towels in the rooms, and a complimentary decanter of local port by every bed, you know a lot of thought has gone into making this place special. I'd plump for the four-poster with access onto the verandah, but if you like your privacy, then go for one in the separate building out the back, which has its own access and small courtyard garden. But it will take a strong will not to be tempted back out for a drink and some lively chat at the bar. And as if that's not enough, Pielow's, an excellent gourmet restaurant, is on the premises.

Rooms: 4: 2 queens, 1 with additional small room attached (suitable for an adult or a child); and 2 twins. All have air-conditioning and baths with shower above.
Price: From R400 pp sharing. Singles + R100.
Meals: Full breakfast included. Dinner available in restaurant from September to April. A la carte menu open Tuesday - Saturday.
Directions: On reaching Tulbagh turn L at the Shell garage into Church Street and R at the church. Next door to information centre.

Old Oak Manor

Salomé and Willem Gunter

7 Church Street, Riebeek Kasteel
Tel: 022-448-1170 Fax: 022-448-1083
Email: cafe-felix@intekom.co.za Web: www.oldoakmanor.co.za

Under long shadows of a languorous summer afternoon, the unhurried tunes of French jazz and a pair of perfectly black cats were wafting through Old Oak Manor's rustic central courtyard. I sensed that, but for its Cape Dutch exterior, the place would be aptly suited to life tucked away deep in rural France. Salomé is a well-known interior designer with a passion for the country, and it shows. Nods to traditional French country design are everywhere. Iron four-posters, creaky wooden dressers, over-sized lamps, old travel cases and the odd slipper bath have all been salvaged from auctions and each room is as original as the next. Whilst Salomé has set the tone, it's the three resident cats, Felix, Julius and Misty, who set the laid-back pace. There's not a hint of don't-touch-me fussiness, not even in the impressive open-plan loft above the café. There's an expansive wooden table for reading (that obligingly doubles up as a cocktail bar) and a giant bathroom with wall-to-ceiling cupboards to chuck the bags into; and a free-standing bath hovered over by an inquisitive oak through the window. Out by the kitchen garden hidden by sprouting vines is another cosy nook, a little Grecian-esque whitewashed cottage. Riebeek provides plenty of distractions: you can climb its mountain, or visit its olive farms and wineries, its antiquey shops and cosy garden cafés. Otherwise, cool off in the fresh-water pool, stretch out on a lounger and snooze.... Felix, Misty and Julius would be first, second and third to approve.

Rooms: 6: 4 doubles in the house, 2 with en-suite shower and bath, 2 with en-s shower; 1 double with extra single with en-s shower in separate guest cottage; 1 double & 1 twin in open-plan loft with en-s bath, living area & DSTV.
Price: R350 - R450 pp sharing for rooms in main house & for guest cottage. R1,500 per night for loft.
Meals: Full breakfast included. Café Felix is on-site restaurant serving breakfast, lunch & dinner. Restaurant closed on Monday & Thursday.
Directions: From Cape Town take N7 & 1st turn-off to Malmesbury, Bokomo Rd. R into R45 towards Wellington/Paarl. 1km past Malmesbury, L to Riebeek. 1st turn-off L into town is Church St.

White Bridge Farm

Paul and Peppi Stanford
Wolseley
Tel: 023-231-0705 Fax: 086-611-5107
Email: whitebridge@ubiqua.co.za Web: www.whitebridge.co.za
Cell: 082-578-7881

Snow on the mountains, sun blazing down on the deck, water roaring through the river below... Mother Nature could not do a better job of showing off other people's wares if she tried (I wonder what they're paying her). White Bridge Farm is a working fruit farm, and if you come at the right time of the year (Nov-Aug), you can work on it too, or at least have a tour. Guests, Peppi tells me, are always amazed when they spot the citrus, pears and plums sporting labels of the well-known supermarket brands of home. But I have to say it would take more than a succulent satsuma to tear me away from one of the two log cabins (there is a more conventional larger cottage too). They really are about as rustic as rustic can be. Bamboos have been cut down to line the walls, trees have been felled to build the tables, even old drainpipes have been used as a bright idea for lighting! Nothing has gone to waste, and you won't want to waste your time here either. With walking, fishing, swimming and bird-watching this is a nature-lover's paradise. A family of otters liked it so much, they decided to stay at White Bridge, and you cannot get a better recommendation than that. For those who like their home comforts (and breakfast with the family hand-made for them) Peppi also has a cosy room next to her house. Guarded by two wooden cheetahs, it has its own fireplace and outdoor seating area within the main garden. Just 90 minutes from Cape Town, the perfect distance for a break from the city.

Rooms: 3 units and 1 B&B bedroom: 2 log cabins with 1 double and 1 twin in loft space, shower only; 1 cottage with double and bunks, and a double futon in lounge, full bathroom; 1 double in the main house with full bathroom.
Price: R500 - R600 per unit per night for self-catering. R250 for B&B pp sharing. Singles on request.
Meals: Meals can be arranged if requested. Restaurant and coffee shop less than 1km away.
Directions: At the junction of the R43 from Worcester and the R46 between Tulbagh and Ceres.

Bartholomeus Klip Farmhouse

Lesley Gillett
Elandsberg Farm, Hermon
Tel: 022-448-1820 Fax: 022-448-1829
Email: info@bartholomeusklip.com Web: www.bartholomeusklip.com
Cell: 082-829-4131

Heavenly scenery cossets this Victorian homestead in its lush gardens and stands of oak and olive. The wall of the Elandsberg Mountains rises up from the game reserve, reflected in the dammed lake by the house. Here guests can have breakfast on the balcony of the boathouse before heading out for an excursion onto the wheat and sheep farm. You are also taken on late-afternoon game drives to see the zebra, a variety of Cape antelope, buffalo, quaggas (a fascinating experiment to reintroduce an extinct variety of zebra), eagles, flocks of blue crane... and the largest world population of the tiny, endangered geometric tortoises. But just to be out in such nature! The spring flowers are spectacular and there are more than 850 species of plant recorded on the property. Back at the homestead you can cool down in the curious, round, raised reservoir pool, sit in chairs on the stoep; or, if you have more energy, bike off into the reserve or go on guided walks in the mountains. Staff are very friendly, food is exceptional and a reason to stay on its own (and all included in the price). I recommend splashing out on at least two nights. A great place indeed and very popular so book ahead of yourself if possible. *Closed June - July and Christmas.*

Rooms: 6: 2 doubles & 3 twins, all with bath & shower. New self-catering cottage that sleeps 8 with 3 doubles and bunk beds.
Price: R1,250 - R2,020 pp sharing. Singles + 20%. Includes meals & game drives. R408 - R1,075 pp for self-catering cottage. 0 - 3 are free, 4 - 15 half price in cottage.
Meals: Coffee and rusks, brunch, high tea, snacks and sundowners and 4-course dinner included.
Directions: From CT take N1 towards Paarl. Exit 47, L at stop. Continue turning L onto R44 signed Ceres. Follow for 30km. Past R46 junction signed Hermon, take next R signed Bo-Hermon. Gravel road for 2km. Bartholomeus Klip signed to L - 5km.

Map Number: 4

Entry Number: 75

Oude Wellington Estate

Rolf Schumacher
Bainskloof Pass Rd, Wellington
Tel: 021-873-2262 Fax: 088021-873-4639
Email: info@kapwein.com Web: www.kapwein.com

There seems to be so much to catch the eye even as you rumble along the 800-metre paved and cobbled road to Oude Wellington: vineyards on both sides, ostentatious peacocks, geese and hadedas, pet ostriches peering over a fence. And that afternoon four pregnant alpacas that had just arrived all the way from Australia were to be added to the menagerie. Rolf is clearly the hospitable type (how else could ostriches find a home on a winery?). It took him two years to restore the whole estate to its former glory as a wine-grape farm. Four rustic double rooms are in the original farmhouse (built in 1790) with high, thatched ceilings, low pole beams, whitewashed walls and yet underfloor heating and air-con; the other two are in the more modern main building (well, 1836!), along with the beautiful farm kitchen with old-fashioned pots, pans and irons, billiard room and bar, and a terrace overlooking the vineyards, where breakfast is served in the summer. There is a partly-shaded pool off to the side of the main house, a brandy still in the barn, and handily on the premises is a restaurant popular with the locals (always a good sign). Guests are also invited to watch wine-making taking place at the right time of year. "I farm and dine and love company," says Rolf in his brochure!

Rooms: 8: all kings/ twins with en-suite Victorian baths.
Price: R450 - R550 pp sharing. Single supplement of R100.
Meals: Full breakfast included. Restaurant on premises, open seven days a week.
Directions: Turn into Church Street (Kerkstraat) in Wellington which becomes the Bainskloof Rd (R301/3). 2.5km out of Wellington on right-hand side follow brown signs to Oude Wellington.

Kleinfontein

Tim and Caroline Holdcroft

Wellington
Tel: 021-864-1202 Fax: 021-864-1202
Email: kleinfon@iafrica.com Web: www.kleinfontein.com
Cell: 072-108-5895

An evening leg-stretch with Tim proved the perfect antidote to a long and stressful day on the road. Guided by a German alsatian, an almost-labrador and an incredibly energetic fluffy white thing we strolled past Jersey cows, through a shaded stream and between rows of sunlit vines. Kleinfontein is just an hour from Cape Town at the foot of the Bainskloof Pass and the Holdcrofts are delightful hosts. And this truly is home hosting at its finest; they'll eat and drink with you, show you their farm and even have you out there clipping the vines or feeding the horses if you show willing (and riding them, too, if you're saddle-hardened). In fact there's enough to keep you busy here for days, from hiking in surrounding mountains and cellar tours galore, to the leisurely delights of a good book beneath magnificent oak trees, or a wallow in the pool in Caroline's fabulous garden. She is of Kenyan stock and Tim's British, but they spent years in Africa and over a superb supper we washed down tales of the continent with home-grown cabernet sauvignon. Like me you'll stay in a roomy, restored wing of the thatched Cape Dutch farmhouse with poplar beams and reed ceilings. Like me you'll sleep like a baby. And, like me, you'll wake to breakfast on the verandah with fresh butter and milk, newly-laid eggs and honey straight from the beehive. Sound idyllic? Well, it is. *Closed June and July.*

Rooms: 2 suites, both with sitting room. 1 with en-suite bath and shower, 1 with en-suite bath with shower overhead.
Price: R1,200 - R 1,500 pp sharing. Single supplement + 20%. Includes all meals, drinks and laundry.
Meals: Breakfast, tea/coffee tray, picnic lunch and 4-course dinner included in price.
Directions: Directions are down dirt roads so map can be emailed or faxed.

Bovlei Valley Retreat

Lee and Abbi Wallis
Bovlei Road, Wellington
Tel: 021-864-1504 Fax: 021-864-1504
Email: info@bvr.co.za Web: www.bvr.co.za

When I arrived at Bovlei Valley, catching a waft of baking lavender cookies and the sound of a beautiful aria drifting in from Abbi's kitchen, I was eager to get inside. It didn't disappoint. I settled onto a squishy sofa near the large fireplace, sipped my tea and tried to resist the sweet-smelling biscuits she had just pulled from the oven. Abbi did a degree in hospitality, and it shows. Her open-plan kitchen is part of the impressive-yet-cosy main room, with high ceilings, sofas and a dining area, and she does all her home-cooking there while chatting to guests. Next door is a comfy TV room with a DVD library and every board game you could possibly desire for a rainy day. But on sunny days it will be hard to leave the pool, whose depths are constantly filled with fresh water from the lips of a rather fetching bearded stone head. And if that wasn't enough to keep you there, a plump, well-stocked honesty fridge under the verandah, catering for every poolside whim, should do the trick. The whole place is a working guava, grape and lavender farm, with its own boutique winery, Dunstone. All you can see for miles are plants and mountains. The highlight of the converted stable rooms is the Lavender Suite, with a luxurious four-poster, and a view over – you've guessed it – waving fields of lavender. Guava Cottage has its own mini-vineyard and stoep, and lies in front of – wait for it – the guava plantation. A granite-topped kitchen with dishwasher and generous range mean you can really self-cater in style… that is, if you can stand a night away from Abbi's home-cooking. The cottage even has its own solar panel-heated pool, garden and braai area.

Rooms: 6: 5 in converted stables: 2 with 1 queen and 1 single bed and shower; 3 with queen beds and bath/shower. Also 1 cottage with 1 double and 1 twin. All have en-suite bathrooms.
Price: Stable suites: R400 - R600 pp sharing, singles R500 - R700. Guava Cottage: R600 - R900 pp sharing.
Meals: Breakfast, freshly-baked cakes and complimentary wine included. Dinner available by prior booking.
Directions: See website for detailed directions.

Roggeland Country House

Gordon Minkley

Roggeland Rd, Dal Josaphat Valley, Paarl
Tel: 021-868-2501 Fax: 021-868-2113
Email: rog@iafrica.com Web: www.roggeland.co.za

The highlight of a stay at Roggeland must be the food! All reports glow with praise: served different wines to taste pre-dinner, an opportunity to chat to other guests and one of the family members; then four mouth-watering courses each with a different wine specially chosen to accompany it. Vegetarians will be particularly happy and you are guaranteed that neither meals nor wines will ever be repeated during your stay, such is the quality of service here. The house is an 18th-century Cape Dutch homestead with large, thick-walled rooms - sometimes huge - with a variety of original features: beam and reed ceilings, thatch, antique furniture. The dining room, for example, is in an old kitchen with its original grate and cooking implements. Some bedrooms are in the main house and some are separate from it, all are lavender-scented and none let the side down. Character abounds: floors slope, beams curve and attractive bright-coloured walls are often uneven with age; and there are always fresh flowers and home-made soaps in the rooms. Roggeland is family-run and the atmosphere is friendly and caring as a result. Farmland and mountains surround the property and the Minkleys will happily organise evening rides on horseback into the foothills. Wonderful hospitality and very good value too. *Children by arrangement. Mountain biking.*

Rooms: 10: either twins or doubles, all with en/s bathrooms, 8 with baths and showers, 2 with baths and showers overhead.
Price: Seasonal R520 – R1,220 pp sharing.
Meals: The highlight is a 4-course dinner with a different wine at each course and wine-tasting, all included in price. Full breakfast too. Lunches on request.
Directions: Approximately 60km from Cape Town, take exit 59 onto R301 towards Wellington. After 8km on R301 turn right at Roggeland sign. Follow sign onto gravel road for 1km.

Belair

Janet Plumbly

Suid Agter-Paarl Rd, Paarl
Tel: 021-863-1504
Fax: 021-863-1602
Email: info@belair.co.za
Web: www.belair.co.za
Cell: 082-572-7062

A straight 300-metre drive up two narrow strips of weathered red brick, past roaming gangs of guinea-fowl and rows of vines, takes you to Belair, a beautiful guest house on its own farm beneath the round dome of Paarl Mountain. The view from the doorstep (and the garden and pool) across the valley towards Franschhoek and the Groot Drakenstein is spectacular... and it is rather lovely inside too. Steps lead up from a large threshing-circle style driveway into the hallway and open sitting room, which mixes antique furniture with comfy sofas and bookshelves bursting with swashbucklers. Behind is the bright breakfast conservatory, which looks onto a rose-filled garden. Janet's light but stylish touch is in evidence everywhere at Belair, from the terraced gardens to the bedrooms themselves, each with its own distinct character. All the rooms are wonderful, but the two new luxury suites, complete with fireplaces, open-plan baths and deep Flokati rugs, are sumptuous! The honeymoon suite has a deck overhanging the rose garden with a double daybed on it, while the other suite has a patio area with a swing couch. From the house, it's a short walk up to the dam where birdlife abounds among the reeds (look out for buzzards when it all goes quiet), a great spot for a sundowner. For the more energetic, Paarl Mountain Nature Reserve is further up the hill, and there are lots of golf courses nearby. *Cape Town Waterfront is also only 35 minutes away and there are great restaurants in Paarl. Bikes for hire.*

Rooms: 6: 2 doubles & 2 double rooms with sitting rooms and air-con, all have en-suite bathrooms with bath and separate showers; 2 new luxury suites with downstairs sitting room and bedroom/bathroom upstairs.
Price: R300 - R700 pp sharing. Singles on request.
Meals: Full breakfast included.
Directions: On Suid-Agter Paarl Rd off R101 (next to Fairview Wine Estate).

Palmiet Valley Estate

Frederick Uhlendorff

Palmiet Valley Estate, Sonstraal Rd, Klein Drakenstein, Paarl
Tel: 021-862-7741 Fax: 021 862 6891
Email: info@palmiet.co.za Web: www.palmiet.co.za

Frederick has scoured not just this land but several in his relentless quest for fine things. There's hardly a nut or bolt in the place that isn't antique - even the loos, showers, free-standing baths and wooden wash-stands are Victorian, not to mention the aged safes and old-school slipper bed pans (that thankfully no-one ever uses!). But this is not a museum, despite the long history of the farm - Palmiet was one of the first to be established outside Cape Town in 1692. Guests come here for the luxury and the romance of the vineyards and mountains that stretch out and up from the old farm. One four-poster bed is positioned so that you can wake up and watch the sun rise over the mountains without moving your head. The beautiful gardens are interwoven with cobbled paths and peppered with numerous dreamy spots to be peaceful. Herbs are harvested and transformed into fresh herbal teas or added to shady lunches by the pool. In summer, candlelit dinners are held under the oaks and are as sumptuous as everything else, with top chefs employed to cook exclusively for residents. With so much character and reflection upon old-fashioned values, it's no wonder this place is a hot-spot for weddings. But you don't need to be married or coupled to enjoy it as I, a happy singleton, discovered.

Rooms: 13: 1 Honeymoon Suite en-suite bath/shower, 1 luxury suite, 1 Presidential Suite, 6 standard twins/doubles en-suite bath or shower, 2 single rooms (double beds) en s shower, 2 family cottages with kitchenette (not fully self-catering) en-s bath/shower.

Price: R756 - 1,900 pp sharing. Single rooms R768 - R1,037 or from R904 per couple. Specials available in winter (stay for 3 nights, pay for 2).
Meals: Full breakfast included. Lunches on request. 3-course set dinner R295 pp.
Directions: Heading away from Cape Town on the N1 take exit 62a (Sonstraal Road), turn first left, straight over 2 crossroads. Palmiet Valley is on left. Airport Transfer R575.

Paarl Rock Suites

Udo and Carmen Mettendorf

64 Main Street, Paarl
Tel: 021-863-3192 Fax: 021-863-3192
Email: info@kapinfo.com Web: www.kapinfo.com

Based on the 'golden mile' of Paarl, ballooning-mad Udo and Carmen are pioneers in placing this "rough-diamond-of-the-Winelands-region" on the map. Golden mile basically means the 'old bit' of Paarl, a historic rush of Victorian houses, tree-lined with old oaks. The original house dates back to 1860 when it featured as part of an old wine estate. Although split into various scattered sections now, you still get to look out over the Mettendorfs' rock garden and succulents, onto regiments of vines beyond. Paarl Rock sits stately in the background, a massive granite feature thrown up by volcanic activity and asking to be biked to, walked around and explored; while the swimming pool in the foreground has been craftily crafted to reflect it. Udo and Carmen are an open book of local knowledge. Originally from Germany, they came and explored as tourists, gathering all the best inside information and wrapping it up with a big ballooning bow for their guests. You'll have to book fast to bag a corner of the basket, however, as ballooning has seriously taken off (if you'll excuse the pun) since Udo and Carmen madly (some believed) introduced it a few years ago. I loved the luxury apartment, with leather sofas, spa bath and marble-topped kitchen - and revelled in being able to rustle up my own meal after two weeks of being cooked for (despite many restaurants within a short walking distance). All three flats, however, qualify as the perfect base to negotiate all the Cape has to offer. *Bikes available.*

Rooms: 3 self-catering apartments: 2 with 1 double bedroom and 1 with 2 bedrooms, a double and a queen.
Price: R460 - R750 for the flat. Prefer a min of 3-night stay. ONLY OPEN FROM OCTOBER TO MAY!
Meals: Fully self-catering, but many restaurants within easy walking distance.
Directions: On the N1 from Cape Town take exit 55 leading into Paarl Main Street. Follow until you reach no. 64 on your left, opposite number 113.

Ridgeback House

Vanessa and Vernon Cole

Langverwacht Farm, Nr. Paarl
Tel: 021-869-8988 Fax: 021-869-8988
Email: ridgebackhouse@mwebbiz.co.za Web: www.ridgebackhouse.co.za
Cell: 072-500-7516

Though the ice-cold Coke that Vanessa greeted me with was just what the doctor ordered, it really should have been a glass of shiraz. For this is the place to come for the complete wine experience. Guests are encouraged to help in any way they want in the production of the gods' favourite tipple, whether it be lending a hand with the harvest or just making sure the bottle's not corked. The latter takes place in a tasting centre in the hub of the farm, with a wooden balcony overlooking the dam – which is home to twenty-five species of wild fowl as it goes. A tour of the cellar is easily and enthusiastically arranged too, and no stone is left unturned in the quest to educate and inform. After a hard day's drinking (sorry, working) I retired to my bedroom, one of five in the converted farmhouse. Four of them have beautiful views down to the vineyards, framed by wild olive trees, the spire of the Afrikaans church in the village protruding through the thick foliage. It was difficult to decide which room was my favourite. I loved my dressing room (found beyond an arched entrance) and waking up to the smell of roses, but then I also adore a bathroom large enough for ten. Meals are served in the cavernous dining room, a short amble from the sitting room lit by wrought-iron chandeliers. Vanessa is a superb hostess and Ridgeback the perfect place to ensure that the 2009-2010 vintage is a fine one. *If you are arriving after 7pm let Vanessa know so the gate can be kept open.*

Rooms: 5: 1 king, 1 double and 3 king/twins. All en-suite, 4 with baths and showers and 1 with shower.
Price: R500 - R600 pp sharing. Singles R750 per night.
Meals: Full breakfast included. Lunches available either at tasting centre or at house on request. Dinners also on request.
Directions: Ridgeback House is just north of Paarl. Phone or look at website for more detailed directions.

Eensgevonden Vineyard Cottages

Sally and Douglas McDermott

Near Brandvlei Dam, Rawsonville/Breedekloof
Tel: 023-349-1490 Fax: 023-349-1490
Email: eensgevonden@compnet.co.za Web: www.eensgevonden.co.za
Cell: 082-829-8923

Often by driving that little bit further in South Africa you find something particularly special. Like Eensgevonden. Winding through vineyards of chardonnay and merlot grapes, I came across this beautiful national monument, the oldest Cape Dutch farmhouse in the Breede River Valley and home to Sally and Doug. We chatted under the shady fingers of a giant oak tree, planted nearly three centuries ago on the orders of Cape Governor Simon van der Stel, sampling a glass of the local wine cellar's finest. Along with four other staff, the couple hand-tend and harvest their grapes, honey bees and organic vegetables and will enthusiastically show you round their farmhouse and vineyards. The farm itself is part vineyard and part natural fynbos with 400 hectares of private nature reserve. A short walk from the farmstead, the spotlessly-clean self-catering cottages are surrounded by an indigenous garden. My favourite was Sunbird with its white sheets and duvets, terracotta flooring, wood fire and vases of cut herbs. Large verandahs have magnificent views and are an idyllic spot for sundowners. Well-marked hiking trails traverse the rugged reserve with stunning views in all directions. Keeping an eye out for klipspringer and honey-badger and 100 identified birds the less energetic can amble up the path through sand-olives and proteas, to a secluded, crystal clear mountain rock pool. Eensgevonden is a very special place, offering a wilder, more genuine wine experience than is on offer in the more touristy towns like Franschhoek and Stellenbosch.

Rooms: 3 self-catering units: 2 with a queen and twin room with 1 bathroom with bath and shower and 1 with a shower; 1 unit with a single room and a queen room, 1 bathroom with shower.
Price: R250 - R350 pp sharing.
Meals: Self-catering. Breakfast in basket with home-made muesli & muffins is available as extra. Cooked dinner or vacuum-packed meats provided on request. Good restaurants nearby.
Directions: Off the N1 between Rawsonville & Worcester. Full directions given on enquiry.

Fraai Uitzicht 1798

Karl and Sandra Papesch

Historic Wine and Guest Farm
with Restaurant, Klaas Voogds
East (Oos),
Robertson/Montagu
Tel: 023-626-6156
Fax: 023-626-5265
Email: info@fraaiuitzicht.com
Web: www.fraaiuitzicht.com

'Fraai Uitzicht' means 'beautiful view' in Dutch - no idle promise as it turns out. The 17th-century wine and guest farm is four kilometres up a gravel road in a cul-de-sac valley ringed by vertiginous mountains. People come from far and wide for the well-known restaurant and the seven-course *dégustation* menu is basically irresistible. Matched with local wine, it features salmon trout, springbok carpaccio, beef fillet with a port wine jus and topped with onion marmalade and decadent Dream of Africa chocolate cake. Shall we just say I left with more than one spare tyre in the car. You could also be entertained by a Xhosa choir who give performances every other Wednesday night. Where to sleep is not an easy decision as you are spoilt for choice. A few cottages take it easy in the garden, each comfortable and pretty with impressionistic oils and views of the mountains, while others offer you masses of character with metre-thick walls and timber interiors; my favourite was the loft bedroom in the eaves. Or opt for one of the garden suites with their own entrances and balconies. Make sure you take a peek at the wine cellar - guests have first option on the (uniquely) hand-made merlot. I can't count the number of recommendations we had pointing us here. *Restaurant closed June to August. Limited menu available for guests.*

Rooms: 9: 4 cottages, 2 with 2 bedrooms (1 queen & 1 twin), 2 with 1 bedroom (queen); 4 suites, 3 with king, 1 with queen, all en/s shower.
Price: Cottages are R780 pp. Suites are R510 - R620 pp. Singles on request.
Meals: Continental breakfast included. Lunch and dinner available on premises.
Directions: On R60 between Robertson & Ashton. Approximately 5km from Ashton and 9km from Robertson, Klaas Voogds East turn-off, 4km on gravel road, turn-off to left.

Olive Garden Country Lodge

Gina and Fernand Van Wassenhove
Klaasvoogds West, Robertson
Tel: 023-626-2028 Fax: 023-626-2028
Email: info@olivegardencountrylodge.com
Web: www.olivegardencountrylodge.com Cell: 082-448-5393

Olive Garden Country Lodge, almost invisibly hidden in a dramatic sea of fynbos, is a destination for those who want to lose themselves in nature... but who don't want to compromise on luxury at the same time. This happy combination is typical of Gina and Farnand who are serious back-to-nature conservationists, passionate about the wild things that crowd round the lodge and especially the extra virgin olive oil that they produce; but also epicurean in their tastes. If my room can be likened to a restaurant it would have a Michelin star - its open fire the oven, its beds a perfect soufflé perhaps. Why all the food analogies? Listen up, I'll only say this one hundred times – they are nothing short of magicians in the kitchen. I just would never have thought that the best sushi I would ever taste would be in a remote olive grove in the South African mountains – and made by a Belgian. Then came the meltingly tender pieces of home-reared mutton; and then more than one slice of fruit tartine. I think a few appreciative expletives may have escaped me at some point, for which I apologize. Good job the lodge has its own hiking trail, winding its way through olive groves and up the mountain that cradles the lodge. Looking back across the view my mouth made a perfect 'o' – and this time it had nothing to do with food. Gina was right, this place is a slice of heaven.

Rooms: 5: 4 queens with separate bath and shower; 1 family suite with 2 twins/ queens and 2 bathrooms. 1 separate bath and shower and 1 outside shower and 1 Jacuzzi.
Price: R450 - R750 pp sharing.
Meals: Full breakfast included. Supper from R180 and picnics on request.
Directions: Directions on website.

Mallowdeen Gardens

Rita and Wim van de Sande
Klaasvoodgs West, Robertson
Tel: 023-626-5788 Fax: 086-509-6764
Email: info@mallowdeen.com Web: www.mallowdeen.com

Driving down a long avenue of olive trees coiled in sunshine, I could have been in the hot heart of southern Spain. Rita and Wim, emerging from their traditional Cape Dutch farmhouse, have the greenest of visions for their little bit of joy caught between the Langeberge mountains and South Africa's finest vineyards. Apparently the smell of rotting tomatoes was overpowering when they first took over, but now all that is cleared and replaced instead with herb and vegetable gardens and an apricot orchard gently fanned by swaying elephant grass. They have grand plans to install a Japanese garden and already the canna flowers are the most vivid of reds. Three rondavels, a little way from the main house, face each other across a portly figure-of-eight swimming pool. One is a breakfast room where you sit at neat tables and chairs (if not outside on the terrace) all hand-made locally or, more unusually, cupped inside giant, hand-shaped thrones. The other two cottages are simple and good. Brush aside a fly-curtain and relax into the earthiness of the floors, walls and a maze-like partition into the bathroom. Ornaments like a miniature baobab tree hint at travels around Africa, where Rita and Wim discovered they had left their hearts on return to Holland. Bird-lovers may prefer the more private flat in the main house, which is close to the dam and from its vine-strangled courtyard the views are of one tree in particular where "a lot happens" around 5 in the morning. *Carpe Diem.*

Rooms: 3 units: 2 cottages (king/twin with full en-suite bathrooms), 1 flat (twin/king with en-suite shower).
Price: R450 pp sharing.
Meals: Full breakfast included. Excellent restaurants.
Directions: 7km from Robertson toward Ashton. Take Klaasvoodgs West turning on the left onto dirt road. Mallowdeen Gardens is 1.5km on the right.

Map Number: 4

Entry Number: 87

Natte Valleij

Charlene and Charles Milner

R44 between Stellenbosch and Paarl, Klapmuts
Tel: 021-875-5171
Email: milner@intekom.co.za Web: www.nattevalleij.co.za
Cell: 079-037-4860

Come and lose yourself in the depths of this wild and fecund garden - or do I mean jungle? Ancient trees such as the rare gingco (the oldest in South Africa, once thought extinct), several 200-year-old oaks and a wealth of growth besides keep the pool, 'moon gate' and old brandy stills secreted in their midst. Guests stay in the simple B&B room next to the main house, its verandah festooned with grandiflora, and eat a breakfast in this most lovely of Cape Dutch homesteads (pictured above), built in 1775. If the weather's fine then you eat out on the patio under its cooling roof of vine. Or you can take one of the cottages lost down garden paths. Vineyard Cottage (pictured below), with direct access to the swimming pool, is the oldest building on the property, its original 1714 reed ceilings still intact. While Cellar Cottage is the most recent addition at 'Nutty Valley', small, cute, rustic, perfect for couples. Walks are in all directions up mountains and into surrounding vineyards. Or guests are welcome to enter the park (the entrance gate is just 50m from Vineyard Cottage) where at the last count 23 wildebeest, 25 eland, 30 springbok, 4 bontebok, 3 kudu, 2 oryx and 10 zebra (among others) can be seen. Come for great charm from house and hosts alike. *Local bird-watching tours with Charles are a speciality and Charles's son is now making wine on the property. Well-positioned on the Stellenbosch and Paarl wine routes. Self-catering available in the cottages.*

Rooms: 3: 1 B&B room, double with en/s bath; 2 cottages (self-catering): Cellar Cottage sleeps 2 (plus 2 kids' beds); Vineyard Cottage sleeps 6 (3 bedrooms and 2 bathrooms).
Price: B&B R250 - R290 pp sharing. Rates for the cottages (i.e. NOT per person) per night depending on number of people and length of stay: R390 - R980.
Meals: Full breakfast included in B&B and an optional extra in cottages.
Directions: From Cape Town take N1 Exit 47. Turn right onto R44. Farm 4km on left.

Lekkerwijn

Wendy Pickstone

Groot Drakenstein, Franschhoek Road, Franschhoek/Groot Drakenstein
Tel: 021-874-1122 Fax: 021-874-1465
Email: lekkerwijn@new.co.za Web: www.lekkerwijn.com

Lekkerwijn (pronounced Lekkervain) is a 1790s Cape Dutch homestead with a grand Edwardian extension designed by Sir Herbert Baker. You would probably have to pay to look round if Wendy didn't live there. It positively creaks with family history. You can tell when one family have lived in a grand house for generations - all the furniture, fittings and decoration look so at home. This is not some country house hotel nor some converted annexe. You share the house fully with Wendy, whose family have lived here since the late 19th century - unless of course you would prefer the privacy of Coach House Cottage. My strongest impressions are of the central courtyard with its gallery and cloister, the yellowwood floors and beams and the towering palms planted by Wendy's grandfather, the informal taste of the nursery bedroom, a wonderful breakfast... and Wendy herself, who is full of character and together with her management team, so caring of her guests.

Rooms: 6: 5 either doubles or twins, all en-suite. 1 single. 1 self-catering cottage for couples either alone or with children.

Price: Seasonal R750 - R950 pp sharing. Quotes for singles on request. Minimum stay two nights. Special offers on occasion.

Meals: Full breakfast included for B&B. You can self-cater in Coach House cottage and breakfast in the courtyard is an optional extra. Other meals can be provided by prior arrangement.

Directions: On R45 at intersection with R310 from Stellenbosch (after passing Boschendal), alongside the Allée Bleue entrance walls.

Map Number: 4

Cathbert Country Inn

Lynne and Aubrey Blignaut

Franschhoek Rd (R45), Entrance on "Vrede & Lust Wine Estate",
Simondium, Franschhoek
Tel: 021-874-1366 Fax: 021-874-3918
Email: info@cathbert.co.za Web: www.cathbert.co.za Cell: 083-3093-675

If warm hosting, gourmet food and eye-watering natural beauty in the very heart of the winelands doesn't sound like your sort of thing then I suggest you turn away now, because Cathbert Country Inn is all of these things. Uprooting themselves from hectic Jo'burg, Aubrey and Lynne have slipped into their new hosting boots down south as if they had been wearing them all their lives. Concerned regulars should relax, though, because they have retained the inn's rustic-yet-comfortable charm… and the food is as good as ever. The dining experience is a major draw card here and has received deserved acclaim. Butternut squash quiche with melting Parmesan crust serves as a mouth-watering example of the totally organic culinary compositions that emerge from the kitchen. What better start to a day than devouring an omelette soufflé from the private terrace of your chalet, while gazing at vineyards, farmland and the reservoir that so immaculately mirrors the Simonsberg Mountains looming behind the property. The best thing though? That you can spend the day hiking up a mountain, attending a historic or gastronomic tour, or perhaps just drinking up the peace and a local vintage by the large pool… and not have to get in the car to find a great meal at the end of it all. This year also sees the arrival of a brand-new self-contained cottage, sleeping up to 4, with a private swimming pool, secluded garden and, naturally, the same wonderful views.

Rooms: 9 suites: 2 standard luxury rooms, 4 luxury suites, 1 executive suite, 1 deluxe suite; 1 separate self-contained cottage. All with en-suite bath and shower. All king-size/twin beds. All air-conditioned.
Price: R635 - R925 pp sharing. Singles on request supplement +50%.
Meals: Full breakfast included. Set menu 4-course dinner, R250 pp. In the cottage meals can be arranged or there is a fully-equipped kitchen.
Directions: From CT take N1, take exit 47, turn R at end of ramp, over 4-way stop, left at next road towards Franschhoek. Pass Backsberg Wine Estate. Just before the T-junction, turn R onto private tar road, following Cathbert Country Inn signs for 2.5km.

Les Chambres

Bill and Sandy Stemp

3 Berg Street, Franschhoek
Tel: 021-876-3136 Fax: 021-876-2798
Email: gg@leschambres.co.za Web: www.leschambres.co.za
Cell: 083-263-4926

So much to take in even as I ambled up the garden path towards the house: the palm tree, reputed to be the tallest tree in the village; the herb garden spilling over with basil, rocket and tomatoes - that stone bench would be the perfect spot to make some progress with a paperback, I noted. Venturing further, I found irises, agapanthus and roses all laid out in bloom upon bark-strewn flowerbeds. And finally the house, a verandah-fronted Victorian gem, with Bill, Sandy and Archie (a cat) and Monty (a dog) forming a reassuring welcoming committee. Refreshed with a cool drink, I was shown through to the breakfasting patio where goldfish and koi waft prettily about in a stone pond and French doors provide easy access to the continental-style buffet: fresh fruits and cereals, home-made granola and bread. Cooked options might include poached eggs on English muffins, or 'Eggs Benedict', or scrambled eggs with smoked salmon-trout. Ze bedrooms of ze title are furnished in a mix of the antique and the contemporary with mahogany dressing tables and wicker bedheads while the bathrooms have travertine tiles, roll-top Victorian baths and separate showers. All rooms have air-conditioning and underfloor heating ensuring tip-top comfort whenever it is you stay. Private courtyards are available to two rooms, red-tiled with whitewashed walls and an overhanging orange tree. There is much to enjoy cloistered behind these walls, not least the heated swimming pool.

Rooms: 4: all king-size extra-length doubles or 2 twins, and all en-suite bath and shower.
Price: R450 - R750 pp sharing. R670 - R1,125 singles.
Meals: Full breakfast included.
Directions: From R45 drive through village of Franschhoek and turn left into Berg Street just before monument.

Clementine Cottage

Malcolm Buchanan

L'Avenir Farm, Green Valley Rd, Franschhoek
Tel: 021-876-3690 Fax: 021-876-3528
Email: lavenir@iafrica.com Web: www.clementinecottage.co.za
Cell: 082-320-2179

Running late with my mobile battery dead, I was touched to find Jef waiting expectantly for me just beyond the low-lying bridge that marks the entrance to L'Avenir Farm. He kindly guided me through the orchards of plums and clementines to meet Malcolm, who runs this 21-hectare, family-owned, working fruit farm. Jef, by the way, is a boerboel, as loyal to Malcolm as Robin is to Batman. In retrospect, my timing was perfect: the sun was setting behind the mountains that frame the Franschhoek Valley and from the stoep of Clementine Cottage, looking out over the pool and the vineyard beyond, the sky was stained a deep red. The only sounds I could hear, as I enjoyed a most welcome cold beer with Malcolm and his folks, were the frogs croaking contentedly in the dam that forms the centrepiece of the farm. If you find the pool too confining, a few lengths of this dam should satisfy any Tarzanesque impulses you may harbour. Being only 3km from the village I was able to enjoy a fine meal at the legendary Topsi's, before returning to the biggest bed I've ever had the pleasure of sleeping in. Recently refurbished in the original farm cottage style, Clementine Cottage has everything you could desire from pool, braaing area and satellite TV to large, stylish en-suite bedrooms.

Rooms: 1 cottage: 1 double with en-suite bath and shower and 1 twin with en-suite bath and shower.
Price: 1st Oct - 31st Apr: 2 people sharing R600 pp per night, 3 pax R500 pp, 4 pax R450 pp; 1st May - 30th September: 2 people sharing R550 pp, 3 pax R450 pp, 4 pax R400 pp. Minimum stay 2 nights.
Meals: Self-catering, but numerous restaurants nearby.
Directions: From Franschhoek Main Rd driving towards Franschhoek Monument turn R. Drive for 2km. Turn L up Green Valley Rd (Clementine Cottage signed). Turn L up 1st gravel rd (signed again). Drive over bdge onto L'Avenir, thro' orchards, pass shed on L, Cottage 150m further on R.

Akademie Street Guesthouses

Katherine and Arthur McWilliam Smith
5 Akademie Street, Franschhoek
Tel: 021-876-3027 Fax: 021-876-3293
Email: info@aka.co.za Web: www.aka.co.za
Cell: 082-655-5308

The parade of flowers and stepping-stones through citrus trees, fig trees, rose bushes and bougainvillaea made a beautiful winter's afternoon even brighter. The airy cottages, which sit detached within the flower arrangements, open out onto private stoeps, gardens and even swimming pools. Vreugde, meaning 'joy', is a garden suite for two that has a neat kitchenette in an alcove and a sofa on the terrace. Oortuiging is a restored 1860s cottage for three that retains the old Cape style with antiques throughout. Uitsig, the newest suite, is a stylish addition to the guesthouse, with a private balcony that looks out over the Franschhoek mountains. And Gelatenheid is a luxurious villa with, again, a private swimming pool and a wide wrap-around balcony. At the end of the balcony, suitably screened by tree-tops, is an outdoor, repro Victorian bathtub in which you can soak while gazing out at the mountain views... then wrap up in a towel from the heated bath rail. Inside, an expansive open-plan studio is home for just two people (although there's space enough for a four-bed house), with high wooden ceilings, Venetian blinds and French doors... a decadent holiday home. As full as a full breakfast can be (including boerewors - a type of SA sausage if you really didn't know) is served under the vines at the homestead. Katherine and Arthur - he was formerly Mayor of Franschhoek and they are both sooo nice - are easy smilers and happy to help with any day-tripping tips.

Rooms: 4 cottages: Vreugde: king or twin on request, en/s bath & shower; Oortuiging: 1 king or twin, & 1 single, both en/s bath and shower; Gelatenheid: 1 king or twin, & en/s bath and shower; Uitsig: 1 king or twin, en/s bath & shower.
Price: R1,000 - R3,000 per cottage.
Meals: Full breakfast included.
Directions: From Cape Town take N1 then R45. Akademie St is parallel to main road in Franschhoek, two streets up the hill.

Plum Tree Cottage

Liz and John Atkins

Excelsior Road, Franschhoek
Tel: 021-876-2244 Fax: 021-876-2398
Email: plumtree@kleindauphine.co.za Web: www.kleindauphine.co.za

The setting could not be more perfect. A sanctum of blooming plum-blossom, vineyards and oak trees spatter dappled shadows as they rock gently in the breeze, while magnificent mountains rise steeply from the Franschhoek valley. The Plum Tree Cottage balcony is the perfect spot to soak up all this serenity. Having run B&Bs for many a year, Liz and John know exactly what people want, and with this newly-built cottage they deliver it in spades. Entirely self-contained (it even has its own separate orchard-lined driveway), it allows you the space to do your own thing. This may be in the elegantly-paved courtyard, cooling off in the invigorating plunge pool, or popping out to the restaurants and wineries in Franschhoek, itself just pip-spitting distance away. The interior is a calming refuge in blues and whites, much like the roses and lavender outside. With each room sharing the magnificent view, you won't know where to put yourself.... I'd choose the corner bath and peek through the oaks at the Arab horse stud behind. By now, Liz will be busy clothing its clotted-cream-coloured walls with wisteria, roses and any other creepers she has creeping around for when she runs out of space in the garden: "I just send the plants up the walls." Perfectly tranquil and delightfully quaint… a proper English-style country cottage.

Rooms: 1 queen with en-suite bath and shower. Mezzanine floor accessed by Swedish ladder (so sensibly made it's almost impossible to fall off) can sleep two children (over the age of 12).
Price: R375 - R400 pp sharing. For additions (up to 2) R100 pp. Minimum booking 2 nights.
Meals: (Strictly!) self-catering.
Directions: Drive through Franschhoek and turn right at the monument. After 1.3km turn left into Klein Dauphine, then follow separate drive to the right for Plum Tree Cottage.

The Garden House

Barry and Annette Phillips

29 De Wet St, Franschhoek
Tel: 021-876 3155 Fax: 021-876-4271
Email: info@thegardenhouse.co.za Web: www.thegardenhouse.co.za
Cell: 083-340-3439

Annette and Barry (who also run the local newspaper - The Franschhoek Tatler) have fully immersed themselves in village life since their impulsive holiday decision to leave London in '01 and buy their Cape Victorian house. I felt their enthusiasm from the moment I arrived. The Garden House, originally called Belle Vue, with views across the valley to the mountains beyond and an abundant garden (with a larger-than-usual swimming pool), well deserves both names; and from there it's just an easy walk to most of Franschhoek's famous restaurants. Guests stay in the air-conditioned and stylishly decorated cottage with its original wood-beamed bedroom and large bathroom with under-floor heating. Occasionally, guests can use the pretty guest room in the main house but the lovely Victorian brass bed is "only suitable for very friendly couples". Come morning, Barry took me on a rigorous ride on a mountain bike – he keeps two for guests – while Annette prepared a smoked trout breakfast for our return. Hiking and biking trails, horse-riding and tennis are all nearby and guests often go with Annette to a nearby 'informal settlement' to feed the cats and dogs. She can also give you plenty of ideas for day trips. *A cot for babies at R100 per day and free internet access on their laptop or guests' own are also available.*

Rooms: 2: Cottage Room: 1 queen with en-suite bath and separate shower; Main House Room: 1 standard double with en-suite bath and shower overhead.
Price: Cottage: R600 in summer; R400 in winter with light breakfast served in the room. Main House Room (summer only): R375. All prices pp sharing.
Meals: Breakfast included with complimentary drinks in the room.
Directions: De Wet Street is 1st L after brown sign to Chamonix as enter Franschhoek from Cape Town direction, & 1st R after BP Station if you come over the Pass. Cross over 3 intersections and The Garden House is the 2nd house on the R.

Map Number: 4   Entry Number: 95

Nooks Pied-à-terre

Lesley and Kevin Dennis
6 Haumann Street, Franschhoek
Email: nookspied-a-terre@hotmail.com Web: www.nookspied-a-terre.co.za
Cell: 079-955-3114

After years of work, Lesley and Kevin finished their perfect home only to be called away to America. Well, their loss is our gain... and boy is it a gain! To describe this as self-catering would not do it justice – this is a personal palace. The second I entered the double-height doors I could see that there were no design compromises: from the turquoise glow of the chef's fridge to the cobalt blue of the mosaicked pool, it is sensational throughout. The back wall of the main room slides away to create a fully open-plan route to your garden, complete with lemon trees, brightly-coloured walls, a delicious pool and an enticing-looking outdoor shower. But it was one of the mezzanine floors that caught my eye: an entertainment area with leather armchairs and every shiny bit of machinery a gadget magpie could ask for. The master bedroom, with its air-con/heating unit, electric-blue bed-head, en-suite underfloor-heated bathroom with free-standing bath and open-plan shower is truly, well... masterful. And that's not to say that the second bedroom is plain. With Chinese black-lacquered fitted wardrobes and opulent fur bedspread they're both idyllic spots to end a wine-soaked evening in SA's gourmet capital.

Rooms: 2: 1 king with en-suite full bathroom; 1 king with own adjacent bathroom & large shower.
Price: Winter (May to October 2009) from R1,400 per night (for 2 sharing) to R1,800 per night (for 4 sharing) for the villa. Summer (Nov 2009 to April 2010) from R1,850 per night (for 2 sharing) to R2,500 per night (for 4 sharing) for the villa.
Meals: Self-catering only.
Directions: From Paarl/Stellenbosch, as you enter Franschhoek, take second turn on left into Uitkyk St (signed to Chamonix). Nooks Pied-à-terre is on the left on the corner of Haumann St & Uitkyk.

L'Auberge Chanteclair

Bob and Leslie Maginley

Middagkrans Road, Franschhoek
Tel: 021-876-3685 Fax: 021-876-2709
Email: chanteclair@mweb.co.za Web: www.chanteclair.co.za
Cell: 083-376-9913

The sun had its hat firmly glued on when I stepped from my car at Auberge Chanteclair and all I could hear was birdsong. The flower garden, fruit trees, vineyards, mountains, swimming pool and the vine-shaded breakfast patio all purred in bucolic bliss. The house was built in 1910-ish, but it has since been transformed into the impressive colonial-feel country house it is now, with its thick white-washed walls, old timbers and sash windows. All the bedrooms are large and cool with vases of fresh flowers, carefully-chosen antiques and immaculate white bathrooms. One has French windows out onto the verandah and mountain views from the bed. The reed-ceilinged Studio in the garden has a 2-metre-high wall that separates the bedroom from the sitting room, where there is a wood fire and piles of logs. Vine Cottage also has its own sitting room and fireplace as well as a private vine-covered stoep. Both Bob and Leslie (hoteliers in a previous life) are bird-watching enthusiasts, and can tell you about all their visiting species, from the paradise fly catcher to the hoopoe. But no specialist knowledge is needed to enjoy the cacophony of birdsong that greets you on the lake. Bob and Leslie are natural hosts and evenings are whiled away in the sitting room, talking to guests over a glass of good local wine. Or take a drink (and Bute the golden lab) to the top of the farm at sunset for the view.

Rooms: 6: 3 doubles, 1 twin, 2 cottages with double beds. All en-suite.
Price: R525 - R775 pp for the Studio and main rooms. R1,250 - R1,750 for Vine Cottage. Singles on request.
Meals: Full breakfast included. Can organise gourmet picnics.
Directions: From Cape Town Airport N2 towards Somerset West, then R300 & N1. Take exit 47 and turn R under freeway. Straight on at 4-way stop, over bridge & turn L signed Franschhoek. At T-jct turn R & straight on (20km) into Franschhoek. At Huguenot Memorial turn R & 1st left into Middagkrans Rd – gravel – Chanteclair is 1 km on L.

Le Domaine Charmant

Bernie and Beth Cox

No. 1 Verdun Road, Franschhoek
Tel: 021-671-6800 Fax: 021-671-6808
Email: info@ledomainecharmant.co.za Web: www.ledomainecharmant.co.za
Cell: 082-492-9940

Le Domaine Charmant means 'the charming estate', yet this seems a modest understatement when faced with the reality. As I drove past the rose hedges, over which peek the peaks of the Hottentots-Holland Mountains, I had already begun to look forward to telling others about this place. The house, partly obscured by a drooping weeping willow, sits on the side of a small lake that forms the centrepiece of the property. With such alluring beauty outside it could be difficult to remain indoors, but no… whether reading in front of the large fire in the sitting room, or having a bath in the decadently large bathroom of the main bedroom, ultimate smugness is guaranteed. The rooms all have double beds and two have a view onto the lake – where the real joy is found. Having put in some extreme hammock time (I'll give you lessons one day), I heroically set forth in the pedalo. Enchanted by the blues and purples of the bougainvilleas and lavender lining the water's edge, I became acquainted with the three swans – two white, one black - and the young family of ducks. On a cooler day I could have fished for trout, which occasionally leapt out of the water in celebration of their brief reprieve. Back on terra firma I wandered round the orchards eating freshly-picked peaches from the trees growing at the feet of the mountains. To crown a stay where I ate and played like a king, I drank my second cup of morning coffee on the tiny beach as the sun drenched me in light. I could have stayed forever.

Rooms: 1 villa with 3 rooms: all with double beds; 2 en-suite bath and shower and 1 separate with bath and shower.
Price: R4,300 - R8,500 per night for whole villa.
Meals: 3-course welcome dinner included. Private chef available according to your requirements. You will be billed for groceries.
Directions: Just outside Franschhoek, 5 mins from Huguenot Memorial. Detailed directions on website.

The Map Room

Jo Sinfield

Cabrière Street, Franschhoek
Tel: 021-876-4356
Email: bandoola@mweb.co.za Web: www.explorersclub.co.za
Cell: 072-464-1240

A treasure hunt for the key led me past stands of aloe vera and a trophy mountain sheep that had wandered down from the green slopes of the Franschhoek valley. Normally Jo will meet you in person to introduce you to his very modern and uplifting self-catering cottage, on the last remaining dirt road in Franschhoek, that brings a little New York cool (even though he's English) to the pretty heart of the winelands. Left of the entrance a spiral staircase ascends through the ceiling, with the bedrooms spreading over the ground floor. The master suite with its huge bed, inventive use of milk pails, faded safari chairs, open bath of sultan-pleasing proportions and en-suite wet room. But upstairs is where it all happens as you emerge through the floor into a wonderfully sociable living and kitchen area. This is blessed by an endless dining table, backed on one side by a curving wall seat and on the other by wicker chairs. Here you can put yourself to work cooking on a smart hob, all the while bemoaning your idle companions who will be lounging about on sofas in front of the flat-screen TV or pouring over the eponymous maps or library of classic movies whilst waiting for their dinner to arrive. Better, let someone else do the cooking, fold open the glass-panelled doors, park yourself on the terrace with a glass of chardonnay and gaze out over the vineyard whence it came and the rugged mountain views. Outstanding walks include Rochelle's Peak for a dramatic picnic and some of South Africa's most renowned chefs ply their trade not five minutes away. *Book well in advance. Jo also owns the Explorers Club, to the rear of the Map Room.*

Rooms: 1 self-catering cottage with 1 king with full en-suite. (Two rooms on request.)
Price: R750 per person per night (for 2); R600 per person per night (for more than 2). Minimum R1,500.
Meals: Self-catering. Excellent restaurants.
Directions: Drive into Franschhoek on the R45, turning right at Reservoir St. and then at T-Junction at the end of the road, turn right onto Cabrière St, a dirt road. The Map Room is the house on the right corner at the end of the road.

The Explorers Club

Jo Sinfield

18 Wilhelmina Street, Franschhoek
Tel: 021-876-4356
Email: bandoola@mweb.co.za Web: www.explorersclub.co.za
Cell: 072-464-1240

As I parked in the shade of the ancient oak outside The Explorers Club, I initially thought, well this is perfect…. Set one street back from Franschhoek's main road you can walk into town in two minutes, yet you are secluded enough to enjoy the tranquil setting. But once Jo showed me through to the open-plan main living space, my thoughts quickly changed to: "In fact I'm not sure I am going to be moving too far from here actually!" Jo is an avid map collector and throughout the house tales of exploration, ancient and modern, are illustrated both by Jo's collection and also in expressive African scenes captured by celebrated photographer Horst Klemm. The bedrooms all have their own individual feel, some with skylights, all adorned with colourful artefacts and prints. For travelling families there is a room with two double bunks where teenagers can natter away into the early hours. The hub of the house is the open-plan lounge-dining-kitchen area, which leads out to a sun-drenched (when it's sunny, of course) wooden pool deck, lap pool and your own private vineyard. I don't know if there is such a thing as contemporary-rustic, but that's what springs to mind! So simple, so very, very comfortable, yet with a state-of-the-art kitchen, aircon, DVD library and plasma screen et al. I imagine cosy evenings around the original wagon-wheel-framed dining table, the fire crackling away in the hearth, as would-be explorers put together plans for future expeditions. *No children under 12. Jo also owns the Map Room, 2 mins' walk from the Explorers Club.*

Rooms: 4: 1 king with en-suite bath and shower, 1 queen with en-suite shower, 1 twin/king with bath, 1 with 2 double bunk beds with bath.
Price: R700 per adult per night, 1/2 price for children. Minimum R2,850 per night.
Meals: Self-catering.
Directions: From Cape Town side take Franschhoek Main Road, after Pick 'n' Pay take 1st right into Reservoir Road, then 1st right into Wilhelmina Road, dark brown house on left side.

The Beautiful South Guest House

Katarina and Peter Stigsson

4 Hospital St, Stellenbosch
Tel: 021-883-8171
Email: enjoy@thebeautifulsouth.de Web: www.thebeautifulsouth.de

Katarina and Peter Stigsson never do anything in half, or even three-quarter, measure. Just hearing them chat about their hobbies was enough to make me want to lie down for a rest… or maybe it was the sight of the sun-beds by the pool. Since taking over the reins at The Beautiful South in 2007 they have poured endless energy and enthusiasm into making it the bright, modern, luxurious guesthouse that it is today. On the outside, the house is quaintly thatched and whitewashed, with Cape-Dutch-style gables and wooden windows and the surrounding garden with its mature trees and large pool is directly accessible from each of the bedrooms. On the inside, however, it's very far from traditional. Katarina's inventive ideas in the bedrooms work a treat, such as the smooth pebbles in the bathroom and the old window-frame reborn as a table. The colours in the 'Austin Powers' room, with its framed retro shirt and gigantic green leaf over the bed, hit you like a sensory bomb; 'Desert Rose' is full of romance, with a deep egg bath in the room; and it's all about the terrace in 'Sunrise' with its views of the Stellenbosch mountains. They are also committed philanthropists involved in local community projects, most notably the creation of a township crèche, which guests are welcome to visit. Breakfast is a special meal at The Beautiful South, with a promise of something different every morning, always home-baked bread, muffins, scones, tomato-mozzarella toast and such specials as 'Catch of the Day' and 'Fruity Djibuti' from the buffet bar. Hosting comes only too naturally to Katarina and Peter.

Rooms: 9: 7 doubles, 6 with en-suite bath or shower, 1 with private shower room opposite; 2 family suites with en-suite bath or shower.
Price: R280 - R590 pp sharing.
Meals: Breakfast included with new 'special' every morning.
Directions: From N1 or N2 take turn-off marked to Stellenbosch. On entering Stellenbosch turn into Merriman Street. After white pedestrian bridge turn 2nd left into Bosman. Take 1st right into Soete Weide. Next left into Hospital Street.

Malans Guest House

Laetitia Malan

4 Keerom St, Stellenbosch
Tel: 021-887-8859
Fax: 086-528-2249
Email: malansgh@gmail.com
Web: www.malansgh.de
Cell: 083-664-1517

Laetitia has uniquely and beautifully decorated each of her guest rooms with antique furniture, kilims on beds, fresh flowers and even proper home-found shower caps in the bathrooms! (Ladies with long hair will know what I'm taking about.) She also collects Voortrekker wedding dresses that date back to the 1860s, while her other lace collections are displayed under glass-covered breakfast tables. And what a breakfast room: antique Chinese vases and vessels, exotic orchids, furniture inlaid with mother-of-pearl, 'grandparent' clocks, newly-painted frescoes and a flower-imprinted Chinese screen. Laetitia admitted that she may have lived in China in a previous life. She also collects porridges (!) after a fashion: try maltabela porridge (a traditional black-corn variety), maize or oatmeal at breakfast. And if you're not a porridge fan (no reason why you should be), there are plenty of mueslis, fresh fruits, bacon, eggs and all. Laetitia and her daughter treated me to their home-made chocolate cake and my first-ever rooibos tea, and sitting on the verandah in the sunshine I felt serene. A rare quote from one of our other hosts in this book: "I have stayed there myself and I often send guests on to her. Incredible value for money and an experience in its own right. A very interesting owner, with staff who know the art of hospitality and the most beautiful antiques." This all turns out to be pretty exact. *Nearby: cycling, horse-riding, golfing, fly-fishing and wine-tasting.*

Rooms: 5: 1 queen and 1 double with en-suite showers; 3 twins with en/s bath and shower.
Price: R290 - R390 pp sharing. Singles R390 - R490.
Meals: Full breakfast included. Restaurants aplenty nearby.
Directions: From Cape Town take N2, then R310 to Stellenbosch. Drive into town, at railway turn right into Dorp St. After right-hand bend turn left up The Avenue, first left to Neethling St and first left again into Keerom St.

Glenconner

Emma Finnemore
Jonkershoek Valley, Stellenbosch
Tel: 021-886-5120 Fax: 021-886-5120
Email: glenconner@icon.co.za Web: www.glenconner.co.za
Cell: 082-354-3510

Looking up at the imposing mountains, which rise on both sides of the property, and surrounded by lush vegetation - including all that wild strelitzia and agapanthus - it's almost impossible to believe that you're just six kilometres from Stellenbosch. Such a spectacular location. Sit with a glass of wine on whichever stoep belongs to you for the night and watch the lowering sun paint the mountains a deep pink. You don't need to do any more than this to lift the spirits by many notches. There are three simple, country-furnished sleeping locations to choose from: the homestead with its four-poster bed, Victorian bath and English country feel; Oak Cottage, with its cosy fireplace, pale blue beams and terracotta tiles, and a patio enclave that crouches beneath a looming mountain and gazes upon Emma's indigenous garden; and lastly the Studio, also a separate cottage with an open-plan bedroom, quaint stripey sitting areas, small kitchenette and second bedroom (with the best in-bed view of the lot). A round, spring-water-fed swimming pool sits directly in front of the homestead and a tan-coloured river is a little further away for paddling, picnics and otter-sighting. And horses graze peacefully on the luminous green grass in the paddocks. If all this is not enough for you, the staggering Jonkershoek Nature Reserve is just down the road with some of the best hiking in SA, from 2-hour to 2-day walks. *Trout-fishing, horse-riding and mountain-biking all available nearby.*

Rooms: 3: 2 self-catering cottages: the Studio has double, twin & bathroom; Oak Cottage has double, twin & single room with one bathroom & a shower room in outside unit; 1 double room in the homestead.
Price: The homestead B&B R420 pp sharing. Self-catering cottages are from R345 pp. Children 2-12 years half rate; 2 and under free. Discounts for stays of 5 nights or longer.
Meals: Continental breakfasts included in B&B or R50 for self-caterers. 5 minutes' drive into Stellenbosch for restaurants aplenty.
Directions: From CT, N2 to Stellenbosch, follow signs to Jonkershoek Nature Reserve. 6km from Stellenbosch turn right and cross bridge on R just after entrance to Neil Ellis vineyard.

Allegria Guesthouse

Annemarie Marti and Jan Zevenbergen

Cairngorm Road, Stellenbosch
Tel: 021-881-3389 Fax: 021-881-3210
Email: info@allegria.co.za Web: www.allegria.co.za
Cell: 076-560-0356

Two things I noticed as I stepped into Jan and Annemarie's impressive garden: the first was an immense 20-metre pool where I pictured myself floating about looking up at a halo of mountains and vineyards; the second was a rather large statue of a cow, an old buddy from Jan's advertising days. It isn't surprising that they called this place Allegria (meaning joy); it's pretty hard to wear a frown when you wake up to that view... and everyone does. Each room has a door onto the back garden, with private patios and windows onto the Simonsberg and Helderberg mountains. Each bedroom is named after an animal and has a corresponding wall-hanging. My favourite was the Elephant Room, with a red elephant lumbering above the bed, a beautiful free-standing bath and the biggest double shower I have ever seen. The main dining and living area is a mix of grand, modern and traditional African design, with high ceilings, a friendly-looking metal rhino and earthy colour schemes. These two take hosting seriously. Jan is so dedicated to good wine that he visits all the local estates himself to double-check that he is only serving the best to guests; while Annemarie will happily give lifts into town for those who don't fancy the wobbly drive home. Breakfast is a sumptuous, healthy feast, with fresh rolls, croissants, muffins and health bread, fruit juices, cereals, muesli, fresh fruit, cheeses, meats, yoghurts, jams as well as eggs and bacon. Their motto is that everything is possible, and they really mean it.

Rooms: 6: 2 'superior' rooms with XL queen beds, en-suite bath & twin shower; 2 'deluxe' rooms with queen or twin beds, en-s bath & shower; 2 'comfort' rooms with queen or twin beds and en-s shower.
Price: R345 - R595 pp sharing. Singles on request.
Meals: Big healthy breakfast included. Light evening meals available: cheese platter and salads (order before 4pm).
Directions: From Cape Town follow N2 until R300 at Exit 22a. After 5km on R300 turn-off at Exit 21 (direction M12 - Stellenbosch Arterial). At lights turn R (direction M12 - Stellenbosch). After 10km on M12, turn L into Cairngorm Rd, driveway to Allegria.

Auberge Rozendal

Joerg Streibing and Karin Howard
Omega Street, Jonkershoek Valley, Stellenbosch
Tel: 021-809-2600 Fax: 021-809-2640
Email: rozendalres@mweb.co.za Web: www.rozendal.co.za
Cell: 071-130-1456

On arrival at Rozendal you might think for a fleeting moment that you had stumbled onto a Walt Disney film set: there are long-lashed milking cows in the paddock, wild flowers everywhere… and then there's 'Truffles' the farm pig who happily grunts a welcome to guests. Here on the organic bio-dynamic wine farm, new owners Karin and Joerg have happily continued Rozendal's tradition of promoting health and well-being. The organic vinegar produced here will give your digestive system a yoga lesson – I'd recommend a swill of the lavender, but you'll have to make your own judgements about the kelp…. It's all about fresh, high-quality produce and the proof really is, as I discovered, in the eating. Meals are served under the vines on the verandah or in the dining room with its gallery of canvases by local artists such as Paul Emsley (a Tate exhibitor) and Larry Scully. The purpose-built rooms are separated from the main house by a short path, which leads past the herb and veg gardens. Each is blessed with magnificent views from private terraces that stretch over vineyards to either Table Mountain or the Botmaskop range. After a wonderful meal, and a chat with Joseph, I retired to my room. Joseph, by the way, has worked here for almost 30 years, is a very quick and easy smiler... and his catch-phrase is definitely 'super duper'. On my way I lost a staring contest with a cape owl, who had perched on a tree just four feet away, and I finally fell asleep to a lullaby of frogs flirting in the rose bushes. My stay at Rozendal was... well, super duper. *Rozendal has been accredited by Fair Trade for its organic produce.*

Rooms: 18: 7 queens, 9 twins, 2 family rooms: 1 queen with 1 single and 1 with 1 queen and 2 singles. All en-suite with shower in bath.
Price: R495 - R695 pp sharing. Singles R695-R895.
Meals: All meals by prior arrangement.
Directions: From CT airport, take N2 for Somerset-West. Exit 33 to Stellenbosch.At the junction turn R. After train station L slide into Adam Tas Road, then 2nd traffic lights turn R into Merriman Avenue. Through 3 sets of lights and over roundabout, 2km turn left into Omega Street, Rozendal is at the end.

Mitre's Edge

Bernard and Lola Nicholls

R44 between Stellenbosch and Paarl, Klapmuts, Stellenbosch
Tel: 021-875-5960 Fax: 021-875-5965
Email: info@mitres-edge.co.za Web: www.mitres-edge.co.za
Cell: 082-400-1092

The sea of welcoming dogs that flowed around my feet as I got out of the car made progress slow, but I managed to wade to the fine front door of Mitre's Edge, HQ for a small but busy vineyard. Bernard and Lola were in the middle of organising the shipment of some of their delicious rosé to some thirsty recipient in Europe. "We're a hands-on and hand-crafted set-up here," Bernard reassured me, "Not some characterless production line." Well, the same can be said for the small self-catering cottage (with breakfast included) found at the top of the garden. The sunshine followed us in through the generous windows and glass door, lighting up an open-plan kitchen and living room, which bristles with restorative activities. The main feature, a dark, wooden dining room table, also doubles as a pool table. Arched bookshelves sagging with books, art and board games cover the walls and a flash of tropical colour emanates from the fish tank. The bedroom (beyond the sauna, obviously) is unfussy and comfortable. Proud mahogany furniture matches the straw matting-covered floorboards. Outside, the stoep (with a pizza oven the size of Naples, an outdoor braai and Jacuzzi) leads on to the swimming pool, which in turn leads on to the mountains, with resilient snow glinting on their summits. I can see why Angela the Vietnamese pot-bellied pig seems so content to call this place her home – I only wish I could. *Wine tours and tasting are available.*

Rooms: 1 self-catering cottage with one bedroom. 1 queen-size bed and separate bathroom.
Price: R900 - R1,100 for the whole unit. R150 for the sleeper-couch.
Meals: Full breakfast included.
Directions: From Stellenbosch take the R44 towards Paarl for 13km. Mitre's Edge is on the left. From N1 take exit 47. Mitre's Edge is on R44 towards Stellenbosch.

Hawksmoor House

Maike Harms (Manager)

Klipheuwel Road/R304
Stellenbosch
Tel: 021-884-4815
Fax: 021-884-4816
Email: reservations@
hawksmoor.co.za
Web:
www.hawksmoor.co.za
Cell: 072-367-4788

Table Mountain shimmered in the distance, my rosé twinkled in the sun and I glowed with contentment as I allowed the charms of Hawksmoor House to wash over me. "The Victoria and Alfred Waterfront is just twenty-five minutes away," Maike told me, something I found hard to believe sitting out here like a Rothschild, gazing across vineyards, cradling my glass of wine, with three charming German pointers at my feet. And yet this fact is wholly appropriate for Hawksmoor, a Cape Dutch homestead built in 1700, where the traditional and rural rub shoulders with the modern and urban to such stunning effect: Georgian and Victorian furniture and old portraits in my left corner; bold turquoises, vibrant oranges and pieces of modern art in my right! Each room has its own identity, whether it be the hard-hitting grey of one of the most recent additions, or the intriguing little curved passageway leading to the shower in another. As for me, I stayed in one of the oldest rooms in the house, with a wonderful four-poster bed and an oval bath. In case you were worried. The dining room, with its opulent table and huge rocking chairs, is a lesson in Victorian splendour, and in the sitting room one can see the signatures of old residents scratched into the glass of the windows. Guests can spend their days by the pool or there are walks through the vines on the 220-hectare farm. Dinner (and what a dinner!) is cooked on the Aga while you watch the pelicans fly over the house at sunset. The Hawksmoor experience is very special indeed. *Wine tasting available on request.*

Rooms: 8: 3 Garden Suites, 5 Manor House rooms: 1 twin, 7 queens; all with en-suite bathrooms, 6 with bath and shower, 2 with shower only.
Price: High season: R1,650 - R825 pp sharing. Singles R1,000 per night. Low season: R1,000 - R500 pp sharing Singles R750 per night.
Meals: Full breakfast and afternoon tea included. 3-course Sunday Cape Malay dinners R250 inc. wine and bubbly. All other nights cheese platters only R150 pp.
Directions: On N1 exit 39 onto R304 direction Klipheuwel. After 1km turn left onto gravel road at Hawksmoor House sign. Drive for 1.5km to gate.

Map Number: 4

5 Seasons Guesthouse

Ralf and Simone Rumpf

60 Van Der Stel Street, Stellenbosch
Tel: 021-886-6159 Fax: 021-886-6159
Email: info@5-seasons.de Web: www.5-seasons.co.za
Cell: 076-410-1903

Simone and Ralf are relaxed, calm, easy-going people. They just are. And you will catch a bit of it yourself as soon as you drive through the Five Seasons gates; in fact the entire jacaranda-lined street seems to be in go-slow mode… no traffic, no noise and all just a five-minute stroll from the centre of Stellenbosch. Initially it took a little while for Simone to prize me away from admiring their exquisite collection of wines and whiskeys, before finally leading me outside (away from the booze) to the herb garden where full Continental breakfast feasts are taken among creeping table grapevines, wild jasmine, mint and rosemary. All bedrooms have their own personality. No cheesy themes, but rather tasteful hints of Africa through a well-placed nguni hide here, or a porcupine-quill lampshade there; and of Europe through a French bath tube, enormous showers and a four-poster bed. Each room has its own completely private deck or terrace, from which vantage you can drink in the view over a silhouetted Helderberg mountain… and of course the odd exquisite wine or whiskey while you're about it. A blooming oasis of gardens surround the heated salt-water pool and communal deck, which allows upstairs guests access via outdoor wooden staircases (pick yourself a fresh fig on the way down). I have a feeling guests don't ask for much here, as every wish is fulfilled before you can express it. I'm coming back in winter for their fondue and red wine evenings in front of the fire.

Rooms: 10: 2 king with en-suite bath/shower, 2 twin one with en-suite shower and one with bath, 4 queen with en-suite shower, 2 family cottages each with king and 2 singles and en-suite bath/shower.
Price: R425 - R650 pp sharing. Cottages: R1,300 - R1,700. Singles R625 - R850.
Meals: Breakfast included, snacks, lunch and dinners on request. Self-catering option available for cottages.
Directions: From N2 take R310 to Stellenbosch. In Stellenbosch turn R at 1st light into Dorp St. At end of Dorp St turn L into Drosty St. At end of Drosty turn R into Van Riebeeck St and continue to circle. In the circle/roundabout turn right into Van der Stel St.

Longfield

Pieter and Nini Bairnsfather Cloete

Fikendal Rd, off R44, Somerset West/Stellenbosch
Tel: 021-855-4224
Email: ninicloete@iafrica.com Web: www.longfield.co.za

Perched on the foothills of the dramatic Helderberg mountains, Longfield occupies a truly sensational vantage that drifts across the Winelands and over to the very tip of False Bay at Cape Point. Dreamy by day and by night (when Cape Town's lights put on their glitzy show), there are three cottages from which to enjoy the view. All are fresh, breezy and decorated in a relaxed country-house style and many of the furnishings are rare, early-Cape family heirlooms. This is luxury self-catering. Comfy beds are made up with the highest-quality, hand-embroidered linen and there are spoiling lotions in the pretty bathrooms and coffee-table books on SA wine, flora and fauna etc, and African *objets d'art* in the cosy living areas with a wood-burner for good measure. Each has its private patio or lawn, and fridges and cupboards are re-stocked each day with breakfast materials for you to help yourself to. You'll probably want to disappear into your own world here, but Nini and Pieter, who live on the mountain with you, are the nicest people you could wish to meet. Formerly wine-farmers themselves, they can arrange exclusive garden and wine tours and will happily point you in the right direction for good restaurants and golf courses, all invariably within easy striking distance. But it's quite possible you won't want to go anywhere, what with the almond trees and olive trees and the immense pool in the rolling hills of their garden. This is a wonderfully secluded spot, serene and calm and ideally placed for many of the Cape's attractions.

Rooms: 3 cottages: 2 with twin beds, 1 with king-size bed, all with bath and separate shower.
Price: R350 - R700 pp sharing. Single supplement by arrangement.
Meals: Continental breakfast on request.
Directions: From CT take N2 past the airport, take exit 43 Broadway Bvd. Left at lights. From the next lights 6.3km exactly, then right into Eikendal Rd. Follow up gravel road, jink left onto tarmac and follow to top and Longfield House.

Map Number: 4

Acara

Fiona and Dave Stafford

Winery Road, Somerset West/Stellenbosch
Tel: 021-842-3161 Fax: 021-842-3159
Email: info@acara.co.za Web: www.acara.co.za
Cell: 084-958-5074

It tells you something about the view here that it only took five minutes of standing on the stoep for Fiona and Dave to decide to move in. Nestled in the valley known as 'Happy Vale', this is a truly tranquil and beautiful spot and, as I wandered through Fiona's garden, it was easy to see why she is the chairperson of the Stellenbosch Horticultural Society. It has a huge variety of plants, from indigenous to the exotic: blossoming almond trees, fig and pepper trees and a pristine vegetable patch (help yourself to the herbs and veggies) and mounds of lavender. But the pièce de résistance is a wrought-iron pergola in a cloud of roses where people can sit and admire her handiwork. The stream that runs by it is also home to a mongoose and a couple of otters, much to the excitement of their ridgeback Bikkie. The Jacaranda Suite underneath their home has its own door out onto the garden, while two thatched cottages offer a cool retreat with their own decks and gardens. All rooms have crisp white walls, wooden beams and modern finishings, not to mention great mountain views. An excellent place for those who want to do everything: right in the mountains, near the beach and on the doorstep of several vineyards. But for lazier days, the hammock in the willow tree is perfect for digesting all that fine food and wine. David and Fiona are so friendly that one meeting wasn't enough. A week on, I caught up with them on a weekend break in Tulbagh and we shared another excellent evening of conversation... and more than one bottle of wine, if you must know!

Rooms: 3: 1 suite & 2 cottages, all with fully-equipped kitchen: Jacaranda Suite: 1 king with en-s shower; Lavender Cottage: 1 queen & 1 twin; Willow Tree Cottage: 1 king & 1 twin, both en-s bathrooms.
Price: Jacaranda suite R720, Lavender Cottage R1,200 and Willow Tree R1,600. All prices per cottage per night.
Meals: Continental breakfast hamper arranged on request.
Directions: Take Firgrove Winery Road off R44 betw' Somerset West and Stellenbosch (exit 43 on N2). Acara on LH side, 1.2 km down Winery Road, just before Stellenbosch Vineyards.

Li Belle Guesthouse

Pieter and Alma Du Preez

4 Begonia Street, Heldervue, Somerset West
Tel: 021-855-1672 Fax: 0866-727-660
Email: libelle@iafrica.com Web: www.libelleguesthouse.co.za
Cell: 082-466-0102

After two years of planning, renovating, sourcing and planting, Li Belle Guesthouse opened its doors six months ago at the time of writing. When Pieter and Alma opened the door for me, the smiles and sparkle in their eyes told me just how proud and excited they are about their completed masterpiece. And who wouldn't be! Alma is fanatical about personal touches and told me, "we didn't want more than four rooms in case any of our guests felt crowded or neglected". The rooms have a French feel with uncluttered straight lines, refurbished antiques, white linen and clever little modifications such as mirrors which slide apart to reveal your flat screen TV. The upstairs suite has a private balcony, which looks out over the entirety of False Bay and the Helderberg mountains. Your en-suite bathroom also boasts a hot-jet tub to bubble away at the day's sunburn… a good place to go into a trance and reflect on the day's events. The guest lounge and breakfast room are separated by a marble vent-free fireplace and lead you through French doors onto the sundowner deck and outside stairs to the pool courtyard. Alma is also a specialist bridal make-up artist, so if a Cape wedding is on the cards booking into Li Belle could kill a flock of birds with one stone. Bride's make-up… tick, romantic honeymoon suite… tick, rose garden photos… tick, relaxed South African hospitality... Tick, tick, tick! *No children under 12.*

Rooms: 4: 1 suite with en-suite bath and shower, 1 double with en-suite shower, 2 twin/kings with en-suite shower.
Price: Prices are per room per night. Suite R1,900 - R2,300, Deluxe R1,100 - R1,350, Standard R950 - R1,250.
Meals: Full breakfast included.
Directions: See website for detailed directions.

Manor on the Bay

Hanél and Schalk van Reenen

117 Beach Rd, Gordon's Bay
Tel: 021-856-3260
Fax: 021-856-3261
Email:
manorotb@mweb.co.za
Web:
www.manoronthebay.co.za
Cell: 082-896-5790

Hanél and Schalk van Reenen are a young couple and their enthusiasm for the job is palpable. In 2000 they poured great vats of time and energy into restoring their property. The results are seriously impressive with Hanél's self-confessed perfectionism apparent throughout the six new rooms and luxurious beauty salon. This is a great place to watch sunsets over False Bay or even whales in spring, and the view is conveniently framed by two large palms. Beach Road, you won't need telling, is just next to the sea, and a hop, skip and a dive takes you across the road and into the water. If you don't fancy the walk, however, there's also a pool out the back. Of the twelve rooms, four of the new units have self-catering facilities. But if you are feeling like being spoilt, then you can still opt for the breakfast, which is either healthy (in Hanél's case eaten after an early run on the beach - you don't have to join her, but you can) or hearty, and is served in the bright dining room or on the terrace outside.

Rooms: 12: 11 doubles and 1 family room with 2 queens. All with en-suite shower and/or bath.
Price: R400 - R620 pp sharing. Singles R550 - R800.
Meals: Full breakfast included. Dinner on request.
Directions: From Strand on the R44, take Beach Rd turning just before BP garage. From N2 take Sir Lowry's Pass to Gordon's Bay and cross over on to van der Bijl St, down to Beach Rd and L.

Overberg Side Dishes

A handful of highly-recommended things to do and places to eat in the Overberg area...

Old Gaol Coffee Shop & Restaurant
My mum loved this place. Set in the grounds of the Drostdy Museum this fantastic coffee shop and empowerment project is run by local Xhosa ladies who produce the most fantastic breads and milk tarts cooked over coals in the tradesmen's yard of the museum. Home-made lemonade, roast vegetables, smoked springbok carpaccio, local cheeses, cajun chicken.... The Old Gaol is also running a more sophisticated restaurant in the evening from Oct - April (open Tuesday to Saturday evenings). The price per main course is between R65 - R105.
Contact: *Judi Rebstein, 8a Voortrek Street, Church Square, Swellendam;*
Prices: *Special of the day R49 - R89;* **Tel:** *028-514-3847; 028-514-3847;*
Email: *info@oldgaolrestaurant.co.za;* **Web:** *www.oldgaolrestaurant.co.za*

Klein River Cheese
Enjoy a delicious picnic lunch on the banks of the Klein River. Baskets are filled with their own award-winning cheeses, home-made breads, crackers, pâtés, pickles, cold meats and salads. Shelley and Riaan are cheese-makers and you're welcome to come and taste their produce and watch it being made at the same time. Don't miss the 10-month matured South African gruyere. There's also a playground and plenty of farm animals to keep the kids entertained.
Contact: *R326 Stanford;* **Prices:** *Picnic basket for two: R190;*
Tel: *028-341-0693; 028-341-0844;* **Email:** *kleinriver@telkomsa.net;*
Web: *www.kleinrivercheese.co.za*

Heaven
I suppose Heaven is a meet and right way to describe the view from the restaurant deck, straight down the Hemel-en-Aarde wine valley all the way to the ocean. Bruce Henderson, a Hermanus culinary institution in himself, and Yolande Steenkamp prepare delicious fresh brunch, lunch and high tea in an intimate atmosphere. Chicken breasts stuffed with mature Dutch cheese and black cherries was my choice... heavenly of course.
Contact: *Bruce Henderson, Newton Johnson Wine Estate, Hemel-en-Aarde Valley;*
Email: *heaven@overberg.org.za;* **Web:** *www.newtonjohnson.com*

Mogg's Country Cookhouse
Just when you think you're lost, a trail of knives and forks appears, painted on trees, leading you safely to Mogg's, a beautiful eatery based on a family farm overlooking the whole valley. The hallway is festooned with fairy-lights and fir cones and Jenny serves up fresh, seasonal food. Everything is home-made, including the bread and ice-cream. By appointment only. Closed Mondays and Tuesdays (except Christmas and New Year).
Contact: *Jenny and Julia Mogg, Nuwe Pos farm, Hemel-en-Aarde Valley, Hermanus;* **Prices:** *R80 - R100;* **Tel:** *028-312-4321;*
Email: *JennyMogg@gmail.com;* **Web:** *www.moggscookhouse.com*

White Shark Diving Co.

The shark makes a swift, surprise pass from below and behind, leaping out of the water making a fascinating appearance from nowhere... and you're in the water!... fortunately watching from the safety of the submerged cage. Shark cage-diving is the fastest-growing adventure activity around and booking with White Shark Diving Co. guarantees you unlimited cage time. For those who prefer to stay dry, they have an upper deck which allows excellent shark viewing.

Contact: Nik Walsh, Kleinbaai; Prices: R1,200 for boat trip, dive, meals and videographer included; Tel: 021-671-4777; Email: www.sharkcagediving.co.za; Web: info@sharkcagediving.co.za

Paul Cluver Wines and Forest Amphitheatre

The guys at Paul Cluver are leading the way in preserving the rich biodiversity of the area. Join them on a rejuvenating hike through bird-rich landscapes, observing endemic plant species and enjoying delicious snacks and wines at the same time. In the evening musical and theatrical performances take place in a natural forest amphitheatre, the most intimate venue imaginable. Stars on show, above and below.... Hikes are normally in spring while amphitheatre shows are in summer.

Contact: Paul Cluver Wines, De Rust Estate; Prices: Guided morning walk, including tea and coffee, snacks, light lunch and great wines R220 per person; Tel: 021-844-0605; 021-844-0150; Email: tourism@cluver.com; Web:www.cluver.com

Ivanhoe Sea Safaris

Jason and Michelle run boat-based whale-watching in Walker Bay, Hermanus, which in the season (June - Dec) heaves with southern right whales that come here every year to mate and raise their calves. They guarantee close-up sightings on every trip and you may also see humpback and Bryde whales, Cape fur seals and penguins too. Trips take two hours, with 40 - 70 minutes with the whales.

Contact: Jason and Michelle Stafford, Gansbaai Harbour; Prices: Adults: R750. Kids 6-12yr: R375. Kids 5 and under: free. Tel: 028-384-0556; 028-384-0556; Email: info@whalewatchingsa.co.za; Web: www.whaleviewing.co.za

Raka

I became a fan of Raka wines long before I made it to the winery. In restaurants, bars and friends' houses, I challenge anyone to find a better shiraz than Raka's Biography. The small, personal, family-run estate is named after Piet's beloved fishing boat. Piet and Elna Dreyer's genius is complimented by a slightly madhatter approach to life. Wonderful people making wonderful wine!

Contact: Piet Dreyer, PO Box 124, Caledon; Prices: R23 for a Rosé to R90 for award-winning shiraz; Tel: 028-341-0676; 086-606-5462; Email: piet@rakawine.co.za; Web: www.rakawine.co.za

Wildekrans Country House

Alison Green and Barry Gould
Houw Hoek Valley, Elgin
Tel: 028-284-9827 Fax: 028-284-9624
Email: info@wildekrans.co.za Web: www.wildekrans.co.za

From the tufts of moss poking out between the old flagstones of the front path I knew that this was my sort of place. The 1811 homestead is raised above its garden and looks down on lawns, abundant roses, pear orchards, the large swimming pool and old oak trees. The scene is magnificent with the 'wild cliffs' ('wildekrans') setting the property's limits, rising from a meadow at the back of the garden. Take a stroll beside landscaped water-courses and lily ponds that neighbour the orchards, and you will encounter wonderful, some might think surreal, sculptures that have been positioned with much thought, and I think argument, where they now stand. They add a touch of the unexpected to this magical garden. Finally a rickety bridge - where one almost expects to pay a troll a toll - crosses a stream. Home-made "Follow your Heart" sculptures (giant metal hearts on poles driven into ground) will romance you to the edge of a mystical wood, where you'll find yourself at the foot of the Groenlandberg mountain. Take a healthy hike up and the Kogelberg Biosphere Reserve will be there for you to explore. And with over 1600 species of plant life, it is no wonder they call it the 'heart of the fynbos'. The authentic homestead bedrooms, each with a four-poster bed, are originally parental gifts to Alison and her many sisters, and offer views out to the garden and beyond. And if the mountains get the better of you, Wildekrans boasts an excellent contemporary art collection and Barry's delicious wine and olive oil is available for tasting in the barn. *Wildekrans is a member of the Green Mountain Eco Route.*

Rooms: 4: 3 four-poster doubles in the homestead all with en-s bath, 1 with separate shower and 2 with shower above (1 has private study); & 1 self-catering cottage.
Price: B&B: R440 - R540 pp sharing. Singles R560. Self-catering: R300 - R465 pp sharing.
Meals: Full breakfast incl'. Dinner from 1-course simple supper R120 to 3 courses R160. Or barbecue at R70. All meals self-served.
Directions: On N2 from Cape Town 1 hour approx, past Grabouw & 12km further turn L signed Houw Hoek Inn. Or 30 mins from Caledon on N2, at top of Houw Hoek Pass, turn R signed Houw Hoek Inn. Thro' HH gate posts, follow road round to L. Farm on R.

Acorns on Oak

Mieke Schuchard and Cecil Barrow
2 Oak Street, Greyton
Tel: 028-254-9567 Fax: 028-254-9569
Email: acornsonoak@telkomsa.net Web: www.acorns-on-oak.co.za
Cell: 082-367-2614

I was only meant to be dropping in on Mieke and Cecil but accidentally whiled away an entire afternoon with them. Drinking fresh coffee out of Wedgwood mugs we sat among a network of lily ponds which extend through their immaculate garden. The garden is a particularly peaceful place, draped in mountain scenery, scattered with oak trees and awash with white roses. I lamented the fact that I wasn't staying the night… this time! The cottages bordering the garden are thatched and beautifully done out in different themes: Tuscany, Provence, Exmoor and now Bergsig ('Mountain View') Cottage, their most recent addition. With slick bathrooms, outdoor showers and private sitting rooms they've created a unique brand of laid-back luxury. In the main house there's a romantic room in the eaves with its own free-standing bath. Breakfasts are a favourite here cooked up by Cecil, who together with Mieke, used to run an award-winning inn in Somerset. They moved here for some peace and quiet… and it really is quiet. For hiking they'll organise you a picnic hamper from the bistro pub at the end of the road. I expect you'll be halfway here by now, but I haven't even started on the river at the end of the garden, where an idyllic braai area has been built after a devastating flood destroyed much of the bank. The bank has been rebuilt with fantastic skill, making it the ideal spot from which to gaze up at the mountains. The view is so captivating it's easy to lose yourself and burn the sausages.

Rooms: 5: 3 kings or twins, 2 with bath and shower, 1 with shower; 1 queen with shower; 1 queen with bath and shower.
Price: R415 pp sharing. Singles plus 25% week days, 50% weekends.
Meals: Full breakfast included, packed lunches on request and braai area available.
Directions: Take the N2 from Cape Town. Turn left 1km before Caledon onto Route 406, signposted Genadendal and Greyton. In the centre of town turn right down Oak Street. Acorns on Oak is on the left at the bottom.

Plum Cottage

Pierre Marais
7 DS Botha Street, Greyton
Tel: 082-870-1988 Fax: 021-880-2820
Email: pierre@wastewater.co.za Web: www.plumcottage.co.za
Cell: 082-440-3991

To be frank, I arrived at Plum Cottage at the end of a long and very tiring day that had relentlessly chipped away at my temperament and energy. But on seeing the purple bougainvillea framing the little door to this delightful cottage I knew that they would be restored. As the warmth flowed from the busy little ceramic stove that had been lit for my arrival, I dimmed the lights, padded across to the bar, poured myself a large drink and surveyed all that was mine for the night. One of the bedrooms is painted a vivacious orange, with matching bed linen, while the other is a dapper grey (as is the rest of the cottage). Both have high white ceilings traversed by wooden beams, while the walls are decorated sparingly, giving those pictures that have made the grade extra presence. After a marathon kip and my morning bath (the water was reassuringly tea-coloured – a sign that it has come fresh from the mountains), I was sprinkled with sunshine leaking through the gaps in the bamboo roof of the kitchen. I savoured my tea on the stoep and admired the garden. I fome to a cacophony of different birdsong - Cape Robins, wagtails and sunbirds jostle for air-time and space on the bottle-brush and yellowwoods – it also brims with colour from the jasmine and abitulon. High above, the mountains faithfully protect you from the humdrum of normal life while pleading for you to pull on your boots and put your explorer's hat on. I challenge you to resist their call. *Minimum booking of two nights.*

Rooms: 1 self-catering cottage with 2 rooms: 2 kings; 1 en-suite bathroom with bath and one separate bathroom with bath.
Price: R425 pp sharing. Singles R600 per night.
Meals: Self-catering.
Directions: From Cape Town take the N2 towards Caledon. Just before Caledon, turn left into the R406. In Greyton turn right at the second stop street. Plum Cottage is at 7 DS Botha Rd.

Rouxwil Country House

Thys and O'nel Roux

Caledon
Tel: 028-215-8922 Fax: 028-215-8922
Email: rouxwil@intekom.co.za Web: www.rouxwil.co.za
Cell: 082-575-6612

Rouxwil is perfectly positioned in the middle of nowhere. I say 'perfectly' because nowhere happens to be in the middle of everywhere. You couldn't wish for a better base from which to explore the region, with Hermanus, the Winelands, Greyton and Cape Agulhas all less than an hour away. The main farmhouse is always buzzing with its traditional farm kitchen, lounge with open fireplace and outside braai area. This is where Thys holds sway, whether grilling oryx sirloins over open coals or dispensing encyclopaedic advice on the surrounding town's best-kept secrets (his is a brain worth picking). Since the closest restaurant is thirty kilometres away, it is an added blessing that food is one of O'nel's great interests and talents. She likes her guests to taste traditional recipes, but regularly throws a wild-card onto her menu... springbok shanks, for example. The rooms are certainly not what you would expect on a wheat and sheep farm. No rusted old plumbing or creaking termite-eaten floorboards here. Rather slate tiles, stainless-steel power-showers and plenty of king-size comfort. Sliding doors open onto gardens of cycads, roses and lavender, zebras, antelope and blue cranes. Come to think of it, with a pool to cool off in, a quad-bike for exploring and a river raft for sundowners, why would you want to leave Rouxwil at all? But apart from the views, food, river and wildlife, what makes this place an essential GG entry are the two charming people at the helm.

Rooms: 4: all doubles with en-suite bath and shower.
Price: R550 pp sharing.
Meals: Full breakfast included: Dinner R165.
Directions: From Cape Town take N2 pass Botrivier, carry on for 8km on N2 and take left turn on to the Villiersdorp R43. After 14km turn right off to Greyton and Helderstroom. Follow road for 1km, Rouxwil Country House signposted.

Beaumont Wine Estate

Jayne and Ariane Beaumont

Compagnes Drift Farm, Bot River
Tel: 028-284-9194 (office), 028-284-9370 (home) Fax: 028-284-9733
Email: info@beaumont.co.za Web: www.beaumont.co.za
Cell: 083-9906-319

Jayne's guests stay in the charming buildings of an 18th-century former mill house and wagon shed, today snug with wood-burning heaters, but left as far as comfortably possible as they were, with original fireplaces in kitchens and hand-hewn, yellowwood beamed ceilings. Outside, you can sit around an old mill stone and admire the antediluvian water wheel (which along with the mill has recently been renovated and is now working as it once used to) while the willow-shaded jetty on the farm lake offers one of the Western Cape's prettiest settings for sundowners and wheatland views. While meandering through the flower-filled garden I realised that there is no real need to move from the farm, despite being only half an hour from Hermanus. While Jayne and her family busy themselves producing their annual 150,000-odd bottles of wine, you can swim in the informal swimming pool – being the lake - under the weeping willows where the weaver-birds make their nests; or you can roam about on their land – they own half a mountain! You can even put the idea of cooking on the backburner and instead arrange to have home-cooked meals delivered to you and wine-taste in the cellar flanked by an old wine press. The estate is a proud member of an exciting bio-diversity wine route which includes tours, tastings, hiking and mountain-bike trails (check out www.greenmountain.co.za). Also, to find horses and horse-riding you only have to trot down the road. The setting is beautiful - well worth spending several nights here.

Rooms: 2 self-catering cottages. Mill House has 2 bedrooms (plus 2 extra can sleep in living room); Pepper Tree has 1 double (again 2 extras possible).
Price: R250 pp sharing for first two people. Extra people R110 pp. Call for high season rates.
Meals: Self-catering breakfast and home-cooked meals by arrangement. All meals are self-served.
Directions: From N2 take exit 92, signposted to Bot River. Follow signs to Bot River and Beaumont Wine Estate is signed off to the right-hand side. Map can be faxed.

Barton Farm Villas

Peter Neill
Barton Farm (Off R43), Bot River
Tel: 028-284-9283/UK +44-1489-878-673 Fax: 028-284-9776
Email: villas@bartonfarm.co.za Web: www.bartonfarm.co.za
Cell: 071-609-7198

In the middle of the Kogel National Park, up a winding avenue of pine trees, I finally found five beautifully-designed Tuscan-style villas scattered across the raised valley of a working farm. As we climbed the track and stood under the arches the beam of my gaze shot straight out of the window, and spread across the vineyards and over the sprawling mountains beyond. The views are spectacular, a rolling canvas of working fields, rows of lavender and fynbos-clad mountains which wraps right around you. Built into and around the rocks the villas all have wide verandahs on which to conduct your feasts and to soak up the views. It's no secret Peter built them to stay in himself and consequently no expense has been spared. Notably the bedding, shipped straight in from The White Company because no other duvets would do! With huge sweeping lounges, open-plan kitchens, long tables, big fireplaces and an emphasis on natural materials, the villas are immaculately finished throughout. Peter has a soft spot for Persian carpets bringing colour and warmth to the airy rooms and I'm told a new one sneaks in on his every visit. With spa baths and swimming pools built into the rocks it's easy to forget this is a working farm abundant with wildlife. Don't miss the opportunity to get involved, especially with the wine grown on the farm. I imagined inviting everyone I knew to come for a week of long sunset dinners, lazy days of swimming, riding, tennis, golf, hiking and landscape painting….

Rooms: 5 villas: Heron, 3 doubles, indoor swimming pool & spa bath; Blue Crane, 2 doubles, 1 twin; Hammerkop, 2 doubles; Plover, 3 doubles; Lousada, 2 doubles, 1 twin & indoor swimming pool. All have en-suite bathrooms, outdoor pools, outdoor spa baths & DSTV.
Price: Seasonal R400 - R575 pp. Peak season from 15th Dec to 15th Feb: R700 pp.
Meals: Self-catering.
Directions: From Cape Town take the N2 towards Somerset West/Hermanus, exit 90. Barton Farm is situated on the R43 Bot River/Hermanus Road just past the Shell petrol Station.

Kolkol Mountain Lodge

Karen and Rudi Oosthuyse
Van Der Stel Pass, Bot River
Tel: 028-284-9568
Email: info@kolkol.co.za
Web: www.kolkol.co.za
Cell: 082-654-5090

It may have been the grass tickling the belly of my car that was making me smile – we'd spent so much time together we'd morphed into one - but I don't think so; more likely the grin on my face as I made my way up to Kolkol Mountain Lodge was one of happy anticipation of what lay at the top of the track. It was entirely justified. The log cabin and two luxury tents enjoy a view of Bot Rivier Mountain and its surroundings that everybody should see. But a lot of hard work has gone in to making it so. Rudi built everything: the large pine double bed, the mezzanine, the stone floors and the showers where the sunlight shining through the bamboo gives you a taster of what the day holds for you. In every season this place is heavenly. I could picture the large sitting room during winter lit by the orange light of the fire and filled with the mouth-watering smell of steaks sizzling in the open-plan kitchen – and whatever the weather, you must try the hotpool on the stoep. Heated by an underwater stove fed with wood, you admire the landscape while you wallow. Also blessed with these natty contraptions are the two luxury tents found further up the mountain. Ideal for couples, they are kitted out with baths, loos and an outside shower. This is what they mean by 'glamping', i.e. camping without any of the little discomforts that can mar the experience. Along with the raucous cries of flighting hadidas and the slight tinkle of the stream, I listened out for the sound of my supper cooking on the braai... until I remembered that I wasn't staying this time and my world collapsed!

Rooms: I log cabin: I double, I twin, 2 beds & a sleeper, I loft room; I with en-suite shower & I with separate shower. 2 luxury tents: I double & I twin, both with bath & outside shower.
Price: Log cabin: R300-R450 pp sharing. Singles on request. Tents: R300-R400 pp sharing per night.
Meals: Continental breakfast available R80 - R100 pp on request; Please book in advance.
Directions: Take N2 from Cape Town towards Somerset West. Take L at Bot River and turn into town. After railway line take Ist R onto Van der Stel Pass. 6.7km down the gravel road turn L up to KolKol Mountain Lodge & follow white arrow.

Barnacle B&B

Jenny Berrisford
573 Anne Rd, Pringle Bay
Tel: 028-273-8343 Fax: 028-273-8343
Email: barnacle@maxitec.co.za Web: www.barnacle.co.za
Cell: 082-925-7500

Come and explore Jenny's seaside idyll. Several natural environments collide right outside her cottage. From the deck at the back – with views all the way to Cape Point – you walk down to 'readers' corner', a private lawny enclave in the marsh reeds where narrow paths lead you to the river and beach. The sea is a hundred yards of the whitest, finest sand to your left; beyond the river, fynbos and milkwood 'forest' climb the mountain, a nature reserve. You don't have to be a kid to love this. There are otters in the river, baboons on the mountain, estuarine and fynbos birds aplenty… and Jenny is a horticultural expert in one of the world's most amazing natural gardens. Rooms are simple, rustic and country cosy, one with a Victorian slipper bath, another with a solid brass bed. The Cottage has a sitting area with its own fireplace which makes it cosy for winter breaks, while both the Cottage and The Sunshine Suite have fully-equipped kitchenettes for self-catering. The whole place is super relaxed… a hidden gem. *Jenny has a canoe to take out on the river. This area has been proclaimed a world biosphere reserve.*

Rooms: 2 units: 1 sleeping 4 with 1 double, en-suite shower, kitchen/dining area and 2 singles; and 1 sleeping 3 with 1 double, en-suite 'slipper' bath, kitchenette and one single bed.
Price: R300 - R500 pp sharing. Single and family rates negotiable.
Meals: Full breakfast included. Restaurants in Pringle Bay.
Directions: From Cape Town along N2 turn towards Gordon's Bay before Sir Lowry's Pass - follow coast road for 30km to Pringle Bay turn - follow signs down dirt roads.

Hannah's View

Hannalie Quass
510 Three Ways Road,
Pringle Bay
Tel: 028-273-8235
Fax: 028-273-8235
Email:
hannahsview@telkomsa.net
Web: www.hannahsview.co.za
Cell: 083-368-8429

How the wind huffed and puffed as Hannalie beckoned me in to Hannah's View, battened down the hatches and brought forth scones and jam. Found at the top of Pringle Bay this is just the kind of place you want to be stuck in during a storm. Could there be anything nicer than retiring to your room, sinking into a free-standing bath, steam billowing from behind the screen that hides it, and reading a book? Wild flowers and fynbos (so abundant, of course, in this area and a real reason to visit) are beautifully arranged by Hannalie and placed on all the bedside tables, lending their vibrancy to the rooms and going some way to assuaging any guilt about not going outside. Flashes of colour are also seen in the array of Persian rugs on the stained wooden floorboards found throughout the house. The wind now abating (scones too…), I climbed out of the cushion-bedecked sofa in the sitting room and, admiring the cast-iron chandelier, went upstairs. In between the two upstairs bedrooms – thick duvets aplenty and stunning views from the windows - is the door to the wooden balcony that runs along the front of the house. Hannalie and I gazed past the town and with the help of the telescope, tried to spot a whale or two. No luck, but with the sun now shining we could make the ten minute-walk down to the beach to get a closer look. For quiet exploration or calm contemplation Hannah's View is hard to beat. *Cycles available.*

Rooms: 3 kings: 1 with en-suite bath; 1 with en-suite bath and shower; the suite has a lounge plus 2 en-suite bathrooms, 1 with a bath and 1 with a shower.
Price: R350 pp sharing. Singles R410.
Meals: Full English, continental breakfast and high tea (book in advance) inc. 3-course dinner & wine depending on what's in the larder (book before 12) R150. Lunch boxes from R50.
Directions: From Cape Town take R44 to Gordon's Bay. From Gordon's Bay take Clarence Drive passing Rooi Els. Turn right into pringle Bay. Follow Hanglip Road and after approximately 2km turn right into Stream Road and left into Three Ways.

96 Beach Road

Annelie and Johan Posthumus
Kleinmond
Tel: 021-794-6291 Fax: 021-794-6291
Email: info@kaapsedraaibb.co.za Web: www.kaapsedraaibb.co.za

When the family bought "the beach house" in 1954, the milk was delivered by bike. Kleinmond still feels like a sleepy little town, but it's hardly surprising that more have fled here since. The house is but a kite-tail's length from the sea, the blue Atlantic stretching forth beyond a strip of fynbos. You can choose to watch the whales passing by (from August to December) from two spots, the sea-side verandah or the upstairs bedroom. The latter runs from one side of the house to the other under a vaulted ceiling and ocean-side the walls stop and the glass starts, forming a small square sitting room jutting out towards the blue. Here there is a soft couch and cushioned chairs, perfect for siestas, sunsets (and of course whale-watching). Downstairs is equally adorable. It feels a bit like a Nantucket Island house: white, light, airy and adorned with simple understated beach furnishings. Interior designers, *nota bene*! It is totally self-catering here, but walk a kilometre west and you'll find some untouristy cafés in the old harbour; a three-minute drive east will take you past a decent restaurant and miles of white, sandy, blue-flag beaches, perfect for kids, flying kites, swimming and walking. There is a rock pool about 50 yards from the house, and apart from that all the swimming takes place at the beach and lagoon which is a 15-minute walk away. Kleinmond is near the Arabella Golf Estate, the Kogelberg Biosphere with its myriad fynbos species, the wild horses of the Bot River Estuary and Hermanus, but avoids its touristy-ness.

Rooms: 1 unit with 2 rooms: 1 double with en-suite shower, 1 twin with bath. Open-plan kitchen/dining/living area. Heating. Kitchen fully equipped with dishwasher & washing-machine. Serviced once a week, more frequently on request.
Price: Max 4 persons. R700 per night plus R200 per extra person. Min 2-night stay.
Meals: Self-catering. Braai areas with firewood provided.
Directions: From the main road, turn down 9th Street and travel right down to Beach Road. Turn left into Beach Road. Cross 8th Street. No. 96 is the second from the corner of Beach and 7th Sts.

The Retreat

Chimmy Anderson
2190 Heron Road, Betty's Bay
Tel: 028 272 9157 Fax: 028 272 9157
Email: retreatbb@ananzi.co.za Web: www.retreatbb.co.za
Cell: 072-072-8100

The Retreat does a fine line in reinvigoration, and there's no one better suited to the helm than Chimmy. Not only is she such lively company, but in previous lives she has trained as a Cordon Bleu chef and lived in a Scottish lighthouse where she spent three years practising meditation. The Retreat – serene, luxurious, calm – is surely the brainchild of so much contemplation? Anyway, I for one felt instantly at home and, while Jane was rustling me up a steak in the kitchen, I sank into a hot tub and greeted the rising moon, which appeared from behind Kogelberg Mountain. You could feel guilty, I suppose… or just go with it like I did! There are only two rooms at The Retreat, which allows for prodigious pampering. The bed and its exuberant headboard were the undoubted stars in my room, though there is a strong supporting cast. I fell in love with a vast Victorian cow and a pair of Sacred Ibis, and the lamps are a visual treat too. From the other bedroom you can gaze up at the mountain or out on to the fynbos garden. I ate my breakfast in a gazebo built, like the rest of the house, in a gorgeous pale-blue-painted timber and equipped with all the cooking gear one needs for a banquet. But for the undiscovered beaches and the penguin colony nearby I would have stayed by the plunge pool all day. I loved it so much at The Retreat that I left my notes behind purely to give me an excuse to return.

Rooms: 2: 1 superior double with queen, and 1 suite with queen & day bed for child; 1 en-suite shower and 1 en-suite bath and shower.
Price: R275 - R350 non-season, R300 - R400 season pp sharing. Singles R350 - R450.
Meals: Full English and continental breakfast included. 3 detox meals a day: R300. 3-course meals on request R150. Wine extra.
Directions: From Cape Town: Take N2 through Somerset West. Turn onto R44 to Kleinmond/Gordon's Bay. Follow coastal road for approx 30km. 3km after Pringle Bay turn R to Stony Point. After 10 roads turn R into Wheeler St and 1st left into Heron Road. The Retreat signposted on R.

Schulphoek Seafront Guesthouse

Petro and Mannes van Zyl
44 Marine Drive, Sandbaai, Hermanus/Sandbaai
Tel: 028-316-2626 Fax: 028-316-2627
Email: schulphoek@hermanus.co.za Web: www.schulphoek.co.za
Cell: 083-346-0695

Waves roll into the bay, five foot high when I visited, and crash against rocks right in front of Schulphoek Seafront Guesthouse. The sitting room has one of the most exciting sea views you could hope for and, naturally, whales steal into Schulphoek Bay during the season for private viewings. The best room, Scallop - I don't think there is any doubt, despite the extremely high overall standard! - is upstairs, the whole seaward wall an expanse of window with a sliding glass door and parapet. The other rooms, although without sea views, have solid, hand-crafted oak or mahogany beds and spectacular bathrooms with double sinks, double showers and spa-baths. As I sunk into mine I laughed, safe in the knowledge that as far as luxury goes you will not find better *anywhere*. Not many places in this area feel the need to provide in-house dinners, but your hosts are not taking chances on outside eateries. Guests who want to guarantee themselves delicious food stay in (4-course menu du jour with herbs, salad and veg picked straight from their vegetable garden) and eat at one long table, on chairs made from vintage wine vats. Dinner is a lively affair, before which you will be led to the exhaustive cellar where you can choose from the finest South African wines. Schulphoek is an intimate, state-of-the-art seaside lodge, but still the sort of place where guests socialise with each other, drinks are on an honesty system and meals are eaten together (although you can eat separately if you prefer).

Rooms: 7 suites: superior, luxury and standard, all with luxurious en-suite bathrooms. I family suite.
Price: R616 to R1,429 pp sharing, includes full breakfast & 4-course dinner on 1st night. Single supp' +50%. Discounted rates for longer stays all year round, plus seasonal rates. Website has more detail. Whole guest house on request.
Meals: Professional kitchen with chef. Dinner every night: 4-course menu du jour. Lunch on request. Wine cellar with 12,000 SA wines. Full breakfast incl'.
Directions: Take R43 towards Hermanus. At Engen petrol station by traffic lights (signed Sandbaai) turn R. At 2nd 'stop' turn L into 3rd Street. L at next stop. Marked by flags – entrance off Piet Retief Crescent.

Villa Blu

Riana & Tino Delle Donne

234 8th Street, Voëlklip, Hermanus
Tel: 028-314-1056 Fax: 028-314-1123
Email: info@villablu.co.za Web: www.villablu.co.za
Cell: 082-4436-340

This place does a strange thing to you. Whilst Tino was preparing my coffee (the best I've had in SA, but then he is Italian), my head began to whirl with happy memories of holidays past where faces are golden, living is easy and time passes idly by. Just another guesthouse this is certainly not. Built around an open courtyard that tinkles, trickles and crashes with the sounds of wind chimes, fountains and waves, Villa Blu inspires within you an invigorating lightness of heart. Be it the beach-time photographs, colourful paintings (some are Riana's own), antique Indonesian furnishings, shells scattered around or the blue-tinted hue, everything feels fresh, homely and so very, very relaxed. With pale-washed Oregon pine furnishings and floors, huge mirror-walls in the bathrooms and doors opening onto private patios, every room is as light and airy as the rest of the house. Head up to the roof terrace for stunning views onto the blue-flag 'Grotto' beach just ahead or the green velvet-swathed mountains which loom large behind. Regrettably, as mine was only a quick visit, I didn't get to swing carefree in the garden's hammock, doze by the pool or try Tino's wonderful breakfast (he is clearly as passionate about food as he is about the guest-house). But I didn't just want to stay here anyway... I wanted to live here. Oh, bring on those lazy, hazy days of summer.

Rooms: 8: 5 kings/twins, 2 with separate bath and shower, 2 with bath/shower, 1 with shower; 3 queens, 2 with en suite bath/shower and 1 with en-suite shower.
Price: R400 - R620 pp sharing. Singles supplement 50%.
Meals: Full breakfast included. Culinary weekends offered in winter months.
Directions: From N2, take R43 into Hermanus. Drive through the town, staying on Main Road as you cross the roundabout. Turn right into 13th Avenue and then right into 8th Street. It's 3rd house on R.

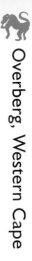

Overberg, Western Cape

Hartford Cottage

Gys and Wendy Hofmeyr
3, 3rd Ave, Voelklip, Hermanus
Tel: 028-314-0102 Fax: 028-314-0667
Email: gyswendyhof@telkomsa.net Cell: 082-897-1773

If you were asked to paint a picture of your perfect country cottage, I suggest it might look a bit like Hartford; white walls, soaring chimney and a perfectly pitched thatched roof, all enveloped by a large, tranquil, lawned garden where I challenge you to find anything out of place. As I sat under the welcoming shade of the umbrella sipping tea and thinking how delicious it would be to live here, Wendy told me - and I didn't register much surprise - that complete strangers have knocked on the door begging to stay, even though originally they only built the cottage for the family. Hiding away from the hurlyburly of Hermanus in a seaside suburb, Hartford is enviably positioned, with mountain walks five minutes in one direction, beach, sea and whales a minute or two in the opposite. Gys is a stickler for detail and a lover of wood and thatch. Door surrounds and light switches were rescued and resurrected from a condemned house in town, while an original yellowwood door hanging on huge hinges is his pride and joy. Don't think Wendy hasn't been busy too. Her eye for interior designs led to the stunning black slate fire hearth, bathroom sink surrounds and kitchen worktops. The open-plan A-frame roof makes it cool and spacious, while the whitewashed walls and an abundance of Cape antique furniture, means it retains all of its delightfully cosy cottage charm.

Rooms: 1 cottage with 1 double room with full en-suite and 1 twin bedroom with separate bathroom. Also a large attic bed/sitter with 3 beds for children. Cottage not available 20th Dec - 15th Jan.
Price: 2 people sharing whole cottage: R900 plus R100 an extra head (May - Aug inclusive). R1,200 plus R200 a head per extra person (Sept - April inc'). Min 2-night stay. Children under 12 free.
Meals: Cottage fully self-catering, including breakfast provisions for your first morning.
Directions: 4km from Hermanus direction Stanford, take 3rd exit off roundabout into 10th St (seafront rd), past CEM Motors & on for 300m. 3rd Ave on R, then thatched house on R. Map faxed on booking.

Entry Number: 126

Map Number: 4

Pebble Beach

Pat Morland

8 Fernkloof Drive, Hermanus
Tel: 028-313-2517 Fax: 088-028-313-2517
Email: info@pebblebeachguesthouse.com
Web: www.pebblebeachguesthouse.com Cell: 083-659-0455

Pat Morland and her family have moved seventeen times since she and her husband got married, so she knows what it takes to make people feel at home. It's no surprise that so many contented guests have now congregated for evening drinks on Pebble Beach's colonial-style, wrap-around balcony to contemplate remarkable views down the tree-lined 25th fairway (that is correct) of 27-hole Hermanus Golf Course… and to pass derisive comment on the golf swings on show. This can be enjoyably achieved with equal smugness on colder days in the Rocky Lounge with its open fire. Others will eschew golf criticism altogether and settle down by the swimming pool among the olive trees. The house, with its Zimbabwean wall hangings and headboards, has a subtle African flavour to it. Natural materials have been used wherever possible, with sunset-slate flooring, stone baths, wooden mirrors and the harmonious result is restful on both eye and spirit. For non-golfers, the front door opens onto the Hermanus Mountains, complete with nature trails through the fynbos, and both beaches and village are close by making it easy to burn off those calories from the mammoth breakfast that Pat, with typical flare and generosity, provides. Pebble Beach has so much to offer both the action man and the poolside potterer.

Rooms: 6: 2 kings, 4 king/twins, 1 sofa-bed for children under 12; 3 with en-suite bath and shower, 3 with en-suite shower.
Price: R480 - R575 pp sharing. Singles R720 - R850. Children under 12 sharing with parents R250.
Meals: Full English and continental breakfast included.
Directions: From N2 take R43 to Hermanus. Go all the way through the village and turn left at the Shell garage. Hug the golf course and turn first right before the school. House is second after the bend.

Selkirk House

Elise Haarhoff

29 Selkirk Street, Hermanus Heights, Hermanus
Tel: 028-312-4892 Fax: 028-312-4387
Email: info@selkirkhouse.co.za Web: www.selkirkhouse.co.za
Cell: 076-587-4753

When William Selkirk landed 'that' 967kg shark onto the rocks of Hermanus in 1922, I doubt he ever dreamt his name would appear in lights that shine quite as brightly as they do at this multi-levelled mountain-side retreat. The exceptional use of space and natural surroundings through levels, landings, terraces and quiet mountain recesses is visionary, not only aesthetically but also functionally. Everything is slick, chic, minimalistic and clean, accentuated by bursts of bright fynbos flower paintings. Chrome balustrades lead you up wooden stairs to your next indulgence, whether it's your room, the pool and first living space, complete with temperature-controlled wine cellar and vent-free fireplace, or the contemporary bar room with outside deck and fireplace, or the roof-top viewing deck which provides 360° views of mountains and ocean. All suites are a spacious dream and completely automated, allowing you to control your immediate environment whether through music, climate or brightness. I think they must have had a bit of a chuckle watching me walking in and out of the various rooms, wide-eyed as a child, as lights magically switched themselves on and off. Although everything really is cutting edge, Selkirk is also welcoming and warm-spirited and you are certainly encouraged to kick off your shoes and make full use of this supa-dupa new creation. Just as I was about to leave a tortoise had made its way down the mountain and into the garden… the race is on!

Rooms: 5: 4 kings with en-suite bath and shower and 1 twin with en-suite bath and shower.
Price: R750 pp sharing, Singles R1,125.
Meals: Full breakfast included, lunch and dinner available on request.
Directions: From N2 take R43 into Hermanus, go through village until 4-way stop, continue over with Marine Hotel on right for 2km, turn left at Shell garage with golf course on right. Take 1st turn right and continue towards mountain, through hairpin bend then left into Selkirk Street.

Sumaridge Vineyard Cottage

Simon and Holly Turner

Sumaridge Wines, Farm 22, Hemel-en-Arde Valley, Hermanus
Tel: 028-312-1097 Fax: 086 623 4248
Email: info@sumaridge.co.za Web: www.sumaridge.co.za
Cell: 072-992-1981

After driving 5,000km all across South Africa – mainly on the Greenwood trail, of course - Simon and Holly finally bought Sumaridge Wine Estate, sandwiched between the mountains and vineyards of the Hemel-en-Aarde wine valley. In less than a year they have transformed the former farm cottage into a five-room 'Vineyard Farmhouse Delight' and opened their doors to visitors. With so much to do here - horses, mountain-biking, hiking, bass fishing and, of course, the wine farm - it would have been some sort of crime not to! At the cottage itself, you have the freedom to go to war on the boules 'court', popping inside for snacks from the fully-fitted kitchen to keep up energy levels, followed by a post-mortem over a glass or several of chardonnay in the verandah Jacuzzi; all this without having to put your shoes on. The main house has four en-suite bedrooms, all with brushed-oak flooring and each gently themed to a local indigenous flower. The extra large rooms also boast private patios and flow into the indoor-outdoor lounge verandah which is the heart of the house and where many unforgettable evenings surely lie in wait. There is also a fully wheelchair-friendly annex, which allows those in need of adapted bathrooms and entrances to share the break with their family and friends. Sumaridge is a place that will entertain kids and parents alike.

Rooms: 5: in the main house: 2 kings with en-suite bath and shower, 1 twin with en-suite bath and shower, 1 twin with en-suite bath; self-catering annex: king with wheelchair-friendly bath and shower.
Price: R350 pp sharing.
Meals: Self-catering. Breakfast on request at R80 pp.
Directions: From N2 take R43 towards Hermanus, left at R320 up Hemel-en-Aarde Valley for about 8 km, Sumaridge on left.

Mosaic Farm

Breese & Kathryn Johnson (owners), Justin & Jolene Boshoff (managers)

Provincial Road, On the Hermanus Lagoon, Stanford
Tel: 028-313-2814 Fax: 028-313-2811
Email: info@mosaicfarm.net Web: www.mosaicfarm.net Cell: 082-825-3211

In 1892, visitors to Mosaic Farm would have had either to cross the lagoon or travel by horse and cart to reach it. Today the journey to this historic house is a bit more civilised. "You can arrive by helicopter if you have one," smiles Jolene as I step from my dusty car. That would be a fitting entrance, for Mosaic Farm has the feeling of a Texan ranch, but sadly I am no wealthy oil baron. This peaceful 1,000 hectare property, separated from boisterous Hermanus by an 8km lagoon (4km of which is in front of Mosaic), is rich both in history and plant and animal life. The silence here is only punctured by birdsong or the splash of a kayak paddle. The main house dates back to 1892 and, in homage to its past, new cottages have been built in the same style; high-beamed ceilings, stacked stone walls and natural finishes combine with modern-day comforts. Hidden in the bush there is far more still to be discovered. Luxury safari-style tents peek out from beneath the canopy of ancient milkwood trees, a plunge pool overlooks the lagoon, and a dining area, complete with thatched roof and canvas flaps, serves up very fine food. There are even plans to introduce game. "You get a real out-of-Africa feel here," says Jolene; this is so true despite the farm's proximity to Hermanus. I really don't think the helicopter is necessary to ensure a massive dose of luxury and romance at Mosaic Farm.

Rooms: 7: 5 luxury tents all en-s bathroom, outdoor shower & private deck; 2 fully-contained self-catering cottages: 1 double & 1 twin with en-s, loft sleeps 5 with downstairs bathroom; & 1 cottage with twin room & loft sleeps 2 kids.
Price: B&B: R695 - R990 pp sharing. Singles R990 - R1,390. Children 4 - 12 yrs R495. Self-catering cottages: R700 - R1,600 per unit per night, additional pp R100 - R225.
Meals: Full breakfast & activities included for Lagoon Lodge guests; & optional extras for self-caterers. Dinner in 1892 Stanford Spookhuis & picnic lunches available for all guests.
Directions: From Cape Town R43 to Stanford. R thro' village then L at Moore St. Straight until becomes farm road. Carry on for 10km, Mosaic Farm Reception signed on R.

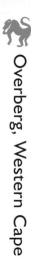

Cliff Lodge

Gill O'Sullivan and Gideon Shapiro
6 Cliff St, De Kelders
Tel: 028 384-0983 Fax: 028-384-0228
Email: stay@clifflodge.co.za Web: www.clifflodge.co.za
Cell: 082-380-1676

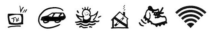

This is the closest land-based whale-watching you could possibly find. I could see the whites of their eyes (I was only shooting with a camera!) and the callosities on their heads. It was as though Gill and Gideon had paid them (in plankton) to put on a special show for me; blowing, breaching, spy-hopping, lob-tailing. I applauded delicately from the royal box. The viewing from my room and from the breakfast conservatory-balcony was don't-turn-your-eyes-away-for-a-minute magnetic. But the fun wasn't just in the looking. As soon as I walked through the door, Gideon, formally a dive-master, whisked me down to the ocean for a swim through the cave (bring shoes you can swim in for the rocks) and Gill kindly booked me a whale-, sea-lion- and penguin-watching boat trip for the following morning. For the 'help-danger' adrenaline rush, there is also the shark-cage diving. The guest house décor is classy and modern and there are whale-spotting terraces for those rooms on the side of the house. The luxurious penthouse suite has a huge balcony and glass-fronted living room for whale-gazing in true style. On the cliff edge there is also a swimming pool area which has recently been given a makeover. Gill, Gideon and the ever-smiling manager Nico are wonderfully hospitable hosts. After the best breakfast you could possibly have - not only because of the food but also the panorama - indulge in an aromatherapy massage organised by Gill, nature reserve walks in front of the house and the nearby flower farm.

Rooms: 5: 1 twin/king with bath & shower; 1 queen with shower over bath; 1 twin/king with shower over bath; 1 luxury suite with king, separate living room, bath & shower; 1 twin/king with shower
Price: R600 - R1,250 pp sharing. Single supplement +50%.
Meals: Full breakfast included.
Directions: N2, then R43 through Hermanus. Past Stanford towards Gansbaai. Turn right at first De Kelders turn-off, then right into De Villiers Rd, left into Kayser Rd and right into Cliff St.

Kleinzee Oceanfront Guesthouse

Lourens and Ilana Myburgh
59 Cliff Street, De Kelders
Tel: 083-650-5156
Email: loumy@mweb.co.za
Cell: 072-748-8463

As Piera welcomed me with her indelible smile and infectious laugh, all my jangly travel-related tension just melted away into the ether as if it had never been. She and Kleinzee just ooze wonderful warmth and character. The house is set on the cliffs of De Kelders, so the focal point of each of the three rooms is the ocean and its seasonal visitors. You can stay in one of two very roomy downstairs bedrooms, each with their own private deck and a shared lounge area separating them. En-suite bathrooms have Victorian slipper-baths and enormous pebble-floored power-showers, essential for blasting out sand from hidden crevices and for buffing up the day's sunburn. Natural textures and colours are evident throughout with exposed stone walls, whitewashed cabinets and soft blue shutters. But the jewel in the crown, so to speak, is upstairs, a private honeymoon floor… not just a suite, but an entire floor. The sleeping/activity part of the room is broken by a half stone wall doubling as a headboard, behind which lies your open-plan bathroom. Again a huge free-standing bath and power-showers, only this time throw in a sea view. The adjoining private lounge and whale-watching deck has a double-sided fireplace. With under-floor heating throughout, a heated splash pool and a hypnotic view, Kleinzee is not only a summer hot spot, but also a cosy romantic winter hideaway.

Rooms: 3: 2 kings with en-suite bath and shower, 1 twin with en-suite bath and shower.
Price: R380 - R420 pp sharing, Honeymoon R650 pp sharing.
Meals: Full breakfast included.
Directions: From N2 take R43 through Hermanus and Stanford. Take 1st right signed De Kelders and follow down to the sea. Turn right into Cliff Street.

Whalesong Lodge

Stanley and Lainy Carpenter
83 Cliff St, De Kelders
Tel: 028-384-1865 Fax: 028-384-1866
Email: stanley@whalesonglodge.co.za Web: www.whalesonglodge.co.za
Cell: 082-883-5793

I sank with delight into a candlelit bath in the midst of a raging sea storm. On a calm day I'd have been bathing before a host of whales. "There were twenty or thirty in the bay this morning", said Stanley casually. I was more than happy curled up with a book, chatting to guests in the cosy, glass-fronted living room. They had a date with some sharks in the morning and tales of these awesome creatures steered the evening's conversation. Stanley and Lainy used to run the Pontac Hotel in Paarl, but I suspect they always hankered after a nice small place where they could give their guests more love and attention, cook for manageable numbers... and be themselves. Whalesong Lodge, with just five rooms, is it. All the bedrooms have sea views, of course, either from a panoramic window or a small, private balcony, and underfloor-heated bathrooms are separated from the sleeping areas by shoulder-high walls. All is slick and modern. Many cookbooks and a well-stocked kitchen loudly trumpet Stanley's culinary expertise. So will he be cooking for his happy hordes? The eyes narrow. "Only if I'm feeling inspired," comes the reply, through a suppressed smile. Luckily for me, that evening he was, and what a feast! Succulent ostrich, a delicious fish caught that morning (sorry Stanley, I can't remember the name?) and other tasty trimmings. All this followed by Lainy's delicious dessert. Breakfast ("from 8 till late") is fresh and all-encompassing, with home-made preserves, fresh fruit, eggs and bacon. Oh yes, and great coffee.

Rooms: 5: 2 twins, 3 doubles, all en-suite bath and shower.
Price: R700 - R950 pp sharing.
Meals: Full breakfast included.
Directions: From N2 take R43 through Hermanus and Stanford. Take first right signed to De Kelders and follow down to the sea. Turn right into Cliff Street. Third house on right.

Klein Paradijs Country House

Susanne and Michael Fuchs
Pearly Beach, Gansbaai
Tel: 028-381-9760 Fax: 028-381-9803
Email: info@klein-paradijs.com Web: www.klein-paradijs.com

Paradise would be a proud boast, so perhaps Little Paradise is a more defensible claim. But you can see why the name stuck: nature on the one hand, man-made environment on the other, and all rounded off by delicious cooking and green fingers. I'll elaborate. The property stretches up a mountain covered in indigenous fynbos vegetation - fifty hectares of which has recently been designated a voluntary conservation site - and nearer the house there is a reed-edged dam with weaver birds, an old camphor tree in the courtyard and an amazing garden whose swimming pool acts as a moat to a tiny island of plant life. Inside, high open spaces are punctuated with lovely things: bright paintings, vases of proteas and pincushions, a stinkwood grandfather clock, for example. A-shaped rooms have soaring thatched roofs, dormer windows, beams, window-seats, balconies and the curtained-off bathrooms are truly luxurious. The Fuchs are Swiss and have brought many talents with them. Susanne was a translator, speaks English, German and French and is a certified tour guide, while Michael is a chef. The proof is in the pudding, as it were, as the guests are treated to restaurant-quality food every evening. *Large dam with canoe and rowboat available on the property. Whale-watching possible nearby from June – November.*

Rooms: 5: 2 twins and 3 doubles all with en-suite bathrooms; 2 with bath and shower, 3 with showers.
Price: R550 - R1,050 pp sharing. Single supplement +50%.
Meals: Full breakfast included. Light meals and dinner by arrangement. The restaurant is fully licensed.
Directions: From Hermanus take the R43 through Stanford and Gansbaai. Go left at Pearly Beach crossing, then 1st left again. The house is on the right. GPS coordinates S 34° 39' 23.5" E 19° 32' 05.7"

Farm 215 Nature Retreat and Fynbos Reserve

Maarten Groos

Hartebeeskloof, Baardskeerdersbos, Near De Kelders
Tel: 028-388-0920
Email: book@farm215.co.za Web: www.farm215.co.za
Cell: 082-097-1655

Farm 215 perches neatly among the fynbos of this private nature reserve. It's not really that remote, yet when I visited absolute silence prevailed, so much so that you could hear the neat pitter-patter of Maarten's dogs following us along the boardwalks. The individual cottages, angled to look rosy-faced into the sunset and onto sea and mountains, squat above the 35 different species of protea that contribute to the vast and wild garden. The conservation of the reserve here is a constant priority and the cottages were very much built with sustainabilty in mind and they have won an award for their efforts (one of very few places in SA that are Fair Trade accredited). Testament to this is the yellow lichen, a sign of air purity, that paints the rock faces of this self-sufficient retreat. The log fire in the restaurant provides the under-floor heating, while solar panels heat the spectacular chlorine-free 25m-lap pool. Maarten is constantly improving his fynbos world and speaks with eager animation of plans in progress. The restaurant is capacious and contemporary with two fireplaces and folding doors that open onto a wooden deck. Here Henki (the chef) produces his incredible food, always steering clear of frivolous gourmet towers. The free-standing suites are luxurious, with cotton linen and large open-plan bathrooms of wood and black slate; or you can stay in the farmhouse rooms with their black-framed historic photographs and wide Persian rugs. With 20km of hiking trails radiating from the door of your cottage, an astonishing number of birds and horse trails on site, there is every opportunity to earn yourself a slice of heaven. *Children over 12 are welcome.*

Rooms: 6: 3 free-standing suites with kings, lounge area & en-s bath & shower; 1 ground floor suite with private garden and 2 doubles in main house, each with en-s bath & shower.
Price: From R750 - R950 pp sharing (for rooms) & from R890 - R1,050 pp sharing (for suite) in house. Fynbos suites R1,070 - R1,300 pp sharing. Singles +30%.
Meals: Full breakfast included. On-site restaurant for lunch & 3-course dinner. Picnic baskets also available.
Directions: At Bot River take turn to Hermanus (R43). After Franskraal L into dirt rd signed to Elim. Follow for approx 10km. Gates to Farm 215 are on L after lake & vineyards.

Map Number: 4

Entry Number: 135

Rothman Manor

Andreas and Franziska Gobel

268 Voortrek St, Swellendam
Tel: 028-514-2771 Fax: 028-514-3966
Email: guesthouse@rothmanmanor.co.za Web: www.rothmanmanor.co.za

With lily-littered dam, salt-water pool and cobbled courtyard Rothman Manor boasts grounds of park-like calibre. The original Cape Dutch house and venerable oak tree (whose shady canopy acts as a parasol for your breakfast table) both date back to 1834, yet fresh, clipped interiors (born of Andreas and Franziska's combined flair for design) shift matters decisively into the present. With pale-blue or cream-hued walls and cloud-white curtain-swept beds, heavenly rooms are earthed by wooden flooring and black-framed artwork, many of which are Franziska's own. Bathrooms sport chequered tiles and African-themed titbits seem to hang suspended in cubby-holes, unique reminders of the grounds and its outdoor inhabitants. Here, in wine-dominated Swellendam, I was bowled over with sightings of zebra and sprightly springbok, all residents of the Gobel's eco-reserve. I was tempted to bag a lounger near the deck-bound jacuzzi where you can keep an eye on any animal action. Each generous room has its own view-treated patio for outdoors delight or spoil yourself indoors with a therapeutic, individually-tailored massage. With easy access to numerous nature reserves, wine farms and Bontebok National Park, Rothman Manor is its own destination and a gateway to others.

Rooms: 6: 3 kings and 3 twins, 4 with full baths, 2 with shower only.
Price: R420 - R875 pp sharing. Singles on request.
Meals: Full breakfast included.
Directions: Turn off N2 onto R60, and then turn R into Swellendam. Rothman Manor on R.

Jan Harmsgat Country House

Brin and Judi Rebstein
PO Box 161, On the R60 between Ashton and Swellendam, Swellendam
Tel: 023-616-3407 or 023 616-3311 Fax: 023-616-3201
Email: brinreb@iafrica.com Web: www.jhghouse.com Cell: 072-279-3138

A true country house, Jan Harmsgat is a breath of fresh air in an often-chintzy genre. Judi (a producer in the film industry) and Brin rescued it from tumbledown oblivion in 1989. They swept out the old rotted beams, mould, even pigs, and set about pouring a cellar-full of TLC into it. It is a beautiful place. The above photo does not lie but what it doesn't show is that the restaurant and its increasingly famous staff are starting to catch the food-media's eye… or that your hosts are so gracious. Past resident Hermanus Steyn proclaimed the Independent Republic of Swellendam in 1795 and farmed wine here originally, but I doubt he dined on butterfish bobotie stacks with coriander. Or perhaps he did! His 25-metre barn-cellar (now the dining room, complete with grand piano) today looks out of a glass wall. Guests are housed in old slave quarters whose large rooms and great comfort might make you forget the history of the place. However, sympathetic renovation means that windows in the clay walls have not been enlarged, and the wonky lintels, wooden shutters and vast beams all play their part in preserving the original character here. Mine was high up in the apex of the thatch, had a free-standing Victorian bath, gilded chairs and come morning I had a colour-me-happy moment when I opened my shutters and was drenched in a sweet citron-scented breeze gusting across from the orchard. Bliss.

Rooms: 5: 1 twin with en/s shower & 1 twin with en/s bath; 1 queen with Victorian bath in room & en-suite loo; 1 king with Victorian bath in room & en-suite loo; 1 king luxury room with full bathroom (bath & shower).
Price: R440 - R910 pp sharing. Luxury room R1,030.
Meals: Full breakfast included. Lunch by arrangement only. The restaurant is open for dinner to the public (reservations essential). Four-course set menu R250 pp.
Directions: From Cape Town on N1 to Worcester turn right into R60 (Robertson) at Worcester. Carry on thro' Robertson and Ashton. Turn R after Ashton and stay on R60. House on left after 21km. From Cape Town on N2 to Swellendam turn into R60. Carry on 24.5km after Swellendam towards Ashton, house on R.

Map Number: 2

Entry Number: 137

Frog Mountain Getaway

Brian and Peter Kilpin
Frog Mountain Getaway, Swellendam
Tel: 028-512-3732 Fax: 028-512-3732
Email: kilpin@mweb.co.za Web: www.frogmountain.co.za
Cell: 083-261-0596

Frog Mountain Getaway is where Peter Pan goes on holiday. I can't prove it - Brian was a model of discretion - but I just know he would love it here. As I drove down the long dirt road that leads into the depths of the Langeberg mountains, I felt my skin soften and my normally retrogressive hairline creep forward with every turn in the road. Those lucky or clever enough to book in at Frog Mountain are blessed with a river to swim, fish and kayak in, mountains to hike about on, bike trails to follow and birds to spot. There is also an overflowing adventure playground equipped with an old tractor, climbing frames, a Wendy house (she's obviously a regular guest as well), a trampoline and a mini football pitch. Even the accommodation offers itself up for adventure. There are four rondavels, each with a double bed, and two singles in an open loft. These were probably designed for children, although I was so high on the Peter Pan effect that Brian had to coax me back down by promising me another go on the tractor. There's a stove for when the weather permits, and a stoep provides the perfect setting for watching the sun disappear, the stars come out and the sausages sizzle on the braai. This really is a place where families and adventurous couples can spend day after blissful day exploring all there is to offer - I urge you to stay for two days or more. See you there.

Rooms: 4 self-catering rondavels sleeping 4: 3 double/twins, 1 king, all with 2 singles on an open loft; all with en-suite showers.
Price: From R600 - R850 per rondavel per night (not per person).
Meals: Self-catering.
Directions: Take N2 until 9km past Swellendam. Turn left at Sparrebosch (directly after the prison). Travel for 9km on dirt road until the end.

Bloomestate

Maarten and Carla Van der Ven
276 Voortrekker Street, Swellendam
Tel: 028-514-2984 Fax. 028-514-3822
Email: info@bloomestate.com Web: www.bloomestate.com

The contrast between Bloomestate (cool, calm, chic) and the dirt roads I'd spent most of the day bumping my way down (dirty, hot, rattly) was clearly demonstrated by the detached fascination with which the van der Ven dogs observed my dust-covered car. This house overflows with originality and is the quintessence of modern living (i-pod stations, wireless internet a given). The seven enormous garden rooms are identical in size and furnishings, with chunky beds looking through French windows to the pool, with its one striking blue wall perfectly framing the mountains beyond. Each room is coded by season or element, with one brightly-painted wall, matching cushions and a spray-painted canvas. 'Spring' is a vibrant green, 'Summer' (where I stayed) a sun-burnt orange, and the honeymooners' 'Fire' a passionate red. In the lounge bar area an L.E.D light projects the time onto the opposite wall, and shattered glass is encased in the bar. The stoep, equipped with designer furniture, provides a perfect viewing platform from which to watch the sun slipping down behind the mountains. The lemons in tall glass vases in the house are from the orchard, and to walk around the many hidden delights of the garden accompanied by its various fragrances is the most enchanting start to any day. Not as enchanting, though, as my breakfast of fruit, scrambled egg and toast. This is a place that naturally inspires and delights. Maarten and Carla have now started offering wellness treatments as well.

Rooms: 7: 4 kings and 3 twins, all with en-suite bath and shower.
Price: R575 - R850 pp sharing. Singles plus 50%.
Meals: Full breakfast included. Picnic baskets, cheese platters, seasonal salads and open sandwiches available on request from R90 pp.
Directions: From Cape Town and N2 take Swellendam West exit (R60) towards Ashton. At the crossroads turn right and Bloomestate is first building on the right.

Schoone Oordt Country House

Alison Walker

1 Swellengrebel Street, Swellendam
Tel: 028-514-1248 Fax: 028-514-1249
Email: info@schooneoordt.co.za Web: www.schooneoordt.co.za
Cell: 082-772-6881

As I sat reaching with monotonous regularity for Alison's unmistakably more-ish home-made biscuits in the palatial conservatory of Schoone Oordt, I felt very definitely at home. This isn't because I'm used to country houses, of course, nor indeed platefuls of biscuits (honest), but because Alison and Roy (partner and friend) are such natural, friendly, put-you-at-your-ease hosts. The house is wonderful too, it goes without saying. The intricate details of the white balustrades against the light umber of Schoone Oordt are beautiful and testament to some very hard - but satisfying, I feel sure - work put in by Richard, Alison's husband, in restoring it to its former glory (a job that took four years). The rooms, separate from the main house among fountains and roses, are furnished with restored antiques: grand old wardrobes stand guard next to the beds, vast mirrors with opulent golden frames adorn the walls, and a thick wool carpet covers the floor. Bathrooms have pale wooden panels, free-standing baths, curvaceous showers with heads the size of satellite dishes, while above the loos the antique cisterns were also restored by Richard. In the honeymoon suite, if you can tear your eyes away from the fuchsias and their kaleidoscope of pinks, you will encounter a beautifully-crafted, slightly-larger-than-king four-poster bed opposite a broad-shouldered fireplace. Look out as well for the antique dresser rescued from an old train. As we chatted by the old Austin truck in the car park, I unfortunately had to turn Roy's offer for brunch down. He promised he'd keep it until next time - I only hope he remembers.

Rooms: 9: 8 king/twins and 1 four-poster king in Honeymoon Suite. 9 en-suite with bath and shower.
Price: R600 - R925 pp sharing. Singles R900 - R1,380.
Meals: Full breakfast included. Other meals can be provided, but only by special arrangement and only for groups larger than 6: about R150 pp.
Directions: From N2, take Swellendam East turn-off. Drive back downhill, thro' 3-way stop. After Koornlands River Bridge turn immediately R. Turn before grass verge with Swellendam written in white brick on it. Schoone Oordt Country House is on R.

Kliphoogte

Herman and Marita Linde

Swellendam
Tel: 028 514 2534 Fax: 028 514 2534
Email: kliphoogte@telkomsa.net
Cell: 084-581-4464

Three kilometres of dusty track bring you to Kliphoogte, one of South Africa's most charming farm B&B's. Herman, absurdly cheerful for a man who gets up at 4:30am, runs a fruit and dairy farm on the banks of the Leeurivier…. while his mother Marita looks after the guest house. Herman represents the fifth generation of Lindes to work the property and will take guests on walks around the farm, or leave them in the company of the boisterous weaver-birds to swim at the small lake. At meal times Marita takes charge and cooks typical South African dinners. Herman will probably then take you in his 4x4 up a nearby hill to look at the stars. The blue main bedroom is a sweet affair, with sturdy old Afrikaner furniture, family photos and rugs made by the farm workers. The other is more functional (though it does have a four-poster bed), but this is not a place where you'll want to spend long in bed; there is too much going on outside. To sit on the Kliphoogte stoep, listening to cicadas, and looking out over the small, lush valley is to know contentment indeed.

Rooms: 2: both doubles; 1 with en-suite shower, 1 with separate bathroom.
Price: R400 pp sharing. Singles available on request.
Meals: Lunch by arrangement only - reservation essential. Full course set menu R150.
Directions: Turn off N2 onto R60 (Swellendam turn-off). After 10km, Kliphoogte (blue sign) is on your left. Then 3km more on gravel road.

Augusta de Mist Country House

Madeleine and Rob Harrisson
3 Human St, Swellendam
Tel: 028-514-2425 Fax: 028-514-2057
Email: info@augustademist.co.za Web: www.augustademist.co.za
Cell: 082-829-1808

Cool, contemporary decor meets rustic heritage architecture at Augusta de Mist, each setting the other off to great advantage. And Madeleine and Rob are grandmaster hosts at this most laid-back of guest houses. Since our last visit two new luxury garden cottages have sprouted in the garden with white-linened, king-sized beds, spa baths and walk-in showers. Under reed-and-pole ceilings you'll find fireplaces, large indigo sofas or chairs and organza curtains billowing in the breeze. The main house is a unique Cape Dutch national monument, dated from 1802. Rob does up old tools and farm implements in his workshop, so all round the house you'll find intriguing wagon boxes, shutters, hinges, doors and once-cherished peasant furniture that has been tailored and restored under his furnace and bellows. The rose nursery garden is a peaceful haven with red-brick paths winding up the hill through banks of lavender towards the swimming pool with its swanky canvas brolly and loungers... and then off to the right over a stream. All the indigenous trees and shrubs mean an abundance of birds. From November to April local wines and cheese/cold platters are available for those who wish to give a full-on restaurant outing a miss. The platters can be enjoyed in the comfort of your own room in front of a log fire or on a private patio overlooking the garden.

Rooms: 8: 3 kings with bath and/or shower; 1 queen, 1 double & 2 twins with en-suite bath & sh'r; 1 queen with adjoining single & bath with sh'r.
Price: R380 – R800 pp sharing. Singles on request.
Meals: Full breakfast included. From Nov-Apr local wines & cheese/cold platters available in the comfort of your own room.
Directions: From Cape Town thro' village centre, past white church on left. As road bends to R, carry on straight for 20 metres. Then L into Human Str. From Garden Route down hill, past Drostdy Museum, over bridge, take R leg of triangle, then L, then R into Human Str.

The De Hoop Collection

Kate Naughton
The De Hoop Nature Reserve
Tel: 086-133-4667 Fax: 028-542-1679
Email: res@dehoopcollection.co.za Web: www.dehoopcollection.co.za

There are eighty-six species of mammals in the De Hoop Nature Reserve and, although I would have loved to see them all (and we did spot bontebok, eland, caracal and Cape mountain zebra on our trip around), for the clarity of my already sprawling notes it was some kind of blessing that we didn't. It leaves some for when I return, which I know will be soon. The accommodation belonging to the De Hoop Collection is as eclectic as the wildlife. I stayed in the De Hoop Village, made up of nine whitewashed cottages with three bedrooms. The table in the rustic kitchen was already laid when I arrived, and as I sat having supper a bontebok strolled past eating his. My double bed - covered in white linen and crowned by a handsome headboard - lay beneath a row of fynbos prints. Similar cottages and a few rondavels overlook the vlei, a stunning landmark of the reserve that turns golden at dusk. Houses, with larger rooms, are dotted amongst the milkwood trees. Luxury lies at the other end of the vlei: a four-bedroom manor house done up to its former glory. The song of some 260 species of birds was the only (!) sound. Hugging the sand dunes that make up the reserve's endless unspoilt beaches are the old fishermen's cottages of Koppie Alleen, making them ideally situated for whale-watching; from the courtyard I could hear their blowholes while I watched the shadows from the fire dance on the drawn curtains. As much as I don't want to share it, I can't help but implore you to go and discover this magical place for yourself. There is a restaurant, bar, deli and shop for provisions.

Rooms: Cottages, houses, manor houses, rondavels & camping spots available. Ring or look at website for details.
Price: R250 - R1,950 pp sharing, depending on accomodation.
Meals: There is a restaurant that provides breakfast, lunch and dinner.
Directions: From Cape Town take N2 to Caledon. Head to Bredasdorp on R316, & then Swellendam on R319. After c. 6km turn R at De Hoop/Malgas sign. Follow dirt road for c. 35km to reserve. For De Hoop Nature Reserve turn R at Buchu Bush sign.

Garden Route Side Dishes

Garden Route Side Dishes

A handful of highly-recommended things to do and places to eat in the Garden Route area...

The Shuntin' Shed

Wendy and Russell took a year to renovate this old railway goods shed, using authentic train paraphernalia. A relaxed ambience of old world charm sets the tone here. Whether it's pizza, ribs or steak you won't find a better vibe, sitting on the deck overlooking the valley. Only problem is, I won't be able to go for a pizza and beer anywhere else again.
*Contact: Wendy Voogt, Bot River train station; **Prices:** Mains R58 - R79, desserts R18 - R25; **Tel:** 028-284-9443; **Email:** shuntingshed@hermanus.co.za*

Outeniqua Adventure Tours

For a "wheely" good time (humble apologies), call Dave and Cheryl. They love the scenery of the Garden Route and Karoo and arrange 2-10 day cycling routes along quiet country roads in order to share it with you. If you don't fancy that, they run more traditional tours that focus on spending the minimum amount of time in the vehicle and the maximum exploring.
*Contact: Cheryl and Dave Griffiths, 29 Tarentaal Street, George; **Prices:** Between R600 - R900 per day depending on tour; **Tel:** 044-871-1470; 044-871-1470; **Email:** outntour@mweb.co.za; **Web:** www.outeniquatours.co.za*

île de päin

As expected with the name 'Bread Island', a variety of serious breads are baked in a wood-fired oven, in full view of regular and out-of-town guests. Chef/owner Liezie Mulder presides over the kitchen and turns the best that nature has to offer in the region into simple, wonderful and healthy meals for breakfast and lunch. The desserts are sublime alongside hot chocolate (made from Grand Cru Chocolate), proper coffees and other hot and cold specialty drinks. Take home some of the goodies and stock up on Ile de Pain's own professional "tools-of-the-trade", including Liezie's recently-published recipe collection. Also opened "Mon Petit Pain" on Corner of Gray and Gordon Streets. Same quality and vibe with lighter, quicker meals. Open 8-3pm Monday - Fridays, 8-1 Saturdays, Closed Sundays, 044-302-5767.
*Contact: Liezie Mulder, The Boatshed no.10, Thesen Islands, Knysna; **Prices:** Breakfast menu items R35 - R55, lunch R40 - R85, pastries R8 - R25, wines R100 - R 250 (and by the glass) breads R10 - R60. Prices may rise 10% a year. Open 8am-3pm, Sun 9-1:30, closed Mondays, May and August; **Tel:** 044-302-5707; 044-302-5706; **Email:** office@iledepain.co.za; **Web:** www.iledepain.co.za*

Oystercatcher Trail

Like the neighbouring Whale Trail in the Overberg, this three- or five-day coastal route leads you through some of the best scenery of the Garden Route. It's fully guided and portered, leaving you to plod happily along endless beaches and awesome cliffs, investigating ancient caves and rock pools, learning about the fascinating habits of the African black oystercatcher, as well as all the other flora and fauna, while soaking up fab Indian Ocean views. There is a good probability of sighting dolphins and whales (in season).
*Contact: Fred Orban; Mossel Bay; **Prices:** R3,550 for 3-day (2-night) hike until 30 Nov '09; R3,250 pp for groups of 9 or more; single supp' R150 per night; min 6, max*

12 hikers required. R5,850 for 5-day (4-night) trips. Prices all-inclusive. Book well in advance. Special quotes for smaller groups; **Tel:** *044-699-1204; 086-555-2604;* **Email:** *forban@mweb.co.za;* **Web:** *www.oystercatchertrail.co.za*

Old Nick Village

The secret's out! If you are looking for some of the best in South African craftsmanship and design, then head to the Old Nick Village. It's about local, about good quality and individuality in textiles, ceramics, clothing and accessories, all linked by the common thread of Africa. After a hard morning's shopping, treat yourself to a slap-up lunch and wander through the surrounding indigenous gardens. Expect special exhibitions, lazy afternoons on lawns or encounters with the odd vervet monkey
Contact: *Janet Holding, N2 Highway, 3km east of Plettenberg Bay;* **Prices:** *From R15 for hand-made soap to R50,000 for custom-designed steel and ceramic water feature;* **Tel:** *044-533-1395; 044-533-0521;* **Email:** *info@oldnickvillage.co.za;* **Web:** *www.oldnickvillage.co.za*

Stormsriver Adventures

When guides Rachel and Leanco asked if anyone had any serious medical conditions, I forgot to mention my vertigo! Somehow, I conquered my fear and zip-wired from yellowwood to yellowwood through the Tsitsikamma forest canopy. Perfect for nature-lovers and adrenaline-junkies alike. Other Stormsriver Adventures activities include abseiling into and tubing down the river or cycling and walking pretty much anywhere.
Contact: *Anneline Wyatt, Darnell Street, Storms River Village;* **Prices:** *Canopy tours R395;* **Tel:** *042-281-1836;* **Email:** *adventure@gardenroute.co.za;* **Web:** *www.stormsriver.com;*

Bramon Wine Estate and Restaurant

Bramon Wine Estate is the Garden Route name currently on everyone's lips and with good reason. Enjoy fresh oysters, meze platters, local wines and cheeses, while the eye rests on the Tsitsikamma Mountains and surrounding vineyards. Is there a better way to spend an afternoon? Peter Thorpe's vision of empowering local communities through his Vukani ("wake-up") wines and the Vukani Trust is one worth embracing.
Contact: *Peter and Caroline Thorpe, The Crags;* **Prices:** *Meze platter from R8 - R40 each. Wines R75 - R100 a bottle;* **Tel:** *044-534-8007;* **Email:** *caroline@bramonwines.co.za;* **Web:** *www.bramonwines.co.za*

Serendipity

The whole dining experience at Serendipity is one that will shine in my memory forever. Here you are unobtrusively pampered. Rudolf is in charge of looking after you while Lizelle (a champion chef) works culinary wonders preparing a five-course table d'hote menu that changes regularly. I was dazzled afresh with each course, from the fireside apéritifs to the Warm Dark Chocolate Mousse, Milk Stout Ice Cream and Mock Coffee Sponge (possibly the best dessert to ever melt in my mouth). Sigh....
Contact: *Freesia Lane, Wilderness;* **Prices:** *R279 for 5-course table d'hôte menu;* **Tel:** *044-877-0433; 0866-843-655;* **Email:** *chef123@mweb.co.za;* **Web:** *www.serendipitywilderness.com*

Waterkloof Guesthouse

Hannes and Christine Uys
Waterkloof Farm, On R324 near Witsand
Tel: 028-722-1811 Fax: 028-722-1811
Email: info@waterkloofguesthouse.co.za
Web: www.waterkloofguesthouse.co.za Cell: 083-270-2348

Ever played chicken with an ostrich? Now's your chance. Admittedly I had the protection of a bull-barred pick-up truck but it was exciting stuff, rattling around the farm collecting still-warm eggs for the incubator and doing our best to avoid overly ruffling their fathers' feathers. Waterkloof is an ostrich farm through and through and there is nothing that Hannes (only the seventh generation of the Uys family to work this land!) doesn't know about these feisty fowl. They use the leather for bags, the eggs for breakfast, the eggshells for lampshades and the meat for supper (Christine is quietly a master of this). Sunk into rolling fields of barley and wheat, this is a hard-working farm but a great place to take it easy. Cool, luxurious bedrooms open onto the garden and fountain, wild fig trees shade benches built for reading on and the pool area has its own kitchen for help-yourself Sunday lunches. And if you feel like a change of scenery (and wildlife), Witsand is the place to see migrating whales. Back at the house Hannes patiently answered my babble of questions as we sank into ostrich-leather-covered armchairs and tucked into Christine's cheesecake - no ostrich in that, I take it. *Leather goods made by Italian designers in Cape Town are sold here for a third of the price too! The bathrooms have just been upgraded with brand-new showers and Victorian baths after a thunderstorm caused a flood in the house.*

Rooms: 4: 2 doubles and 1 twin all with bath and shower, 1 twin with shower.
Price: R280 - R450 pp sharing.
Meals: Full breakfast included. Dinner on request.
Directions: From the CT and the N2 turn R onto R324 after Swellendam 32 to the farm. From Mossel Bay take R322 to Witsand. At the crossroads turn R. Farm is on the L after 17 km.

River Magic

Bosky and Paul Andrew
Reservations: 35 Pear Lane, Constantia, Cape Town, Physical address:, Riversdale/Vermaaklikheid 7806 Tel: 021-794-6294 or 028-713-2930 Fax: 021-794-6294 or 028-713-2930 Cell: 082-732-3003 Email: rivermagic@zsd.co.za Web: www.vermaaklikheid.co.za

"Welcome to the centre of the universe," said Paul, as our tubby little rowing boat sliced through the early morning mist, its oars stirring the clear cola-coloured water and groaning in their rollocks. We bumped gently against the jetty and then hopped out onto a dew-damp riverbank, the best and, for that matter, only way to arrive at River Magic's 'Glory Be'. Silence. I fumbled for an appropriate superlative. What a spot... what a find. Two low, stone-built, thatched cottages, buried in the folds of brush-carpeted, ancient sand dunes and, without doubt, the most enchanting place I had yet encountered. I longed to return with a gang of pals, threading our way between the banks of Spanish reed, ferrying supplies across the river, fishing for grunter from the jetty (or canoes) and sharing beers and a braai around the huge outdoor table on the even more enormous shaded verandah. Inside, the cottages are comfortably (not extravagantly) kitted-out with wooden furniture and all kitchen essentials. There are beds for as many as you can muster, some secluded, others tucked into tents or in sociable four-man rooms. On a hot tip, I wheeled mine outside to sleep under the stars where I lay heaped in a duvet, inventing constellations, listening to hadedahs in the blue gums and scribbling notes by torchlight. Sound alright?

Rooms: 3 cottages: Glory Be sleeps 12 in 5 bedrooms (3 en-suite); Back Track sleeps 6 (1 double and 1 twin en/s shr, 1 twin bed in tented hut); Base Huis sleeps 8 - 10 (2 twins, 1 double, 1 x 4-bed, 1 separate bath and shower).
Price: From R150 - R170 pp sharing. Min R500 - R600 per cottage per night. Min R500 - R800 over long weekends and R800 - R1,500 over Christmas.
Meals: Self-catering, bring your own towels and torches. Wood for sale. Seafood restau' nearby.
Directions: From Cape Town 50km after Swellendam & 3km before Heidelberg turn R at 'Port Beauford: Witsand' sign. 6km down tar rd, turn L at dirt rd signed Vermaaklikheid. 14km turn L at T-jct, cross Duivenshok River over causeway. Follow signs to Vermaaklikheid & on to River Magic.

De Doornkraal Historic Country House

Jacolette De Necker (Olivier)
8 Lang Street, Riversdale
Tel: 028-713-3838 Fax: 028-713-3050
Email: dedoornkraal@mweb.co.za Web: www.dedoornkraal.com
Cell: 082-958-0622

If the hectic pace of today's world leaves you feeling out of breath, or even slightly nauseous, I couldn't think of a more suitable antidote than a stay at De Doornkraal. Formerly a doctor's surgery (operations can still legally be performed on the premises!), this Cape Dutch beauty dates back to 1746 and is one of the oldest buildings in Riversdale. Also found here is a 200-year-old vine, the oldest on the Garden Route and still providing grapes for the breakfast jam. Listen carefully and you can almost hear the history echoing through these walls; you can certainly see it anyway. After a painstaking restoration, the original yellowwood and Oregon pine floors and ceilings, blackwood furnishings and the stunning rosewood front door are now revealed in all their former glory. Understatedly elegant rooms have simple, neutral-coloured upholstery so as not to upstage the beautiful woodwork throughout. Original paintings add splashes of colour, the work of a well-known artist, Johannes Meintjes, who previously lived here. They also share a fine drawing room with honesty bar, the ideal place for an after-dinner nightcap. Across the road are two comfortable and airy cottages set by a large willow-shaded pond and the Syrah vineyard that rolls towards the river's bank. Honeymooners can contentedly picnic under the oaks here, while children could acquaint themselves with the aquatic and farm animal neighbours. Happily, I sat listening to the fountain murmur in the tea garden, lost to the outside world; its only reminder hoots from the twice-daily steam-train that runs through an otherwise sleepy town.

Rooms: 15: 3 in Meintjes House (2 queens & 1 twin, all en-s bath/shower, sharing lounge); 9 in annex (3 queen, 6 twin, all en-s bath/sh'r) Ceder Cottage (1 queen, lounge & en-s sh'r); Willow C'tge (1 queen, en-s bath/sh'r, 1 twin en-s sh'r, lounge & kitchenette).
Price: R425 - R860 pp sharing. Single supplement +50%.
Meals: Full breakfast included. Lunch and dinner on request. Restaurant open for private functions.
Directions: N2 from Cape Town to Riversdale, L into town at the main entrance, follow signboards. Turn L just before you leave town into Lang Street. 100m on LHS.

Riversong Farm

Piers Sibson

Waterblom Avenue, Stilbaai (Still Bay)
Tel: 028 754-3427
Email: pierss@mweb.co.za Web: www.riversongfarm.co.za
Cell: 082-374-8274

Rustic, down-to-earth and outdoorsy. If these words jump out at you, then this is a truly great find. Sheltered by reeds and milkwood trees on the banks of the Goukou River, Riversong Farm is the ideal spot to relax, get outside and experience nature's simple pleasures. In fact it would be shameful not to spend at least most of the time by, in or on the river or off exploring the farm's kloofs, dams and bushman paintings as it stretches back into the fynbos backlands beyond (also ripe for investigation). Not that the indoors is not for enjoying as well. The three wooden chalets are comfortable, unfussy and cosy affairs, one of which sits on the river's edge. Each has a well-equipped kitchen, open fire and verandah from which you can follow the river as it idles its way down to the Indian Ocean. Braais in the chalets and on the lawn by the reed-lined deck provide ample opportunity to cook up the day's catch. Also living on this working farm are Simon and Manuela, both very knowledgeable about the area's wildlife, particularly the abundant bird life. Barely had I stepped out of the car before I had seen two eagles! So, with all this on hand and surfing, golf, 4x4 trails, and horse-riding nearby, I promise there won't be a dull moment. *Pets welcome!*

Rooms: 3 chalets: Thames sleeps 4 (1 double bed, plus 2 single bunk beds, en-suite bathroom); Orange sleeps 4 (2 rooms - 1 double bed with en-suite shower/loo, 2 single beds with en-suite loo); Jordan sleeps 2 (1 double bed with en-suite bathroom).
Price: Seasonal. R120 – R155 pp sharing. Min R450 per chalet. Min 2 nights. Special rates for longer stays on whole farm..
Meals: Fully self-catering. Fishing and boating permits are available from the local village.
Directions: Between Riversdale and Albertinia on the N2, take the Stilbaai turn-off towards the sea. Once in town R over bridge, then immediately R into Waterblom Avenue. Farm clearly named about 12km upriver.

Map Number: 2

Sandpiper Cottages

Fred Orban

Boggoms Bay, Mossel Bay District
Tel: 044-699-1204 Fax: 044-699-1951
Email: stay@sandpipersafaris.co.za Web: www.sandpiper.co.za
Cell: 082-550-4788

This secretive beachside spot is creeping shyly onto the map with Sandpiper's budding cluster of thatched white-walled fishermen's cottages. Fred, a developer by trade, started building with his children in mind but, like swallows, they have flown to Europe, leaving you to take up residence instead. My favourite was Fred's most recent project, the honeymoon cottage, christened 'Sea Mist'. Here a tender haze emanates from the affectionately planned and implemented interiors. Red clay tile floors are ornamented with yellowwood and Oregon pine furniture, while a sleeper-wood worktop and recycled timber staircase showcase Sandpiper's originality and your host's particular love of old wood. An extraordinary hearth gathers you with fire-warmed fingers into its seated inglenook and a three-roomed bathroom flaunts its own lounge. Hugely roomy yet indisputably cosy, the varied cottages combine an atmosphere of the past with luxuries of today. Fred himself is a truly lovely chap and, although the cottages are fully self-catered, he can sort you out with a 'real Boggoms breakfast' and even dinner as well. You will certainly need the energy if you want to make the most of the superb Fred-built sports centre and spa and hike the dazzling, Fred-established Oystercatcher Trail. Untamed fynbos encourages bees, buck, rabbits and birds to gather in the garden; the vegetation extends from your cottage to the beach where sand and rock scuffle with the sea, vying for attention with the distant Outeniqua Mountains.

Rooms: 5 cottages: 2 with 2 beds, and 3 with 3 beds. All have multiple bathrooms.
Price: Self-catering R290 - R550 pp sharing; B&B R350 - R630 pp sharing. Singles on request. Minimum 2-night stay.
Meals: Meals on request. Full or continental breakfast can be delivered to self-catering cottages for R75 pp. Evening meals R125 pp (excluding wine) ordered 1-2 days in advance.
Directions: From Cape Town along N2 towards Mossel Bay, turn R 34km after Albertinia at Boggoms Bay junction. Continue for 11km before L into village. More detailed directions can be emailed.

Botlierskop Private Game Reserve

The Neethling family

Little Brak River
Tel: 011-696-6055 Fax: 044 696 6272
Email: info@botlierskop.co.za Web: www.botlierskop.co.za
Cell: 082-563-8226

The Garden Route is best known for its scenery and sea life, so the last thing I expected to see as I navigated the back roads was a rhino. But there it was, chewing the cud like a contented cow. Botlierskop is a private game reserve that brings the big five south. It's not as wild as its northern counterparts (the lions are in a sanctuary) but it's a magical place to stay, set in 3,000 hectares of grassy plains and forested sandstone hills. The park is open to day visitors, though they use a separate day centre. A real highlight is Sam and Tsotsi, orphaned elephants - now proud parents - who are trained not only in giving rides, but also as actors. Did you see *Far of Place*? Or *Elephant Boy*? Trust me they were great! Morning coffee with the rhino is also a must and personally I found nibbling on live termites pleasantly minty. Overnighters are appointed their own private guide and I had Billy, an animal almanac and rock art aficionado. From the cavernous hilltop restaurant, he ushered me into a dinghy and we drifted off down the wooded Moordkuil River before showing me to my tent. More of a marquee than a tent, each is set above the river, giving a splendid view of both the water and the hills opposite. Inside it's luxury with a capital 'L'; deep armchairs, a writing desk and a room-for-two bath accompany the mosquito-netted four-poster. One tip though: zip it closed when you leave for the swimming pool – the vervet monkeys have a penchant for coffee and cookies.

Rooms: 15 Luxury, Deluxe and Executive Tented Suites. All with en-suite bath and outdoor showers; Executive has its own lounge and outdoor splash pool. A solar-heated pool is available at the lodge.
Price: R2,107 - R3,112 pp shg (inc. 2 game drives, meals & drinks). Singles R3,160 - R4,668. Child (6-12) 1/2 adult rate. 2-day stay incl. free horseback ride and 3-day stay incl. free helicopter ride.
Meals: Breakfast and dinner included and lunch as well if staying 2 or more nights.
Directions: From Mossel Bay and CT on N2 take Little Brak River exit (401). Heading inland turn R to Sorgfontein. Continue 4km and after causeway turn R for 4km along gravel road to Botlierskop.

Map Number: 2

Malvern Manor

Sandra and Michael Cook
Nr Fancourt, Blanco, George
Tel: 044-870-8788 Fax: 044-870-8790
Email: info@malvernmanor.co.za Web: www.malvernmanor.co.za
Cell: 084-867-6470

If you are having any difficulty understanding why the area is called the Garden Route, well, have a trundle up Michael and Sandra's drive. Much more colourful and vibrant than anything visible from the public thoroughfares. I drove past cows and dams onto a redbrick road overflowing with thick tangles of foliage that hide Malvern from view - and all this perfectly framed by the imposing Outeniqua Mountains. Here is another English couple who fell in love with South Africa, upped sticks and bought their country idyll. They are both of farming stock, so this 21-hectare dairy farm was perfect. But despite being just a hop, skip and a jump from George, it was no easy task converting the Manor House, the keep at the heart of the farm, into a guest house. But it's all come together so nicely. My room opened onto the garden through French doors, and lavish Greek-style pillars pick out the bath – the perfect place to unwind after a round of golf at Fancourt (recent host of the President's Cup). For non-golfers, two dams offer blue gill and big-mouth bass fishing and there's endless scope for pre-breakfast walks or watching DVDs on the newly-installed players. Play your cards right on your return and Michael might don his apron and prepare his speciality 'chocaccino'. Delightful people in an enchanting setting.

Rooms: 3: 1 queen, 1 twin or king, 1 double with single bed. All have en-suite bath and shower.
Price: R550 - R750 pp sharing. Singles on request.
Meals: Full breakfast included. Restaurants nearby and deliveries can be arranged.
Directions: From N2 take George airport exit onto R404 and follow signs to Oudtshoorn for approximately 8km. After Fancourt Golfing Estate, sign to Malvern Manor on left. Follow signs.

Fairview Historic Homestead

Philda Benkenstein

36 Stander St, George
Tel: 044-874-7781
Fax: 086-603-7840
Email:
benkenstein@mweb.co.za
Web:
www.fairviewhomestead.
com
Cell: 082-226-9466

This picturesque, listed Cape Georgian house on the eastern edge of George is an intriguing place to stay. With its high ceilings and abundant Victoriana, Fairview has the feel of an old English rectory, although the vivid colours owe more to African than Anglican themes. The bedrooms are a treat: they still have their original 1880s floorboards, beams and fireplaces; the Orange Room, complete with dashing white trim, bathes in afternoon sunlight; while the Yellow Room soaks up the morning. The sitting room has the same high ceilings and wooden floors, with shuttered sash windows and enormous linen press. Alternatively, a cosy (self-contained) self-catering double offers guests a quaint, private garden with braai facilities. The whole place has a happy family atmosphere, enhanced by the original home features, which have been retained wherever possible. Philda loves to host and have people in her beautiful home. She will cook too and if you do eat here, as the GG guests visiting were, then you'll enjoy mainly South African fare. She's an intrepid hiker too and following her advice I soon found myself on a mountainside with sweeping views over George. Husband Desmond is a green-fingered doctor and the creative force in the glorious garden. There are fruit trees, an immaculate veggie patch, swathes of clivia and plans for much more.

Rooms: 3: 1 double with en-suite shower; 1 double with en-suite bath and shower; 1 double self-catering (B&B optional) with en-suite shower.
Price: R400 - R500 pp sharing (B&B); R300 - R400 pp sharing (self-catering). Singles plus 40%.
Meals: Full breakfast included. Dinner by arrangement: R100 pp for 2 courses, R150 pp for 3 courses. Prices exclude wine.
Directions: Take York St exit off N2. Go up York St to roundabout in front of museum. Go toward Knysna on Courtney Rd past High School & over rwy bdge. L at 1st lights after rwy bdge into First St; over Stop St & R into Stander at T-jct. From Knysna R at 5th lights (just before bridge) into First St & over Stop St & turn R into Stander at T-jct.

Map Number: 2 & 5

Entry Number: 151

Acorn Guest House

Colin and Esther Horn
4 Kerk St, George
Tel: 044-874-0474 Fax: 086-610-7854
Email: info@acornguesthouse.co.za Web: www.acornguesthouse.co.za
Cell: 083-539-7398

With birds chirping in the tree-lined street and church bells chiming (kerk is Afrikaans for church), I approached the pink, ivy-clad walls utterly unaware of the riches hidden within. Acorn Guest House is a veritable treasure trove and Esther was quick to explain: "as some people go to casinos, we go to auctions." Almost everything in this Edwardian house is second-hand and antique. Persian rugs are strewn over bare floorboards; battered wooden trunks are scattered throughout the bedrooms; mirrors and ornaments adorn the available wall space; every nook and cranny arrests the eye. The bedrooms are equally ornate, the master room boasting a large en-suite bathroom separated from the grand sleeping area by a gold-coloured curtain. Had I stayed a little longer (and deprived the Horns of even more of Esther's delicious home-baked cake), I could have joined Colin on a fishing trip… although not the leisurely pipe-and-picnic fishing I had envisaged. "If guests are able to swim 4km in the sea with a snorkel, they're welcome to join me," he proclaimed, re-emerging with his weapon of choice, a spear gun. If all this sounds a bit too James Bond for you, he also offers more serene tours of the Garden Route. Those with spoils to share come evening do so on the braai, while bargain-hunters furiously jot down Esther's top tips.

Rooms: 8: 2 twins with en-suite bath and shower; 2 doubles with en-suite bath/shower; 1 double with en-suite bath and shower; 1 family unit with en-suite shower; 1 twin/king with full disabled provision, spa bath & shower, 1 double with en-suite shower.
Price: R275 - R650 pp sharing. Singles +50%.
Meals: Full breakfast included. Picnic basket and dinner by arrangement. Self-catering facilities available.
Directions: Take York Street exit off N2 towards town. Go through town on York Street until the roundabout. Turn right (signed to Knysna) and Kerk Street is third turning on left. Second property on right.

The Waves

Liza and Iain Campbell

7 Beach Rd, Victoria Bay, George
Tel: 044-889-0166 Fax: 044-889-0166
Email: thewaves@intekom.co.za
Web: www.gardenroute.co.za/vbay/waves/index.htm

Iain and Liza have an amazing photo from 1906 when The Waves was the only house on the beach, used as a holiday home by an Oudtshoorn farmer. It is not surprising a few others have since joined the club. The hamlet is closed to vehicles – only residents hold the key to the gate, so you can park your car securely at night. I'm no surfer, but the waves here are enticing, rolling up the perfect arc of the small bay at a height that is challenging, but not scary. Iain will arrange a wetsuit and surfboard or fins and a snorkel. Or if you like your activity less damp, there is horse-riding nearby, dolphin- and whale-watching in season and walks along the bay front. The house is right on the sea (see above) to which all three bedroom suites (each with its own lounge) look out, although you may spend more time on the verandah watching the waves roll in. They are hypnotic. Breakfast is served here in the sunshine and often goes on for hours. Both Iain and Liza are consummate hosts, love what they do and share a great sense of fun. Bay life could be addictive. *Fully non-smoking everywhere. Children over 12 only.*

Rooms: 5: 3 B&B rooms, all doubles, 1 with en-suite shower, 2 with en-suite bath and shower; 1 cottage and 1 suite available for self-catering.
Price: R550 - R900 pp sharing out of season. R750 - R1,000 in season.
Meals: Full breakfast included.
Directions: From Mossel Bay on N2 past George exits where highways merge. 1km signed Victoria Bay to right - follow down hill 3km. Park and walk along beach road to collect the key for the gate.

Map Number: 2 & 5

Entry Number: 153

Porcupine Pie Boutique Lodge

John and Judy McIldowie
10 Mile Lane, Wilderness Heights
Email: john@porcupinepie.co.za Web: www.porcupinepie.co.za
Cell: 083-447-6901

You really are on top of the world here - even the air smells different at this height! Porcupine Pie, nestled at the end of a winding, climbing road, has some simply breathtaking views. The Wilderness Nature Reserve and the Outeniqua Mountains unfurl before you, and a wedge of stunning blue sea looks out out between its foliage-fringed peaks. A rare commotion of birds provides possibly the best on-site birding around. You don't even need to leave the deck, just whip out a pair of bino's and watch. In the time it took me to munch just one of their biscuits, I had seen an eagle and two resident jackal buzzards. I arrived on a freakishly hot winter's day (30 degrees!), so I braved a swim before warming up in a candlelit bath. And when I looked up mid-bath, there was that view again. Each bedroom unit is a stilted wooden chalet with a patio that hovers mid-air. Judy's artwork hangs on the walls including, of course, a porcupine. During the home-made supper of chicken stuffed with feta, I had to ask, why Porcupine Pie? The morning after they laid the guesthouse path, John explained, they found a small pair of porcupine prints in the wet concrete. So really the place named itself. They do all the cooking (don't miss Judy's breakfast bran muffins), including portered picnics in the river valley below. Dozing off that night with the French windows wide open, the bush-frogs ribbeted me to sleep. No understatement here... it was the best night's kip I'd had in months.

Rooms: 3: all kings with en-suite bath and shower.
Price: R450 - R750 pp sharing.
Meals: Full breakfast included. Two-course dinners approx R100 pp.
Directions: From George follow N2 to Wilderness. Turn L into Wilderness Village, follow road past Protea Hotel to T-junction. Turn L and travel up Heights Rd for 3.8km. Do not turn off tar until you reach T-jct marked 'Old George/Knysna Road'. Turn R onto gravel road and after 1.6km turn R onto 'Ten Mile Lane'. Follow Porcupine Signs for 3.4km.

Whale's Way Ocean Retreat

Tim Ivison and Ali Drummond

858 6th Avenue, Wilderness
Tel: 044-877-0482 Fax: 044-877-0436
Email: themagic@whalesway.co.za Web: www.whalesway.co.za
Cell: 076-371-4601

According to Tim and Ali this is "a place where magic happens". It certainly seemed like an optical illusion when Tim first showed me to my room, opening a door marked 'Ocean' onto a world of white. It was like entering the delicate vastness of a giant seashell, one that comes equipped with king-size bed and spa bath. Both ends of the room are more windows than walls and frame a different view, while the high white-beamed ceiling hovers gently above. You can lie, mesmerised by the wide expanse of sea from the wide expanse of your bed or wallow in the jacuzzi admiring the mountainous backdrop of Wilderness Nature Reserve. Left to unpack I suppressed urges to cartwheel from one end of the room to the other (I calculated a good 10 would do it) opting for the more socially acceptable practice of quietly playing my guitar. When I chose to rejoin reality, Tim proved himself a faultless host and conversation flowed freely into the night. Ali is qualified in Ki massage, a wonderful added bonus in situ. Unfortunately she was away when I visited and I missed out on one of Whale's Way's many heavenly experiences. Warmed by an evening's food, drink and chat I dived beneath waves of cotton and floated gently into sleep while promises of a sunrise bathe whispered soothingly from the sea.

Rooms: 4 kings with en-suite bath and shower.
Price: R500 - R1,200 pp sharing. Singles by arrangement.
Meals: Full breakfast included.
Directions: Travelling from George, stay on the N2, passing the turn-off to Wilderness on your left. Continue driving for about 3km. Turn right at the Wilderness Beach Hotel. Turn left at the small roundabout behind the Caltex garage and follow the signs to Whale's Way.

Moontide Guest Lodge

Maureen Mansfield
Southside Rd, Wilderness
Tel: 044-877-0361 Fax: 044-877-0124
Email: moontide@intekom.co.za Web: www.moontide.co.za

It's a rare pleasure for us to stay somewhere on holiday and to experience it over a period of days. And Moontide was a palpable hit with all five of us. Its position is hard to beat, right on the banks of the lagoon, its wooden decks shaded by 400-year-old milkwood trees. Here you can sit out for bountiful breakfasts or with an evening drink from your bar fridge, and watch giant kingfishers diving for fish – well, we saw one anyway. Birdlife is profuse on the lagoon. The long, white-sanded Wilderness beach is only a two-minute walk from the house, but you can also take a canoe straight from Moontide up the lagoon into the Touw River and then walk along forest trails to waterfalls to swim in fresh-water rock pools. Whatever we did it was a pleasure to return, play cards in a relaxed sitting room, or read in the cool of a bedroom. I was delighted with 'Milkwood' because I'm a sucker for dozing on a futon, in a loft, under thatched eaves, with river views by my head. But I would like to return and try them all. Since we descended en masse, Maureen has built herself a tree-top sanctuary. The deck, day-bed, even the free-standing bath, look out across thatched roofs to the river. Sportingly, she's decided it's too nice to keep for herself!

Rooms: 8: Moonriver Luxury Suite (king, 2 twins, bath, sh'r); Treetops (qu, bath, outside sh'r); Milkwood (king/twins & queen upstairs, bath, sh'r); Stone Cottage (twins, sh'r); The Boathouse (d'ble, bath); Moonshadow 1 & 2 (kings, baths & sh'rs); Nest (king, shower).
Price: R440 - R825 pp sharing. Single +70%.
Meals: Full breakfast included. Self-catering option available in the Nest.
Directions: From George on N2 ignore Wilderness turn-off. Cross Touw River bridge, first left signed Southside Rd. Moontide at the end of cul-de-sac.

Slanting Acres

Pam Ross
Bitou Road, Hoekwil, Wilderness
Tel: 044 850 1195 Fax: 044 850 1195
Email: reservations@slantingacres.com Web: www.slantingacres.com
Cell: 082-907-2404

Horses were chewing, birds were roosting, ducks were swimming, cats were purring, chickens were foraging, peacocks were displaying by the new tennis court and the guinea fowl… were just being guinea fowl. Animals are everywhere on Slanting Acres' slanting seven and a half acres, plenty of room for everyone. The immaculate lawns sweep around this white-washed, wood-decked house, hoisted high on the Hoekwil hillside, with far-reaching views over Wilderness and into the wilderness of the deep-blue Indian Ocean. Equally blue is the figure-of-eight-shaped pool, where a waterfall is a constant cooling sight and sound. If lazing by the pool is not enough to occupy your mind, there is always the 18-hole putting green and the brand-new tennis court. Personally I would prefer to sink one in the nautically-themed bar inside. Iain is a ship's captain in the merchant navy and he'll happily tell you all about his life at sea… that is if he is not actually at sea when you visit. Pictures of the various ships he's skippered fill the walls. Pam will keep you entertained in his absence. She's the driving force behind Slanting Acres. The bedrooms are small, but perfectly formed with white cotton sheets, pine wardrobes and plenty of light. And Pam now has a new Peacock Suite (graced by the roaming presence of those colourful beauties) in addition to the honeymoon Garden Suite, with king-size bed, spa bath and stunning views of mountains and sea from the private decks. Homely comforts in a very friendly house.

Rooms: 5: 2 doubles and 1 twin, all with en-suite showers; 1 king with en-suite spa bath; Peacock Suite: 1 queen with en-suite spa bath, TV, bar fridge, air-con, sea and mountain view from private deck.
Price: R350 - R550 pp sharing B&B. Singles + 25%.
Meals: Full breakfast included. Lots of restaurants nearby.
Directions: From Cape Town take the N2 past George and 2km past Wilderness turn L to Hoekwil. Pass the lake and go over railway, up hill and turn R at 1st brown B&B sign.

Kingfisher Country House

Sue Millard

1030 Dumbleton Road, Wilderness
Tel: 044-877-1955 Fax: 044-877-1955
Email: info@kingfish.co.za Web: www.kingfish.co.za
Cell: 082-808-4379

Bring your camera to breakfast as you sit on the covered verandah overlooking stunning gardens. This is the best seat in the house for catching sight of, among other startlingly beautiful birds, the Knysna loerie, whose red velvet wing feathers tease and tantalise no less than three times a day when they come to feed. Ideally situated on the edge of the Wilderness National Park, this is a paradise for birds and for those who watch them. The forest too comes right down to this family home, the sunlight dappling through the trees onto floral and feminine nuances throughout. The rooms are just like Sue: warm, gentle and immediately relaxing. Oil lamps hang low, bringing lustre to assortments of coloured bottles and pretty boudoirs. Linen arches drape over friendly beds while curtains are full of summer, complemented by fresh flowers and still-life pictures of potted trees and plants, courtesy of Sue's daughter, Alexandra. Enjoy the feel of cocoa butter soap on the skin as you rejuvenate in the shower, before wrapping yourself in soft bath robes, choosing then perhaps to lean over the stable door, hung with tiny herb garlands, to wave hello to your neighbour. Victorian christening robes float in the hallway next to African baskets and Sue loves her frills, but she has toned it down for the more 'masculine' rooms. I took tea with her in the quirky living room where she delighted in filling my diary full of canoe and hiking trips, as well as dinner reservations in a handful of excellent restaurants.

Rooms: 4: all twin/king with en-suite shower bathrooms.
Price: R275 - R400 pp sharing. Singles on request.
Meals: Full breakfast included. Plenty of good restaurants.
Directions: Take Wilderness turning from the N2 and follow Waterside Road around the far side of the lagoon. Continue for 2km until signpost to Kingfisher Country House on the right, followed by a turning immediately to the left. The house is 200m from here.

The Dune Guest Lodge

Gary and Melisa Grimes

31 Die Duin, Wilderness
Tel: 044-877-0298 Fax: 044-877-0298
Email: info@thedune.co.za Web: www.thedune.co.za
Cell: 083-941-1149

Gary Grimes is both consummate host and chief breakfast-maker at The Dune and when I pulled up (carefully avoiding parking in the space marked "for my girlfriend/wife") he and Melisa had just finished feeding the hordes with a man-stopping fry-up. "Anything you can do with eggs, I do it," he tells me. I made a note to arrive a little earlier next time. By most standards, he is greedily tall, but at 6'7" he insists he was pretty average among his basketball contemporaries and after years as a pro in Switzerland he dropped the ball in favour of a dishcloth, dinner plates and the wildness of Wilderness. If you're looking for a beach-house then you couldn't get much more beachy than this. As the name suggests it's smack-bang in the dunes and, to be numerically fastidious, exactly 85 wooden steps lead down to 7.5km of pristine sandy beach stretching away to both east and west. The whole place has a wonderfully soothing, seaside feel. Walls hung with seascape oils are whitewashed or sea-blue. Driftwood sculptures surround the fireplace and bedside sofas look south through wall-to-wall windows for round-the-clock whale-watching. Best of all though, wherever you are in the building, you can hear the surf heaving, sighing, thumping and crumping against the beach.

Rooms: 5: 2 doubles, 2 twins with 3/4 beds, all with en/s bath and shower. 1 self-catering cottage.
Price: R350 – R800 pp sharing B&B. Singles +R200.
Meals: Full breakfast included.
Directions: From CT pass Wilderness on N2. Cross the Touw River and turn right into Die Duin 700m later. Take the right fork and The Dune is first on the left.

Serendipity

Phillip and Elsabé Kuypers

Freesia Avenue, Wilderness
Tel: 044-877-0433 Fax: 0866-717-992
Email: info@serendipitywilderness.com
Web: www.serendipitywilderness.com Cell: 082-4499-701

Where else can you dine in arguably the best restaurant on the Garden Route and then wander upstairs to snuggle into bed beneath goose-down duvets? This is a place whose name is breathed in quiet reverence all along the coast. Other Wilderness guesthouses flatly refuse to cater. "What's the point?" they say with community pride. Brushed up crisply for dinner after a three-chapter-long soak in the bath, I stepped from underfloor-heated tiles onto the shared balcony, to watch geese flighting across a sunset lagoon. Then it was an easy meander down to the guest lounge for an apéritif, where Rudolf, husband to head-chef Lizelle (her culinary accolades, which hang in the loo, are very encouraging indeed), gave a sensuous description of a South African-inspired menu combined with European haute cuisine. Agonising, I finally plumped for snoek mousse and loin of springbok, variously interspersed by an amuse-bouche of kudu carpaccio and delicious butternut soup. The intimate restaurant discreetly backs onto a fireplace flanked by sheer windows looking out onto the water. For dessert I cracked into an exquisitely fruity crème brûlée, even as my waiter taught me the basics of Xhosa. Following a breakfast in ebullient sunshine I found myself discussing semantics and champion deep-sea angling with owners Elsabé and Phillip, who had originally planned to run only a guesthouse... that was before they invited their daughter to cook.

Rooms: 4: all twin/king with en-suite shower bathrooms.
Price: R380 - R640 pp sharing. Singles +50%.
Meals: Full breakfast included. Dinner in restaurant by prior arrangement.
Directions: From N2 at Wilderness turn North at Caltex garage following George Road to T-junction in front of Protea Hotel. At T-junction turn right, travel along Waterside Road for 1.2km. Turn right into Freesia Avenue. Serendipity 4th house on right.

Lodge on the Lake

Frank Brauer

746 North Street, Wilderness
Tel: 044-877-1097 Fax: 044-877-1097
Email: info@lodgeonthelake.co.za
Web: www.accommodation-wilderness.com Cell: 084-383-7766

Übercool has come to Wilderness. Frank used to be in film production and his eye for precision design underlies every detail in this grandly Tuscan villa, which sits resplendent on its many pillars above the lake. As I skirted the central courtyard fountain and entered beneath the portico, something magic seemed to happen. The walls suddenly disappeared, the outside was inexplicably coming inside... but most mesmerising of all was the lake that had effortlessly risen, without a ripple, to the rim of the pool and forged a seamless sheet of the deepest liquid blue, only finally interrupted by the mountains. I suppose that's what you call German engineering. There's a Zen-like tranquillity here, a faraway sound of trickling water, which recently attracted a pair of authors; no one's sure whether they wrote anything. More than likely they discovered the delights of the in-house spa where three treatment rooms employ the mineral wealth of the sea to leave you feeling as fresh as the surf. Naturally the rooms, reached by a winding staircase, are mindful of weight, colour and proportion to the enth degree. Thick carpeting softens a solemnity of dark wooden bedsteads, cupboards and ingenious concertina doors, with a sense of playfulness creeping into striking patterns, stalactite pillars, open tubs and creative positioning of mirrors. Each has its own fabulous private balcony.

Rooms: 5: 4 doubles, 1 twin; all en-suite bath and shower.
Price: R350 - R900 pp sharing.
Meals: Full or continental breakfast included.
Directions: Emailed or faxed on booking.

Wilderness Manor

Gerald Hoch and John-David (JD) Janse van Rensburg

397 Waterside Road, Wilderness
Tel: 044-877-0264 Fax: 044-877-0163
Email: wildman@mweb.co.za Web: www.manor.co.za

Gerald and JD have a flair for interiors. You won't need one of the hundreds of books (African art and history, its wildlife and architecture, war memoirs, children's classics and psychology texts) that rub sleeves throughout the house to find this out. Overlooking the lagoon, the glass-encased sitting room is carpeted with Afghan kilims, a low-slung ivory sofa and a pair of Morris chairs, given to the Governor of Gauteng. There's an old billiard table, too, somewhere under a pile of maps. African artefacts have been begged, borrowed or bought: Ndebele pipes and beads, bartered-for carvings and stones from the Cradle of Mankind. The bedrooms have similar horn-and-hide hues, all the luxurious trappings you could wish for, and room for Indonesian chairs and chests, chocolate leather sofas, slipper baths and dark canopied beds with reading lights. In the morning, linen tables were dressed with bone-handle cutlery and lilies in a square metal vase placed on an old country bench next to fruit and muesli. Your hosts are discreet and attentive, and after serving up a faultless (and greaseless) breakfast, will give you a map and bountiful beach-bag and set you off to explore your surrounds. Birdlife is rampant in the area and walks in the surrounding forests are a must. It is only a five-minute stroll along lagoon-side boardwalks to the beach, town and some good restaurants.

Rooms: 4: 3 lagoon suites (2 kings and 1 twin with bath and shower en-suite) and 1 garden room (king/twin with shower en-suite).
Price: R300 - R650 pp sharing. Singles on request.
Meals: Full breakfast included.
Directions: Turn into the Wilderness Village from the N2 and follow road to the T-junction. Turn right into Waterside Road and find Wilderness Manor on your left after 1km.

Teniqua Treetops

Robyn and Viv Patz

Sedgefield
Tel: 044-356-2868 Fax: 088-011-356-2868
Email: queries@teniquatreetops.co.za Web: www.teniquatreetops.co.za

This really is unique! Few guesthouses warrant such an accolade, but to let you think of Teniqua Treetops as a handful of tree-houses would be like dismissing the Sistine Chapel as a handful of murals. Descriptions and photos won't do it justice. You could call Viv and ask him about his handiwork, but you'd still need to see it (he's too modest for that sort of thing). Robyn gave me a tour, unassumingly pointing out how eco-friendly they are here: dry-composting toilets, rainwater harvesting, low-energy everything. I saw eight tree-houses set deep in the forest canopy, created in natural gaps or spaces left by carefully extracting non-indigenous trees. Each is different, but outdoor braais, chill zones, tented double beds and electric blankets are the norm (ignore flashbacks of damp camping, nothing's flimsy). Showers, worktops and bedside tables are carved from reclaimed yellowwood with shapes begging to be stroked, while the four honeymoon suites are very spoiling indeed with lavish corner baths. Privacy, here, goes without saying. Seats, decks and turrets have been positioned to make the most of views which cast their own spell on me. Majestic yellowwoods stretch above the rest of the forest canopy, which plunges into the 160-metre-deep gorge of the Karatara River, long wisps of Old Man's Beard clinging to every light-exposed branch. Trails allow serious hiking in this otherwise impenetrable chunk of nature. A wonderful, romantic and tranquil hideout. Go and visit!

Rooms: 8: 4 honeymoon suites with baths and overhead showers; 2 rooms sleeping four with showers; 2 family rooms, bunk bed and queen, with shower.
Price: From R595 to R1,870 per tree-house. Single rates on request.
Meals: Self-catering, although meals can be provided with prior arrangement.
Directions: Coming from Cape Town on the N2 turn off at the brown boarded 'Teniqua Treetops' sign. Follow the signposted tar road for 15 minutes until you reach the treehouses.

191 Nirvana

Madi Butler

191 Rheenendal Road, Rheenendal, Knysna
Tel: 044-386-0297 Fax: 044-386-0297
Email: madibutler@cyberperk.co.za Web: www.191nirvana.co.za
Cell: 084-826-2266

Who would have thought you could make a couple of self-catering cottages out of two water reservoirs? Evidently Madi Butler did. (First you have to empty out the water of course.) Her two circular, thatched properties now stand proudly on the top of the hill. The position, at the hub of outstanding panoramic views that stretch from the end of the Outeniqua Mountains, across Knysna Lagoon and into the surrounding forest, was just too good to waste. You won't quite know where to gaze first. This is one self-catering place where you can be 100 per cent independent, yet still have the reassuring presence of a very friendly hostess just at the bottom of the hill. On top of all the added extras you require (Madi supplies beautiful white bed linen, towels, firewood and tit bits such as organic salad), a basket of home-grown herbs and veggies (depending on the season) will find its way onto your doorstep each morning. The indoor fireplace doubles up as a braai area which - and this is my favourite part - becomes virtually outdoors when you 'roll up' the walls (made of canvas blinds) at the front of the cottage. What's that? Roll up the walls? I assure you it's possible, you'll just have to come and see for yourself.

Rooms: 3 self-catering units, both sleeping two couples or two small families.
Price: Basic price for the cottage: R950 - R1,500 (for up to 4 people and children under 13). Add R150 per extra person.
Meals: Self-catering.
Directions: Heading to Knysna from George on the N2. Before you enter Knysna turn left into Rheenendal Road. Follow the road for 1.6km and the entrance to 191 Nirvana is on your right.

Lindsay Castle

Jean and Allan de Souza
Noetzie, Knysna
Tel: 044-384-1849 Fax: 086-611-5111
Email: knysnacastles@kingsley.co.za Web: www.knysnacastles.com

There is something peculiarly invigorating (and perhaps just peculiar) about trudging through sand and over glistening rocks, in salty sea air, crashing surf on one side, lush hillside vegetation on the other, to your own beach-marooned, stone-turreted castle. King Arthur meets Robinson Crusoe and all this just a few minutes away from the activity of Knysna and Plettenberg Bay! My enchanted eyes feasted on the view from the castle: the ocean, bordered with intensely coloured rocks, gold and orange, the gentle curve of the wide beach, the fine sand and the wild, lush coastline of Noetzie. At one end of the beach, a path leads directly to the Sinclair Nature Reserve. That night dinner was served by candlelight in a stone-walled tower around a medieval-looking table made from railway sleepers. Later, having reached my turret by a wooden ladder and cosily enveloped in crisp, white sheets, I listened for a long time to the waves breaking against the rocks below and contemplated the starlit sky through my arched window. Whales (in season) and dolphins cavort in the bay and there are otters, bushbuck and the rare oystercatcher too. You can hike, fish and swim in the estuary or sea. The castle seduces the visitor with its unique atmosphere. Romantics only need apply.

Rooms: 4 doubles with en-suite bathroom, 2 in turrets, 1 honeymoon suite. (1 tower room has indoor bath with outdoor shower with an awe-inspiring view from outside top deck). 1 extra room on ground floor with separate bathroom.
Price: from R700 to R1,250 pp sharing. No single supplement.
Meals: Full breakfast included. Lunch and dinner by arrangement. R225 for dinner.
Directions: From N2, 3km east of Knysna, is the Noetzie turn-off. Take sand road for 5km to public parking area. On LHS is private road with boom pole, drive down & park on L. 10m further is beach - Lindsay is c. 250m across it, 7th castle on far R. Call from N2 so you can be met with your bags. No cell phone signal on beach.

Blackwaters River Lodge

Pam and Colin Emmett

N2, Goukama Valley, Knysna
Tel: 044-383-0105 Fax: 044-383-0021
Email: info@blackwaters.co.za Web: www.blackwaters.co.za
Cell: 072-136-7241

The name 'Blackwaters' comes from the tannins that make for the distinctively dark waters of the Goukamma River, from whose bank this rambling guesthouse emerges. It's all pure, though, and the water you drink comes fresh from the river. You can also jump into a canoe from here and make your way deep into this gorgeous valley, home of wild pigs and leopards and a superabundance of birdlife. There's a room for every need. Children are well accommodated, as are honeymooners in a suite that smoulders with African romance, from the delicate embroidered designs to the huge bed, fireplace and generous-sized tub. Below the balcony that looks out onto palms trees, Colin cooks his famous fish braai, although he is even better known for his lectures on the southern skies, which can be observed through his own telescope. Pam, too, is the most thoughtful and caring of managers. The entire lodge has only recently been completely refurbished ("down to the last teaspoon" says Colin). Each room has been uniquely decorated and finished with subtle African touches. The breakfast room is an inviting, sunny spot with views of the river and pool, while for lunch you should take a picnic outside on lawns that unfold from the river, rising up to a pedestal pool. All of this is beautifully floodlit by night. I could see myself reliving a 9-hole round of golf in the communal lounge, the place to gather in the evening with its honesty bar stocked with wines and spirits, comfortable sofas, books, magazines and large plasma screen TV.

Rooms: 10 rooms, all en-suite (2 shower only, 8 bath and shower). Two are family suites.
Price: R320 - R550 pp sharing B&B. Self-catering from R550 - R970 for whole room.
Meals: Full breakfast included. Lunch and dinner available on request.
Directions: 10 minutes outside of Knysna along the N2 toward George, opposite sign for Buffalo Bay.

Springtide Charters

Evelyn and Stephan Pepler

34° South Jetty, Knysna Quays, Knysna
Tel: 082-470-6022
Fax: 044-382-5852
Email: info@springtide.co.za
Web:
www.springtidesailing.com
Cell: 082-829-2740

As I took the helm on board the Outeniqua, 50 feet of shimmering beauty somehow suddenly under my command, and sailed her across Knysna lagoon at a leisurely six knots, I felt very special indeed. The Outeniqua is sailed daily by Greg or Stephan and their young friendly crew who clearly love what they do, and it's not hard to see why. The coastline around Knysna is spectacular, with regular sightings of marine life and pelagic birds. The vessel itself is also exceptional, and I'm not just saying that because Stephan spent four and a half years building and fitting her out! Every immaculate thing on board, excluding the hull, is his own work. Anyone who has climbed aboard will agree. The day starts with a call to the harbourmaster to raise the bridge, as you head off across the lagoon to the Heads, two majestic sandstone cliffs that lead out to the open sea and a whole world of excitement. Various day trips include a 4-hour day sail with lunch, a 2.5-hour sail and the 3-hour sunset cruise where you can indulge in Knysna's famous oysters, seafood and sushi, all washed down with a fine South African bubbly. Evenings are spent anchored in the calm lagoon where a private chef conjures up a gourmet dinner from the galley. A wonderful experience. *Advance bookings essential.*

Rooms: A 50ft yacht comprising 3 double cabins, 2 heads (toilets), a galley and saloon.
Price: Day (2-3 hours) dinner, sunset and champagne breakfast cruises: R400 - R640 pp. Overnight charter with gourmet chef & 3-course dinner: R2,550   R3,600 pp D, B&B.
Meals: Various packages available (see above).
Directions: Next to Deli 34° South at the Knysna Quays Waterfront.

Narnia Farm Guest House

Richard and Stella Sohn
off Welbedacht Lane, Knysna
Tel: 044-382-1334 Fax: 044-382-2881
Email: narnia@pixie.co.za Web: www.narnia.co.za
Cell: 083-325-2581

Narnia combines just about every element we search for in a place to stay. It's defiantly itself - the style (luxuriously ethnic, but never overdone) is so unusual and so genuine that you know it is the extension of real people, not some pretentious interior design job. Stella (graphic design graduate, potter, mother of two) is one of those people and Richard (lawyer, 'architect' and father of four) the other. Narnia is entirely their creation, a dream slotted round one or two key requirements: the house should have a deck with a clear view to the Knysna Heads; and there should be a big, open, friendly entrance hall. Otherwise the house has grown organically into some mad ship with wooden decks, gangways and staircases, swing chairs, heavenly colours of tropical brilliance ("In a previous life I must have been a Mexican," says Stella), a prize-winning garden, and smaller surprises everywhere. The decking-clad, black-painted pool (of swimming - as opposed to plunging - dimensions) shares the same long views in all directions as the fully-serviced self-catering cottages. Stella and Richard amaze me with their great energy and skill with people, despite holding down so many jobs. *Bushbuck are often spotted by the dam on the farm and visitors to the garden include porcupine, blue duiker, steenbuck, monkeys, bushpigs, lynx and 85 species of bird.*

Rooms: 3 units: 1 family suite with 1 double and 1 twin room, both with en-suite bathroom (B&B basis). 2 self-catering cottages: 1 with double room, en-suite bathroom & optional pull-out beds for kids; 1 sleeps four (1 double & 1 twin with shared bathroom).
Price: B&B: R475 - R600. Self-catering: R75 less pp sharing. Children under 12 half-price.
Meals: Full breakfast is included for the B&B apartment. For self-catering full breakfast is R75 and continental is R50. Not available high season.
Directions: On N2 from George turn into Welbedacht Lane just before Knysna. Then follow signs to Narnia Farm Guest House.

The Bamboo Guesthouse

Jaynie Court and Gordon Turrell

9 Bolton Street, Hunters Home, Knysna
Tel: 044-384-0937 Fax: 044-384-0937
Email: bamboo@abs.org.za Web: www.bambooguesthouse.co.za
Cell: 082-812-8838

I had to call three times for directions (each time cringing a little more deeply), but Jaynie finally got through to me with, "and if you don't make it this time you forgo the bottle of red under your pillow". Moments later I arrived and closed the door on the hubbub of Knysna. All around me wooden slatted walkways divided and ordered a jungle of plants and fountains, a pool, a pond and a boma (in this case a homely outdoor restaurant and bar). Jaynie and Gordon have transformed an ordinary garden of lawns and flowerbeds into their own mini-Eden, burying seven spotless rooms in a relaxing garden that grabs the senses and deceives the eye. Guests and hosts alike benefit from the tranquility, manifest in Jaynie's smile (as warm as they come) and Gordon's obvious contentment as he braais away behind the bar. But beware: from his work-station come rustic feasts to challenge the most voracious appetite, wines to lure the most disciplined off task, and stories to leave the most hardened traveller incredulous. There's something of Mick ("Crocodile") Dundee about Gordon and I felt a tad pale and urban next to him. This was not helped in any way by accepting a two-hour full-body massage with Catherine (an exceptional visiting masseuse). But I got over it. A night drifting to sleep on a mountain of cushy bed pillows, vaguely aware of frogs croaking one minute and birds chirping the next, made this weak urbanite feel terrific.

Rooms: 7: 5 king/twins with en-suite showers; 1 queen with en-suite shower; 1 family room with queen and twin sharing en-suite shower.
Price: R280 - R445 pp sharing. Singles R425 - R595.
Meals: Full breakfast included. Anything on request. Roasted vegetables and rib braai, R45, highly recommended.
Directions: From N2 in Knysna (heading to Plett) turn right down George Rex Drive. After lights take 2nd left into Howard St; at the golf club house take central road signed Bolton St, continue over 2 speed bumps and you'll see no.9 on your right.

Noetzie Cottage

Richard Davies

Noetzie Cottage, Noetzie, Knysna
Email: richard@dav l es.co.za Web: www.dav l es.co.za
Cell: 072-679-7473

You must come for the setting. The first glimpse of the view appears at the crest of the dirt track approach, a sudden expanse of corrugated sea out of nowhere. Once you've caught your breath and ensconced yourself in a wicker chair on the open, pillared stoep, you'll find yourself gazing at the protected forest of the Sinclair Forest Reserve to your left, whose headland tapers into craggy fingers of rock clawing into the ocean. Directing your focus down, if you've a vertiginous imagination you'll start eyeballing the drop and calculating how many hundreds of uninterrupted yards you'd cover in a mighty leap before hitting the beach below (otherwise an eight-minute walk round and down). Out front and to the right, it's deep, deep blue as far as the eye can see. Of course the hues are susceptible to change, but the distinctness remains constant, adopting whatever persona the weather dictates. On a previous visit, I was transfixed by the ferocity of a late-winter storm as the elements lashed the castles of Noetzie beach below - quite a sight to behold. Indoors, think Cornish cottage, i.e. black-and-white photos, maps, wooden beams and flowery curtains, and you won't be disappointed. Clean-living, functional, cosy, comfortable, light, bright, warm and welcoming all come to mind, the thrills being a central stone hearth and (now here's a quirk) free-standing baths within the shower alcoves.

Rooms: 3: 1 twin with separate bath & shower; 1 queen with en-suite bath & shower; 1 queen with child's single & en-suite shower.
Price: R2,200 - R3,600 per night (minimum stay 3 nights, 7 in high season). Please direct all initial enquiries to Richard's email: richard@dav l es.co.za
Meals: Self-catering only.
Directions: On N2 to Plettenberg from Knysna, turn right 5km after Knysna (signed to Noetzie). Follow dirt road through all bends until you crest a hill. As descend towards sea, look out for brown house on right-hand side (just before car park).

Buffalo Hills Game Reserve and Lodges

Tony and Maria Kinahan
Plettenberg Bay
Tel: 044-535-9739 Fax: 044-535-9480
Email: buffalohills@mweb.co.za Web: www.buffalohills.co.za
Cell: 082-771-9370

Fluttering its eyelashes in my direction, an inquisitive giraffe, intently cleaning its face with its tongue, stopped me in my tracks on the road. Fresh from the beach (Plett is a mere 15km away), I was taken aback to find myself so deep in the 'real' Africa of my imagination as I drove through the bushy reserve to the camp. Although more traditional accommodation is available, for a true outdoorsy experience the tented rooms here are a must. Replete with big proper beds, plump pillows and wooden furniture, tents have certainly come on a peg or two. These ones even boast their own spa baths. As the sun set, I discovered the pleasure of kicking off walking boots, hanging up binos and re-living events of the day watching fire-flames dance in a sheltered boma. Here, Tony cooked up a hearty feast on the braai - being a reserve, local game is his speciality - whilst regaling us wide-eyed lot with heroic tales involving rhino scuffles and marauding buffalo. After supper, it was facial contortions all round as we sampled shots from the reserve's very own distillery - its liquors are sold in Harrods. I had a great time at Buffalo Hills and, above and beyond the tents and all the animals, this is down to the friendly and inspirational way the place is run. Tony constantly looks to bring his guests closer to nature with individuals benefitting from active, intimate experiences, on bike or foot. Ask about his Elephant Gorge Portered Trail and expect more offerings in this vein to come.

Rooms: 13: 11 tents, all twin/doubles with en-suite spa baths with shower over; 1 cottage with 1 double/twin and separate full bathroom; 1 lodge with 3 en-suite rooms, 3 with shower only, 1 with full bathroom.
Price: R700 - R1,300 pp sharing. Game drive and guided walk included in price.
Meals: Full breakfast and dinner included. Lunch extra.
Directions: From Cape Town take N2, turn L 4km after Plettenberg Bay onto R340. Turn L after 4.9km, then R after 1km onto Stofpad & follow signs.

Fynbos Ridge County House and Cottages

Liz and Brian Phillips
Plettenberg Bay
Tel: 044-532-7862 Fax: 044-532-7855
Email: info@fynbosridge.co.za Web: www.fynbosridge.co.za

Fynbos Ridge is a botanical paradise where new owners Liz and Brian have continued an eco-conscious mission to remove all invasive alien vegetation. Painstakingly, a wide variety of indigenous trees and shrubs have been reinstated to create a haven where Cape flora (fynbos) and fauna can flourish. There are birds here that you will only see in the fynbos. These green-fingered nature lovers will cushion your stay with super-down duvets, pure cotton sheets and a hearty breakfast in the light-filled, alfresco-esque dining room. Lucky self-caterers can choose from newly-refurbished cottages in 'gazania' yellow, 'clivia' peach or 'aristea' blue, all inspired by indigenous flowers and fully and sensitively equipped to satisfy any modernist yearnings... I, for example, particularly liked the minimalist stone baths. They can also pick their own vegetables, but please do let Brian cook for you at least once. This private nature reserve cries out to be walked in, though unfortunately I only made it as far as the ozone-purified swimming pool (no chemicals here - just a weird-sounding contraption doing its bit to keep the establishment and all guests 100% carbon neutral). Follow the natural borders and discreet signposts to this oasis amongst the fynbos to take a dip. Hidden within the depths of a private nature reserve and contemplating the meeting of the Outeniqua and Tsitsikamma mountains, you could easily spend the whole day here languishing with a book. Now where did I pack my swimming togs? *Children 10+ welcome.*

Rooms: 9: 6 rooms in the house: 4 luxury doubles, 1 superior luxury double and 1 self-catering studio, all with en-suite bath and shower; 3 self-catering cottages, all sleeping 4-5 with 1 bathroom & 1 shower-room.
Price: B&B R495 - R895 pp sharing. Self-catering R400 - R675 pp sharing. Singles on request.
Meals: Full breakfast included in B&B price or R85 for self-catering. Lunch and dinner on request.
Directions: 23km along N2 from Knysna heading towards Plettenberg Bay. Take L into 'Blue Hills Bird Farm'. Bear L where road forks to Fynbos Ridge.

Cornerway House

Dee and Robin Pelham-Reid

61 Longships Drive, Plettenberg Bay
Tel: 044-533-3190 Fax: 044-533-3195
Email: cornerwayhouse@mweb.co.za Web: www.cornerwayhouse.co.za

Robin and Dee moved from my Wiltshire school-town (as it happens) to start Cornerway House, and fantastic hosts they make too. Robin will ably point you off to the beach with sundowners or to the Robberg Peninsula walk, an exhilarating experience. Meanwhile Dee can give you a different and rewarding perspective on Plett as Chairman of The Plettenberg Bay HIV & AIDS Foundation. Her dedication has set in place home care work and a safe house for abused women and children (aptly named Invicta House); attached to this is also a day hospice. After drinks in their English drawing room, we repaired for dinner, where wine flowed and conversation roamed. Dee uses what she can from the garden, herbs of course, but artichokes and strawberries too on the day I visited. When a professional cycling team came to stay they were so well fed they failed to win a single race (… not that professional then!). I retired to my room - wooden antiques, comfy bed and sash windows looking onto the garden – and at dawn joined Ocean Blue to spot whales, dolphins and sharks, returning to a proper breakfast, courtesy of Robin. Throughout the house there are colourful quirks, to wit the yellow-washed and lilac shutters of the house, the petunias bathing in a bath, a purple TV/sitting room with bright blue cushions and the pink and yellow mohair in the garden suite. I left Robin and Dee among the frangipani, gardenia and orange trees as I wrenched myself away. *See owner's website to make an online booking.*

Rooms: 5: 4 twins and 1 double; 2 with en-suite shower, 3 with en-suite shower and bath.
Price: R250 - R540. Singles plus 50% in low season, per room in high season. Low season rates can be negotiated.
Meals: Full breakfast included. Lunch and dinner can be arranged with prior notice.
Directions: From N2 heading east, turn right into Plett. Continue to the circle and go straight over. Road descends to river and crosses it. Over circle, turn right onto Longships Dr. Continue down 0.9km to Cornerway House on right.

Bosavern

Vivienne and Gerald Dreyer
38 Cutty Sark Ave, Plettenberg Bay
Tel: 044-533-1312 Fax: 044-533-0758
Email: info@bosavern.co.za Web: www.bosavern.co.za
Cell: 082-922-4721

The striking S-shaped waves of Bosavern's timbered ceiling mimic the sea and combine with minimalist white interiors and mirrors to strike a harmonious note with the blue ocean far below. Glass doors lead off the open-plan sitting room and onto the balcony where you can treat yourself on wicker chairs to a regal cliff-top view of the Robberg Peninsula and the white beaches of Plettenberg Bay. Powerful binoculars will pick out whales and schools of dolphins which are (can be!) plentiful in the clear water. The bedrooms downstairs have the same sliding doors that disappear smoothly into the wall and the sea breeze wafts in through a square gap of sky as if from a bright blue painting. The view from your room and private balcony is no less spectacular. Comfort is a priority, with goose-down duvets on enormous beds, fine cotton sheets, a welcoming bottle of Nederberg, gowns and slippers. Vivienne and Gerald are natural hosts, who provide great breakfasts and also picnic hampers for the beach or Robberg hikes, and mountain bikes and canoes for the madly active (a pool caters for loungers). They will also point you in the right direction for golf and recommend a number of restaurants within easy walking distance.

Rooms: 5: 4 twins/doubles & 1 double; 3 with en-suite shower, 2 with en/s bath and shower. All rooms and bathrooms all have heated towel rails and underfloor heating.
Price: R565 - R895 pp sharing. Singles on request.
Meals: Full breakfast included and served from 8am - 9am.
Directions: From Knysna take N2. Right at Shell garage into Plettenberg Bay. Turn 1st right into Cutty Sark Ave. Follow road round, then turn right again into cul-de-sac. House on left.

Beacon Lodge

Al and Clo Scheffer

57 Beacon Way,
Plettenberg Bay
Tel: 044-533-2614
Fax: 044-533-2614
Email:
info@beaconlodge.co.za
Web:
www.beaconlodge.co.za

This is a small (just two rooms), personal, friendly and involving B&B – and I mean B&B in the proper sense where you share the house with your hosts. Both rooms have their own separate entrances, mind you, if you want to slip about more furtively. The patio, for breakfasts, garden bird-watching or reading, has long views out to sea and it's only a short walk to the beach and the lagoon, presumably where you will want to spend at least some of your time. To this end Al and Clo have all beach necessities at the ready – umbrellas, towels and the like. The larger of the two rooms was my favourite (and also the more expensive) with sea views through a huge window and anti-glare solar blinds. There is seagrass on floors, plenty of immaculate seaside white in walls and towels and colour is added in the form of fresh flowers. The Scheffers take the greatest care of their guests. *Fridge facilities provided. Great restaurants within walking distance. Whales and dolphins in season. Closed mid-Dec to mid-Jan and either June or July. Enquire first!*

Rooms: 2: 1 twin and 1 double, both with en-suite bathrooms with showers.
Price: R225 - R450 pp sharing. Singles on request.
Meals: Full breakfast included. There are good restaurants in town for other meals.
Directions: From Knysna take the N2. Take the third turn into Plett at the Engen 1-stop garage. The house is 600 metres on your left.

Map Number: 5

Entry Number: 175

Southern Cross Beach House

Neill and Sue Ovenstone
1 Capricorn Lane, Solar Beach, Plettenberg Bay
Tel: 044-533-3868 Fax: 044-533-3866
Email: info@southerncrossbeach.co.za
Web: www.southerncrossbeach.co.za Cell: 082-490-0876

... and relax. With this dreamy, whitewashed, wooden house at the quiet end of Robberg Beach's long arc, it is impossible not to. Plettenberg Bay is a lively town, with lots of restaurants and bars, but people really come here for the sea, and you would seriously struggle to get closer to it than at Southern Cross. During the Christmas holidays the beach is packed, but for the rest of the year there are more signs of life in the sea. Dolphins race by all year round, revelling in their position at the head of the food chain, with southern right whales often wallowing just in front of the house from June to November. The house itself is just up a wooden gangway from the beach. Wood predominates, with blues and white echoing the ocean. The brochure says 'plantation style', but I would plump for classic Massachussetts beach house. Wooden decking looks across the bay to the Tsitsikamma Mountains to the left and the Robberg Peninsula opposite, which is geologically identical to the Falklands, bizarrely… and a fantastic place to walk. Inside is the breakfast room and living room, and set around the garden on the ground floor (Sue and Neill live upstairs) are the five lovely rooms. Barefoot, laid-back luxury.

Rooms: 5: 1 double, 1 queen, 2 twins, 1 king. All have en-suite shower, 2 with baths as well.
Price: R395 - R775 pp sharing. 30% single supplement.
Meals: Full breakfast included. Kitchenette available for putting together salads and light meals.
Directions: From dolphin roundabout in main street descend the hill past Central Beach, over Piesang River bridge. Straight over the roundabout, past shops (kwikspar) to your left and take the first right into Longships Dr. 2km over 3 speed bumps turn left into Gris Nez Dr. Over stop street (Rothersands) turn left into Gemini St. Turn right then left into Capricorn Lane.

Bitou River Lodge

Sue and Paul Scheepers

R340 Bitou Valley Road, Plettenberg Bay
Tel: 044-535-9577 Fax: 044-535-9577
Email: info@bitou.co.za Web: www.bitou.co.za
Cell: 082-978-6164

For well-heeled South Africans "Plett" is the place to summer and its sophisticated buzz can border on the frenetic. Which is why Bitou River Lodge is such a find. Just east of town, it's close to Plett's glass-plated beach houses, bijou shops and restaurants, yet feels a million miles away. Paul and Sue wanted to make the most of the natural environment and have created a peaceful haven for nature lovers. The drive sweeps past a citrus orchard and horse paddock to the whitewashed lodge, which sits on five hectares of neat flower-filled gardens, with pool, chipping-green and river frontage. Behind pepper trees and honeysuckle, stable-style bedrooms have river-facing patios, where dazzling sunbirds congregate. The lime-washed, painted-pine rooms have slate-floored kitchenettes and bathrooms, and sliding doors keep them light-filled. Farmhouse feasts are served in the breakfast room, which adjoins a warm lounge where you can settle into birding books (there are 134 species in the area to tick off). Outside, the liquid-smooth lawn gathers all before it – boulders, benches and flowerbeds – as it slips silently toward the lily-leafed river. While away some time out here, watching busy weaver birds build upside-down nests and lazy ones sway in the reeds, while the ripple of canoe paddles, the splash of a kingfisher and whizz of a fly-reel provide a soothing summer soundtrack. *In season the bay hosts whales, dolphins and seals.*

Rooms: 5: 3 kings and 2 twins, all with en-suite bath and shower.
Price: R375 - R595 pp sharing. Singles on request.
Meals: Full farmhouse breakfast included. Plenty of restaurants in nearby Plett.
Directions: Head east from Plettenberg Bay on N2. Immediately after bridge, turn left onto the R340. Bitou River Lodge is signed on left, 4.2km from the N2.

Emily Moon

Simon and Diane Valentine
Rietvlei Rd, Plettenberg Bay
Tel: 044-533-2982 Fax: 044-533-0687
Email: info@emilymoon.co.za Web: www.emilymoon.co.za
Cell: 083-266-2994

I stooped under Emily Moon's 400-year-old Jaipuri doors and stumbled into a far-flung bazaar in some foreign land: gold-inlaid masks on the wall, cattle skins for carpets, African bao board games and mammoth pewter candlesticks. Sipping rooibos tea, I steadied myself and worked my way along family portraits of muscle-bound men sporting over-sized fish and Blixenesque women who could pour a G&T then shoot a marauding lion without blinking an eye. And then the view… past the glass-fronted restaurant the River Bitou scrawled an 'S' through reeded wetlands before halting at the foothills of the Outeniqua Mountains. Was I hearing things? Or was the wind really carrying the low grunting of buffalo and wildebeest herds that must have grazed here centuries before? I'd clearly watched one too many repeats of 'Out of Africa', but thankfully Simon rescued me from my reverie. You're more likely to see a tortoise (60 at the last count!) than a grumpy buffalo here; but the birding has warranted the establishment's very own guide. He showed me the huge rooms with their fawn-coloured walls, dark wooden furniture, open fires and deep, deep leather sofas. My favourite was the split-level family room with its panoramic view. When it's free, Simon takes a cold beer down to watch the flock of sacred ibis which fly past in a 'V' at sundown. The outdoor shower in every room is also worth a mention, although it did cause a problem for one German husband who complained bitterly when his wife refused to get out! *Two golf courses 1.5km from the lodge.*

Rooms: 8: 2 twin/king, 5 king all with en-suite baths and showers. 1 family room with en-suite shower.
Price: Low Season: May 2009 - September 2009: R1,070 per lodge B&B sharing. High Season: October 2009 – April 2010: R1,105 per person sharing B&B.
Meals: Full English or Continental breakfast incl'. A table is automatically reserved for guests at the restaurant in the evening.
Directions: On N2 from Cape Town pass main Plettenberg Bay turn-off, then L at Penny Pinchers supermarket. Carry straight on. Drive up steep hill & follow signs.

Anlin Beach House

Dermot and Fran Molloy

33 Roche Bonne Avenue, Plettenberg Bay
Tel: 044-533-3694 Fax: 044 533 3394
Email: stay@anlinbeachhouse.co.za Web: www.anlinbeachhouse.co.za

Like a moth to a lamp, the first thing I did here after dropping off my bags was head to the beach, irresistibly close (100 metres away) and tantalizing from the top-floor balcony. A run along the soft sands all the way to the Robberg Peninsula was exhilarating at sunset. Beneath cobalt blue skies, I passed only seals and surfers cresting the smooth ocean rollers. The beach really does seem to slow you down as both Dermot (a wine-marketer) and Fran (a trained counsellor) will attest. As we passed the quirky outdoor shower, Fran commented that she always wanted the place to be ultra up-to-date in terms of design, but comfortable at the same time, "I don't want guests to think: 'I can't sit on that'". The style is therefore contemporary, with walls and furnishings in natural colours imitating the beach, the ocean and dramatic rocky outcrops. The bedrooms have tiled floors and cream-coloured furniture drenched in light from the private patios and vast windows. Dermot's an avid collector of South African art so expect to see some interesting pieces. If you can, book the upstairs room. The view, which sweeps the ocean to the Outeniqua Mountains, finally persuaded Fran to go for the house; "when a school of dolphins swam past, I knew I had to sign!" The kitchens, with their polished-cement surfaces and hi-tech gas hobs, all come well stocked with tea, coffee, soup and other goodies. Don't forget to ask Dermot for his autograph either. He once worked as an extra on Zulu Dawn!

Rooms: 4: 1 upstairs apartment (potentially 2 units) with 3 beds and 2 bathrooms, 1 with bath/shower and 1 with shower only; 2 garden apartments, both sleep 3 with 1 shower bathroom each.
Price: From R385 pp to R765 pp. Singles +25%.
Meals: Self-catering but continental breakfast can be served on the patio for R40.
Directions: From N2 heading east, R into Plett. Continue to circle & go straight over. Road descends to river and crosses it. Over circle, R onto Longships Dr then left into Roche Bonne Avenue, which has a brown B&B sign. Anlin Beach House is 50m on R.

Piesang Valley Lodge

John Elliott
Piesang Valley Road, Plettenberg Bay
Tel: 044-533-6283 Fax: 044-533-4477
Email: info@pvl.co.za Web: www.pvl.co.za
Cell: 072-5190-244

If ever a place resembled its owner, this is it. Unpretentious, laid-back, friendly and personal, John has bestowed these qualities on a lodge, part of which he built with his own hands using a special vertical construction technique (just nod and make understanding grunts). These are also the rooms of choice where pine and timber frame a scene of dark wood furniture, inviting beds and earthy rugs, soothed by white-washed walls and alabaster bathrooms. All open breezily onto the garden. There's a refreshing youthful energy here as well, something else you'll notice about John, who leads a tremendously healthy life. I challenge anyone to guess his correct age. When we met he had just returned from rescuing his new houseboat that had slipped its moorings. After many years in the hospitality industry, it was his dream to start his own guesthouse and where better than on family ground, whose hill-top seat looks all the way down the valley into Plett and out to the Indian Ocean. There are plenty of good restaurants in the area, but you're welcome to bring your own grub and cook lunch and dinner in the kitchen. That's if you're still hungry after a bonanza breakfast with the birds. The garden is a great place to kick back with a cold beer and enjoy a gently sloping verdant scene of lawn, bush and tree, across which playful house hounds tumble. "It's convenient and tranquil," says John. It's very good value too.

Rooms: 6 rooms: all queen doubles or twins (2 bath/shower and 4 shower en-suite).
Price: R320 - R470 pp sharing.
Meals: Full breakfast included. Guests are welcome to cook their own lunch and dinner in the kitchen.
Directions: Take Piesang Valley Road turn-off from N2 into Plettenberg Bay. 1.4km down the road the lodge is on your right-hand side.

Gulls View

Noel and Pam Mills

31 San Gonzales Street, Plettenberg Bay
Tel: 072-343-7217 Fax: 044-533-3498
Email: info@gullsview.co.za Web: www.gullsview.co.za

Gulls View is named for the feathered athletes who riot and curl in the thermals that funnel up the cliff at the sea-facing end of the garden. From the verandah, upstairs main bedroom and front rooms there are views in bands of searingly simple colour; a spread of blue sea, white beaches on the peninsula, then the green of a lawny (and wholly indigenous) garden filled with birds including the Knysna loerie. Noel and Pam (who also have a (GG) guesthouse (Rockwood) in the Cederberg) have coaxed the second oldest house in town into the 21st century and built a whole new one too. This way you can live in the new house if there are only two of you, or use both if you are more numerous. The new house has an open feel with polished timbers, nice curvy wicker chairs, soft white, cream and turquoisey-green tones and billowy ivory-coloured curtains framing the view. All of which are right and proper for the sea. The little things haven't been forgotten either; TV and DVD, stereo set, CD player and, of course, a top notch kitchen. The house is equidistant to several beaches (down a fairly steep hill) and a five-minute walk to the vibrant and trendy town where there are excellent restaurants. Louann lives next door and will meet and greet you and look after you as much or as little as you wish.

Rooms: Self-catering house let as a whole, with 6 bedrooms.
Price: Low season: R800 per night for 2 sharing, + R100 per extra person; Mid: R1,000 per night as above; High (1st Dec – 20th Jan): R3,000 per night. Rates include week-day servicing.
Meals: Breakfast ingredients can be supplied on request at a cost of R30 pp.
Directions: Turn off N2 into Plett at Shell Garage. Turn right at the roundabout, then left into San Gonzales St. Gulls View is 2nd last house on the right before Signal Hill.

Bella Manga

Fiona and Ray Berresford

Country House, Uplands, Plettenberg Bay
Tel: 044-535-0053 Fax: 044-535-0053
Email: info@bellamanga.co.za Web: www.bellamanga.co.za
Cell: 072-272-7890

Leaving free-range turkeys and security systems back in Hertfordshire, Fiona and Ray harnessed their passion for all things rustic and revitalized this 100-acre farm. Determination - and a little madness? - have transformed ruins and tangled vegetation into what now proudly stands as Bella Manga. Its name, meaning 'beautiful nonsense' in Zulu (says Ray), pays tribute to a Jonny Clegg song describing a place "where the world began" (says Fiona). Amid the quirks, original keystones have been left exposed and a section of mud-brick wall has been framed. A fireplace from a labourer's cottage is now a braai; a colossal fire pit looks poised to spit-roast elephants; and acre upon acre of overgrown wattle has been lovingly developed into grounds that now display four types of lavender, wild mistletoe, a colony of weavers, guava and pepper trees, with handy benches dotted about for sedate contemplation. Fidgets can dive into the 2.8m deep pool, chase the Rhodesian Ridgebacks or jump on a quad. The toughest part of your stay will be deciding which sleeping option to go for: rondavels with double power showers; self-catering bliss (long stoeps, hammocks, a pool, a pond, a boat and wildlife); or the Lavender Suite with huge bathroom/double power-shower; or the Yellowwood Rooms with truly stunning yellowwood floors and lavish en-suite bathrooms. Whatever your fancy, Fiona and Ray will make you feel like you've always belonged here... and you will eat like royalty. These are hosts who fully appreciate the meaning of fun.

Rooms: 13: 2 rondavel king/twins, en/s showers; 1 family rondavel (king, 2 bunks & en/s bath); 7 king/twins with en/s bath or shower; 3 self-catering lodges with queens or king/twins and en/s double showers.
Price: R300 - R795 pp sharing. Single supp' 50%.
Meals: Full breakfast incl' (just like mum makes it!). Dinner on request (24hrs notice, but it's well worth it): R100 - R200 for 3 course meal, wine separate.
Directions: From N2 after Plettenberg take R340 left to Uniondale. Follow the bends up hill for 11km then take a gravel road left to Uplands and Bella Manga is signed to the right after 1.5km.

Sandbanks

Jill Mellis

No. 13 Bowtie Drive, Plettenberg Bay
Tel: 044-533-3592 Fax: 044-533-3592
Email: stay@sandbanks.co.za Web: www.sandbanks.co.za
Cell: 072-360-9989

I arrived at Sandbanks to find a fellow guest sunbathing on her private balcony and deeply engrossed in the Greenwood Guide (…I've read it, it's great!). She promised that she had not been set up to impress me… but I was already impressed anyway. Sandbanks is fabulous, modern, chic and creatively in harmony with Plettenberg Bay and the sea; and all the good taste and design flair belong to Jill. Bedrooms are all painted a soft white, except for the king suite in the penthouse upstairs. There, the white four-poster and faded furniture stand out against wallpaper of green and gold and dark wooden floorboards. In the upstairs sitting room decorative pots and bowls on shelves can be admired from white sofas topped with luxurious cushions. The rooms downstairs are reached by a separate entrance, reached by passing a stunning infinity pool sunk in wooden decking, its furthest edge an indistinct silvery line where the pool water gives way to the dazzling view of the bay glittering below – a view of such prefection that Jill could have composed it herself. Back inside, we were surrounded by objets d'art and pale furniture. With a kitchen of stone tops and state-of-the-art appliances – including a mammoth gas braai outside - self-catering is an option; but a fully-trained chef from a restaurant in town is available if you wish. As we said our goodbyes by the black-topped bar upstairs I couldn't help but envy all those that would stay here when I had gone.

Rooms: 6: 3 kings, 2 queens and 1 double; all en suite, 2 with baths and showers and 4 with showers.
Price: R250 - R750 pp sharing. Single supplement plus 50%.
Meals: Full breakfast included. Other meals on arrangement.
Directions: From PE travel on N2 towards Cape Town. Take 1st off-ramp into Plettenberg Bay & onto Beacon Way. Follow road past Market Square shopping centre on R. Half way up hill and R into Julia Ave. Take 1st left onto Bowtie Dirve. Sandbanks is 2nd house approximately 100m on L.

That Place

Jo and David Butler

The Crags
Tel: 044-534-8886
Email: info@thatplace.co.za Web: www.thatplace.co.za
Cell: 082-578-1939

This is 'that place', you know the one you talk about for years after you've been there. "Do you remember the time we went to South Africa and stayed in 'That Place' where we watched the elephants wandering through their paddock across the valley, where we hazily dreamt in the hand-crafted sauna. We braai'd and feasted for hours on the deck, the kids duck-diving and splashing in the waters of the private pool - do you remember?" Jo and David have created a memory-building, self-catering home. And that's just what it is - a home. It's not grand or pretentious, just comfortable and happy to have you. I was shown around by a very modest David who failed to mention that the great wooden table and chairs, the sauna and the three cheeky fish sculptures suspended on the wall (amongst other details) had sprung from his own gifted fingers. I met the dogs too, all six of them. Right from John Keats the Great Dane down to McGregor the feisty Jack Russell. Don't worry, these chaps live next door and won't bother you unless you want them to. But if you want them to…! "You named your dog after a poet?" I asked Jo. "David did," she replied, "he's very into his poetry." Sounds like the perfect man to me - unfortunately already taken by Jo who is equally wonderful.

Rooms: One 3-bedroom self-catering cottage let as a whole: 1 king with en-suite bath and shower and 2 twins (1 ideal for children).
Price: From R750 - R1,500 per night for the whole house.
Meals: It's possible to pre-order dishes from a company specialising in Continental cuisine by prior arrangement.
Directions: Travelling in the direction of Port Elizabeth on the N2, 20km east of Plettenberg Bay. At The Bramon Wine Shop, turn right off the N2 and follow the signs to 'That Place.'

Lily Pond Country Lodge

Niels and Margret Hendriks

R102 Nature's Valley Road, The Crags
Tel: 044-534-8767 Fax: 044-534-8686
Email: info@lilypond.co.za Web: www.lilypond.co.za
Cell: 082-746-8782

From the moment I met Niels and Margret I was confident of a great stay. Whilst their lodge is a monument to mathematical modernity (straight lines and strong angles prevail), its slickness is balanced by the natural surroundings (beige and terracotta walls contrast strikingly with the greenery of Nature's Valley). Everyone benefits from the tranquility and abundant birdlife here. The lily ponds provide a lush home to a mesmerising array of flora and fauna. The frogs serenaded me with their croaky chorus as I braved a mid-winter swim in the black infinity pool. Warming up in my polished concrete bath, I soaked up the garden suite's quirky design. Think African colonial (tribal paintings, gauzy curtains and kudu-skin rugs) with every bit of stuffiness surgically removed and replaced with funky exposed brickwork, slick crete-stone floors and a bright ochre-and-white colour scheme. In summer, the lilies outside are a carpet of colour and balmy evenings are set aside for drinks and nibbles followed by a many-coursed, mouth-watering meal in the (equally angular) restaurant. Margret, a supremely good cook, has trained a marvelous Xhosa chef, Vincent, who has a flair for flavour fusions; he crosses oriental and European dishes, and is fond of African Bobotie Wonton starters and Sushi Ice desserts. All the staff are friendly and, for people who "never meant to run a guest house", Niels and Margret are doing a seriously good job. *Massage treatments on request.*

Rooms: 10: 4 en-suite rooms (2 queens & 2 king/twins) & 2 luxury suites (2 king/twins), all en-s bath & shower; 3 luxury garden suites (all extra-length king/twin) & 1 honeymoon suite (extra-length king/double), all en-s bath & sh'r plus outdoor sh'r.
Price: R425 - R1,075 pp sharing (sing supp 50%).
Meals: Full breakfast included. Fusion kitchen with 4-course dinner R195 (vegetarian on request). Light lunches available.
Directions: 22km east of Plettenberg Bay. From CT take first exit to Nature's Valley. From Port Elizabeth take 2nd exit Nature's Valley (14km after toll) to L. Then follow R102 for 3km and R at sign.

Map Number: 5

Tarn Country House

François and Hendré Lenferna de la Motte

N2, The Crags
Tel: 044-534-8806 Fax: 044-534-8835
Email: info@tarn.co.za Web: www.tarn.co.za

Ah, this is the life… 100 acres of bucolic bliss. Picture the scene if you will: frogs croaking contentedly, birds chirping merrily in the afternoon sun, and a smug inspector enjoying the top tea spot on the Garden Route. From the shade of a pine tree I overlooked the reservoir onto a forested valley and up to the Outeniqua Mountains stretching away into the hazy distance. My thoughts were only lightly disturbed by a lone guinea fowl clucking about in search of food and an ephemeral twinge of guilt as ruddy-faced guests returned from hikes through the foothills of the nearby Tsitsikamma Mountains in time for a fireside apéritif and a hearty dinner. But I quickly discovered that I'd also somehow earned a three-course François special. The restaurant enjoys the same views as my favoured tea spot, through the full-length French doors that flood the room with morning sunshine. Blissfully settled beside the ceramic wood-burning fire, I chomped my way through camembert-filled filo pastry parcels, a succulent fillet of beef with a mustard cream sauce, sorbet rounded off with grilled plums, and all washed down with a local wine from Tarn's extensive collection. The sprawling, bungalowed building is surrounded by a brilliant moat of flowers, and as I slopped around in my over-sized tub, contemplating the king-size bed that awaited me, I realized that after only a few hours here I already felt refreshed, revitalized and raring to go.

Rooms: 8: 3 kings, 3 queens and 2 twins all with en-suite bath and shower.
Price: R570 - R890 pp sharing. + 50% single supplement. Children welcome.
Meals: Full breakfast included. Light lunch on request. 3-course dinner at in-house restaurant from R150 - R250.
Directions: On N2, 15km east of Plettenberg Bay, sign to the left. Coming from PE direction, 19km from Toll Gate, sign to the right.

At The Woods Guest House

Bev and Marco Coetzee

Storms River Village, Isitsikamma
Tel: 042-2811-446 Fax: 042-2811-550
Email: info@atthewoods.co.za Web: www.atthewoods.co.za
Cell: 082-3282-371

If you go down to the woods today, you're sure of a big surprise. After nine months - and seventy-five thousand bricks! - Marco should give himself a big pat on the back. He personally oversaw and renovated the property all the way down to its reclaimed skirting-boards, doing a great deal of the work himself. "He likes to build, this man," Bev laughed as she passed me some home-made bread. In addition to its relaxed atmosphere, earthy colours and African background music, At The Woods also has all the mod cons of the contemporary guesthouse. The rooms have king-size extra-length beds with Oregon pine headboards, white linen, funky lighting and colourful mohair blankets. The bathrooms, meanwhile, have bamboo ceilings and walk-in showers. My favourite room had blue painted chairs, and a patio with a view across to next-door's macadamia plantation. When staying, make sure you take full advantage of Bev's extensive Garden Route know-how. She worked at Knysna Tourism for six years. The highest bungy jump in the world is only 20km away (my answer to that is a simple no, so don't even ask), plus there's the nearby canopy tour, where you slide through the Tsitsikamma Forest's indigenous treetops. Storms River is the adventure capital of the Western Cape and Bev and Marco will help you make the most of it.

Rooms: 8: 5 kings, 3 twins, all extra-length and all with en-suite with showers.
Price: R350 - R495 pp sharing. Singles: 50% supplement in summer, none in winter.
Meals: Breakfast includes cereals, yoghurts, fruit salad, cooked breakfast and toast & croissants. Home-cooked two-course dinner available on request.
Directions: From Cape Town turn off the N2 at Storms River. At The Woods is 600m in on your right.

The Fernery Lodge and Chalets

Meg and Frans Gerber

Forest Ferns, Blueliliesbush, Tsitsikamma
Tel: 042-280-3588
Fax: 041-394-5114
Email: reservations@forestferns.co.za
Web: www.forestferns.co.za

You've heard us harping on about beautiful views before, but this time I need an even stronger superlative! As I cradled my welcome G&T, I watched an enormous waterfall relentlessly plummet 30 metres down a river gorge before making its way to the sea. Beyond the forest I could see all the way to the ocean. On certain clear days, whales and dolphins complete an impossibly picturesque scene here. It's not surprising, then, that The Fernery focuses on this natural visual treasure, from lodge bedrooms to dining areas, jacuzzis and pools. Decks and towers offer yet more angles for kloof-gazing to sundowners. I stayed in the main lodge, which was the perfect place to relax after another leg-achingly long drive. Here you will find yourself on the end of some serious pampering, with large inviting rooms leading to even larger bathrooms. Up the hill from the lodge are the wooden chalets, which have traditional wood-burning heaters and outdoor braais to give them a back-to-nature feel... and no TVs. But fear not, there is entertainment at hand for chalet guests, including a pub, pool, and canopied jacuzzi overhanging the waterfall valley. And beyond these is Frans' gift to tandem couple travellers: the luxury twin self-catering chalet. Thought through to the last detail, two sleek suites branch off a central kitchen and dining area like arms off the nave of a church, while gliding walls allow each couple to retreat into plush privacy in one swift swoosh. At last travelling couples can have their cake and eat it.

Rooms: 16: 6 doubles with en-s in lodge; 6 double/twin B&B chalets en-s bathroom; 2 self-catering chalets with doubles & twins with 1 bathroom; 2 luxury S-C twin chalets each with 2 full en-s bedrooms.
Price: B&B lodge suites: R790 - R1,180; B&B chalets: R570 - R690; S-C chalets (sleep 4): R1,330 - R1,600 per chalet; 12 luxury S-C twin chalets with en-s bathroom & double showers: R2,200 - R2,640. All prices pp sharing. Extra for singles & use of bicycles.
Meals: Full breakfast incl' for B&B chalets & lodge suites. 4-course dinner available for all guests, or 3-course dinner braai (meat, fish or vegetables).
Directions: Bluelilies Bush turn-off, 4km from PE side of Storms River bridge, then 7.5km down signed track from road.

Karoo Side Dishes

A handful of highly-recommended things to do and places to eat in the Karoo area...

Prince Albert Country Store
William and Collen have opened up their dream in a true country store. Take an inspiring browse through their unique collection of antiques, vintage items and local Karoo products. All this is surrounded by an exquisite tea garden offering buffet lunches, award-winning cheeses, fresh flowers and so much more.
Contact: *William and Colleen Penfold, 46 Church Street, Prince Albert;* **Tel:** *023-5411-053;* **Email:** *penfold@mweb.co.za*

The Plough Restaurant
Internationally known Chef de Cuisine Christina Martins' new restaurant is sure to include some favourites from her worldwide top-three School of Food and Wine. Bill and Christina serve up superb food, incorporating local produce, and have kept the restaurant relaxed and welcoming to all. As Bill says, "we want to keep it accessible to the locals, so that a farmer can feel comfortable coming for lunch in his gumboots." I greatly enjoyed this image! They will also be running culinary getaways this year.
Contact: *Bill and Christina Martin, Corner of Burger and Schoeman Streets, De Rust;* **Tel:** *044-241-2214;* **Email:** *info@housemartin.co.za*

Karoo Connections Tours and Transfers
The Karoo is a South African must-see, but where do you start? David and his team at Karoo Connections know this vast expanse like no other. Take a historical tour through the architectural gem of Graaff-Reinet, visit Nieu-Bethesda or the fantasy world of the famous Owl House; do a Township Walkabout and learn about Xhosa culture; take a game drive in the Camdeboo or Mountain Zebra National Park; or my personal favourite, the Valley of Desolation Sundowner tour. A special place needs special people to show you around.
Contact: *David McNaughton, 7 Church Street, Graaff-Reinet;* **Prices:** *From R200 - R550 depending on the tour;* **Tel:** *049-892-3978; 049-891-1061;* **Email:** *karooconnections@intekom.co.za;* **Web:** *www.karooconnections.co.za*

Meerkat Magic
You simply can't miss this. Grant has been studying meerkats for an unhealthily long time and has even learnt all of their calls. Head out with him on a dawn or dusk visit and watch as he starts chirruping and chirping. The meerkats come streaming out to see what's going on and you get the most fantastic close-up inspection of these intriguing animals as well as an amazing explanation from "The Meerkat Man" on their social structures and behaviour.
Contact: *Grant McIlrath, around Oudtshoorn* **Prices:** *R750 includes all entrance fees and meerkat DVD. No cameras please;* **Tel:** *044-272-3077; 044-272-3077;* **Email:** *gmmcilrath@mweb.co.za;* **Web:** *www.meerkatmagic.com*

Housemartin Guest Lodge

Bill & Christina Martin
16 Schoeman Street, De Rust
Tel: 044-241-2214 Fax: 044-241-2317
Email: info@housemartin.co.za Web: www.housemartin.co.za
Cell: 083-342-6456

Arriving at the gates of this Victorian homestead and lodge, though the heavens wept outside for the first time in months, inside there were nothing but smiles and laughter. Unmistakably the heart and soul of the guest lodge, the deep-red, high-beamed restaurant bustled with life. As I tucked into a hearty bobotie, jolly guests on the next table had the right idea, ordering a fresh round of Irish coffees. Bill and Christina, whose School of Food and Wine in Durban is world-renowned (my lunch was superb), bought the lodge 'on a whim' after falling for the charms of De Rust and the taste of village life it offered. And you can try a bite of it too. All rooms are similar affairs with original corrugated roofs and Klein Victoria coloured windows decorating each private verandah. Percale bed linen, mohair blankets and under-floor heating add a little luxury to the airy and tastefully decorated rooms. After a day spent exploring the dramatic Swartberg, collapse on your verandah, admire the abundant fruit garden, sample some local muscadel and then wait in anticipation of the culinary delights ahead.

Rooms: 12: all queen/twin with en-suite showers and air-conditioning.
Price: R380 - R500 pp sharing. Singles from R465 - R625.
Meals: Full breakfast included. Restaurant on site.
Directions: De Rust is just past Oudtshoorn on the N12 on route to Beaufort West, and is just 1hr from George. Guest Lodge is well sign-posted on main road through town.

De Zeekoe Guest Farm

Paula and Pottie Potgieter

R328, road to Mosselbay, Zeekoegat Farm, Oudtshoorn
Tel: 044-272-6721 Fax: 044-272-6721
Email: info@dezeekoe.co.za Web: www.dezeekoe.co.za
Cell: 082-551-3019

I'm going to come straight out and say it: I'm smitten! You'll find the house in a desert cauldron, whose dusty plains are ringed by mountains holding back the coastal cloud. I arrived on a sultry afternoon and took refuge in the cool of the tile-floored farmhouse, among soft leather chairs, vibrant oil landscapes and low Oregon pine windows. Next door, a large dining room that overlooks the Outeniqua Mountains and riverbed promised a memorable supper and the slick in-house rooms lured me in from the indigenous gardens, source of many of the ingredients for meals. Beyond the saltwater pool is a wall of reeds where a fish eagle nests, and beyond that a river - the farm is named after the hippos once found here - where you can quietly canoe under a reliable summer sun. The farm is stretched over 2,000 hectares, home to springbuck, ostriches, cattle and alfalfa stretching as far as the eye can see, so borrow a bike and introduce yourself. But I really lost my heart to my waterfront cabin. In a washed-blue dawn, the mountains now faintly outlined like mascara, bright birds busied about the reeds (there are 250 species to spot). I sat on the deck, its legs planted firmly in the dam, as my neighbour cast his line. So beautiful, so peaceful…. De Zeekoe completely relaxed me and I long to return. *Biking, hiking, canoeing and birding opportunities abound on the farm's reserve. There is also a meerkat project in the reserve, run by TV's Meerkat Magic man Grant McIllrath (See Karoo Side Dishes). If you're lucky you might even spot one of the shy five (tours cannot be guaranteed).*

Rooms: 16: 12 in-house (king, twin and double), 6 with en/s bath and shower, 2 with en/s shower, 5 kings and twins with en-suite bath, shower and outside shower. 4 x two-bedroom cabins, all with shared showers and kitchenette.
Price: Rooms R450 – R1,200 pp sharing. 5 new rooms are at R1,200 pp sharing.
Meals: Full breakfast included. 4-course dinner available at R185 - R200 pp, excluding wine. Braais, light meals and organic salads also available.
Directions: Head west from Oudtshoorn (toward Calizdorp) on R62. Turn left at sign to Mossel Bay on R328. After 7km turn right on dirt road, for 2km to De Zeekoe on left.

Map Number: 2

Entry Number: 190

Red Stone Hills

Petro and Hermanus Potgieter
Oudtshoorn
Tel: 044-213-3783 Fax: 044-213-3291
Email: redstone@pixie.co.za Web: www.redstone.co.za

The humbling sense of the passage of time pervades this 3,000-hectare veld, whose desert colours swirl with Van Gogh vibrancy. The current Potgieters are the fifth generation to farm this land (ostrich, vineyards, cattle, fruit), but that lineage is put into perspective by the red stone hills. They date to the enon-conglomerate period, formed 120 million years ago when the earth twisted and a torrent of sanguine mud-stone settled and solidified; a few million years later, bushmen hid in the hills' stone pockets and painted wildlife; and in the 1790s Karoo cottages completed the picture. It's all been authenticated by erudite visitors: botanists, geologists and a chap from Roberts who identified 204 birds here, including eagles, black stork and five varieties of kingfisher. But you'll find Hermanus and Petro plenty knowledgeable themselves. We drove out along dusty tracks leading past the schoolhouse that his father donated to the mixed community (which still congregates there), through babbling brooks to Chinese lanterns and blankets of fynbos and medicinal succulents. Hermanus will name them all. Petro says he lives in the past, whereas she's an artist facing the future. Also in the pipeline are geological, botanical and fossil tours. There are many ways to enjoy the scenery, cycling, hiking, riding, fishing… and ostrich-obsessed Oudtshoorn is minutes away. When you're tired out, your sleepy cottage, with original Oregon pine doors and floors and farm-made furniture, awaits.

Rooms: 6 cottages: all fully self-contained with 1, 2 or 3 bedrooms and shared or en-suite bathrooms with baths and/or showers.
Price: R190 - R320 pp self-catering. Singles and special family rates on request.
Meals: Full breakfast R65, Continental breakfast R48. Formal dinners or informal semi-prepared braai packs on request.
Directions: Halfway between Calitzdorp & Oudtshoorn on R62. Head west from Oudtshoorn 28km, then Kruisrivier turn-off. Red Stone 6km down this road. Another entrance between foot of Swartberg mountain & Cango Caves via Matjiesrivier.

The Retreat at Groenfontein

Marie and Grant Burton
Calitzdorp
Tel: 044-213-3880 Fax: 044-213-3880
Email: info@groenfontein.com Web: www.groenfontein.com

A tiny gravel road twists along the sides of one idyllic to another yet more secluded valley, past old Cape Dutch farm buildings which line the route and eventually arrives at the Burtons' Victorian-colonial homestead. They ran a popular wilderness lodge in Namibia before trawling southern Africa for a new Eden, and it took years to find Groenfontein. It was worth the wait. The view from the verandah, where meals are served (and where I sampled a mouthwatering smoked snoek mousse, followed by ostrich casserole with gem-squash), crosses a valley and climbs the Burtons' own mountain before joining the vast Swartberg Nature Reserve, now a UNESCO World Heritage Site. What with hiking trails to intimate rock pools and excellent mountain trails, the opportunities for merry traipsing are limitless. When it gets hot, you can swim in the river or pool, or collapse inside the gloriously cool house with its original marble fireplace and pine and yellowwood flooring. There are 2 luxury rooms with slate floors and reed-and-mud roofs and 2 brand-new suites built away from the house with French-window views, which have been done in similar style. Airy bedrooms benefit from simple combinations of yellow, beige and cream. It is an incredible area to explore with kloofs, mountain wilderness, half-forgotten roads, with many animals to look out for. But, best of all, you come back to award-winning hospitality: delicious dinners, welcoming hosts and a truly relaxed household. Give yourselves 2 nights!

Rooms: 8: In main house; 1 king, 1 queen & 1 twin with shower & 1 twin with bath/shower; also 4 luxury rooms away from house, all kings/twins with views, bath & shower except 1 with shower only.
Price: R400 - R810 pp sharing, includes 3 or 4-course dinner and breakfast. Singles on request.
Meals: Full breakfast & 3 or 4-course dinner (without wine) ind'. Fully licensed. Light lunches & picnics from R35.
Directions: From Oudtshoorn take R62 towards Calitzdorp for 30km. Turn R to dirt rd signed Kruisrivier. After 17km keep L at fork as rd gets narrower & follow 10.7km until sign for The Retreat to your R. From Calitzdorp L at Groenfontein sign - 19km to house. Drive slowly.

Les Hauts de Montagu Guest Lodge

Myriam and Eric Brillant

Route 62, Montagu
Tel: 023-614-2514 Fax: 023-614-3517
Email: info@leshautsdemontagu.co.za Web: www.leshautsdemontagu.co.za
Cell: 083-529-3389 (Myriam) 083-528-9250 (Eric)

If you set your sights solely on staying in Montagu itself you would completely miss this little oasis of all things fine and French nestled three kilometres further along the road. As I slunk slowly up the long driveway past the helipad (sadly the Greenwood chopper was in for a service), Les Hauts De Montagu revealed itself in all its glory. It is not difficult to see why Eric and Myriam (both Congolese by birth but with years of Parisian industry experience) instantly fell '*tête over talons*' with this place; its setting is sensational. Perched high on the hillside it enjoys expansive views of the valley and its ripening vines. The main Cape Dutch farmhouse dates from 1865 and it has taken two years of painstaking restoration to bring the dilapidated building back to life. Inside, under 21 huge beams that hold up the roof, I dined on food that was fabulously French - garlic snail ravioli and creamy blue cheese with green fig preserve to name just two of the four scrumptious courses. With stomach bursting at the seams I crunched more heavily than usual along the loose stone path past beds of lavender to my cottage. A soaring chimney encourages the fire beneath on cold winter nights, while the huge glass doors allow refreshing breezes on hot summer ones. The glorious outside shower the following morning meant washing in the full view of Montagu... I was thankful it was those three kilometres away!

Rooms: 10: 1 twin, 7 kings and 2 superiors, all with en-suite baths with outside showers.
Price: R500 - R800 pp sharing. Singles on request.
Meals: Full breakfast included. Restaurant on premises, 4-course set menu from Oct-Apr.
Directions: Pass Montagu, stay on R62 for 3km. Hauts de Montagu on R. Helipad and airstrip also available.

Collins House

Tessa Collins
63 Kerk St (Church St), Prince Albert
Tel: 023-541-1786 Fax: 023-541-1786
Email: collinsh@tiscali.co.za Web: www.collinshouse.co.za
Cell: 082-377-1310

Collins House stands out on Kerkstraat, unusual as a fine two-storey Victorian townhouse among so many Cape Dutch gable buildings. The open-plan kitchen/sitting room is the warm heart of the house - check out the beautiful tile and wood floor - and when I arrived Tessa was in her 'office', an old desk in the middle of the room, creating wire topiary and listening to the cricket on the radio. There are french doors out to the flower garden, and the very large swimming pool and air-con in all the bedrooms are a blessing during Karoo summers. The town is full of Cape Dutch national monuments and snoozes right at the foot of the spectacular Swartberg Pass. You must not fail to experience this and Tessa takes guests up there with evening drinks - or you can hire your own scooter in town. Collins House is long on luxury. Bedrooms are upstairs (almost a rarity in itself in South Africa) and you are mollied and coddled with fine-quality linens and lotions. Tessa herself has been with us from the start, is refreshingly outspoken and likes grown-ups who she can have a drink with and get to know. Luxury is one thing, but character is inimitable... and Tessa and Collins House have that in spades. *No children. DSTV is available in the upstairs guest sitting room.*

Rooms: 4: 3 twins, 1 with en-suite bath, 1 with shower and 1 with bath and shower; 1 double with en-suite bath.
Price: R350 - R450 pp sharing. Single supplement R100.
Meals: Full breakfast included and served till 9.30am.
Directions: On Kerkstraat in the middle of town.

Onse Rus Guesthouse

Lisa and Gary Smith
47 Church St, Prince Albert
Tel: 023-541-1380 Fax: 023-541-1064
Email: info@onserus.co.za Web: www.onserus.co.za
Cell: 083-629-9196

The official pamphlet does a good job of conveying the delights of Onse Rus, but it modestly fails to bear testament to the biggest plus, the Smiths themselves. They fell in love with Prince Albert and the 150-year-old Cape Dutch Onse Rus in 1999 and their enthusiasm for both town and house has not abated since. Guests who have come down over the Swartberg Pass are given a whisky for their nerves and trips to The Hell, a famously isolated community 57km down a dirt track, are easily arranged. Back at the house, the large living room is hung with a permanent exhibition of local artists' work. The five thatched bedrooms all have private entrances, high ceilings, white walls and simple Karoo furnishings. One used to be part of the bakery, another was the printing room for a local newspaper. The house has some history! Outside there's a brand-new swimming pool (a thing of particular beauty in such a hot climate) and also a gazebo, a focal point for relaxing in the garden. Here guests are brought food and drink while leisurely hours are whiled away with good books. If the weather permits – which it usually does – you can sit out on the verandah and enjoy fig ice cream in the shade of the Cape ash and Karoo pepper trees.

Rooms: 5: 3 doubles and 2 twins (one twin sleeps 4). 4 with en-suite shower, 1 with en-suite bath and hand-shower.
Price: R330 - R370 pp sharing. Singles prices enthusiastically given on request.
Meals: Breakfast included. Traditional dinners on request
Directions: On the corner of the main street (Kerk or Church St) and Bank Sts.

Lemoenfontein Game Lodge

Ingrid Köster
Beaufort West
Tel: 023-415-2847 Fax: 023-415-1044
Email: lemoen@mweb.co.za Web: www.lemoenfontein.co.za

Lemoenfontein, in the shadow of the Nuweveld Mountains, is one of those places where whatever your mood on arrival – and after a tiring drive down the N1 mine was ropey - a calmness envelops you like magic vapour. I was suddenly enjoying a cool drink on the vast wooden verandah, gazing over measureless miles of veld and chatting happily to Ingrid about the history of the place. It was built as a hunting lodge in 1850, then became a sanatorium for TB sufferers (the dry Karoo air was beneficial), a farm and finally (and still) a nature reserve. Everything has been done well here, no corners cut and the result is a most relaxing, hassle-free stay. Rooms are stylish and understated with top-quality fabrics and completely comfortable beds. Outside, lawns, a pool, bar and braai area and the veld are all segregated by high dry-stone walls. You *must* go on a game drive through the reserve before dinner - to look at all the buck and zebra of course, but also to be out in such scenery as the sun goes down. And one final thing: dinner when we got back was at first mouth-watering, then lip-smacking. A real South African experience. *All rooms are air-conditioned.*

Rooms: 12: 7 doubles, 5 with en-suite bath and shower 2 with just shower; 5 twins, 2 with en-suite bath and shower and 3 with just shower.
Price: R360 - R400 pp sharing. Singles R450 - R480.
Meals: Full breakfast included. A set dinner is available every night for R130.
Directions: From the N1, 2km north of Beaufort West. Turn onto De Jagers Pass Road at the Lemoenfontein sign. Go 4km up dirt track, following signs.

Eastern Cape

Eastern Cape Side Dishes

A handful of highly-recommended things to do and places to eat in the Eastern Cape area...

Alan Weyer, Spirits of the Past Historical Tours

If you think you knew little of South Africa before coming here, just think about the droves of Europeans who set sail for these lands in the 1880's. The colonisation period is a facinating story of adventure and hardship, of determination and gritty humour and it's one Alan Weyer tells captivatingly. He's a knowledgeable historian and a great raconteur.
Contact: Alan Weyer, PO Box 490, Grahamstown; *Tel:* 046-622-2843;
Email: info@spiritsofthepast.co.za; *Web:* www.spiritsofthepast.co.za

Beachcomber Horse Trails

Experience the exhilarating freedom of galloping through the surf on deserted beaches, or if you are a novice walk sedately on fit, safe, well-trained horses. When it comes to equestrian adventure Jono is your man. He also organises game reserve rides (no lions here, in case this was a worry!) and, if you are a competent rider, I highly recommend the two- or four-night horse-safari. This is mainly on the beach with two river crossings, but you will also cross some game reserve with big-game viewing opportunities.
Contact: Jonathan Arnott, Kenton-on-Sea; *Prices:* R150 for one and a half hours' ride. Game reserve rides dependent on reserve;
Email: beachcombers@mtnloaded.co.za; *Web:* www.beachcomberhorsetrails.co.za

Nanaga Farm Stall

From humble beginnings 40 years ago, Nanaga is now one of the top farm stalls in the country. With jams, marmalades, relishes, chutneys, rusks and roosterkoek all on offer, it's really all about their pies which have reached iconic status. Whether frozen to take home, fresh for on the road or to enjoy in the country setting of Nanaga, you simply have to try the lamb and mint, or perhaps the wild boar, or the turkey and cranberry, the venison, the lamb curry, the spinach and feta... get the picture?
Contact: Leigh MacKenzie, N2 Highway; *Tel:* 041-468-0183; 041-468-0920;
Email: nanaga.farmstall@mweb.co.za; *Web:* www.nanaga.co.za

Wicker Woods

Joel Malkinson taught himself to cook and, having got to grips with South Africa's traditional cuisine, has given it a good shake-up in his own restaurant, an old house with open fires in winter and essential air-con in summer. An innovative menu is chalked up on a blackboard and there are seafood and grills galore. This is still one of the most popular restaurants in Port Elizabeth - booking long in advance is essential and only telephonically.
Contact: Joel Malkinson, 50 6th Avenue, Walmer, Port Elizabeth;
Prices: Average price for a 3-course meal R160 - R180; *Tel:* 041-581-1107;
Email: wickerwoods@mweb.co.za

Sederkloof Lodge

Thys and Alice Cilliers

PO Studtis, Baviaanskloof, Willowmore District
Tel: 049-839-1122 Fax: 049-839-1081
Email: thysbaviaans@mweb.co.za Web: www.sederkloof.co.za

Who dares, wins. The dust road that links the World Heritage Site Baviaanskloof Wilderness Area to the rest of the world also keeps it undiscovered. Old ways endure here. Warped and riven rocks line your passage through this spectacular valley, cracking open to reveal deep ravines and long forgotten roads into the earth. Do not be daunted. The lodge is as far as front-wheel drive will take you, though at times I would cut the engine anyway and step out into the awesome silence. Met by a very welcoming Thys and Alice, I was trundled up by 4x4 to the top where the air, rarified and fynbos-sweetened, blesses six mountain chalets discreetly built in glass and local stone. They are deceptively simple. I had barely stepped onto polished floors before I was burying myself in the folds of luxuriously white duvet that covered my four-poster bed... and slipping into a hot tub with mountain views and even eagles swirling beyond my toes. It was too early for a glass of port... but why not? Suddenly I was the gentleman traveller of old. Thys loves showing you his playground, for now that he has retired this is his passion, reintroducing oryx, impala and wildebeest onto the farm. A drive into the wilderness offers sightings of fabulous Knysna loeries and very rare black rhino. Let local guide, Kiewiet, walk you into the Sederkloof itself, famous for its old cedars and wild beehives. The personal attention is exceptional. Guests are treated to Alice's fine dining in the communal lodge, set to an epic vista that drops away from beyond the pool. But best of all is the 'surprise treat' to which you are led blindfold. Unforgettable.

Rooms: 6 mountain chalets with king-size beds, en-suite baths and outdoor showers.
Price: R1,500 pp sharing including all meals and activities.
Meals: All meals included.
Directions: Detailed directions on request.

34 Lovemore Crescent

Monica Johnson

St. Francis Bay
Tel: 042-294-0825 Fax: 042-294-0825
Email: dolfinvu@intekom.co.za Web: www.b-b.co.za
Cell: 082-695-3395

34 Lovemore is an unpretentious B&B and an absolute delight. This has everything to do with Monica's warm hospitality and the character of her home, built 20 years ago, though the beachside location is an added bonus. A cuppa appears on arrival and you are then shown up to your quarters, two large rooms under a high thatched roof, with a living area between them, all looking out to sea. The aloe-filled back garden is a bird-watcher's paradise where even the neighbours pop over for the viewing. The front garden has weaver-birds' nests in the trees and possibly Africa's most southerly baobab tree, a tenacious little thing brought down from Zimbabwe by the family in the '80s. And on the other side of the garden there is another separate flat, which can be rented on a B&B basis or as a self-catering unit (but you'd be missing out on an unforgettable breakfast of delicious home-made breads, scones, jams and all…). It lacks the sea views, so Monica feels duty-bound to offer it at give-away prices. With a sweeping vista across St. Francis Bay, where southern right whales can be seen in season and dolphins year round, you cannot fail to relax here. Keen surfers will be interested to note (they will in fact salivate over the news) that Bruce's Beauties are at the end of the garden.

Rooms: 3: 1 double with en/s shower and 1 twin with private shower and bath; 1 flat sleeping up to 6 with 1 bathroom.
Price: Rooms in the house: R250 - R350 pp sharing. Flat: R200 pp self-catering (or R240 with breakfast.)
Meals: Full breakfast included for B&B in the house.
Directions: From the Humansdorp road take 1st right into Lyme Rd South, then 3rd right onto St. Francis Drive, then 5th left onto Lovemore Crescent. 34 Lovemore is sign-posted at each of these turns. 34 is the last house on the left.

The Dunes Country House

Chantelle and Brent Cook
St. Francis Bay
Tel: 042-294-1685 Fax: 042-294-1687
Email: reservations@dunesstfrancis.com Web: www.dunesstfrancis.com
Cell: 082-324-3484

After fourteen years in the madding metropolis of LA, St. Francis Bay represented a vivid and welcome contrast for Chantelle and Brent: 600 hectares of thrumming nature on the doorstep and tranquillity in abundance. At the end of a sandy road through coastal fynbos, the guest house sits surrounded by indigenous garden with thick grass - the kind that crunches underfoot - aloe trees and strelitzias. Brent is a walking guide and takes guests through the reserve on foot. He explains what they are doing for nature conservation while pointing out and expanding your knowledge of any critters spotted en route. A two-hour walk takes you through the sand dunes, where you follow in the footsteps of the Strandlopers who lived in the region hundreds of years ago. Ancient middens, archaeological artefacts and endemic fauna and flora are part of this fascinating tour. Tea, scones, lunch or a well-earned sundowner will be waiting for you on your return. Reminiscent of an old Cape farmhouse, the guest-house is part of the conservation effort with its Oregon wood floors, doors and window frames all reclaimed from an old school. The theme of comfortable splendour extends into the bedrooms, with their marble counter tops, percale linens on beds, underfloor heating, ball-and-claw baths and French doors that open onto the verandah. For even more comfort book a moonlit massage at their new outdoor bush spa... relaxation never felt so sweet. *The Dunes are implementing responsible tourism practices and gradually becoming fully eco-friendly. They have also recently introduced a frogging safari.*

Rooms: 7: 6 doubles with en-suite bath and shower, and 1 family cottage with full bathroom.
Price: Doubles: R650 - R1,250 pp sharing. Cottage: R500 - R625 pp sharing (based on 4-pax occupancy), R250 - R350 per child sharing. Winter specials available on request.
Meals: Full breakfast & afternoon tea & scones incl'. Light lunches R24 - R50. Dinners by arrangement.
Directions: From the N2, take St. Francis Bay/Humansdorp exit. Follow signs to St. Francis Bay on R330. Go thro' traffic circle - drive for approx 800m. R at The Dunes sign & continue to gate.

Cottage on the Hill Guest House

Anne and Rob Eaglesham
63 Assissi Drive, St. Francis Bay
Tel: 042-294-0761 Fax: 042 294-0016
Email: cottageonthehill@telkomsa.net Web: www.cottageonthehill.co.za
Cell: 076-563-5662

Cottage on the Hill has been awarded five stars, which, paradoxically, might have been quite off-putting for GG. But on this occasion we would award five stars too! This is because all the luxury is fully backed up by some very warm, attentive and characterful hosting from Anne and Rob. Leading me away from their sumptuous yellowwood bar, the ever-animated Eagleshams (followed closely by their two no-less-animated dachshunds) showed me to my enormous suite, Francolin. White furniture makes for a beachy atmosphere, as does the voile drape over the bed and the exposed thatched roof. You can absorb the sea view from the black-footed Victorian bath, although I remained dry and admired it from the expansive balcony. Then below there is Mongoose Suite with its dark granite surfaces on top of white cupboards and Persian rugs on the floor and original oil paintings. The shower has a door leading to an outside bath (always a sure-fire winner with me) and braai area. A sink thoughtfully placed next to the braai meant that I could prepare the record-breaking yellow-finned tuna I'd caught earlier that day. Further round, there's a bird hide hidden by indigenous plants. And across a courtyard, past the natural rock swimming pool and some metal heron sculptures, is Guinea-fowl Cottage with its mahogany bed and cane furniture. I long to return and eat my breakfast among the lavender and aloes. If you're wondering if I really did catch that fish, you'll have to go to Cottage on the Hill and find out for yourself....

Rooms: 2 suites and 1 bedroom in the cottage: 2 king/twins, 1 queen; All with en-suite bath and shower (bath outside in Mongoose).
Price: Guinea-fowl Cottage: R395 - R550 pp sharing.Mongoose and Francolin: R550 - R840 pp sharing. Single rates on request.
Meals: Full breakfast and afternoon tea included.
Directions: From N2, take St. Francis Bay/Humansdorp exist. Follow sign to St. Francis Bay onto R330. Go over roundabout, past the golf course and drive for approx. 600m. Turn left into Homestead Rd. Turn right onto Assissi - Cottage on the Hill is no. 63.

Thunzi Bush Lodge

Mark and Trenwyth Pledger

Maitland Road, Maitlands, Port Elizabeth
Tel: 041-372-2082 Fax: 086-5030-698
Email: places@thunzi.co.za Web: www.thunzibushlodge.co.za
Cell: 072-597-4810

Ex-engineer Mark has been building treehouses since he was three (well, as soon as he could co-ordinate his hands with any intricacy) and Thunzi's flawlessly planned and finished chalets are standing proof of his skill. Many personal touches are integrated within; baths wrapped in wooden decking, sinks stationed on sealed, sniffle-free sneeze-wood (strangely enough, a beautiful wood that makes you sneeze when you work with it); and a medley of wholesome games and entertainments. The completely private cabins, linked only by gravel walkways, peep timidly through indigenous forest onto the De Stades River Wetlands where an abundance of birds have been listed. Over 352 wacky-named species flock to this eco-diverse area where coastal forest, thicket and wetlands meet (try narina trogon, African rail, Knysna loerie and the often-heard buff-spotted, red-chested and striped flufftails for size). Take the night walk through the forest and you'll be greeted by a hypnotic symphony of nocturnal sounds and even a few wandering antelope. By day relaxation comes easy (the spa packages sound blissful), but should you want a little more activity simply pop down the road to Maitland's impressive duned beach, the most isolated and untouched Port Elizabeth has to offer. Here you can hike, snorkel, whale-watch or sand-board (oh yes - the dunes really *are* that big). Personally a lamp-lit dinner beneath the star-lined silhouette of canopy would be enough, but I suppose one really should work up an appetite first.

Rooms: 3 chalets: 2 twin/kings, both with en-suite bath & shower; 1 family unit with 1 queen & 1 twin room with en-suite bath and shower.
Price: R525 - R795 pp sharing. 40% supplement for singles.
Meals: Full breakfast included. Light lunches and 3-course dinner on request. R165 for dinner, an extra R165 for private open-air dining experience.
Directions: Thunzi Bush Lodge is signed from the N2. More detailed directions can be emailed on request.

Aquasands

Richard and Deborah Johnson
No. 7, 11th Avenue, Summerstrand, Port Elizabeth
Tel: 041-583-3159 Fax: 041-583-3187
Email: greenwood@aquasands.co.za Web: www.aquasands.co.za
Cell: 082-462 6774

Aquasands is glamorous. The welcoming, vibrant Deborah is also glamorous. By the time I left, even I felt a bit glamorous too. She is a food stylist and husband Richard is a philatelist (a stamp dealer - but glamorous too!); they excel in their acute sensitivity to each guest's needs. And their open-plan contemporary home is a repository for an ever-changing, rotating collection of fine art. The guest rooms, with their own separate entrances, are blessed with crushed velvet or silk bedspreads, percale cottons and mohair blankets, red gerberas in fish-bowls and cactus-style soap dishes, an echo of the real cactus garden out there next to the tranquil koi fishpond. Breakfast is served on the architecturally spectacular grey, slate-tiled patio under steel and wood, offset with cheerful splashes of pink, purple and cobalt paint blocks. This is surrounded by a lush garden where palm trees intermingle with indigenous plants and giant aloes... and beyond is the ocean, with safe bathing and sandy beaches a mere two minutes' walk away. If that's too far there's always the large heated saline pool, sauna and steam room within flopping distance of the breakfast table. I met Grandpa too - another asset of the house - a champion fly-fisherman with photos to prove it. Come here for a holiday and not just a stopover!

Rooms: 4: 3 king/twins and 1 queen. All with en-suite bath and shower.
Price: R500 - R650 pp sharing. Singles from R600.
Meals: Full breakfast included.
Directions: From Cape Town take N2 to Port Elizabeth. Take exit 751B at sign for Settlers Way, follow signs to Summerstrand. Keep left onto Marine Drive along the sea front until 11th Avenue.

Forest Hall

James and Hilary Bolton

84 River Road, Walmer,
Port Elizabeth
Tel: 041-581-3356
Fax: 086-660-4848
Email:
foresthallbb@telkomsa.net
Web: www.foresthall.co.za
Cell: 072-020-9595

As I approached Forest Hall I couldn't help wondering how my car had taken such a dramatic wrong turn as to end up somewhere in the Home Counties. Built by a British architect who already owned a house in England by the same name, the building is over a hundred years old and was one of Walmer's first farms. But don't worry... no old eiderdowns or Victorian plumbing here. These rooms have all the modern comforts you could ask for: slate-floored bathrooms with frameless, open-plan showers and some seriously sumptuous bed linen. The three self-catering rooms have neat, compact kitchens and can accomodate families, while the smaller bed and breakfast room is more old English in style, with paintings of fox hunts on the walls. Nothing is too much trouble for James, who will even happily take people to Addo Elephant Park. He may not be a qualified guide, but he has a minibus and plenty of enthusiasm and knowledge. And it's not just James who'll do anything for you. Every member of the family is involved in some way. Hilary is the gourmet cook and James's mum Ann makes the home-made rusks, which you will find in your room. Even their three kids like to get involved, especially if there are other children looking for bouncing accomplices on their ground-level trampoline. The peaceful, beautiful, 1-acre, sun-filtered, park-like Forest Hall garden also recently won the corporate section of the Garden of the Year competition for Port Elizabeth. Good hiking and mountain-biking trails are a five-minute walk away, with free use of the Forest Hall bikes.

Rooms: 4: all king/twins, all with en-suite bath, shower and kitchenette.
Price: R400 pp sharing.
Meals: Full Continental breakfast included. Dinner served on request.
Directions: From Port Elizabeth airport turn L at 1st traffic circle into 3rd Ave Walmer. Turn left at 1st set of lights into Heugh Rd. Go up until 9th Ave lights. Turn right into 9th Ave. Go down this across the traffic lights in Main Rd until you reach the last road off 9th on left. Turn into River Road. Sign 'Forest Hall' outside gates.

Lupus Den Country House

Priscilla and Noel Walton

Addo/Sunland
Tel: 042-231-0447 Fax: 086-626-7380
Email: info@lupusden.co.za Web: www.lupusden.co.za
Cell: 072-1814-750

Priscilla and Noel have not needed to learn any tricks about how to host. They are just naturally hospitable people who make you feel instantly at home and relaxed. When I arrived, lunch was waiting on the table and, with a home-made lemon drink in hand, I already felt part of the furniture. They have been living in their farmhouse for 40 years now – although the land it stands on has been in the family's hands since 1894 – and have made some adjustments to make the rooms all the more comfortable for their guests. The latest of these - three new large rooms, each with its private entrance - are in Garden Cottage. Two have outdoor showers and all have air-con. Their citrus and cattle farm is found on the friendly dirt roads between Addo and Kirkwood. And when I say friendly, I mean locals waved hello to me all the way there! The garden, surrounded by citrus groves, blooms with bougainvillaea and an abundance of other flowers and trees. The tiled swimming pool and an enormous tipuanu tree are two of the gardens' greatest assets, while vine-shaded terraces are the perfect places of repose after a rendezvous with the elephants in Addo (only 20 minutes away). When staying at Lupus Den you can be a tourist by day out in the parks and feel a local when back in the fold. Breakfast includes freshly-baked bread (naturally). A true farm B&B with home cooking – hard to beat.

Rooms: 6: Homestead: 1 twin & 2 doubles, 2 en-s bath & shower, 1 en-s sh'r; Garden Cottage: 3 doubles/twins, all en-s bathrooms, 2 outdoor shower. All rooms own entrance, patio & aircon.
Price: Homestead rooms: R250 - R300 pp. Singles R325 - R390. Garden Cottage rooms: R400 - R425 pp sharing. Singles R520 - R550. Ask re kids' rates.
Meals: Full breakfast included. Adults & children 12 years up: light lunch R50 pp; set 3-course dinner R150 pp. Younger children's meal rates reduced (depends what they have).
Directions: From PE R335 towards Addo. Cross railway in Addo, then L onto R336 towards Kirkwood. At Sunland R at Lupus Den B&B sign & follow signs.

The Elephant House

Clive and Anne Read
Addo
Tel: 042-233-2462 Fax: 042-233-0393
Email: info@elephanthouse.co.za Web: www.elephanthouse.co.za
Cell: 083-799-5671

The bush telegraph gave advance notice of the many charms at Elephant House. Many tourists and other guest house owners had urged us to visit with a sincerity you could not ignore. It's a stunning house, the brainchild of one night's sleepless pondering by Anne who mapped the whole thing out in her head – a small, lawned courtyard surrounded on three sides by thatched and shady verandahs. The house is, in a sense, inside out. The drawing room leads to a dining room outside on the verandah (with antiques and Persian rugs). All the bedrooms open onto the verandah too and dinner (advertised with an African gong) is served there on silver and crystal. Evening meals are lit to stunning effect with lampshades made of Tuareg bowls. Lawns, indigenous trees and the racehorse stud (Clive used to run one in Natal) surround the house and when I was there the paddocks were full of mares with their foals. The bedrooms are luxurious with antique furniture, carpets, thick duvets and deep beds; and morning tea or coffee is brought to your bed, if so desired. There are also the Stable Cottage and the Family Suite, which, separate from the main house, retain the same charm, but are just a little cosier. The Elephant House also runs open-vehicle game drives in Addo, a few minutes away, morning and afternoon. *There is now a seasonal on-site masseuse who can conduct treatments inside or outside (Mon - Fri, Oct - May).*

Rooms: 15: 9 rooms in the house; 4 twins and 4 kings, all with en-suite bath and shower and one family room that sleeps 5. Also 2 cottages that both sleep 4 and 4 cottages that sleep 2.
Price: R660 - R1,450 pp sharing. Cottages R500 - R600 pp sharing.
Meals: Full breakfast included in Elephant House and Stable Cottages. Lunch & dinner provided. Three-course dinners R220. Or a la carte at Wine Bar & Café (near the Stables).
Directions: From P.E. R335 through Addo 5km on the road towards the park - you will see a sign off to your left for The Elephant House.

Hopefield Country House & Guest Farm

Kobus Buys and Gerhard Maritz

Off the R336, between Addo and Sunland
Tel: 042-234-0333 Fax: 086-566-0152
Email: info@hopefield.co.za Web: www.hopefield.co.za

Known in the Addo area as The Music Boys, Kobus and Gerhard have been upping the tempo in the Sundays River Valley. They've both done time in the fast-paced record industry in Gauteng, but now they've repaired to Kobus's family home (along with three pianos and an organ) to do what they love best: playing music, gardening and entertaining (don't miss out on dinner - the cooking is sensational!). Outside, the garden continues the musical theme. A bust of Beethoven surveys the perfect lawn and several of their 54 varieties of roses have composers' names, Edward Elgar and Benjamin Britten among them. Their palpable creative urges are certainly not confined to just music-making though. Rooms are all uniquely decorated, with one-off paintings, beautiful antique furniture and slaved-over original wood floors. Whatever happens, they don't want it to look like a catalogue: even the baths are all different, with free-standing Victorian tubs and time-warping spas. There is a fully-licensed bar with a well-stocked library next to it, as well as an open sitting and dining area, overlooking the baby grand. Guests have even commented that the affable Horatio and Ophelia, their well-loved miniature schnauzers, were more of an attraction than Addo's elephants!

Rooms: 5: 1 king with en-suite shower, 2 queens with en-suite bath, 2 king/twins with full bathrooms en-suite. All rooms are air-conditioned.
Price: R350 - R550 pp sharing. Singles rates on request.
Meals: Full breakfast included. Set 3-course dinner available on request.
Directions: Signed from the R336 between Kirkwood and Addo. More detailed directions can be emailed.

The Colonial on Arundel

Molly and Conor O'Hagan Ward

Arundel Farm, Rietfontein Road, Addo
Tel: 042-234-0871 Fax: 086-689-8649
Email: info@thecolonial.co.za Web: www.thecolonial.co.za
Cell: 082-558-9896

When it comes to character The Colonial on Arundel is not in short supply: from the elephant feet that proudly stand on the porch (they are authentic, Molly tells me) to the huge wooden rhino statues that grace my bedroom fireplace and the framed butterflies that decorate the wall. And then of course there is Conor, a delightful story-teller, conservationist, game driver and self-confessed lover of colonial history. Brimming with colourful anecdotes he tells me over tea and cake that the house was originally owned in the 1930s by an English gentleman from Arundel (hence, of course, the name). The couple have kept much of the original design but have also added a myriad of treasures from the game lodge that they used to run in KwaZulu Natal. Zebra, giraffe and buffalo prints decorate the bedrooms, while wildlife and history books are stacked on the table in my private lounge. There's a sense of care and attention here which extends to the garden too. Lemon and orange orchards surrounding the homestead, a herb garden packed with marjoram, thyme and parsley is bursting into life, and there are Molly's roses too, to be showcased at the Addo rose festival. For me, though, the hidden treat is The Wallow, an enchanting outdoor bath. "It's not just for honeymooners," Molly smiles. "Guests have been known to race back from the elephant park to be the first ones in there!" Guided by the light from the full moon, I later creep across the garden to enjoy my very first wallow. Ah, yes. It really is something to rush home for! *3-day package available. Ask for details.*

Rooms: 2: luxury suites, both with queens and en-suite shower and outdoor bath.
Price: R395 - R475 pp sharing.
Meals: Full breakfast included. A set 3-course dinner available on request.
Directions: Detailed directions on website.

RiverBend Lodge

Marius Malherbe
Off Zuurberg Road, Addo Elephant National Park
Tel: 042-233 8000 Fax: 042-233-8028
Email: reservations@riverbendlodge.co.za Web: www.riverbendlodge.co.za
Cell: 084-503-3189

Within one hot hour of PE airport I was supping a nectareously refreshing lemonade, squeezed from one of eight variants of citrus plantations at RiverBend. Within another hour I'd moved on to vetkoek (a traditional 'doughnut' bread, in this case oozing with gourmet ingredients from 7-course-chef Chris), followed by a fanned power kip and a reviving speed-dip in the pool. And now six of us, newly acquainted, were out spotting on a game drive – the sun, scent and space of the bush already working their magic, dissipating the rest of the world into the dust clouds behind us. I've been to Addo already and I've also been lucky enough to experience several other game drives up and down the country, but in this 400-odd-minute taster of the Nyathi section of the park - to which this lodge enjoys private access - I felt I could have been freshly landed from Heathrow. Under our Addo-born, extremely approachable ranger Justin, we learned anything from how the leopard tortoise is the only member of its family able to swim, to the cause for the genetic recession of female elephants' tusks in this area. We also fell into a trance at the beauty of a herd of 50+ ellies crossing grasslands under our noses. As Marius explained, folks don't come here for 'big five kills', nor is Addo comparable to Kruger or Botswana (where his years of experience were accrued). This park knows its draw-cards and RiverBend specializes in providing guests with an effortless, enchanting and affecting experience to take away with them. It is also very luxurious!

Rooms: 8: 4 luxury family rooms; 3 executive rooms with private outdoor showers & verandahs; 1 honeymoon suite with private verandah, outdoor shower & plunge pool. An additional exclusive use villa sleeps up to 6.
Price: R1800 - R3200 pp sharing. Singles +40%. Private villa: R2000 - R3200 pp sharing (sleeps & fully caters up to 6, & includes private chef, guide, vehicle, laundry service).
Meals: Full cooked breakfast, lunch (a la carte), high tea and 7-course dinner all inclusive.
Directions: Allow a good hour from PE; see owner's website for detailed directions.

Idwala Game Lodge

Ernst and Alida Du Toit

Adjacent to Lalibela Game Reserve, Sidbury
Tel: 046-622-2163 Fax: 046-622-2163
Email: enquiries@idwalalodge.com Web: www.idwalalodge.com
Cell: 083-277-7235

I was very excited when I first discovered Idwala. This was not just because of their introductory cocktail, complete with floating pebble (in case you're wondering, it's because Idwala means 'rock'), but because this was a real family-run lodge, as luxurious as all its corporate competitors. Mother and daughter team Claudine and Alida have created their own unique take on bush lodge décor, hand-picking every detail of the rooms, right down to the rock soap dish. Taxidermy is pastiched with carefully-chosen pieces of local art and craft. Animals made from wire paper and beads are lit from beneath, wardrobe knobs are shaped like tortoises' backs, and a beautifully gnarled knobwood tree branch wound its way to the top of my thatched ceiling. The glass doors in each room slide all the way back, so you can be completely open to the unfenced wilds beyond, and the shower has a glass wall out onto the bush. But you needn't worry about privacy. Every room is surrounded by greenery and reached by its own Indiana Jones-style walkway. The only creatures sneaking a peak through the curtains will be of the distinctly wild variety. And to get really close to them, Idwala's magnificent game drives are worth every minute of the early wake-up. *Airport transfers are available as well as star-gazing with trained ranger using on-site telescope. The lodge can also be rented out exclusively. Ask Alida for details.*

Rooms: 4: all can be double or twin with en-suite showers.
Price: R2,500 - R3,750 pp sharing. 50% supplement for singles.
Meals: All meals, local drinks and game drives are included.
Directions: Take the N2 from Port Elizabeth to Grahamstown. Exit at Sidbury turn-off. The Idwala Lodge is 7km further.

The Cock House

Richard Anker-Simmons and Jean-Louis Fourie

10 Market St, Grahamstown
Tel: 046-636-1287 Fax: 046-636-1287
Email: cockhouse@imaginet.co.za Web: www.cockhouse.co.za
Cell: 082-820-5592

The Cock House offers a friendly welcome and fine dining in the setting of a historic old house in downtown Grahamstown. Nelson Mandela has stayed three times and former President Thabo Mbeki has also been a guest (their visits are recorded in photos on the walls of the bar in case you don't believe me). Former owner Belinda Tudge worked hard with her late husband Peter to build up a business to be proud of, and it is really nice to see a staff who are so obviously genuinely proud to work there. With new owner Richard, manager Jean-Louis and his team carrying on the Cock House tradition of friendly hospitality there is always an opportunity to strike up a conversation in the delightful yellowwood bar. The house dates back to 1826 and was one of the first built in Grahamstown. A stone-floored verandah stretches along the front of the house (mirrored by a wooden balcony upstairs) and the interior is full of yellowwood beams and broad-planked floors. I can recommend Norden's restaurant, which offers an international cuisine with a South African flavour and has its own herb garden, using local and seasonal ingredients wherever possible. The home-made bread is a particular treat. The two large rooms in the main house have glass doors opening onto the balcony, while modern apartments and seven converted stables open onto the garden. Personal and fun.

Rooms: 13: 7 doubles, 2 twins; all with en-suite bath and shower; 4 x 2-bedroom apartments with bath and shower.
Price: R395 - R475 pp sharing. R415 - R475 singles.
Meals: Full breakfast included & served any time. Lunch & dinner available in Norden's restaurant (except Mon lunch). Dinners on request if not incl'.
Directions: From P.E. take 2nd exit from N2 signed "Business District/George Street". Take off-ramp L, turn L at bridge into George St. Continue down long hill into Grahamstown. At 4-way stop with Market St turn R & will see Cock House on R corner.

Map Number: 6

Entry Number: 210

Dovecote

Angela Thomas
17 Worcester St, Grahamstown
Tel: 046-622-8809 Fax: 046-622-8809
Email: anthomas@imaginet.co.za Web: www.grahamstown.co.za/dovecote/
Cell: 082-695-4262

From the charming garden cottage off her quiet Grahamstown street, Angela runs a good old-fashioned B&B: very comfortable and very friendly. Even as I drove up Worcester Street, I knew I was going to like Dovecote – joggers, dog-walkers and garden potterers all offered a nod and a wave. Angela, an avid bridge player, was the most friendly of the lot, opening up her cottage to guests simply because she loves doing it. And guests quickly become devoted. Her most famous returnee, Emeritus Archbishop Desmond Tutu, often stays when he's in town – there's a photo of him and his wife standing in the Dovecote garden. Perhaps it's this small garden with pebbled paths and a stone table in the shade of the bougainvillaea; perhaps it's the quiet privacy of the studio-style cottage, with its stable door and small kitchenette; or perhaps it's Angela's delicious home baking that lures him back time after time. Big, warm, freshly-baked scones were just one small scratch on the surface of Angela's impressive breakfast repertoire. I surreptitiously held one back to savour later in the day, they were so good. All of this has certainly whetted my appetite for a return visit.

Rooms: 1 cottage with twin beds and sleeper-couch and en-suite shower.
Price: R240 - R260 pp sharing. Singles on request.
Meals: Continental breakfast included. Selection of restaurants in Grahamstown.
Directions: On N2 from PE take first Grahamstown exit signed Beaufort Street. At lights turn left into Summerset Street. Go over three stop-streets and, as road curves left, turn left into Worcester Street.

Kichaka Luxury Game Lodge

Keith Craig
Assegaai Bush, Grahamstown
Tel: 046-622-6024 Fax: 046-622-6028
Email: info@kichaka.co.za Web: www.kichaka.co.za
Cell: 083-236-0754

The rhinos were minding their own business, but in my over-excitement at seeing them, I missed my turning. I was able to retrace my steps, though, and was received at the lodge in fine style. A cool face-towel and a fruit cocktail were followed by a glass of chilled white wine and a buffet lunch tantalizingly described by one of the waiters. After lunch, manager Keith, who is bursting with enthusiasm for Kichaka, took me on a tour. First stop was 'hippo station', a large deck that extends over a small lake in front of the trimly-thatched lodge; here an infinity pool permits the illusion of basking with the hippos as they grunt and shuffle below. Each rondavel suite is exquisite, mixing African tones with European sophistication. Neat shutters at one end partition off vast baths and showers from equally enormous beds, while at the other French windows lead out onto a private stoep inset with your own pure-blue plunge pool. Upstairs in the main lodge you are well served by a huge flat-screen TV and literary bookshelves, but it was as Keith described the gourmet dinners served each night that I really began slavering. I noticed him frowning over the (complimentary) house wine. "It's just too good," he said shaking his head. With all this you might forget that you were in the bush, but daily game drives (all the so-called big five and much much more are here) with expert guides ensure that you won't. The message was loud and clear. Kichaka is about very fine living in an exciting bush setting. *Children from the age of 8 are welcome.*

Rooms: 10 suites, all king/twin with en-suite bath and shower and plunge-pool.
Price: R2,750 - R3,950 pp sharing (single +50%) inclusive of all safari activities, meals and drinks (local beers and spirits, house wines and soft drinks).
Meals: Full board including refreshments on game drives.
Directions: Take the Assegai Bush/Kichaka turn-off from the N2 (30km from Grahamstown toward PE) and then drive 3.5km along gravel road to lodge entrance.

Map Number: 6

The Safari Lodge on Amakhala

Justine and Mike Weeks
Amakhala Game Reserve
Tel: 046-636-2750 central reservations
Fax: 086-694-9454
Email: centralres@amakhala.co.za
Web: www.amakhala.co.za
Cell: 082-966-5696

As I soaked in my double bath, candles lit, the late sky glowing pink with pleasure, birds twittering, bush buck barking in the surrounding hills and lions roaring from afar (or so I chose to think…), it crossed my mind that this was perhaps not the toughest assignment of my life thus far. Amakhala Safari Lodge is surely the luxurious way to experience the game parks of the Eastern Cape. Beds, equipped with mosquito nets, are super-comfortable and there's a sofa area inside each thatched hut whose canvas fronts and terraces look onto the valley brush and the waterhole below. The bedrooms and the communal hut are decorated with Cape antiques and furniture carved from the wood on Mike's farm. Mike and Justine aren't always at the camp, but their friendly rangers are sure to take good care of you. After a delicious meal – usually served round the fire outside – and a good night's sleep, an early wake-up call takes you to Amakhala Game Reserve (now a big five reserve) with its beautiful and varied scenery of bushveld, savannah, cliffs and lots and lots of animals. Back at the lodge I prefered to loll by the pool before an afternoon game drive took us back out to those magnificent animals. Justine and Mike deserve to feel proud of their establishment, which has now been Fair Trade Accredited since 2008. *Day trips to the neighbouring Born Free Foundation and Addo Elephant National Park are included in a 3-day package. Children 9+ are welcome.*

Rooms: 11 luxury doubles with en-suite double baths with shower attachment, outside showers and private plunge-pools.
Price: R2,580 pp sharing - R3,780 pp sharing. Singles plus 30%. All-inclusive (meals, local beer & house wine, safari activities).
Meals: All included.
Directions: From PE take N2 for 60km towards Grahamstown. Turn left on gravel road to Paterson and follow signs.

Reed Valley Bush Lodge

Rod and Tracy Weeks
Reed Valley Bush Lodge, Amakhala Game Reserve
Tel: 042-235-1287 Fax: 042-235-1263
Email; reedvalley@amakhala.co.za Web: www.amakhala.co.za
Cell: 082-783-2506

Built into the bush at the top end of an open valley, Rod and Tracy's latest venture offers their guests a large helping of unspoilt wilderness... without forgetting, of course, to accommodate fully your appetite for luxury and creature comfort at the same time. Guests are welcomed at Reed Valley Inn before being whisked away to the Bush Lodge and the Amakhala Game Reserve. Talking of creature comfort, giraffe, antelope and elephants are your neighbours here, slowly foraging their way about on the open plains under a great sweeping sky. Rooms at the lodge keep as close to nature as they can with thatched roofing, tented walls, outdoor showers and wooden flooring. Each earth-toned room - white linen, plump cushions, air-con, oval bath, fireplace - also has its own decking, complete with plunge pool, so that guests can keep an eye on the comings and goings of the animals in great comfort. Although only 15 minutes' drive from Reed Valley, the Bush Lodge is a world away. Peace and tranquillity reign, but this is also a fun, sociable place. Evening meals are served at long tables in the main building with guests and staff mingling to create a laid-back, all-in-it-together sort of atmosphere. An inviting pub with wrap-around bar is an enticing addition, and perfectly designed for late-night story-telling with its elevated wooden platform opening out onto the bush. The lodge only opened in December 2007 and is an exciting new addition to the Amakhala scene.

Rooms: 4: all doubles with en-suite bath and outdoor shower. Each room/tent has its own private plunge pool.
Price: R2,580 pp sharing May to August; R3,780 pp sharing September to April. All-inclusive with light lunch, dinner, B&B and two game activities. Single supplement 30%.
Meals: All meals and game drives included.
Directions: From PE take N2 for 60km towards Grahamstown and see sign to Reed Valley on the right.

HillsNek Safaris

Brent and Chantelle Cook

Amakhala Game Reserve
Tel: 042-294-1685 Fax: 042-294-1687
Email: reservations@dunesstfrancis.com Web: www.dunesstfrancis.com
Cell: 082-779-9575

The banks of the Bushmans River lie but a few metres away; to the front, expansive plains sprawl hectare upon hectare; and behind, at the foot of cliffs, an entire fossilized skeleton of a paranthodon was discovered in 1845. Welcome to HillsNek, an exclusive-use, family-owned safari lodge cocooned in the Iguanodon Hoek at Amakhala. Though encircled by a big five game reserve, there's not a fence in sight. Instead, three luxury tents, outdoor showers, wrap-around decks, a thatch-and-stone lodge, open bar and pool, are bound at the seams by raised walkways; other than that they stand free. The managers, Brent and Chantelle, prefer things this way, while their ranger, Andy, has known it no other. His job is to look after the reserve's black and white rhino, which, much to the envy of his peers, involves him being all but part of the herd. A local East Caper with a degree in Nature Conservation, there's little this guy can't tell you about the region and its inhabitants, and his patience is equally admirable. You'll need a minimum two-night stay, in which he'll take you on unlimited open-top game drives with plenty of other activities and chill-time in the mix. A special moment for me was watching Andy quietly at work, tracking his animals with a telemetry set before monitoring and recording their behaviour at a distance. The terrain, with its raised ridges, open plains and deep gorge, lends itself perfectly to this low-key, unobtrusive approach to animal observation, a sometimes forgotten contrast to those up close and personal encounters!

Rooms: 3 luxury safari tents, all kings with open-plan baths, child pull-out beds, raised verandahs and outdoor showers.
Price: R1,650 - R2,500 pp sharing, based on a minimum 2-night stay for 4-6 people; R1,950 - R2,750 pp sharing, based on a minimum 2-night stay for 2-3 people.
Meals: Full breakfast & all meals, snacks & drinks incl'.
Directions: From Port Elizabeth, travel N2 towards Grahamstown. Turn right at the Amakhala/Woodbury Lodge gate. Proceed through gate to Conservation Centre where you will be met by your ranger.

Woodbury Lodge

Jennifer, Giles, Richard and Cathy Gush

Amakhala Game Reserve
Tel: 046-636-2750 Fax: 086 694-6895
Email: centralres@amakahala.co.za Web: www.amakahala.co.za

I'm more accustomed to being welcomed by barking dogs than by a giraffe nonchalantly chewing on the treetops. And was that an elephant doing its best to blend into the undergrowth? With Jennifer's eagle eye, more and more animals became apparent in the shimmering distance, and I'd hardly left the N2. Though don't worry, you'd never know it. The stone-and-thatch buildings huddle against rocky hills, and the rooms (reached via steps dug into the hillside) are hidden from each other by palms and wild vegetation. The yellow walls of my simple room were dotted sparingly with local art, though the window offered the most striking sight – a 'dazzle' of zebra gently following the curves of the river while a raptor rode the thermal currents above. I knew I could never forget Amakahala. And all of this from my bed, whose crisp white linen promised a sound night's sleep later on. Heading back down to the deck outside the dining room, I feasted on the high tea with a ferocity that worried a fellow guest, impelling him to warn me against ruining my supper – how kind, but how mistaken, he was. After the game drive, and drinks by the outside fire that had been lit in our absence, all three courses of supper were hungrily dispatched on the long dining table with Richard (Jennifer's brother-in-law), our genial host. With the glowing embers of the fire slowly dimming before going out all together we made our way to bed. My new friend looked aghast when I expressed how much I was looking forward to breakfast.

Rooms: 6: all with twin/kings and en-suite baths and showers.
Price: R2,080 - R2,580 pp sharing. 30% single supplement.
Meals: Full breakfast, high tea and dinner included. Drinks also included.
Directions: 80km from Port Elizabeth on the N2 towards Grahamstown. Turn right at Woodbury Lodge sign.

Sebumo Tude Nature's Lounge

Doris and Ronald Dettke
Southwell, Kenton-on-Sea
Email: info@sebumotude.co.za Web: www.sebumotude.co.za
Cell: 072-490-6035

Those who know South Africa well and feel in need of the nurture of nature come here to unwind. When the wind stills, the music begins in this valley; it possesses an acoustic wonder. Every note emitted from the vast register of indigenous bush is somehow amplified and echoed, so that as I sat on the decked verandah petting Sebu and Mo (gentle-giant brother and sister Great Danes), I found myself tuning in to a remarkably sharp, natural, surround-sound system. This, I thought, is what is meant by Nature's Lounge. Doris and Ronald left Hamburg with a dream and a plan: to scour Namibia, Botswana and Zimbabwe for inspiration before creating their own haven not too far from the ocean. Thatched lapas and chalets mushroom from the predominantly green bush, which may be decorated by yellow acacias in summer or orange aloes in winter; red spring corals were the motif at the time of writing. Inside, the theme is quite simple all year round… luxury. Headboards are coddled in suede, mattresses are super-sponged and sand-crete walls metamorphose into satin-crete in all the en-suite bathrooms. With a romantic touch the latter also open on to outdoor showers. Those seeking even closer contact with the elements should opt for the tented camp (15 minutes away by 4x4) where, once the sun sets below raised verandahs, there's a fair chance of spotting that weirdest of creatures, the aardvark. Oh, and the food here is so sought-after that the restaurant recently had to be shut to a fuming public just so that resident guests could be properly looked after.

Rooms: 8: 2 chalets, comprising 2 kings en/s shower & 2 queens en/s shower; 1 queen en/s shower in main lodge; 3 separate tented queens en/s showers.
Price: Chalets: R650 - R980 pp sharing. Tents: R550 - R700 pp sharing. Singles + 25%.
Meals: Full breakfast included. Lunches, picnic baskets, braais or dinners on request.
Directions: From Kenton on R72 L to Southwell (from Port Alfred take next R to Southwell). Follow gravel rd for 8km (past sign to Sibuya Stores) until crossrds; R to Sebumo Tude. After 4.5km look out for entrance to reception.

Sibuya Game Reserve

Jenni van Wyk

39 Eastbourne Road, Kenton-on-Sea
Tel: 0861-SIBUYA (742892) or 046 648 1040 Fax: 046-648-1443
Email: reservations@sibuya.co.za Web: www.sibuya.co.za

The Sibuya team greeted me quayside in Kenton, then transported me upstream on a wholly exciting journey into the wild. I felt like one of those early adventurer-pioneer chappies. You may be only half an hour from Kenton, but you'll think you're in another, pretty idyllic world of singing birds, splashing fish and rustling leaves. The flat-bottomed boat will take you to your new home, an intimate tented camp with tents on stilts protected above by a wooden roof. They are scattered among the trees, sharing the space with hammocks and hanging chairs. Beds inside are enticing with crisp, white cotton sheets and oh-so-snug green-fleece blankets for chillier nights. But Sibuya is all about being outside, even when it comes to your en-suite bathroom. A flight of stairs takes you up into a wood-decked affair where you can shower and wash your teeth while looking into the bush and wondering if anything is watching you watching them. By night the camp relaxes in the mellow glow of paraffin lamps and roaring log fires, while a fine feast of game is prepared for you. Nights will pass star-gazing and strange-sound-identifying, while days can be spent on game drives (now 2,500 hectares with rhino, elephant, leopard and buffalo) or messing about on the river. A unique reserve experience! *Children 6+ are welcome.*

Rooms: 13 tents: 8 in the forest camp and 5 in the river camp. All doubles or twins.
Price: R1,700 - R2,550 pp sharing. Price includes boat transfers and cruises, game drives (unlimited), all meals and local alcoholic and non-alcoholic drinks.
Meals: Breakfast, lunch and dinner included.
Directions: 120km from Port Elizabeth & 150km from East London on R72. Turn into Kenton and follow the signs.

Bushmans View

John and Karen Ling

41 Fourth Avenue, Riversbend, Bushmans River, Kenton-on-Sea
Tel: UK: (+44) 01728-861-889
Email: 3lings@eurotelbroadband.com Web: www.bushmans.co.za

'Bushmans View' offers superb bird-watching opportunities, according to John and Karen. A plethora of birds are constantly spotted, including the Knysna loerie, hadidas, spoonbills, Goliath herons… to name but a few. The house, with its white wooden slats and two good-sized verandahs, reminded me of a Nantucket holiday home. The main living area is upstairs and open-plan. On the upstairs verandah you'll find a wicker sofa and other garden furniture from which to enjoy a panoramic view; on the lower, a dining table for al-fresco meals and a portable braai to use on the lawn alongside. There is a mature front garden and also a rear lawned garden with lime, lemon and pawpaw trees which is a fun place for children to play. The bedrooms are of a decent size with wooden floorboards, white linen and rustic lampshades. True to the house's name, the windows have fantastic views past the garden's aloes and across to the Bushmans River, with its thickly-forested banks. Brochure cliché though it is, this place really does 'have it all'. The beaches at Bushmans River Mouth and Kenton-on Sea are a mere five-minutes' drive away; and the Kariega and Sibuya Game Reserves are either a ten-minute drive or boat trip away. Beach and beasts within a quarter of an hour – beat that.

Rooms: I house: 2 doubles, 2 singles, I twin; all share bath & 2 showers; open-plan lounge/dining area & kitchen; garage space for I car. I booking at a time.
Price: Whole house: May to Aug R800 per day; Feb to Apr/Sep to Nov R950; Dec, Jan & Easter week R1,500. N.B. Mini-breaks of 2-3 days can be booked outside high season of Dec/Jan & Easter Week.
Meals: Self-catering. Well-stocked supermarket in Kenton-on-Sea.
Directions: From Kenton, R72 towards Alexandria. Over bridge, take 1st R at top of hill to Riversbend & follow signs for Sandbar Restaurant. House 1st on L at bottom bend of 4th Avenue, next to river.

Wings

Marijke and Mike Kirby

21 Elliot Road, Kenton-on-Sea
Tel: 046-648 1834 Fax: 086-515-5181
Email: wings@casbusol.co.za Web: www.kenton.co.za/pop_wings.htm
Cell: 083-626-4172

Mike's parents named this homely B&B Wings because "they used to like watching the birds drifting over the sea," Marijke tells me as I stand mesmerised by the expansive sea view. "We like to think we give our guests wings too," she laughs. And it would seem they do. According to Marijke the last guest sat in front of this very same window and wrote a whole book during his stay. I waited for similar inspiration to strike me too, but was soon distracted by the large, inviting sofas in my private sitting room and the shelf-load of games, puzzles and books. There is everything here you need for a comfortable stay; a private garden overlooking the sea, a large open-plan kitchen and breakfast bar, and cosy sea-facing bedrooms. Mike and Marijke are delightful hosts and their generosity is far-reaching; they also take an active part in their community, involving themselves in a number of Outreach programmes. A Continental breakfast can be provided in the downstairs apartment, but guests are also welcome to nip upstairs and enjoy Marijke's morning cooking... which is what I did. As I lingered over another pot of coffee her friends started arriving armed with paints and brushes and I soon found myself in the midst of their weekly art group. I was urged to stay and spend the day painting the stunning view. I got my wings in the end.

Rooms: 1 unit: 2 doubles with en-suite baths and 1 twin.
Price: R250 - R275 pp. No singles surcharge. Single party lets only.
Meals: Breakfast R45, frozen meals on hospitality basis from R20.
Directions: Turn into Kenton, drive to Ocean Avenue and turn R. Continue along to yellow circle, turn R into River Rd. 1st turn on L into Elliot Road, number 21 on right.

Whitnall's

Gail and Mike Whitnall
36 Elliot Road, Kenton-on-Sea
Tel: 046-648-2138 Fax: 086-544-0691
Email: whitsend@wol.co.za Web:
Cell: 072-231-0451

Gail seems to magic out of nowhere a cafetiere of piping hot coffee and a selection of the finest cakes this side of the Bushmans River. And she's insistent I try each and every one… and I am sadly weak with cakes. This is a lady who seems instinctively to know exactly what her guests require, especially when it comes to kids (there are board games for the bored and boogie-boards for the beach). This is self-catering where everything is catered for. Can't be bothered rustling up the breakfast? Gail will be there again, serving up either in the dining room or outside on the patio. Personally I would be outside all the time. The garden is a riot of life with an abundance of colour, birds, sundials, lush grass, chattering guinea fowl and the occasional inquisitive mongoose. Gail and Mike perform no mean feat keeping it this way. The Latin-tagged trees have adopted many weird and wonderful poses that work to shelter this little haven, perfect for peaceful days around the plunge pool. Whitnall's may be a matter of metres from the beach, but it would take more than that to tear me away from this sun-soaked idyll.

Rooms: 1 cottage with 2 doubles and 1 twin; 1 with en-suite bathroom, 1 en-suiteshower room.
Price: R275 pp sharing self-catering. R300 pp B&B. No singles surcharge. Single party lets only.
Meals: Full breakfast by prior arrangement. Fully equipped kitchen for the self-catering option. Several restaurants are within walking distance.
Directions: Turn into Kenton, 3rd right into Ocean Avenue. Continue across stop of River Road, continue up until last house on right (before turning in to Elliot Road).

The Lookout

Louise and Alan Corrans

24 Park Rd, Port Alfred
Tel: 046-624-4564 Fax: 046-624-4564
Email: info@thelookout.co.za Web: www.thelookout.co.za
Cell: 073-273-2912

It was only after I returned to the office that I found Louise's answer-phone message inviting me to join her and Alan for lunch. Shame... I know I would have eaten well. And also as it turned out, I'd only limited time to explore everything the Corrans have done with their perfectly positioned pad. After sifting through the old photos, I can see that they've done a lot. Not for nothing is The Lookout so named, with a sight line down to the Indian Ocean over the head of a toy town Port Alfred fragmented over its harbour islands below. Each of the alluring suites downstairs opens directly onto the garden, where a royal palm and an aloe bainesii sway above the pool. While the Corrans may be up in the world (they live on the 1st floor), that doesn't mean they have forgotten about you down below. In fact they'll come knocking on your door every morning with your breakfast basket, a system Louise and Alan have now perfected. Although each guest has their own tiled verandah from which to soak up the views, I can recommend a natter around the sun-baked braai area, where patio doors lead through to the pub where I would be on 'The Lookout' for a cooling drink to match a magnificent sunset. Each unit has a well-fitted kitchen suitable for preparing light meals.

Rooms: 3 units: 1 king, open-plan dining/living/kitchen with en-s shower; 1 twin with private bath and shower and open-plan dining/kitchen/lounge area; 1 twin with en-s shower and open-plan dining/kitchen/lounge area. All have additional sofa-beds.
Price: R275 - R435 pp. Singles on request.
Meals: Includes full English/Continental breakfast. Self-catering option available.
Directions: R72 from PE into Port Alfred. Turn first left after bridge into Pascoe Crescent, then immediate right into Park Road. House is signposted on the right.

Sheilan House

Joan Buckley and Mike Beaumont

27 Prince's Ave, Port Alfred
Tel: 046-624-4076 Fax: 046-624-4722
Email: mikeb@sheilanhouse.co.za Web: www.sheilanhouse.co.za
Cell: Joan 082-894-1851; Mike 082-895-9671

I may have been on a high as England emerged victorious from the World Cup, but that still didn't bias my admiration of ultra-modern Sheilan House. Instantly my eyes were drawn upwards to an intricate web of white-painted beams fanning out around the roof. The architect had done a stunning job of converting what was just a humble bungalow into this super-cool enclave and now similar designs are beginning to pop up all over Port Alfred. High vaulted ceilings dominate throughout while an abundance of glass and light heightens the sense of serenity. The bedrooms too have a Zen-like quality with their white walls, white-tiled floors, and in some, white wardrobes and white furniture - minimalist and peace-inducing without ever being Spartan. Pastel-shaded duvets add the only colour they need. Bathrooms are big, the showers enormous, while each of the four rooms benefit from their own private gardens for those times when you just want to get away from it all. Breakfast the following morning provided an ample opportunity to sample Joan's speciality, springbok carpaccio. As I munched mouth-watering morsels in the terracotta-tiled, glass-walled dining room, I looked out across the neat garden to an alluring blue swimming pool. A kingfisher sat on the decking calling a mate for a quick dip or so I understood it. If the weather had been nicer, I would have happily obliged.

Rooms: 4: 3 doubles & 1 twin. All en-suite, 2 with bath and separate shower, 2 with shower only.
Price: R395 - R550 pp sharing. Singles on request.
Meals: Dinner on request.
Directions: On the R72 cross Port Alfred Bridge heading in Port Elizabeth direction and turn L into Wesley Hill. Then take 3rd turning to R into Prince's Ave. Pass two streets on left and property on left.

Fort D'Acre Reserve

Mel and Rory Gailey

Fish River Mouth, Port Alfred
Tel: 040-676-1091 Fax: 040-676-1095
Email: info@fortdacre.com Web: www.fortdacre.com
Cell: 082-559-8944

When the sun's gone down, you're running late and, whether you admit it or not, are ever so slightly lost, some sort of a signal is much appreciated. On cue, the Fish River Lighthouse that stands in the middle of the reserve lit up the night sky like a beacon to guide me in (or so I like to think). The lodge, where guests stay, is not actually a fort but a mammoth thatched affair, entered via heavy, sliding glass doors from a pretty redbrick garden path. It's immediately obvious that this was a lodge designed for hunters: the rustically tiled floor is strewn with animal skins and the local taxidermist has not been idle. Even the great central hearth is framed by elephant tusks. A galleried landing overlooks the communal lounge, where a cavernous leather sofa almost prevented me from making it to bed that night. The next morning I was able to see the Fort D'Acre Reserve in all its glory. Opening the curtains in the bay windows that dominated my bedroom, I looked beyond the milling herd of zebra to the Great Fish River stretching out below me towards the Indian Ocean and the reserve's private stretch of beach. I enjoyed my breakfast on the sun-drenched terrace, but the open-walled, thatched, outside bar could be equally appealing. Down on the beach is a new lapa from where whales can be watched, sundowners drunk and romantic picnics consumed. Guided horse rides through the reserve and onto the beach now available at additional cost.

Rooms: 4: 3 doubles and 1 twin, all with en-suite showers.
Price: R450 - R495 pp sharing. Whole lodge available for self-catering (sleeps 8, plus a kid's room): R3,500 per night, minimum 3 nights. Game drives an optional extra.
Meals: Full breakfast included (B&B). A selection of restaurants nearby.
Directions: On R72 20km from Port Alfred towards East London. First turning to right after Great Fish Point Lighthouse.

The Beach House

Janine Handley

80 West Beach Drive, Port Alfred
Tel: 046-624-1920
Fax: 046-624-1920
Email:
info@thebeachhouseportalfred
.co.za
Web:
www.thebeachhouseportalfred
.co.za Cell: 082-662-5720

If you fancy a luxurious getaway in the sun, where the pace of life is… very… slow, and where you can stare all day long at a blue-flag beach from your doorstep, then head immediately for the Beach House at Port Alfred. "We love holidays and like to see others kick off their shoes too!" says Janine. With this in mind, she and her husband moved here a few years ago - from not-too-distant Bathurst - to reap the benefits of the sea air and an utterly chilled pace of life. As I strode from one open verandah to another, their admirably simple life plan kept resonating in my head. All six rooms have sunny balconies and a pair of white, wooden 'sun-thrones' (four of these are sea-facing, so whale-watching is a very real possibility); sliding glass doors allow uninterrupted views out, even from the soft depths of your plumped-up bed, and all have wireless connections and satellite TV. Downstairs, more spongy sofas and bright, open spaces feature in an L-shaped sitting room, which sweeps in to a breakfast hall and out on to a shaded porch, eventually meeting the generous deck surround of a cobalt-blue pool. Janine has thought of everything and, to top it all, has a wonderfully relaxed hostess, Lisa, who will greet you with a smile on arrival. *Children 12+ welcome.*

Rooms: 6: 1 king/twin and 2 queens with en/s showers; 2 king/twins and 1 queen with en/s baths and showers. All have balconies with seating.
Price: R510 - R650 pp sharing. R720 - R1,300 singles.
Meals: Full breakfast included.
Directions: On N2 from PE towards East London turn right down Causeway Road before the Kowie River. At seafront T-junction turn right up West Beach Drive and continue over bumps passing West Beach, Kellys Beach and Shelley Beach on your left. #80 is to the right on the corner of Curfew Crescent.

Cottage 51

Dee Simpson

50 Snipe Drive, Kaysers Beach
Tel: 043-781-8564
Email: deesimpson@telkomsa.net
Cell: 072-634-1337

Dee could see that I was feeling a little travel weary. So she sat me down with a glass of freshly-pressed lemon juice and told me to have a nap while she prepared lunch. I happily drifted off to the rhythm of the surf and the dusty miles just slipped away from me. And this is why her guests love coming here. I had barely closed my eyes for twenty minutes and already I was feeling lighter in myself. Seizing the telescope I surveyed the sea; Cottage 51 is blessed with a rugged sea-front and long untrampled beaches and beautiful shells are to be found in some of the bays. But sadly on this occasion, no trace of dolphin or migrating whales. I had to be content with landlubber buck which emerged from the bush to graze near Dee's largely indigenous garden. Lunch was an organic treat of delicious soup followed by locally-reared lamb and the meal was washed down with a good wine. I almost found myself taking a second siesta in one of two light and fresh bedrooms, the most enticing of which is sea-facing with sparkling parquet floors and its own private balcony where a table and chairs have been appealingly stripped down by the salt air. A separate bathroom is home to playful nymphs and a gentleman rabbit, an artistic quirk that continues into the en-suite bedroom. Dee has claimed as her talisman the nautilus shell that she found on the beaches here (of both geological and historical interest) and now rests on a weathered cabinet in the guest living room. Simply touch it to unwind…. A perfect stop-over en route to or from the Wild Coast.

Rooms: 2 rooms: 1 double (with private bathroom), 1 twin (with shower en-suite).
Price: R280 - R380 pp sharing.
Meals: Breakfast included. Dinner and light lunches on request. Self-catering is an option.
Directions: From P.E. along the R72, take the DR 104 turn off. From East London, take the MR 500 turn off to Kaysers Beach. Either way follow the tar and gravel roads to find Cottage 51 - it is on the right at the end of the last road along the seafront.

Kob Inn Beach Resort

Daan van Zyl

Willowvale Area, Wild Coast, Qhorha Mouth
Tel: 047-499-0011 Fax: 047-499-0016
Email: info@kobinn.co.za Web: www.kobinn.co.za
Cell: 083-452-0876

This is not called the Wild Coast for nothing. Barely thirty exhilarating metres from my chalet, waves pounded the rocks in huge swells and rips that have been the demise of many a stricken vessel. Xhosa chieftains have traditionally owned this unspoilt land, which, leased to the Kob Inn, ensures a close relationship with local communities. You may even recognise in your bedroom mural one of the village scenes that you pass on the 32km drive from the highway to get here… including wandering cattle, so go slowly. Soon after arriving I was guided through a labyrinth of thatch, firstly to the earthy comfort of my room… and then to a bar whose deck juts out like a prow. Sunday night was braai night and, having heaped my plate, I joined a Durban couple that come every year because they love the lack of commercialism. Waking from the sleep equivalent of the Mariana Trench, I took breakfast to the sound of laughter from a group of elderly travellers who epitomised the prevailing informal atmosphere. The Kob Inn staff are passionately keen and were only too happy to guide me to one of their favourite places, the mouth of the Jujura River. Honeymooners will love the privacy of deserted lagoons, but with so much to do on and off the water (kayaking, boating, quad-biking, games room, etc), this is a brilliant place for families and children will be exceptionally well looked after.

Rooms: 45 rooms: 29 doubles (twin/king), 14 family and 1 honeymoon suites, 1 cottage. All en-suite bathrooms, mostly with bath and shower.
Price: R460 - R700 pp sharing. Full board. Certain activities extra.
Meals: All included. Lunch and dinner set menus. Saturday-night seafood buffet. Sunday-night braai.
Directions: Turn off N2 at Dutywa following signs to Willowvale. It's 32km from the highway along a dirt road to Kob Inn, which is signposted all the way. Make sure to branch right after 12km.

Umngazi River Bungalows & Spa

Michele and Graham Walker

Wild Coast, Port St Johns
Tel: 047-561-1115/6/7 Fax: 047-564-1210
Email: stay@umngazi.co.za Web: www.umngazi.co.za
Cell: 082-321-5841

The wild coast may be South Africa's most spectacular and yet least touristy region with its rocky coastline, indigenous forests, secluded coves and many river mouths. And all this is on your doorstep at Umngazi, a lively family holiday resort where the only time you will spend indoors will be to sleep and eat. The relaxed and informal lodge is on the banks of the Umngazi Estuary so you can choose between swimming in the pool, the river or the sea, fishing off rocks or boats, and walking in the forests. Bird-watching cruises are also organised for sunset. Ferries transport guests over to the beach from a river jetty. Meanwhile, back at home you will be missing out on tennis, snooker and table tennis. I guarantee that a week here, however lazy you are, will see the colour back in your cheeks and a bit of muscle on the arms and legs. And your sense of time will go haywire. Children are well catered for with trampoline, fort, sandpit and designated dining room. You have a choice of sea-, river- or garden-front cottages, four honeymoon suites with spa baths and double outside showers, and the new Ntabeni (two luxury open plan palapa suites with panoramic views across the estuary, a buggy service, in-house pampering and canapes served at 5pm). You can fly in from Durban at 500 feet above sea level along the coastline, a great start to a holiday. *The spa offers (among other things) Swedish massage and a peppermint sea twist wrap while you look out on 180-degree views of the Indian Ocean.*

Rooms: 69 bungalows: 67 twin/doubles, all en/s bathrooms, most baths & outdoor showers; 2 luxury king suites with spa treatments & golf buggy service.
Price: Bungalows: R620 – R930 pp sharing all-inclusive. 40% sing supp. Fly-in package R7,720 – R8,910 pp for flight, 7 nights, all meals & transfers from Port St Johns. Luxury suites R1,150 - R1,400 pp sharing; fly-in package R10,450 - R12,200.
Meals: All included.
Directions: From south, Umngazi 90km due east of Umtata. From north, via Flagstaff to Port St Johns on tarred rd. Transfer service from Umtata & private flight service between Durban & Port St Johns.

Leliekloof Valley of Art

Dries and Minnie De Klerk
Burgersdorp
Tel: 051-653-1240 Fax: 051-653-1240
Email: sanart@lantic.net Web:
Cell: 083-760 7851 (please leave a message)

What a place! Magnificent Bushman art and high-altitude wilderness to nourish the soul; log fires and home-cooked meals to look after earthier parts. The river here has chiselled a tortuous gorge through the sandstone and ironstone hills and the many caves host thirteen remarkable sites of Bushman rock art, many of the paintings of indeterminable age. Dries took me for an exhilarating morning drive and we visited two of them, Eland and Dog Shelters. The quality of the paintings is superb, Dries a full reservoir of information about both the images and their artists. There is also a two-day scenic 19km hike around the valley, and two large dams for canoeing and trout/fly-fishing. Art apart, the countryside will extract from you superlatives you never knew you had. The De Klerks now live in the main house with their guests, but don't worry, they're great company and there's plenty of room for everyone! The magnificent main room is 22 metres long, with sitting area, DSTV, yellowwood bar, fireplace and huge antique Oregon pine dining table. You can self-cater, but given the stellar quality of Minnie's food (and the variety of things to do), I strongly suggest that you ask her to prepare your meals. *Two nights minimum stay recommended.*

Rooms: 1 farmhouse with 2 bedrooms (1 double with child's bed and 1 double with child's bed and 1 cot, 1 with en-suite bath, 1 en-s shower); plus a loft sleeping 4; also 1 extra bathroom with bath & shower. Only one couple/group booking at a time.
Price: Full board rates: R430 - R490 pp (for three or more). R450 - R510 pp for 2 people. Self-catering options available. Singles on request.
Meals: Breakfast, lunch and dinner included. Dinner is 3 courses - bring your own wine.
Directions: 6km south of Jamestown on N6 turn towards Burgersdorp. Turn R after 9.7km. After another 5.6km fork R again and Leliekloof is another 1km. Just follow Leliekloof signs. Map can be faxed.

The Stagger Inn

Ann Bryan and Rosy Balela

Carnarvon Estate, Sterkstroom
Tel: 045-966-0408 Fax: 045-966-0408
Email: carnarvon@worldonline.co.za
Cell: 082-445-1032

So nice to arrive somewhere and instantly know that the people there will make your stay all the more enjoyable. I wasn't even asked if I'd like lunch… it was assumed and presented. Tea? That came too. Smiling, warm faces are a given at the Stagger Inn and all those living and working on the estate exude a contagious enthusiasm for it. So here you are in the great outdoors with 25,000 acres of pristine wilderness at your beck and call. You can bird-watch, fish for large-mouth bass, swim in the weirs of clear spring water, go boating on the dams, do some clay-pigeon shooting and spot some of the fifteen species of antelope on game-drives (also lynx, jackal, genets, black eagles, fish eagles and vultures). Or you can just walk among the indigenous shrubs and wild flowers. Ruddy-faced and hungry from the fresh air and activities, guests cosy up by the blazing log fire before a hearty, healthy dinner of home cooked produce fresh from the farm (cows, sheep, pigs, sawmill and a dairy). And then to bed, hunting-lodge-style in farmhouses with comfortable (rather than luxurious) rooms for a well-needed night's sleep. As I discovered in the morning, the quality of light up here is a phenomenon, and the views breathtaking. The rolling ridge-country and grassy plains reach as far as the eye can see. Make sure you stay for long enough.

Rooms: 6: 2 doubles, 2 twins with en-suite bathrooms; 2 doubles for self-catering with en-suite shower.
Price: R250 – R300 pp B&B. R175 pp self-catering.
Meals: Full breakfast included. Lunch and dinner by request.
Directions: From Queenstown, take N6 for 50km and turn right on the R344 towards Dordrecht and follow signs to Stagger Inn (gravel road for 13km).

Redcliffe Guest Farm

Johnnie and Carol Morgan
Tarkastad
Tel: 045-848-0152 Fax: 045-848-0152
Email: info@dtours.co.za Web: www.dtours.co.za

Johnnie and Carol kindly adopted me for the night when I couldn't - or rather didn't want to - leave their unspoilt country idyll in the depths of the Winterberg Mountains. Not many tourists have yet found the Winterberg, but surely it is only a matter of time. This is an escape from everything apart from cows, sheep, birds and the natural environment that supports them. The simplest way to enjoy the area is to go for a hike across the rolling grassland hills. The gorge on a neighbouring farm is, I think, the most spectacular spot I have been privy to in South Africa and it goes virtually unvisited. The plateau folds in on itself and plummets hundreds of metres down, waterfalls dropping from terrace to terrace. Or you can go swimming, trout-fishing, mountain-biking, horse-riding, bird-watching, or play tennis back at the house. Carol may cook you her speciality stuffed leg of lamb for dinner and Johnnie will happily show you around his shearing shed. He is especially proud of his Merinos whose pure white wool is used to make smart Italian suits. Guests here have all the space they could need both outside and inside the five-bedroom farmhouse, including a light-filled sun room. A real home and the area of highland farms is still to be discovered even by the more adventurous overseas traveller.

Rooms: 1 farmhouse: 5 twins, 3 en-suite and 2 with private bathrooms.
Price: R595 pp lunch, dinner, bed and breakfast or R200 pp self-catering, minimum 2 people for both options.
Meals: Breakfast, lunch and dinner on request. Self-catering also an option.
Directions: On R344 between Tarkastad and Adelaide. Directions faxed or emailed.

Cavers Country Guest House

Kenneth and Rozanne Ross

R63, Bedford
Tel: 046 685-0619 Fax: 046-685-0619
Email: ckross@intekom.co.za Web: www.cavers.co.za
Cell: 082-579-1807

I can't be the first to call Cavers an oasis, but it is irresistible. There in the distance a stand of tall oaks shimmers unconvincingly in the haze. And then suddenly you are among well-watered and mature gardens, an Eden of lawns and vivid flowers. The fine stone, ivy-encased farmhouse was built in 1840 and has been in Ken's family for four generations (now exclusively for guests). The bedrooms, with wooden floorboards, high ceilings and voluptuously draped windows, are refined and elegant. From one of the upstairs rooms I got an impression of living in the trees with an hadeda nesting at eye level and yellow orioles twittering and fluttering about. Two grand upstairs rooms with pressed-metal ceilings have balconies overlooking the profusion of flowers below. The thatched cottage also has long views over the lawns and up to the Winterberg Mountains. Rozanne is a maestro in the kitchen, cooking with fresh produce from the farm and the surrounding area and all her meals are mouth-watering feasts. The memory of that salmon cheesecake is even now a Pavlovian trigger that gets the mouth watering. There is a clay tennis court, hiking and riding or even cricket on the magnificent ground nearby. Swimming is in the pool or a big round reservoir.

Rooms: 5: 4 rooms in the manor house: all king/twins, 2 en-suite shower, 1 bath, 1 shr & bath; 1 cottage has 1 twin & 1 double sharing bath & shower.
Price: R450 - R595 pp sharing.
Meals: Full breakfast included. Dinner and light lunches on request.
Directions: 8km from Bedford on the R63 towards Adelaide, turn left at the sign and follow the dirt road for 8km.

Die Tuishuise

Sandra Antrobus

36 Market St, Cradock
Tel: 048-881-1322 Fax: 048-881-5388
Email: tuishuise@eastcape.net Web: www.tuishuise.co.za

Unique accommodation indeed! Sandra has a raptor's eye for historic detail, laced with an antique-dealer's nose and the heart of an interior designer - unparalleled in my experience of South Africa. There are 25 houses along Market Street, all antiquely furnished to reflect different styles, eras and professions. The houses were once lived in by bank managers, teachers, wagon makers etc, and you step into their 19th-century shoes when you stay - although the bathrooms, perhaps, retain a little more modernity. Each house is an antique shop in its own right, but modern comforts include fans, heaters and fireplaces. I was lucky enough to visit them all and it is no exaggeration to say I was struck dumb - reason enough for Sandra to have gone to the effort (some might feel). The hotel, a Victorian manor at the end of the street, has a further 19 rooms similarly done out in the style of the time and sherry is served in the drawing room before buffet dinners (my Karoo lamb was delicious). Sandra and her daughter Lisa are dedicated to presenting South African history in a way you can touch and feel. They do cultural performances epitomising the Xhosa and Afrikaner culture - ask in advance. *Closed 24th & 25th December.*

Rooms: 25 restored 19th-century houses, each rented out as one 'unit'. There is also a hotel.
Price: R250 - R850 pp.
Meals: Breakfast included (unless you choose to self-cater) and served 7 - 9am. Traditional dinners served between 7pm and 9pm.
Directions: From PE take N10. When you arrive in Cradock at 3-way stop turn left into Voortrekker St. Die Tuishuise is 4th block on left. Reception is at Victoria Manor.

Wheatlands

Diana, Arthur, Kirsten and David Short

Route R75, Graaff-Reinet
Tel: 049-891-0422/4 Fax: 049-891-0422
Email: wheatlands@wam.co.za Web: www.wheatlands.co.za
Cell: 076-377 4026 or 072-251-9022

Guests at Wheatlands are thoroughly spoilt. I had read that the main house had been built on the profits of ostrich feathers in 1912 (a so-called 'feather palace'). I'm not sure why, but this led me to expect a humble farmhouse… and to get my shoes muddy finding it! But no. I found instead a gigantic manor house with a façade dominated by three extravagant gables. The house, designed by Charles Bridgeman, mingles Cape Dutch and Edwardian styles with a lovely white-pillared verandah at the back and then a green lake of lush lawn where heritage roses grow like weeds. Park your wagon (or whatever you are driving these days) in the huge sandy courtyard and enter a long, cool, wood-panelled hall, an instant pleasure as you leave the desert heat of the Karoo. It's an appropriate home for the piano, all the antique furniture and the Persian rugs. The corridors are lined with books, there is a snug for reading and guest bedrooms are not converted outhouses, but an integral, lived-in part of the house. There are wonderful wanders to be had in the revelation of a back garden. The Shorts are astoundingly nice people, brimful of the hostly arts. Diana and Kirsten cook delicious dinners, which are eaten at one large oak table. Arthur and David, meanwhile, are serious wool and mohair farmers and cricketers… they even have their own ground.

Rooms: 3: all twins, 2 with en-suite bath and shower, 1 with private bath and shower.
Price: R380 - R420 pp sharing.
Meals: Full breakfast and dinner included (Karoo lamb a speciality).
Directions: 42km on the R75 south of Graaff-Reinet, Wheatlands turn-off to the left, 8km up a gravel road.

Abbotsbury

Sue Scott
Graaff-Reinet
Tel: 049-840-0201 Fax: 049-840-0201
Email: abbotsbury@cybertrade.co.za Web: www.abbotsbury.co.za
Cell: 072-486-8904

A three-kilometre drive on a dirt track takes you up into the land that time forgot, a small, perfectly-formed valley that Sue calls home. She is there to greet you in her improbably lush and well-tended garden, which seems immune to the Karoo sun's forbidding glare. An ingenious old water furrow running down from the dam must take some of the credit for this, although a fence has also been added to protect the garden's aloes and roses from midnight-feasting kudus… of which there are plenty, despite the privations. You can relax under the trees in the tranquil gardens, or hike up the valley in search of the ten species of antelope and other Karoo wildlife on the farm. Back at base, guests either stay in a lovely old cottage, circa 1880; or a twin-bedded suite attached to Sue's own, even older house; or the luxury garden suite with its sweeping views of the garden and wild valley in the distance. None lack for character, with polished yellowwood floors, restored old furniture and photographic prints and artwork on the walls. Sue takes your supper orders when you book so as to have a fresh farm supply at the ready (springbok and Karoo lamb specialities) and you are served in your own private dining room with solid silver cutlery, bone china and service bell! Breakfasts are also a royal affair. *Nearby: the sculpture garden of the Owl House, historic Graaff-Reinet, and the awe-inspiring views of the Valley of Desolation.*

Rooms: 3 units: 1 cottage with double & en-suite twin and separate bath with shower attachment; 1 cottage with king and en-suite shower; 1 twin suite with en-suite bath and shower. All have private lounge/dining room

Price: R350 - R400 pp sharing B&B.

Meals: Full breakfast included. 3-course dinner on request: R110. Meals are served privately to each cottage.

Directions: 27km north of Graaff-Reinet on N9, turn left onto 3km farm track to Abbotsbury.

Cypress Cottages

Hillary Palmé
76 Donkin St, Graaff-Reinet
Tel: 049-892 3965 Fax: 049-892-3965
Email: info@cypresscottage.co.za Web: www.cypresscottage.co.za
Cell: 083-456-1795

After a hot and particularly bothersome drive to this historic Karoo town, it came as a huge relief to wearily step through Cypress Cottage's heavy wooden doors and immerse myself in the quiet coolness lurking within. Minutes later, cold beer in hand and propped up on a stoep with a magnificent mountain view, my recent hardships evaporated into the heat-hazed sky. Both cottages are of the beautiful early 1800s Cape Dutch variety and are understatedly decorated with a highly developed taste for the natural and comfortable. Thus, the bedrooms display high reed ceilings, solid pine and slate floors, antique chests, fresh flowers and free-standing baths. Fresh and perfectly wholesome breakfasts are laid up on the terraces - free-range eggs from the house chickens, succulent figs, peaches, prunes and apricots straight from the orchard. You can escape the heat by splashing in the bore-hole-fed reservoir that has been converted into a swimming pool. Across the sleepy street, a familiar smell wafted over from the other cottage, where guests were merrily braaiing under the shade of its vine-covered pergola. The main garden is an extraordinary feat of will and clever engineering - desert has been transformed into an oasis of lush vegetation despite the difficulties of brackish water. Historic Graaff-Reinet is worth at least a two-day stopover in my opinion - Cypress Cottages many more.

Rooms: 6: 4 doubles and 2 twins. All with en-suite bathrooms, air-con and heating.
Price: R350 - R550 pp sharing. Singles on request.
Meals: Full breakfast included.
Directions: From south enter town and pass police academy on L and go over bridge. Two filling stations on L - take road between them (West St). Follow to very end, turn R into Donkin St, guest house first on L. From north: R at T-jct (Caledon St). 4th Left is Donkin St. House last on R.

Melrose Guest Farm

Campbell and Karen Scott
Graaff-Reinet
Tel: 049-891-0532
Email: melroseguestfarm@telkomsa.net
Cell: 082-380-1569/083-580-2753

Melrose Guest Farm is a very welcome stop on the long R75 south. As I stepped from my overheated car, Karen and Campbell were already on hand to usher me onto their shady porch. Looking out over the vast, flat Karoo landscape and huge African sky, I felt my road weariness dissolve and my languishing spirits revive. The Scotts are a delightful young couple and, although they may be new to the business, they are natural hosts. After a restorative cool drink and an enormous plate of Bourbon biscuits, I was shown into a deliciously cool lounge; no need for air-con here as the wooden flooring and high ceilings keep everything at a perfect temperature. A lot of care and attention has gone into restoring this farmhouse to its original self. Campbell has stripped every door and window and sanded down every surface to leave a smooth polished finish. Meanwhile, Karen has been busy putting an unerring eye for design into furnishing the dining room and lounge in appropriately simple, comfortable fabrics and soothing cream and white tones. The units are equally appealing with good-quality white linen and a sleep-inducing serenity that makes you want to flop straight onto the beds. Those with more energy, however, can dive into the reservoir, go in search of antelope or take the 8km walk round the farmland. As for me… that huge Karoo sky performs some sort of magic trick and I ended up staring hypnotically into a picture-perfect landscape.

Rooms: 2 units: 1 with double and twin and en-suite bath and shower. 1 with double and twin and en-suite shower.
Price: R300 pp sharing. Single supplement R100.
Meals: Includes full breakfast. Dinner R80, braai on request.
Directions: Email for directions.

Ganora Guest Farm and Excursions

JP and Hester Steynberg
Nieu-Bethesda, Near Graaff-Reinet
Tel: 049-841-1302 Fax: 086-505-4184
Email: info@ganora.co.za Web: www.ganora.co.za
Cell: 082-698-0029

JP and Hester, along with visiting palaeontologists and guests, are thrilled with the historic finds on their farm, which together demonstrate a South African heritage spinning back in time from the Boer War to the Bushmen dynasty, to the pre-dinosaur era. 'Give us one day and we will give you 240 million years', says the brochure. They originally bought their 4,000-hectare Karoo property to farm Dohne-Merino sheep, famous for their fine wool (shearing and grading fleeces demonstrated in the shearing shed) and excellent meat. Then JP hit the Jurassic jackpot, so to speak, finding a horde of fossils in an ancient mud slide; and a tip-off from the previous owner led to Louis and Reiner (JP and Hester's teenage sons) finding a cave with not only the engravings from an escapee of the Boer War, but also bushman and Khoi paintings. Hester pointed out the image of a tortoise, the only one found in SA, and explained to me the methods and significance of the art. If history is your thing (and it will be), you can bundu-hike up the Compassberg Mountain, swim in the Karoo river pools, go on township visits or drop in on Helen Martins' weird and wonderful Owl House. Guests stay in newly-renovated former labourers' cottages, with bare stone walls and large, powerful showers. After an activity-filled day, a four-course supper and a bout of star-gazing, a good night's sleep is had by all.

Rooms: 1 self-catering cottage sleeping 6 with 2 bathrooms, a kitchen and lounge with patio and braai facilities. Meals available.
Price: R800 per night for the whole cottage. Visits to Boer War engravings, bushman rock shelter, fossil museum/walk and woolshed visit from R40 each.
Meals: Full breakfast and dinner available on request from R85 each.
Directions: Off N9 between Graaff-Reinet and Middleberg, turn towards Nieu-Bethesda (second turning to Nieu-Bethesda if coming from Graaff-Reinet). Directions on web or emailed.

KwaZulu Natal

KwaZulu Natal Side Dishes

A handful of highly-recommended things to do and places to eat in the KwaZulu Natal area...

Mo-zam-bik
Undoubtably the closest thing to actually scoffing down real Mozambiquan grub on the beach in Vilanculos. Mozambik is hot! Peri-peri, combined with chicken, prawns and other fresh seafood options, is king here. For those who aren't into fiery fare, there are many tamer tastes available. Feel free to kick your shoes off and wash it all down with original Laurentina beer.
Contact: Brett Michielin, Shop 4 and 5, Cnr. Jack Powel Street and Compensation Road, Ballito; Prices:Starters around R40. Mains around R95; Tel: 032-946-0979; 032-946-0995; Email: admin@mozambikrestaurant.com; Web: www.mozambikrestaurant.com

Spiga D'Oro
It's very seldom that you come across a place that gets everything right: food, atmosphere, service, everything! Dine inside or out on the pavement while the Santoniccolos make you feel like old friends. This bustling Italian trattoria is an absolute must if you are in Durban.
Contact: Marco, Giuseppina, Sergio Santoniccolo, 200 Florida Road, Morningside, Durban; Prices: Average R100 per person; Tel: 031-303-9511/2; 031-303-2241; Web: www.diningout.co.za

Evan Jones
As military historian and a Badged Member of the Guild of Battlefield Guides, Evan Jones is so enthusiastic and engaging you will feel as though you are back in the original melée as he takes you to any of 68 battle sites in the area and ignites your imagination about what took place. There is hardly a thing he doesn't know.
Contact: Evan Jones, 90 Victoria St, Dundee; Prices: R480 per person; Tel: 034-212-4040; Email: battleguide@telkomsa.net; Web: www.battleguide.co.za

Ardmore Caversham Gallery and the Bonnie Ntshalintshali Ceramic Museum
The legendary story of Ardmore Ceramic Art is one of inspiration and hope, with Fee Halsted-Berning and her students essentially redefining the term 'ceramic art'. Through her unearthing of talent and teaching of those whose futures held little, Fee has been described as a 'creator of artists'. "The Zulu people have a wonderful sense of colour, rhythm and design. All they needed was an opportunity." Open Mon-Sun 8 am - 4.30 pm.
Contact: Fee Halsted-Berning, Caversham Road, Lidgetton; Tel: 033-234-4869; Email: contact@ardmoreceramics.co.za; Web: www.ardmoreceramics.co.za

Café Bloom

Simple, fresh wholesome fare, with flavour and feeling in a stunning setting. Locally home-smoked trout on fresh salad greens and garden herbs, Danish feta and chives was a real winner. Whether you are looking for a light meal, coffee, cakes or bakes, Café Bloom is a comfortable place of ease and pleasure. Superb ceramics and paintings by Mick and Sally help furnish this family-run affair.

Contact: Mick and Sally Haigh, Nottingham Road; Prices: Breakfast R24 - R48. Lunch R30 - R80; Tel: 033-266-6118; Email: kraalart@vodamail.co.za

Trattoria La Terrazza

Buried behind the South Coast banana plantations this is quite a find. A covered loggia with an open lower deck looking onto the Umkobi Lagoon and the Indian Ocean. The surf beats rhythmically on the rocks and washes up on the beach, setting the scene perfectly for Massimo and Nicci Negra's innovatively varied but Italian-at-heart menu.

Contact: Massimo and Nicci Negra; Outlook Rd; Southbroom; Tel: 087-805-9400; Email: nicolanegra@gmail.com

Impulse by the Sea Curry Restaurant

After 17 years, Impulse by the Sea is the ultimate Indian restaurant. Subtle decor, soft Indian instrumentals, warm hospitality and - most importantly - mouth-watering curries served in traditional brass and copper kadais create the complete Indian experience. World-renowned food and wine connoisseurs Erica and John Platter comment thus: "... in Michelin-guide speak, their prawn curry is still holding pole position." So I suggest booking a sundeck table, gazing out at the sea... and getting curried away.

Contact: Neville and Shamen Reddi, Tinley Manor Beach, North Coast; Prices: Average curry price R70; Tel: 032-5544-626; Email:impulse@telkomsa.net;

Natal Sharks Board

Sharks get pretty bad press and the NSB work hard to dispel that. Come here and learn all about these awesome fish. There are regular shark dissections too, so you can find out how they work (and smell!) inside too. Alternatively join the Sharks Board team in the early morning boat trips along Durban's waterfront, checking the shark nets that line the beaches and protect swimmers.

Contact:1a Herrwood Drive, Umhlanga; Prices: Adults R25. Kids R15. Boat trips cost R250; Tel: 031-566-0400/0435; 031-566-0499 Email: hargreaves@shark.co.za; Web: www.shark.co.za

Four Rivers Rafting and Adventures

The Fourie family have an effervescent zest for adventure and had been into canoeing and rafting for years before finally turning a hobby into a business. Aside from the river-based activities, they organise kloofing (my favourite), quad bikes, archery, zip lines (not at the same time!) and abseiling and much more....

Contact: Fourie Family, Central Drakensberg, GPS: S28°57.208 E29°31.157, Winterton; Prices: Rafting Day Trip R460 incl. braai and refreshments. Quads one & half hours outride R420. Zip Line R40; Tel: 036-468-1693; 036-468-1336; Email: info@fourriversadventures.co.za; Web: www.fourriversadventures.co.za

Plumbago

Mick and Libby Goodall

546 St Ives Ave,
Leisure Bay
Tel: 039-319-2665
Fax: 086-689-3993
Email:
info@plumbagokzn.co.za
Web:
www.plumbagokzn.co.za
Cell: 082-561-6993

I think the coast of KwaZulu Natal gets better and better the further south you head, and Leisure Bay is testament to that. It's just stunning and buried in the banana plantations between bush and beach is easily missed by those hammering along the N2 to more on-the-beaten-track destinations. Plumbago itself is on the crest of a hill on sandy St Ives Avenue (just off Torquay Avenue, naturally), a gentle stroll from the sea. It's an airy double-storey home, hidden from its neighbours by the thick foliage of Libby's indigenous garden, indigenous that is "except the rosemary and the lemon tree for G&Ts," she admits. The birds are amazing and hop around right under your nose, and while they chattered in the trees, we chattered (over lunch) at a long, central dining table made from an old jetty post. Downstairs the house is open-plan with large windows, high ceilings and soft, blue walls the perfect antidote to sizzling summer days. Upstairs a wrap-around verandah keeps the main bedroom equally cool and if you do get over-heated you can just jump in the outside shower. There are endless sea- or land-based activities to keep you busy in the area, but with a beautiful beach on hand, well, I'd be just as happy focusing on some serious R&R.

Rooms: 3: all doubles, two with bath and shower, one with bath, outside shower also available.
Price: R290 – R380 pp sharing. Singles on request.
Meals: Full breakfast included. Dinner on request.
Directions: Follow N2 and R61 south from Durban towards Port Edward. About 5km north of town take the Torquay Ave/Leisure Bay turn off. Follow Torquay Ave to the crest of hill and turn L into St Ives Ave. Plumbago is 100 yards down on the R.

Figtree Lodge

Paul and Barbara Reynolds

30 North Ridge Road, Southbroom
Tel: 039-316-6547 Fax: 039-316-8211
Email: sbelite@lantic.net Web: www.figtreelodge.co.za
Cell: 082-421-1172

Figtree Lodge is one of those laidback places where guests can B&B, self-cater or do both. The three self-contained lodges come with a private pool, honesty bar and a fully-equipped kitchen. Saying that, it would be an act of foolishness to miss out on Paul and Barbara's breakfast. But before being treated to a slap-up 'full English', I was first shown around. First up was 'Figtree Lodge', which is shaded by the eponymous ("yonks old") tree. Up the outdoor stairs, the wooden deck looks out across the swimming pool and covered lapa. Inside, the living and kitchen area is open-plan. The bedrooms have white linen embroidered with butterflies and wooden furniture. Over the road is the Reynolds' own house, with 'Kingfisher' attached which comes with its own kitchen and lounge. Crossing back, we passed a coral tree. "When Southbroom was divided into plots, they staked branches from these trees into the ground to mark boundaries," Barbara explained. "Now most older properties have one, and the monkeys love sucking their nectar!" Finally Barbara showed me 'Swallows Nest', the large family house next door with a double-deck and great views up the Imbezane River. After breakfast, we jumped into the car for a whirlwind tour of Southbroom. The beach is only four minutes' walk away, so bring your binoculars (whales go by from May to October) and leave your watch behind. *Within easy reach of six top golf courses.*

Rooms: 3 Units: 'Figtree Lodge': 3 bedrooms, 2 bathrooms (1 en-suite), both with showers; 'Swallows Nest': 4 bedrooms, 4 bathrooms en-suite, 3 with showers, 1 with shower and bath; 'Kingfisher': 1 bedroom with en-suite shower and bath.
Price: R310 pp sharing (self-catering) - R360 pp sharing (B&B).
Meals: Ingredients for a braai can be provided.
Directions: Faxed or emailed when you book.

Ivory Beach Lodge

Massimo and Nicci Negra

379/1 Outlook Road, Southbroom
Tel: 039-316 8411 Fax: 086-615-4304
Email: ivorybeachlodge@gmail.com Web: www.ivorybeachlodge.co.za
Cell: 082-440-9489 or 082-331-3202

Overlooking a stretch of protected indigenous reserve and the Indian Ocean just fifty yards away, Ivory Beach Lodge boasts easy access to wide sandy beaches and warm seas. The lodge is a plum pad for entertaining, with fabulous open-plan spaces, which provide for entertaining both indoors and out and includes a large pool room with built-in leather-clad sofas and a grand sandstone fireplace. Al fresco attractions include soaring lapas, interlacing wooden walkways, sun decks and an indigenous garden. Three massive suites each have something to vaunt, a double shower and mammoth dressing room, a private deck, corner spa baths or the outdoor shower for rinsing off after a day on the beach. "The Cottage" which floats in a leafy canopy is a self-contained bungalow featuring two more bedrooms and a private deck overlooking the gently sloping garden, salt-water rock pool below and out to sea. More like a "bush-lodge-by-the-sea", this beach house was built with rest and relaxation in mind. It has been impeccably thought out, everything original and custom-made. Artefacts are not just displayed here. The fixtures and furnishings have become articles of interest themselves, from the huge front stable-door, hand-carved wooden architraves and pigmented floors, to the Indian window which has morphed into an intricately-latticed coffee-table. The Negras' award-winning Trattoria La Terrazza is the obvious place to eat, just a 10-minute stroll away from the homestead. Enjoy!

Rooms: 3 large suites with private balconies and en-suite bathrooms with luxury fittings (2 with corner spa-baths and showers), master suite with fireplace and spectacular sea views.
Price: B&B: R400 - R600 pp sharing. Self-catering for lodge (sleeps 6): R3,500; self-catering for whole lodge and cottage (sleeps 10): R5,000.
Meals: Both B&B and self-catering options available.
Directions: Take the N3 south. Exit at Southbroom South, travel 400 metres, turn first right into Outlook Rd and follow for 2km (approx). Look for number 379/1 down a driveway on your left.

Lindsay Loft

Caroline and Pepi Jankovich
26 Lindsay Avenue, Morningside, Durban
Tel: 031-207-1634 Fax: 031-208-3227
Email: caroline@lindsayloft.co.za Web: www.lindsayloft.co.za
Cell: 083-490-0963

If your loft is anything like mine it's a dark and dusty dumping ground for old junk. Caroline's loft, I can enviously assure you, is NOTHING like mine. It's enormous. Walls are whitewashed and go up forever, floors are tiled to keep it cool in summer and there's a lengthy, decked verandah, of which more later. Actually no, I can't wait. The verandah is great, accessed from both the living- and bedrooms it peaks through the trees and across the city from its hill-top look-out. The stunning view stretches right up through the Umgeni Valley and gorge, which transforms into a starry, bright-lit cityscape by night. Back inside, the bedroom is cavernous and calming with (besides a bed of course) caramel armchairs and a beautiful old writing desk. The living area too is dotted with mahogany antiques and separated from the kitchen by a breakfast bar. For the chef, there's all the cooking kit you need and Caroline will supply the essentials to get you started. This is a great base from which to explore KZN. The Drakensberg mountains are a few hours inland, the game reserves a short drive up the coast and there are excellent beaches and golf courses.

Rooms: 1 double/king with en-suite combined bath and shower with optional spare single bed for extra family member in adjoining room. Air-conditioned.
Price: R400 pp sharing. R700 singles.
Meals: Starter supplies and a health breakfast provided on arrival. Otherwise, fully self-catering.
Directions: From M4 to Durban take exit 2, Moore Rd. Follow to traffic lights and turn R into Manning Rd which becomes Essenwood Rd. 100m after feeding into Montpelier Rd take Lindsay Ave up a steep hill. Lindsay Loft is just over the brow.

Ntengu Lodge

Andrew and Kathryn Buchanan

24 David McLean Drive, Westville, Durban
Tel: 031-266-8578 Fax: 086 505-9839
Email: info@ntengulodge.com Web: www.ntengulodge.com
Cell: 083-777-2644

That Andrew was sloping around barefoot was an immediate sign of the pace of life at Ntengu: gloriously slow. A couple of recently-arrived guests were enjoying the quirky spa package; another, here on business, was tapping away on his computer (they now have wireless internet). Everyone seemed happily ensconced as if in their own homes. Like so many of the owners in this book, here is a man too creative for the corporate world who has opted for a change of tack and these days spends his time hammering and sawing in his workshop, building striking kiaat wood furniture to fit his house. And he's got his work cut out after expanding from one to six rooms in as many years. Ntengu Lodge is a two-storey house squarely planted on one of the jungly ridges that fold back from Durban's beachfront. Up here the trees rustle with a constant breeze that makes for a welcome escape from sweltering city-centre summers. In fact, the city couldn't feel further away. The breakfast room opens onto the decked pool and a wall of greenery, and from wrought-iron bedroom balconies there is a stunning view down into the Palmiet Nature Reserve that protects the surrounding hillside. Staff are easy smilers, service is impeccable, rooms have silk curtains, walk-in showers or other twists of luxury. Andrew is also the chef, adding the ability to excite your tastebuds to his other many talents.

Rooms: 6: 2 king/twins with en-suite walk-in shower; 2 queens, 1 with en-suite bath and shower and 1 with en-suite bath/shower; 2 doubles, 1 with en-suite bath and shower and 1 with shower only.
Price: R380 pp sharing. Singles R530.
Meals: Full breakfast included. Dinner on request.
Directions: From Durban International Airport follow N2 north towards Stanger. After 20km exit L on N3 towards Pietermaritzburg. Take next exit, M32 to Pavilion Shopping Centre & turn R at top of ramp to Westville. Continue 2.1km to T-jct, turn R. Proceed for 1.2km to BP station. Turn L into David McLean Drive and house is number 24 on L.

Fairlight Beach House

Bruce and Michele Deeb

1 Margaret Bacon Avenue,
(Corner South Beach Rd),
Umdloti Beach
Tel: 031-568-1835
Fax: 031-568-1835
Email: bdeeb@mweb.co.za
Web: www.fairlight.co.za
Cell: 082-775-9971
or 082-443-8529

I got my first taste of Bruce and Michele's laid-back hospitality as soon as I arrived. It was another hot KZN day and I was bustled off for a joyous dip in the sea just across the road – "We can talk later." And we did. This newly-refreshed 'inspector' was soon sipping a cold beer by the pool and tucking into some delicious Lebanese pastries and thoroughly South African boerewors as Bruce tended the braai. The garden behind the house is dominated by a large milkwood, a great place to shelter from the sun, although there are also sun-loungers around the swimming pool. The front of the house has a wooden deck running all along it, from where you can watch the surfers - 6 of the rooms open onto it. Dolphins love the surf too, and if you're lucky you can swim with them. Bruce can lend you a boogie-board and flippers. Inside, it is effectively a family home and luxury guest house rolled into one – plenty of light and air as befits a beach house, family snaps on the wall and a warm, welcoming vibe to it. Rays of positive energy emanate from Michele, Bruce and Denise, their very charming manager. Soak it up, then go forth and fish, surf or swim with a big smile on your face. Ten miles of heaven, a.k.a. Umdloti Beach, are but 40 paces from the house. *Durban and the airport are both within half an hour's drive.*

Rooms: 9: 6 with en-suite bath and shower, 3 with just shower (all are fully air-conditioned and have sea views).
Price: R525 – R675. Singles on request.
Meals: Full breakfast included. Limited self-catering facilities available.
Directions: N2 exit to Umdloti. Follow down to roundabout. Keep right past Total garage and Fairlight is 500 metres along South Beach Rd.

Seaforth Farm

Trevor and Sharneen Thompson

Exit 214 off N2, Salt Rock, Umhlali
Tel: 032 525-5217 Fax: 032-525-4495
Email: info@seaforth.co.za Web: www.seaforth.co.za
Cell: 082-770-8376

Seaforth Farm is a full-blown treat of a guest house. Trevor and Sharneen have many interests, talents and motivations and Seaforth is a constant source of stimulation. Sharneen is a water-colourist and has also won medals for flower-arranging, so the house blooms with extravagant displays and paintings. Trevor is both an official tour guide and a skilled craftsman and much of the furniture has been made in his workshop (his latest piece, a huge lychee-wood bed) – and it is highly accomplished work. The garden is lush and wild and envelops everything at Seaforth in tropical colour. The produce from the new organic garden will always make its way to the breakfast table, in the inventive form of zucchini and feta fritters (when in season, of course) or fried mielie cakes! The cattle is now pure Nguni (the painted cattle of Africa), chickens run among the pawpaw and sweet and soursops trees and then there's the dam with its abundant bird life. Trevor is coaxing it in with a cunning plantation of pond weed, lilies and islets. The guest house provides large, well-equipped bedrooms, a pool and thatched summerhouse with dam- and sea-view for heavenly breakfasts and candle-lit curry evenings. Finally, the staff have a stake in the success of their venture. A pioneering guest house indeed…. *Zulu spoken.*

Rooms: 4: 1 family suite with 2 bedrooms, each with en/s shower; 2 doubles and 1 twin with en/s shower and bath.
Price: From R380 pp sharing. Single supplement R100. Family suite from R290 pp (min R1,020). First child free.
Meals: Full breakfast included.
Directions: From Durban take the N2 north. Exit on the 214 signed Salt Rock. Go 200m and take the 1st right into Old Fort Road, then 1st left into Seaforth Ave - the house is at the end.

Nalson's View

Wendy and Kelvin Nalson

10 Fairway Drive, Salt Rock
Tel: 032-525-5726 Fax: 032-525-5726
Email: nalsonsview@3i.co.za Web: www.nalsonsview.com
Cell: 083-303-1533

After a long, long (long, long) day on the road I finally emerged from my car at Nalson's, wild-eyed and mud-besmattered. I couldn't have pitched up anywhere more perfect. Kelvin and Wendy welcomed me as if I had been living there for years. This was my room, these my beers and friends… I owned the place didn't I? A fantastic shower washed off the mud (don't ask) and I was invited to dinner. I couldn't tell who were guests, who were family friends, such is the open-house air of friendship here, and the meal was out of this world. Kelvin and Wendy have an oyster and mussel licence (guests can go with them and pick their own) and these were by FAR the best I've had in SA. Nalson's is one of those places where guests stop over for one night and have to be prised out of the place days later. Breakfast was sensational (both local baker and butcher are true servants of the community!) and, joy oh joy, freshly-squeezed fruit juice. Guests who make the correct decision to stay more than one night will get involved in the sea activities – dolphin- and whale-watching on boats, fishing, bird-watching and the ten kilometres of beautiful Christmas Bay Beach. There's plenty to do on dry land too, including golf galore, walking-distance restaurants and the Sibaya casino just 10 minutes away. *Ask about children.*

Rooms: 4: 2 doubles, 1 family and 1 double/twin; 3 with en-suite shower, 1 with en-suite bath and shower.
Price: R350 - R400 pp sharing. Singles on request.
Meals: Full breakfast included and served when you want it. Dinners by prior arrangement. Price depends on what you have.
Directions: From Durban take N2 north. Take exit 214 (Salt Rock/Umhlali). Right at T-junction signed to Salt Rock, follow road round to the right past Salt Rock Hotel (on your left). Fairway Drive is next right.

Comfort House

Ray Leitch

27 Dolphin Crescent, Shaka's Rock, North Coast
Tel: 032-525-5575 Fax: 032-525-8775
Email: comfort@iafrica.com Web: www.comforthouse.co.za
Cell: 082-556-9795

"I'm afraid I'm going to be a terrible host and ask you to get yourself a drink", was how Ray introduced herself to me. Within seconds I was drink in hand, utterly at ease and ready to get to know my terrible new host. As a former advocate for the government and prosecutor for some years in the Cape, there's not much on the streets Ray hasn't seen or heard before ("everything you can possibly imagine… and also what you can't!"). She's certainly straight-talking, but also very down-to-earth, a quality mirrored in her lovely manager, Val, and the anything-goes, everybody's-family feel to the place. This is a home and there's no attempt to conceal it. A Red Bear surfboard leans on a depiction of The Annunciation by the front door; family collages adorn the landing; greetings arrive in handfuls from the golden retriever and spaniel (with eyelashes longer than I believed possible). Even the four rooms are named after Ray's children (who fled the nest some time ago): Sarah, Jessica, Nicholas and Alexander. Yet none of this is overbearing. It's just what the label says: Comfort House. Each room opens on to a large communal balcony, so that guests fall into conversation and sun-loungers with equal ease, while taking in the turquoise pool below and the deep blue sea beyond. Honeymooners, of course, get the extra-special candle-lit treatment, and I admired the gorgeous dark-wood sleigh bed and intimate Jacuzzi on the private verandah… almost worth getting married for!

Rooms: 4: 2 kings, 1 queen and 1 twin, all with en-suite baths and showers.
Price: R350 - R550 pp sharing. Single supplement R100.
Meals: Full breakfast included. Dinner on request, at about R100 for 3 courses.
Directions: From Durban take N2 north until off ramp 212 to Shaka's Rock Road. Turn towards the sea and continue 3.5km to a T-junction. Turn left into Ocean Drive and then 2nd left in to Dolphin Crescent.

KwaZulu Natal

One On Hely

Ann and Mike Walters

1 Hely Hutchinson, Mtunzini
Tel: 035-340-2498 Fax: 035-340-2499
Email: admin@oneonhely.co.za Web: www.oneonhely.co.za
Cell: 079-509-4256

Ann describes the Walters family's relocation to Mtunzini as a 'calling'. Swapping the industrial chimneys of Newcastle for the rolling Indian Ocean they have much to teach about bravely following your instincts. Mtunzini is an up-and-coming town on the tourist map. Its main street leads to the greenery of the Umlalazi Nature Reserve and on to miles and miles of virginal beach. "Oh dear, it's busy," Ann remarked as we walked onto the white sands and counted five people dotted between us and the horizon. With its burgeoning independent café and shop scene, Mtunzini is a gem waiting to be discovered. Here you can fish, surf, bird-spot, wind-surf, walk and water-ski to your heart's content – although if I were you I'd factor in some time flopping by the pool at One On Hely, which has been set in wooden decking high above a flood of greenery. A stone's throw from town, this modern guest-house is surrounded by its own lovely garden, but from upstairs views are out over forest, reserve and sea. All the bedrooms have pristine beds and linen, while pictures of shells and wild flowers in dark wood frames remind you that the sea and green of the reserve is just outside your private balcony. As the Walters also own The Fat Cat in town they frequently raid their own café for prawns, calamari, fresh fish and lamb. In fact, it seems, you can dine on pretty much whatever your belly is rumbling for. Get there before everybody else does.

Rooms: 9: all king/ twin all ensuite. 7 with bath and shower and 2 only shower.
Price: R600 - R700 pp sharing. Single R850 - R950.
Meals: Full breakfast included. All other meals on request.
Directions: Take N2 from Durban exit at Mtunzini toll plaza exit. Turn right, and One on Hely is 1km on your right.

Chase Guest House

Jane and Jonathan Chennells

Eshowe
Tel: 035-474-5491 Fax: 035-474-1311
Email: thechase@netactive.co.za Web: www.thechase.co.za
Cell: 083-265-9629

Jane and Jonathan have so much to offer their guests that you hardly have to leave the premises. The weather-boarded house is gargantuan (Mrs Chennells senior had a penchant for large, open spaces) with long views of the farm's sugar cane plantations on overlapping mounds of distant hills. On clear days you can even see 90 degrees of sea. They also have ducks, chickens and (Nguni) cows like a proper farm should, of course. Also a pair of resident spotted eagle owls. The garden is an orgy of barely controllable tropical growth, lush and colourful (check out the tulip tree and the Indian mahogany), its trees often weighed down by parasitic ferns and creepers. Birds are equally irrepressible and there are 70 species in the garden and 280 (!) in the Eshowe area. Kids will love the walled-in swimming pool (13 metres long) where you can swim by floodlight at night too. A hammock swings from a tree, a trampoline is stretched at ground level and there is a hard tennis court. Chennells Chase is an involving, very comfortable, incredibly good-value family home, with huge amounts of space inside and out. Pack a sense of humour and a pair of binoculars. *Bikes are available for use.*

Rooms: 2: 1 double with en-suite bath; 1 twin with en-suite shower. Also a self-contained farm cottage with 3 bedrooms and 2 bathrooms, plus 2 double self-catering flatlets.
Price: R300 - R400 pp sharing. Singles R380 - R459. Self-catering cottage (sleeps 5), R600 - R750.
Meals: Full breakfast included (except in the cottage and the flatlets - by arrangement only) and served any time. Dinners on request.
Directions: From Durban take N2 north for 1 hour. Turn off at Dokodweni off-ramp R66 to Eshowe. Half an hour to Eshowe. Take first left signed to Eshowe, house 1.8km signed on left.

Chennells Guest House

Graham Chennells

36 Pearson Avenue, Eshowe
Tel: 035-474-4919 Fax: 035-474-2691
Email: info@eshowe.com Web: www.eshowe.com
Cell: 082-492-6918

The Chennells family have been an integral part of the Eshowe community for four generations, so it was no surprise that everyone waved at us as Graham and I drove through town. We were heading to the steep Signals Hill that looks across the valley to enjoy a welcome sundowner and watch the evening cane fires. As the sun bade us farewell, he told me of his passion to put Eshowe on the tourist map. After all, it was from here that the King Shaka built the Zulu empire. The family home has been elegantly converted with three light and airy bedrooms. Here the gentle morning sun will caress you from your king-size bed and the sizzling of bacon will draw you to the mahogany breakfast table. You may well spend your time back at the guest house reading on the black-and-white tiled stoep, sipping Graham's award-winning Zulu Blonde beer or diving into the pool that looks out into the hills. But I highly recommend getting out and about and taking advantage of what this wonderfully generous family have to offer. Depending on your mood, you may find yourself whisked off to the Zulu Kings Reed Dance, or strolling through the Dlinzi Forest Aerial Boardwalk… or do as I did and spend the most emotionally uplifting afternoon of your life with the children at the AIDS orphanage, learning Zulu songs. The memories I took from my stay here will undoubtedly remain with me forever.

Rooms: 3: 1 double with bath and shower; 2 doubles with shower. Also, a separate self-catering unit with 1 double and 2 twin rooms and 1 bathroom with separate bath and shower.
Price: R600 - R800 pp sharing. Singles on request.
Meals: Breakfast included. Light lunches plus 3 course suppers on request.
Directions: Enquire on booking.

Thula Thula Game Reserve

Françoise and Lawrence Anthony
D312 Heatonville, Buchanana, Ntambanana
Tel: 035-792-8322 Fax: 035-792-8324
Email: francoise@thulathula.com Web: www.thulathula.com
Cell: 082-259-9732

Pouring down the dirt roads, dust billowing, I cursed myself for being late for my first game drive... but I needn't have flustered. Within minutes of entering the park, an elephant ambled across my path. Moments later, after wiping a cool towel over my dusty face and a fresh fruit cocktail was placed into my thirsty grasp, I was whisked into a 4x4 and found myself virtually nose to horn with Heidi the rhino. Françoise and Lawrence are wonderfully entertaining and like their friendly staff, passionate conservationists. Here, human and animal lives are intimately intertwined as I discovered upon meeting a giraffe practically sunbathing on my stoep. Thula Thula is home to elephant, rhinoceros, leopard, giraffe, zebra, nyala, hyenas, crocodile, kudu, wildebeest and no fewer than 350 bird species. The tented camp with its outdoor showers, laid-back meals and luxury tents big enough for King Shaka and his entourage are perfect for families. A couple of kilometres through the bush, the lodge is equally breathtaking with cathedral-sized, African-themed rooms lavishly decked out with four-posters, zebra rugs and huge doors leading to the stoep. Not bad for the bush! Meeting other guests around a candlelit pool I was guided into the boma, complete with mesmerizing fire ("nature's TV" whispered Françoise) and presented with a four-course extravaganza. While feasting on chicken with chilli chocolate sauce and a sensational impala pie, Lawrence offered to remove one of my wheels so that I would be forced to stay another night. Temptation just made leaving even harder.

Rooms: 16: 8 lodges all king/ twin, 2 standard with sh'r, 4 luxury & 2 royal all en-s bath & sh'r. 8 luxury tents, 6 deluxe king/twin with bath & sh'r & outside sh'r, 2 family with bath & sh'r.
Price: Lodges: R1,500 - R2,750 pp sharing. Tents: R1,200 - R1,350. Full board, inclusive of all game drives & bush walks.
Meals: Includes all meals & gourmet 4-course dinner.
Directions: From N2 R34 to Empangeni. Thro Empangeni R towards Heatonville. Follow 10km crossing 3 rail tracks. Turn L at next T-jct onto dirt rd for 8km. Turn R for 2km to Thula. 2 hrs from Durban. Map on web.

African Ambience

John and Laura Engelbrecht
124 Pelikaan Street, St Lucia
Tel: 035-590-1212 Fax: 035-590-1416
Email: lejon@digitalsky.co.za Web: www.africanambience.com
Cell: 082-372-1769

Having brushed through lush, rain-shiny jungle foliage, I finally banged on the enormous door to African Ambience, which opened to reveal two large wooden elephants and a beaming John ready to show me round. He and Laura built and designed the place from scratch and, after living in St Lucia for 23 years, they certainly knew what they wanted. The thatched roof is set high above the well-proportioned rooms with their cream walls and big log furniture, all built by a local carpenter. "Are you child-friendly?" I asked. "You'd hope so, I've got at least six of my own," he laughed. There was indeed a real family feel to the house with guests and kids coming and going and everyone chatting around coffee mugs waiting for the rain to stop. John's passion is boat chartering and if you're lucky he might have caught a fish or two to braai for your supper. This takes place in the garden - where John keeps an impressive collection of koi carp in a series of raised ponds - around a candlelit figure-of-eight-shaped pool. Inside, the maids were scurrying around in brightly-coloured African aprons while I was learning about the resident fruit bat that dropped off its mother and decided to stay on as a permanent guest. Whatever you get up to in St Lucia, African Ambience provides a lively base that's bound to be eventful.

Rooms: 6: 1 honeymoon suite with king, private entrance, patio and en-s shower & spa bath; 3 luxury king/twin rooms with sofa-bed option and en-suite shower; 2 doubles with en-suite shower; 1 family room with 1 king and 2 singles with full bathroom.
Price: From R320 - R450 pp sharing. Family room R1,200 per night. Singles on request.
Meals: Full breakfast included. Dinners on request (speciality fish braais).
Directions: From N2 take R618 at Mtubatuba turn-off, following signs to St Lucia (approx 28km). Over bridge, turn R at T-junction into McKenzie St. At next roundabout veer L into Albacore Rd and then 2nd L into Pelikaan St. African Ambience is 1st house on L.

Lidiko Lodge

Dirk and Lyzette Kotze

95 McKenzie Street, St Lucia
Tel: 035-590-1581 Fax: 035-590-1581
Email: lidiko@wetlands.co.za Web: www.lidikolodge.co.za
Cell: 082-940-7184

At the end of the Lidiko Lodge's long lawn, I finally reached the verandah, just in time to see jugs of fruit juices disappearing to the kitchen and white wooden furniture being manoeuvred back into position. I was partly consoled for having missed out on what was clearly a sumptuous breakfast by the sight of Lyzette coming out to join me with coffee. African music wafted out with her. The last of the raindrops were dripping off the roof as we sat admiring the view across the wetlands. Once settled, I was soon quizzing Lyzette about the visit from the Zulu king. "Everyone was so nervous and excited, especially the staff!" she said proudly. Dirk and Lyzette are natural, gifted hosts and it was hard to imagine them as lawyers in Pretoria. They've turned the main house, an original 1930s colonial structure, into a gallery of local arts and crafts. A silky plum sofa occupies centre spot, surrounded by paintings, elaborate beading and hand-made jewellery – much of it so tempting I had to force myself to look away. The rooms, found by meandering through the back garden, past mango, banana and papaya trees, are decorated with contemporary African fabrics, wicker chairs and rugs, French doors from each lead out to the pool. The honeymoon suite (where the king slept) is an octagonal, thatched hut in the garden with Persian rugs and old colonial furniture. I was tempted to find a sun-lounger under a shady tree, but the nearby creatures of the wetlands needed finding and admiring first! *Bikes can be borrowed from the lodge.*

Rooms: 16: 12 twin/king with en-s bath and showers; honeymoon suite with en-s bath and shower; 2 family units sleeping 4, 1 with shared en-s bath, 1 divided with separate en-s showers.
Price: From R450 pp sharing. Honeymoon suite from R950 per couple. Singles plus R100. Kids on request.
Meals: Full breakfast included, dinners on request. Tea garden open for à la carte lunch & tea til 5pm.
Directions: Cross the bridge into St Lucia. At the first roundabout turn right into McKenzie Street. Lidiko Lodge is 800m down McKenzie Street on L.

Mtubatuba Boutique B&B

Ida Scheepers

243 Celtis Drive, Mtubatuba
Tel: 035-550-4265
Fax: 035-550-4019
Email: ida@bnbmtuba.co.za
Web: www.bnbmtuba.co.za
Cell: 082-494-6077

Ida is doing research in community psychology and was away at the time of my visit. But luckily, her effervescent, gregarious (aptly-named) manager Talent and big-hearted chef Fikile (who had been dancing and singing the previous evening from 9pm to 8am with her gospel choir and was still going) were there instead with ready smiles and open arms. These are exceptional people and the B&B a delightful secret with all the attractions of nearby St Lucia at their disposal, but without the crowds. As the three of us laughed, chatted and admired our way from room to room my pen had trouble keeping up. In Red and Green, light-coloured walls and generous proportions provide the perfect backdrop for antique mini-chandeliers, lavish velvet-covered benches, contemporary African art and white-washed kudu horns. If you fancy a laid-back beach house atmosphere with antique wooden bed and picture-frames then go for the Blue Room with its own lounge and kitchenette opening on to a wide patio. The love and fun invested in this special place is evident in the heart-shaped, hand-made pillows in the family room and the buckets of toys waiting Santa-style at the foot of the beds. Fikile is a fantastic - albeit far too modest - chef. I defy anyone not to count their blessings whilst dining by the pool, or strolling across the bridge and through the aloes and countless fruit trees in the garden.

Rooms: 5: 3 standard doubles and 1 executive suite with king. All en-suite bath and shower. 1 family room with 1 king and 2 singles with 1 bathroom and separate shower and toilet.
Price: R450 - R700 pp sharing.
Meals: Full breakfast included. Dinner on request.
Directions: Traveling from Durban on the N2 take the turn-off to Mtubatuba/St Lucia on the R618. Continue for 1km and take the first turn-off on your right onto Celtis Drive. The road curves to the right and the B&B is the first house with a driveway leading down on the right.

Makakatana Bay Lodge

Hugh and Leigh-Ann Morrison

Mtubatuba
Tel: 035-550-4189 Fax: 035-550-4198
Email: maklodge@iafrica.com Web: www.makakatana.co.za
Cell: 082-573-5641

Makakatana Bay Lodge is sensational and I can do little to improve on these photos, which do not lie. If only we had space for ten shots, to show you every aspect of the lodge: the gleaming wooden interiors; the bedrooms (including the wonderful honeymoon suite), connected by walkways through the forest, with their gargantuan slabs of glass and warm, earthy African colours; the pool encased in decking and raised above the grasses of the wetlands; the lake itself and the extraordinary St Lucia waterways. Guests are taken on drives into the wetlands to search for birds (360 species), crocodiles and hippos. You can also be taken to the beach for snorkelling and swimming or out on a game drive to a nearby reserve before returning to a sumptuous dinner with your hosts in the outdoor boma. Safari drives to Hluhluwe Game Reserve are also available if you have a hankering to see the Big 5. The family's old 'Crab House' is the only part of the lodge not raised above the tall grasses. This was once a storeroom for crabs caught in the lake, now a wine cellar with a giant tree growing out of its roof. Huge sliding doors throughout the lodge open onto wooden decks with views over the lake, and the absence of railings just adds to the feeling of openness to nature. The lodge is beautifully welded to its environment. An absolute treat.

Rooms: 6: 1 honeymoon suite with extra single bed, 2 king suites, 3 twin suites; all with en-suite bath and outside shower.
Price: R2,680 pp sharing, honeymoon suite R2,990 pp sharing. Singles R3,395 Children (aged 8-12) R1,750. All meals and in-house activities included. Drinks for own account.
Meals: Fully inclusive of all meals and safaris.
Directions: Take N2 north from Durban for 250km to Charter's Creek. Follow road for 15km (14km on tar) to fork. Take right fork and follow signs to Makakatana Bay Lodge (4 more km or so).

KwaZulu Natal

Hluhluwe River Lodge and Adventures

Gavin and Bridget Dickson

Greater St Lucia Wetlands Park, Hluhluwe
Tel: 035-562-0246/7
Fax: 035-562-0248
Email: info@hluhluwe.co.za
Web: www.hluhluwe.co.za

A short drive through dense bushveld takes you to this friendly, informal, adventure-orientated lodge overlooking the shores of Lake St Lucia. Although the shallow waters of the lake have receded in recent years there is rumour that they will be back, along with the hippos, in the near future. On arrival, I dumped my kit in a wood-and-thatch chalet and headed straight for the big deck, the centrepiece of the lodge, for some orientation and to drink in the view across the Hluhluwe River flood plain. There's a plunge pool lost in the trees, but most will want to make full use of the all-seeing, all-knowing guides (including sometimes Gavin himself) who will take you exploring in this remarkable region. There are drives through the Wetland Park sand forests, or to Cape Vidal National Park, but I visited nearby Umfolozi-Hluhluwe Park. And what a trip, my first real game drive and we spotted a leopard! You can also go quad- or mountain-biking, horse-riding through False Bay Park or take botanical trips and guided walks to old fossil banks. A highlight here are the meals: breakfast, lunch and fabulous candlelit dinners were all excellent when I last visited. Whatever you choose to get up to this is an intimate, sociable place with small numbers and knowledgeable guides making the experience personal and rewarding. The focus is on the topography, the birdlife and the wetland environment as a whole, rather than just the 'Big Five'.

Rooms: 12: 8 twins & 2 family rooms, all with en/s shower; 2 honeymoon suites (pictured) with shower & bath. For honeymoon suites, ask when you book.
Price: From R1,940 - R2,600 pp DBB and one game drive. From R1,600 – R2,255 pp sharing for DBB. Winter special (1 April to 31 July) R1265 - R1,790 pp sharing DBB and 1 game drive. Prices from R1,095 - R1,600 pp sharing DBB. Additional activities extra.
Meals: Full breakfast and dinner included. Lunch/ high tea on request from R65 for DBB guests.
Directions: From the N2 take the Hluhluwe off-ramp and pass through Hluhluwe town. Take the R22 signed towards Sodwana Bay. 3.4km after crossing the railway line turn right onto D540. Follow 5km signs to lodge. The gate guard will also direct you.

Bushwillow

Julian and Liz Simon
Hluhluwe
Tel: 035-562-0473 Fax: 035-562-0473
Email: info@bushwillow.com Web: www.bushwillow.com
Cell: 083-651-6777

Game reserves can be an expensive stop-over, so for visitors on a tighter budget we've uncovered some more affordable gems that still offer great access to local highlights. Bushwillow is one such, set in Kuleni Game Park. With 170 hectares to explore (on foot) you'll spot plenty of wildebeest, zebra, warthog and giraffe, setting the mood for the 'Big 5' at Hluhluwe-Umfolozi or the Greater St Lucia Wetlands Park (recently renamed Isimangaliso Wetland Park, which means 'wonder' or 'miracle') just half an hour away. It's hidden in the sand forest and while it can be reserved for your exclusive use, here you will always find an interesting array of people with whom to spend your time. I arrived on a blisteringly hot day and, passing a greedy 'sounder' of warthogs, was only too glad when Julian shepherded me inside to the cool of the fans. The three forest-green chalets blend into the bush perfectly, cunningly positioned a stone's throw from a water-hole so you needn't go further than the deck to spot the local wildlife. The air-conditioned bedrooms are peaceful and private and just a few steps along the boardwalk from the living area, with its granite worktops for the chef, and a eucalyptus dining table that supports excellent home-cooked meals. It seems they've thought of everything.

Rooms: 3 chalets (king or twin) with bath and shower. All bedrooms now have air-con.
Price: R725 (B&B), R895 (DB&B) pp sharing. Self-catering R2,100 per night (sleeps up to 6). Single group bookings available. Long-stay discounts. Ask about all-inclusive deals, e.g. 3-nights (DB&B) + 1 game drive + 1 boat trip (R3,300 pp).
Meals: Dinner and breakfast are only available for DB&B (see above); or breakfast only for B&B guests (as above). No meals available for self-caters.
Directions: From the N2 take the Hluhluwe off-ramp and pass through Hluhluwe town. At the bottom roundabout take the R22 towards Sodwana Bay. Continue 16km after crossing the railway line and Kuleni Game Park is on the L. Bushwillow is signed within the reserve.

Thonga Beach Lodge

Paige and Brett Gehren

Isibindi Africa Lodges, Mabibi, Greater St Lucia Wetland Park (now known as the Isimangaliso Wetland Park)
Tel: 035-474-1473 Fax: 035-474-1490
Email: res@isibindi.co.za Web: www.isibindiafrica.co.za Cell: 079-491-4422

I had been eagerly looking forward to my visit to Thonga Beach Lodge since before I had even left Cape Town. I knew it would be great because all the Gehrens' places are (see Isibindi Zulu Lodge, Kosi Forest Lodge and Rhino Walking Safaris) but I didn't expect it to be QUITE so beautiful! Thonga Beach is sandwiched between forested dunes and ocean, an hour's sandy drive and 4x4 trail from the nearest tar road. Huts are connected by snaking, wooden walkways and in each a huge mosquito net hangs from high rafters, separating the bed from the bathroom, a design marvel in itself. One single piece of sculpted concrete flows past glass-bowl sinks and chrome taps into an oval bath. After unpacking, I took a quick dip in the sea before being whisked out for a breath-taking sundowner on Lake Sibaya. An elegant supper followed and my perfectly light fish accompanied by a soft white wine sent me to my hut for a long, much-needed sleep. Come morning, I was raring to go for a sunrise stroll. The sky was a soft pink, the surf breaking onto footprint-free sand and, looking back to the lodge, I could just make out the thatched tops of each rounded room, twelve in all, poking out through milkwood brush. This is as luxurious and romantic a destination as you'll find anywhere, but it's super-relaxed too. All staff are hugely friendly, the birding, diving, walking and wildlife are superb and – a rare bonus – it's majority community-owned so your pennies help support the local economy.

Rooms: 12: 10 twins, 2 doubles, all with bath & sh'r, air-con, mosquito nets & sea or forest view.
Price: R1,950 - R2,300 pp sharing. Includes all meals, guided snorkelling, guided walks & kayaking. Spa treatments & scuba prices available on request.
Meals: Full board.
Directions: From Durban take the N2 north to Hluhluwe and then follow signs to Kosi Bay (Kwa-Ngwanase). 30km beyond Mbazwana follow signs right to Coastal Forest Reserve. Thonga car park (and lodge pick-up point) is now located at Coastal Cashew factory, 4.7km from tar rd. For 4x4 vehicles you will have to go 32km on along sandy road.

Kosi Forest Lodge

Paige and Brett Gehren
Isibindi Africa Lodges, Kosi Bay Nature Reserve, Kosi Bay/KwaNgwanase
Tel: 035-474-1473 Fax: 035-474-1490
Email: res@isibindi.co.za Web: www.isibindiafrica.co.za
Cell: 082-873-8874

Kosi Bay is the sort of place that novelists map out and then construct adventures in. You are picked up by a four-wheel drive, which can negotiate the sand tracks criss-crossing the region. You park up not just your car, but also the modern world you are now leaving. There is no tar and no electricity here. Instead you enter a landscape of raffia palm groves, primary sand forests, mangroves, water meadows, interconnecting lakes (yes, hippo and crocodile like it too and are regularly sighted). And then there are day trips to the sea and the mouth of the river for snorkelling, swimming and fishing in 'perfect, white sand coves with huge overhanging trees' (says the lodge brochure). The reed-thatched camp itself perfectly balances the wild (your chalet is in the middle of a boisterous forest) with the romantic (candlelit meals and outdoor baths and showers). I loved the deep stillness of the early-morning guided canoe trip and other activities include boat cruises across the lakes, turtle tracking (seasonal), forest walks and bird safaris. I consider Kosi Forest Lodge one of the most rewarding (and therefore best-value) places I have stayed in SA. I recommend a minimum of two or three nights.

Rooms: 8: 1 family 'bush suite'; 5 twins and 2 honeymoon doubles; all with outdoor bath and shower.
Price: R1,350 - R1,530 pp sharing. Guided canoeing on the lakes and walks in raffia forest included. 1 full-day excursion included in stays of 2 nights or more.
Meals: All meals included. Dinner, bed and breakfast rates available on request.
Directions: From Durban take the N2 north to Hluhluwe and then follow signs to Kosi Bay (Kwa-Ngwanase). From JHB pass Pongola and turn R at sign Jozini. In Jozini thru' town, L over the dam and follow for 37km. Turn R at T-jct and follow for 67km to Kwangwanase. Pass through town to end, go to Total Garage for pick from lodge (9km).

Ghost Mountain Inn

Craig Rutherfoord
Mkuze
Tel: 035-573-1025 Fax: 035-573-1359
Email: gmi@ghostmountaininn.co.za Web: www.ghostmountaininn.co.za
Cell: 082-569-0596

I'd been looking forward to visiting Ghost Mountain, if only for the name, but how my excitement increased when I pulled into the car park and saw 26 pristine vintage Bentleys warming up for a day's adventure. NOT what I had expected to find deep in the heart of Zululand! This is definitely a hotel (50 rooms) and thus not a typical GG entry. But I have no doubts about its suitability for this guide. Craig, who is the very charming owner, will instantly make you feel at home. In fact, I cursed myself for not organizing to stay the night after he informed me, over a particularly rich and dark shot of coffee, that there was a boat trip to watch elephants drinking at nearby Lake Jozini or a trail in Hluhluwe-Umfolozi Park on offer if I wished to join them. I didn't even have time to sample a massage in the luxurious on-site health spa. Oh unhappy hour! I did, however, get to wander through the vast gardens that look up to Ghost Mountain (with its spooky history) and admire the fantastic double-trunked sycamore fig tree that stands next to a deep and inviting swimming pool. Naturally the rooms are also top notch: flat screen TV's for sports lovers, reed lampshades that cast gentle shadows across soft white linen and a private patio looking across to the Lebombo Mountains. I cast a green eye on those beautiful Bentleys as Craig escorted me back to my car. His phone rang and he apologetically made his excuses. A Zulu princess was expected for lunch and arrangements had to be made. *Bikes are available for guests' use.*

Rooms: 50: 23 standard twin/doubles en-suite bath/shower; 26 executive rooms en-suite bath/shower; 1 executive suite with king, 2 en-suite bath/shower + outside shower.
Price: R510 - R875 pp sharing. Singles R630 - R1,535.
Meals: Lunch à la carte and 3-course dinner set menus at R145 pp.
Directions: Enquire on booking.

Dusk to Dawn

Johann and Gudrun Engelbrecht

Farm Wagendrift, Piet Retief
Tel: 017-821-0601 Fax: 086-514-0237
Email: dtd@ptr.dorea.co.za Web: www.dusktodawnbedandbreakfast.com
Cell: 083-627-6454

I'm ashamed to say that I saw neither the dusk nor the dawn on Johan and Gudrun's splendid farm. After missing sundown when my three-hour hop from Jo'burg turned into a five-hour slog, I was sorely tempted by Gudrun's description of sunrise over the distant Kommetjie-Kop seen from the balcony of my room, Egret's View. Unfortunately, my alarm clock failed me yet again! I blame the four-poster bed, with its soothing white linen, not to mention the telescope, which had me glued to the startlingly starry night-sky far past my bedtime. The real culprit though, was the seriously deep bath complete with huge candles, which were bright enough to light a cathedral. Luckily breakfast is served until 10... and the whole pace of Dusk to Dawn is geared towards unwinding overnight, hence the name. It's the perfect stop-off point if you're travelling between KZN and the Kruger. Breakfast is a healthy spread of smoothies, juices and, of course, fresh coffee - Gudrun is a trained nutritionist. Over dinner, meanwhile, I tasted some prime Dusk to Dawn pork. All the meat and most of the veggies come from the farm. There are plenty of marked paths if you fancy a wander or Johan will happily show you around. He is also an expert on the Zulu Wars and the local German community which settled here over a century and a half ago. Use the farm as one-night stopover if you must, but if you can spare the time stay for two. They have just completed at the time of writing a new cottage, Robin's Rest, which is free-standing with wonderful views and its own kitchen, lounge, patio, DSTV and aircon.

Rooms: 5: Egret's View: 1 twin, 1 x 4-poster with en/s bath; Hadeda's Nest: twin, en/s shower; Sunbirds View: 4-poster en/s bath & sh'r; Barbet's Corner (self-catering): queen en-s bath & shower; Robin's Rest, king en-s bath & shower, lounge.
Price: R535 pp sharing. Singles available on request.
Meals: Full board. Barbet's Corner self-catering. Full English breakfast or healthy smoothies. Dinner is soup, home-baked bread & choice of fish & meat. Picnics on request.
Directions: Signed off the N2, 35km south-east of Piet Retief and 65km north of Pongola.

Map Number: 14

Isibindi Zulu Lodge

Paige and Brett Gehren

Isibindi Africa Lodges, Rorke's Drift/Battlefields, Dundee
Tel: 035-474-1473 Fax: 035-474-1490
Email: res@isibindi.co.za Web: www.isibindiafrica.co.za
Cell: 082-896-0332

Driving up to Isibindi in the early evening, the way ahead was intermittently illuminated by a spectacular thunderstorm. It seemed to be following me. Ignoring the portents, I pressed on Homerically to claim my prize, a night at the wonderful (the first line of my notes just reads 'Wow!') Isibindi Zulu Lodge. It's on a hill in the middle of a 2,000-hectare nature reserve on the Buffalo River, with six secluded chalets looking out over the bush, a modern spin on the traditional Zulu beehive hut. The best view is reserved for the pool, a great place for daytime dozing before an afternoon game drive with lodge managers who are extremely passionate about the bush. The game wasn't playing ball on our evening outing but we heard plenty of snuffling about in the twilight as we walked back under the stars to the lodge. For those not barmy about the bush there are Zulu dancing evenings laid on. Personally though, the tour of the nearby Isandlwana and Rorke's Drift battlefields are the highlight. Walking the 50 yards of Rorke's Drift, having the battle described to me as the rain fell and the local Zulu choir had their weekly rehearsal in the church on the battlefield itself, was a highlight not just of my trip, but will remain one of the most extraordinary experiences of my life. Nature, history and culture… Isibindi has it all.

Rooms: 6: 4 twins, 1 double, 1 honeymoon suite; all in the traditional beehive shape with en-suite bath and shower.
Price: R1,150 - R1,250 pp sharing. Singles plus 30%. Price includes 3 meals & 1 game activity per day plus a Zulu Boma Evening. Battlefield tours, Zulu homestead visits and panoramic day trips are optional extras.
Meals: Full board includes breakfast, lunch and dinner and all teas and coffees.
Directions: Take R33 from Dundee towards Greytown for 42km, then turn left onto dirt road at Isibindi Eco Reserve/Elandskraal sign. Follow signs to Isibindi which is 21km from main road.

Mawelawela Game and Fishing Lodge

George and Herta Mitchell-Innes

Fodo Farm, Elandslaagte
Tel: 036-421-1860 Fax: 036-421-1019
Email: mitchellinnes@mweb.co.za Web: www.mawelawela.co.za
Cell: 083 259 6394 or 082-734-3118

George and Herta are a natural, down-to-earth couple whose veins of hospitality run deep… and staying with them is to enjoy a few days awash with incidental pleasures. Herta, a bubbly Austrian, moved out to South Africa 28 years ago and married George, who is a beef farmer – his boerewors is delicious. He is also a keen historian and leads tours out to the site of the battle of Elandslaagte. His study is full of Anglo-Boer war prints and weighty tomes including a collection of the London Illustrated News. (Ask him to show you his father's beautiful collection of bird-eggs too.) If you stay in the main house the rooms are very comfortable and the bungalow across the jacaranda-filled garden is perfect for families or groups. A short drive away from the farm itself you'll find the thatched hunters' cottage on 1500 wild hectares set aside for game. There is a trout dam at the front into which George has built a waterfall, and there's a shower and a plunge pool to one side. The cane-sided shady braai area faces dam-wards and you can watch the eland and kudu come to drink in the evenings and with the big five just a seven minute drive away you won't forget you're in animal country. Finally a toast to Herta's cooking which is wonderful! Many of the ingredients are home-grown and all is served on her collection of fine china and family silver. *Bookings essential.*

Rooms: 4: 2 twins (1 with en/s bath, 1 en/s bath & shower); 1 apartment with double, twins & single (self-catering or B&B); 1 self-catering game lodge sleeps 7.
Price: R300 - R400 pp sharing B&B. Singles on request. Self-catering R250 pppn.
Meals: All meals are in the main house. Full breakfast included. 3-course dinners (excluding wine) R100 (booking essential). Main and coffee R50.
Directions: On N11, 35km from Ladysmith, 70km from Newcastle. Also entrance on R602, 35km from Dundee towards Ladysmith. For B&B look for sign to Fodo Farm.

Map Number: 13

Montusi Mountain Lodge

Anthony and Jean Carte
Off D119, Near Alpine Heath, Bergville
Tel: 036-438-6243 Fax: 036-438-6566
Email: montusi@iafrica.com Web: www.montusi.co.za

Montusi feels a bit like a hotel, which just happens to be run by your aunt and uncle. You know… you haven't seen them for years, but no sooner have you stepped from the car than they've got your bed sorted (well, your thatched, Conran-style, country cottage complete with fireplace, selected DSTV and view!) and are fixing you a sundowner on the patio. Yes, the views are every bit as good as the photo suggests. Ant bought wattle-strangled Montusi Farm in the early 1990s. Being a man of X-ray vision, he saw through the undergrowth to a lodge perfectly positioned to catch the surrounding view, he saw fields of galloping horses and he saw lakes to fish in. So he did away with the wattles (via a community project) and a new Montusi emerged. Meals are superb… some examples: lamb with chargrilled lemon and mint, ostrich fillet with garlic and marinated peppers, malva pudding, custard cups. There are many ways to burn off the calories with limitless and fabulous Drakensberg hiking on your doorstep (we walked up stunning Tugela Gorge, but the Cartes can help with suggestions). But there's also horse-riding for all levels of experience, mountain-biking, swimming in the wonderful pool and fishing. But best of all is ex-skiing pro Chris's circus school! It is as professional as they come, with trapezes, bungies, nets, ropes and they sometimes put on shows too. Montusi impressed me because it's a happy, family-run place with plenty of style. *Relaxation massages are now being offered by local ladies as part of a community project. Picnics at waterfalls can be arranged.*

Rooms: 14 cottages: 4 are kings with en-suite bath and another twin with en-suite shower next door. 10 are kings with shower and bath.
Price: R1,000 pp sharing per night. Singles R1,200. Rate includes dinner and breakfast.
Meals: Full breakfast & 4-course dinner incl' (wine extra).
Directions: From south head north thro Pietermaritzburg, Estcourt & turn L signed Northern Drakensberg. Continue 80km thro Winterton & Bergville on R74. Follow signs (some small) to Montusi. From north use Harrismith and R74.

Vergezient Drakensberg Mountain Retreat

Hosts: Keith and Jenny Meyer; Owner: David George
Northern Drakensberg, Bergville
Email: info@drakensbergretreat.co.za Web: www.drakensbergretreat.co.za
Cell: 082-302-0406

It hadn't rained for seven months when I arrived at this serene retreat, but it was doing its damnedest to make up for lost time! Thunder bellowed, rain spat and the lightning gods put on a show to rival anywhere in Vegas. Totally over-excited about the storm, I was ushered inside by Dave, the retreat's congenial owner/builder, through the conservatory with its arum lilies and granadilla vines ripe with fruit and we plonked ourselves down in front of a roaring fire, cup of tea in hand. The first thing I noticed, apart from Baloo the Staffy jumping onto my lap, was the space. The communal living room is as long as the building itself and the windows stretch across the back of the house, giving a panoramic view of the night-time show. Dave's theory? "I have so much space, I'd feel guilty if people didn't use it." It is this generosity that makes Vergezient Drakensberg Mountain Retreat so special. There's no agenda here. So whether it's hiking to New Beginnings Cave, sinking into one of many books piled high in the library or tinkling away on the baby grand Steinway, your time is your own. Supper, however, is compulsory! Over three delectable courses (what a pork dish that was!), Dave and I exchanged old stories, wine flowed, candles flickered, songs were sung. The next morning, after a deep, soft-cottoned sleep, the storm had cleared and I awoke to a view so spectacular I nearly fell out of bed: miles of imposing Drakensberg Mountain, the Tugela Falls in full flight and mist still sleeping in the valley. Now I saw why Dave had to share this. It's too beautiful for one man.

Rooms: 8: all doubles. Four with en-suite bath/shower and four with en-suite shower. They have also literally just opened the "Zonderntwyfel" Barn House for affordable dinner, bed & breakfast.
Price: R450 - R750 pp. Singles on request.
Meals: Breakfast and 3-course dinner included. Light lunch on request.
Directions: See website or enquire on booking.

Spion Kop Lodge

Lynette and Raymond Heron
R600, Drakensberg and Battlefields Area, Ladysmith
Tel: 036-488-1404 Fax: 086-647-8134
Email: spionkop@futurenet.co.za Web: www.spionkop.co.za
Cell: 082-573-0224/5

Soon after arriving, we were off on a late-afternoon game drive in the park next door, winding our way through thick grasses towards a vast lake, then glowing pink-blue under the setting sun. We had the place to ourselves, if you don't count the animals, who seemed to be everywhere, including a nonchalant rhinoceros who munched his way uncomfortably close to our vehicle. Safely back at base, I began exploring. The lodge is now a 700-hectare eco-reserve with 278 bird species and a mass of flowering aloes in June and July. You can stay either in stone cottages, which are snug with fireplaces for winter and verandahs for summer; or in the colonial farmhouse with its polished floorboards and library full of history books. But the main heart of the lodge is the 108-year-old stone converted barn, now a massive glass-walled dining room with sinuous blonde branches creeping from floor to ceiling… and breath-taking views. After an excellent dinner with much red wine and merry-making, we embarked on a night safari in search of leopards and porcupines. Raymond is a registered guide, a raconteur par excellence and an expert on the tragic movements of the Battle of Spionkop. His battlefields tours are so riveting and brilliant that they are often reported as highlights, not just of a stay at the lodge, but of peoples' whole trips in South Africa. Both he and Lynette are wonderful hosts and will ensure you have an eventful stay. With horse-riding, boat cruises, fishing, birding and bushman art on offer as well, there's enough to keep you entertained for a week.

Rooms: 8 doubles, all en-suite with bath and shower. Plus 2 self-catering cottages: Aloe has 1 double, 1 twin and a bath; Acacia has 3 bedrooms and 2 bathrooms.
Price: R990 – R1,100 full board pp sharing. Aloe R890 per cottage per night. Acacia R1,100 per cottage per night.
Meals: Full breakfast, lunch and 3-4 course dinner included. Meals available on request for self-caterers.
Directions: On R600 betw Ladysmith & Winterton. Signed off R74 & N11. Gravel rd for 1.5km. (N3 from Durban or Jo'burg). See web site for map.

Zingela

Mark and Linda Calverley

Weenen
Tel: 036-354-7005/7250 Fax: 036-354-7021 or 086 650 8950
Email: zingela@futurenet.co.za Web: www.zingelasafaris.co.za
Cell: 084-746-9694 (out of range 99% of the time)

Hiking, fishing, abseiling, rafting, swimming, game-viewing, hunting, quad-biking, horse-riding… perhaps I'd be better off listing the things you can't do at Zingela. Mark and Linda are delightful and, over twenty years or so, have built up their home/riverside bush camp to offer everything and anything, all the more astonishing given their location. This really is wild country. From a rendezvous in the wee village of Weenen it was an hour's 4x4 drive (not for the faint-hearted) past isolated Zulu villages and down to the Tugela River - worth every bump. There are five palatial double tents overlooking the river, all open to the elements. Showers are more outside than in, branches provide the towel rails and each tent has hefty, iron-framed beds and beautiful wooden furniture from Zanzibar. Those on the romance beat will love the 'hitching post' with doubtless the world's largest headboard, a vast, mattress-to-canvas slab of sandstone. There's electricity and gallons of hot water but Zingela is essentially bush living ("don't-forget-the-loo-roll-or-matches kind of country," says Linda). When I visited the place was alive with families (there are zillions of kids' beds in extra dormitory tents). Some youngsters were preparing for a rafting adventure and everyone was thoroughly enjoying the endless fresh air, filling grub and lashings of good, wholesome fun. The thatched oil-lamp camp is now open!

Rooms: 5 bush tents: 3 doubles and 2 twins, all with shower. Self-catering option available.
Price: R950 pp includes all food plus game walk, abseiling and rafting. Eco-friendly quad-bike trails, horse-riding and stalking are extra. Transfers from Weenen for those without 4x4 are R100 pp.
Meals: Full board.
Directions: Faxed or emailed on booking.

Ardmore Farm

Paul and Sue Ross

Champagne Valley, Central Drakensberg
Tel: 036-468-1314 Fax: 086-503-3453
Email: info@ardmore.co.za Web: www.ardmore.co.za

Just in time for scones and tea on the lawn, the rain clouds parted and I was able to savour the stunning views of the three highest peaks in South Africa: Mafadi (highest at 3450m), Injisuti Dome (second highest at 3410m) and the majestic Champagne Castle (third highest at 3377m). The Drakensberg National Park begins just down the road so bring your hiking boots. Ardmore is a super-relaxed, freewheeling sort of place. Sociable and delicious dinners, eaten by lantern light at long tables in the yellowwood dining room, draw on the farm's organic produce - eggs from happy, roaming chickens and fruit, vegetables and herbs from a pesticide-free garden. Paul will tell you all about the art here, all created by the local Zulu community, much of it from the new Zulu cotton-weaving factory and the world-renowned Ardmore Pottery at the end of the garden. Here bright blue ceramic elephant teapots sit next to green giraffe egg cups and a red leopard prowls out of a huge urn. This imaginative empowerment project now sells work at Sotheby's, no less. There is masses to do at Ardmore: hike to waterfalls and mountain peaks; watch the rare bald ibis that makes its home here; fish, canoe, mountain-bike; the game farm nearby (1/2-hr drive) offers cheap horse-riding to see the rhino, zebra and giraffe; the Drakensberg Boys' Choir performs on Wednesdays at 15h30; and there are many rock-art sites in the area too. The small thatched rondavels are sweet and cosy and the bigger ones have fireplaces. Garden furniture is set out under the giant liquid amber tree, an important focal point for the property, where you can take tea and contemplate the mountains.

Rooms: 9: 6 cottages and 3 rondavels. 2 cottages with 2 doubles both ensuite. 4 cottages with 1 queen 4-poster, 1 double/twin and 1 twin. 2 ensuite. Rondavels all queen. All with shwr & bath sep.
Price: R385 - R485 pp sharing.
Meals: Full breakfast and 4-course dinner with wine included.
Directions: From the N3 take the R74 to Winterton and go south along the R600 towards the Central Drakensberg for 18km. You'll see a sign on your left, 5km up partly dirt road for Ardmore.

Hartford House

Mick and Cheryl Goss

Hartford House, Mooi River
Tel: 033-263-2713 Fax: 033-263-2818
Email: info@hartford.co.za Web: www.hartford.co.za

The Gosses, owners of Hartford House, humbly refer to themselves as "custodians of one of Africa's most treasured legacies". General Botha assumed command of the Boer forces here in 1899, and it was also home to Sir Frederick Moor, the last prime minister of the Colony of Natal. The deputy prime minister, Colonel Richards, established the world-renowned Summerhill Stud on the property, which today hosts stallions for the rulers of Dubai. Aside from all this history, the Gosses also rightly revel in the beauty of this spectacular place… and so will you. Spread across seemingly endless landscaped gardens, the fourteen rooms have been decorated with dark wood antiques from India and West Africa. Scraping my jaw off the floor, I surveyed the four lakeside suites which are nothing short of spectacular. I was especially taken with the aptly-named "Siyabonga" ("thank you" in Zulu) with its twin egg baths and private pool. The beaded chair, the wooden cow heads on the wall and the building materials are all locally sourced. An emperor-sized round bed dominates the Inkanyesi Suite, while "Nhlanhla" ("good luck") combines Asian furniture with bold green and rich red furnishings and a bright copper bath glints in the bathroom. Made entirely out of hay bales, this amazing example of sustainable luxury accommodation is so close to the dam it is practically floating. Oh, and by the way, the restaurant was in the top ten at the 2008 Dine Awards. Just go.

Rooms: 14: 4 lakeside suites all king with bath and wet room; 4 garden/ pool suites all with bath and shower; 3 standard kings with bath and shower and 3 twins with bath and shower.
Price: R840 – R1,555 pp.
Meals: Full 3 course breakfast included. A la carte lunch and 5 course set dinner. Restaurant in Eat Out top 10.
Directions: Please refer to website.

The Antbear

Andrew and Conny Attwood

Fernhust Farm, Moor Park – Giant's Castle Road, Estcourt
Tel: 036-352-3143 Fax: 036-352-3143
Email: info@antbear.co.za Web: www.antbear.co.za

As soon as I arrived at The Antbear (with its hilltop location and stunning Drakensberg views), I was already cursing my schedule and wishing I could stay longer. Although Andrew and Conny are a polymathic couple with many interests between them, it became as transparent as the clear mountain air that their guest house is top of the list. Around the tenth time that Andrew had to confirm that yes, he also made whatever it was I was pointing at, did I finally accept that everything here is created by the couple with such imagination and flair that it makes Willie Wonker look like a drudge. Here, the mundane becomes exciting as doorknobs become feats of engineering and hand-carved, over-sized hinges works of art. Glinting mosaics of African women enliven bathrooms and wooden dragonflies rest on bedroom walls. The recently-built rooms were all made using eco-friendly methods and 'truth windows' reveal the walls are stuffed with straw. Each night guests congregate at the yellowwood table (Andrew-carved, naturally) to swap tales of their day's adventures, one of which is sure to be flying in the Antbear microlight over 5,000 hectares of game reserve. 100% organic (unless the horses, tortoises or chickens have raided the garden!), the food here is amazing with flavours borrowed from Zulu neighbours or from across the globe. With so much to do in this magnificent place (rock-art sites, river-rafting, battlefield tours, local arts) you'd be a fool to stay for just one night.

Rooms: 5: 4 en/s doubles in renovated tractor shed, all with showers and jacuzzi bath; 1 separate double with en/s shower and jacuzzi bath.

Price: Dinner, bed and breakfast from R610 - R860 pp sharing. No single supplements. Children under 11 half price.

Meals: Lunch on request from R40 pp. Dinner usually 3 courses (excluding wine).

Directions: Take exit 152 on the N3 signed Hidcote for 7km. At T-junction turn right towards Giant's Castle. After 14km turn right towards Moor Park onto dirt road. After 5.5km you will see The Antbear sign to R. The thatched cottages are 2km up the farm rd.

Loxley House

Angie Hunter

Loxley House, Clifton School Road, Nottingham Road
Tel: 033-266-6362 Fax: 033-266-6026
Email: welcome@loxleyhouse.com Web: www.loxleyhouse.com
Cell: 073-228-2099

Sitting in the shade of the gazebo, chatting with Angie and nibbling crusty-on-the-outside-yet-somehow-soft-and-melty-on-the-inside home-baked cookies, it was obvious to me that Loxley is a dream come true. Following in her father's hotelier footsteps, Angie spent years managing some of South Africa's smartest and busiest hotels. But as soon as she clapped eyes on Loxley House, shielded from the road by a large garden and flowering trees, Angie gathered up her Dutch husband Jan, their five cats and three dogs and returned to her home town. Stripping the house and re-clothing it in stylish earthy colours, with matching burgundy cushions in snug window-seats, Angie and Jan have made it their own... and their guests'. Each of the eleven lovely bedrooms has intimate touches such as a sprig of fresh spring flowers in front of a mirror and candles round the bath proving that hospitality is not only in Angie's training, but also in her blood. It is at meal times when the team really shows its mettle, as Angie and Jan prepare and serve their guests locally-sourced food either out on the lawn or in the African dining room. Word to the wise... the fillet stack is a special treat. It's then up to you whether you want to be further furnished with drinks by Jan from his fly-fishing bar or head to your enormous bed with one eye on some early-morning mini-golf, croquet or even trampolining in the garden! *Wifi internet available. Fees apply.*

Rooms: 11 rooms: 6 king/twins with en-suite
shower in bath; 4 with en-suite separate shower and
bath; 1 with en-suite shower only.
Price: From R450 pp sharing. Singles from R550.
Meals: Full breakfast included. Lunch and dinner on
request. Afternoon teas (including home made
chocolate cake and crunchies) also on request.
Directions: From N3 take Nottingham Road exit.
Right into village opposite junction and right again
under railway bridge. 1 km turn left onto Lower
Loteni Road. Loxley is 100 metres on left.

Fordoun

John and Richard Bates

R103, Nottingham Road
Tel: 033-266-6217 Fax: 033-266-6630
Email: info@fordoun.com Web: www.fordoun.com
Cell: 082-334-2189

Tranquillity is infused with oxygen at this one-time farmyard, reborn in 2005 as a boutique hotel and spa par excellence. On arrival I ascended into a state of serenity. After ohhhing and ahhhing at the indoor and outdoor pools, gym, saunas, steam and flotation rooms, my happy (but perhaps not that serene) exclamations continued throughout my tour of the rooms. These used to be the stables and are arranged in a horseshoe around a traditional courtyard. Each bedroom is elegantly decorated with matching French curtains and bedspreads, providing the perfect place to float away after a hot stone massage or facial. Guests can also have a private consultation with exalted sangoma (spiritual healer) and medicinal healer Elliot Ndlovu. Elliot's traditional Zulu treatment rooms are in gardens that are home to over 120 types of medicinal plants used in treatments and in the hotel's complimentary lotions and potions. Skye Restaurant expertly achieves the seemingly impossible, a fusion of healthy and yet utterly indulgent cooking. To borrow words from one happy guest: "True hospitality gives to life what true cooking gives to eating. Fordoun excels in them both". This place is not only for spa- and food-lovers. Fordoun is also perfectly positioned for those who wish to explore spectacular rock art, golf courses, fly-fishing sites and hiking trails. After a morning massage (mais oui!) I was relaxed and revitalised and ready to take on the world.

Rooms: 17: 10 luxury and 7 deluxe. All kings/twins with en-suite bathroom with separate bath and shower.
Price: R600 - R1,100 pp sharing. Singles R800 - R1,500.
Meals: Full breakfast included. Lunch and dinner a la carte.
Directions: N3 Highway, one and a half hrs from Durban or 4hrs from Johannesburg. Take Nottingham Road off-ramp (Exit 132). At stop turn right towards Nottingham Road. Fordoun driveway is 3km from stop on the r/h side.

Engeleni Lodge & Mayfly Cottage

Graham and Sue Armstrong
Nottingham Road
Tel: 033 267 7218 Fax: 033-267-7103
Email: engeleni@futurenet.co.za Web: www.engeleni-lodge.co.za
Cell: 082-854-2338

To experience fully all that the KZN Midlands has to offer, this place should be high on your 'must-do' list. For not only is Sue a delightful host, but she is also an experienced, home-grown tour-guide who is dying to share her local knowledge with you. So whatever sparks your fancy, from private gardens, horse-studs, San rock paintings, air-ballooning (take-off point, the lawn) or Zulu spiritual healing... Sue will sort it out. There are also superb birding and fishing opportunities right here on the farm. And the accommodation is tip-top too. After years spent outcast and overgrown, the lodge has been welcomed back, and wonderfully restored and now radiates country warmth from each room. Full of beautiful original artworks and with fishing rods and binos dotted around, Engeleni is one of those places where I immediately felt right at home. From the huge wood-panelled kitchen with wagon-wheel light-fittings hanging from the rafters, to the flower-filled dining room, cosy pub, cheery bedrooms, book-filled corridors and snug living room (with traditional Gallic fishing-boat above the log-fire!), this deceptively large house, dwarfed by its magnificent setting, is a knock-out. I absolutely loved the smaller, slightly more 'African' Mayfly too; so cosy that Sue sometimes uses it as her own secret R&R retreat. Romantic couples, keen beans and lazy idlers all... I'd recommend you stay at least two nights.

Rooms: Engeleni Lodge: 5 king/twins, 1 with en-suite shower, 2 with en-suite shower & bath, 2 rooms share bath (Engeleni can only be taken by one group at a time); Mayfly Cottage: 1 king/twin with en-s double shower.

Price: Dinner, bed and breakfast R650 - R680 pp; B&B R485 - R530, singles R700 - R750. Self-catering rate R400 - R460 pp. Mayfly Cottage sleeps 2.

Meals: Meals by arrangement at time of booking.

Directions: From Durban/Jo'burg, take Mooi River Toll Plaza off N3. L onto R103 to Rosetta, then R into Kamburg Rd for 18km. R into D314, then 3.7km on dirt road following signs to lodge.

Rockwood Forest Lodge

Tom Hancock
Karkloof Nature Reserve, Howick
Tel: 031-303-5162 Fax: 031-312-4872
Email: info@rockwood.co.za Web: www.rockwood.co.za

I half-expected a trail of breadcrumbs to lead me up to Rockwood Forest Lodge One, a wooden 'gingerbread' house snuggled among green stinkwood, Cape quince and moss-covered blackwood. Creeping up the Oregon pine stairs and ducking under the low slanting roof, I could have sworn that seven dwarfs were snoozing in the four-poster bed, their heads propped up on feather pillows. On second inspection, Dopey and co were nowhere to be seen, or heard. All was silent except the gurgling River Godwini. Passing cupboards and door frames painted in reds and greens, I retraced my steps to the large outdoor braai deck. Propped up on stilts, there's enough space here to host a Grimm's fairytale reunion. Inside, an open fire, spotted cow rugs and slouching sofas beckon when the sun sets. If you prefer open spaces, though, the solar-powered Lodge Four is in a natural clearing with views across to Howick. Karkloof Nature Reserve is on your doorstep here, a mere 2,800 hectares of endemic flora and fauna, which is open to lodge guests alone. Grab your binos and look out for samango monkeys, bushbuck (I saw three on my drive up there), blue duiker, Cape parrots and crowned eagles. If you want a closer encounter, take the Karkloof Canopy Tour, where you swing through the forest on a zip slide. Elsewhere, there are mountain-biking trails aplenty, plus fishing dams and swimming weirs. Enough to put a smile on the face of the grumpiest of dwarves! *Construction begins in Feb 2009 of two new units in equally secluded grounds and of course to the high standard that Rockwood guests have come to expect.*

Rooms: 2 units: Lodge One: 1 king and 2 twins, with 2 bathrooms (bath and shower); Lodge Four: 1 king and 2 twins with 2 bathrooms (bath and shower).
Price: Lodge One: R460 per person per night – R2,000 per unit per night; Lodge 4: R370 pppn – R1,800 per unit per night.
Meals: Self-catering.
Directions: Check website for directions. 4-wheel drive is essential during wet conditions.

Stocklands Farm

Eve Mazery

4 Shafton Rd, Howick
Tel: 033-330-5160 Fax: 086 685 5657
Email: stocklands@iafrica.com Web: www.stocklandsfarm.co.za
Cell: 082-975-2298

The warm welcome that I received as I tumbled out of my car, late and weary, is undoubtedly typical of Stocklands. Eve and Roland are natural hosts, thoughtful and funny, and they have put a lot of love and plenty of style into the wonderful old house. The argument goes that half-measures are not really in keeping with Stocklands, and you can see their point. The walls of the original 1850s Voortrekker Cottage, for example, are over 50 centimetres thick and the belhambra tree at the front of the house is no-less-than enormous. Birds come in droves – they love Roland's indigenous trees, "a small forest", and bank upon bank of stunning flowers. I loved the fuchsia tree myself (it flowers in January). Down near the tennis court there is a koi pond and many guests like to savour a slow, hot afternoon in the thick shade on a blanket here after a picnic. The four rooms, like the cottages, are meticulously decorated in individual themes, all with a cosy, English-cottage feel about them. Eve has found hand-embroidered linen and original works by local artists to decorate and nothing is left out including teddy bears in all rooms and a generous helping of liquorice allsorts. Oh, and if you want to know more about local history, ask Eve – she's writing a book on the subject. Choose from a range of breakfasts including The Military Breakfast and the Stocklands Smoothie. All cooked breakfasts are made with eggs laid by Eve's own free-range hens. *Game can be viewed right next door, by the way. French spoken.*

Rooms: 7: 2 suites & 2 bedrooms: one of each with en-suite bath and one of each with en-suite shower. Also 3 cottages: 1 with 3 bedrooms and 2 bathrooms; 2 with 1 bedroom and shower en-suite.
Price: R310 pp sharing. No sing' supp. Self-catering R250 pp per night. Extra breakfasts on request
Meals: Full breakfast included or you can self-cater in cottages. Excellent café next door & more in area.
Directions: From Jo'burg N3 to Durban. 1st exit to Howick signed Howick/Tweedie. At Stop sign L to Howick. Thro lights to bottom of hill, L to Karkloof. 100m, R into Shafton Rd. Stocklands 1km. From Durban N3 to Jo'burg. 3rd Howick turn-off as above.

Map Number: 13

Entry Number: 275

Waterfall Cottage

Lizzie Purbrick

D51, Dargle
Tel: 033-234-4606 Fax: 033-234-4606
Email: cortaflexsa@gmail.com
Cell: 082-342-8217

A hell-raiser with a heart of gold, Lizzie Purbrick, former England eventing champion and army wife, scandalized the riding world and beat a retreat to South Africa, where she now trains sons and horses in a gorgeous slice of the Natal midlands. From the verandah of the main house an undulating panorama converges on the tip of a sumptuous hill known in Zulu as the maiden's breast (scaled yearly by the famous Michaelhouse boys' school). It was here that I also witnessed a massive fire-breaking exercise; a livid red swathe across a darkening landscape. Youngest son George put his famous chocolate pudding on to simmer and before I knew it my fifteen year-old chauffeur was driving me towards a wall of flame. Of course this will have greened up again by the time you get there. Normal rules don't apply here, but you can escape the furore of parrots, dogs, marauding eagles, horses of course (lovely riding available), chickens (who provide breakfast eggs) and boys by retiring to the haven of calm and uncluttered beauty that is the old 1860 original granite farmhouse. Light the fire and sink into a book before tripping along stone floors, ducking under low doorways, into a simple kitchen on your way to a good lather in the bath, courtesy of Lizzie's own hand-made lavender soap that leaves the skin feeling butterly soft. There are walks aplenty from your doorstep that take you up through pristine indigenous bush onto high ground where herds of blesbok run free; endangered blue and wattled cranes lumber skywards. Rumour has it that the first miserly owner buried his wealth somewhere on the property - bring provisions to stay longer than you planned.

Rooms: 1 cottage with 1 double and 1 twin bedrooms, kitchen, sitting room and bathroom (bath only).
Price: R295 pp sharing.
Meals: Fully self-catering.
Directions: Contact Lizzie for directions.

Inversanda

Tom and Lucinda Bate

Howick
Tel: 033-231-1321 Fax: 033-234-4751
Email: bate@nitrosoft.co.za Web: www.inversanda.co.za
Cell: 082-781-3875

It's true that GG owners are a welcoming bunch, but the Bates go far beyond the call of duty. Actually, I don't think they see it as a duty at all. In fact, I know they don't! Hemmed in by mountains and a meander of the Mgeni River, the farm is in a world of its own, but in easy reach of the major routes. All four Bates (plus assorted hounds) are utterly charming and you're encouraged to participate in their farm and life as much or as little as you like. Talk about a welcome! We were hardly out of the car before we had a greedy calf and a bottle of milk in hand. Half an hour later we were bringing the horses in for feeding. Then just time for a bobble over the fields looking at pregnant cows before a delicious and greatly entertaining dinner with the family. Tom and Lucinda are serious horse-lovers, breeding and schooling polo ponies. Polo players are more than welcome for a weekend knock-about on the makeshift riverside pitch. Otherwise you can fish, walk or swim pretty much anywhere you want. The farmhouse itself (1800s) goes on forever and guests have the choice of their own wing, a pot-planted patio with stunning views across the valley, two enormous twin rooms and a basic kitchen; or a brand-new cottage which also has a large verandah with a commanding view over the valley and two large bedrooms. But even if you had to lie on a bed of spikes, I'd still recommend Inversanda! This is a place that allows you to unburden yourself of the tourist mantle and truly feel part of what's going on.

Rooms: 1 self-catering wing of the house with two twin rooms and shared bath and shower; 1 cottage with 2 rooms, 1 double and 1 twin. Both have en-suite bathrooms, 1 with shower and 1 with bath and shower.
Price: R240 - R280 pp self-catering.
Meals: Meals available on request.
Directions: Faxed or emailed on booking.

KwaZulu Natal

Duma Manzi Private Game Reserve

Donald and Brenda Perry

District Road D60, Richmond
Tel: 086-148-4848 reservations Fax: 031-568-1874
Email: info@dumamanzi.co.za Web: www.dumamanzi.co.za
Cell: 082-653-3475 (Donald); 082-449-4799 (Ruth)

This can be an exhausting job, but as I drove through Duma Manzi's gates, my final destination after a few dusty weeks on the road, I knew instinctively that this lodge was going to be the jewel in the crown. Leaving my car, phone and computer behind, I climbed aboard a 4x4 and as my fists and busy mind unfurled, I sat back and drank in some astonishing views over the Spitz Kop hills and way, way (way) down to the Umkomaas River. As we rumbled along my friendly guides told me the history of the 5,000-hectare conservancy. Once 16 separate farms (one of which was Cecil Rhodes' cotton farm) the Perry's are re-introducing the wild animals whose home this really is. After viewing a herd of buffalo as well as numerous buck, zebra, giraffe and warthog I devoured a home-made scone at a vertiginous viewing site before our descent to the lodge itself. Camouflaged against the sandstone cliffs and balancing on the edge of the 'Thundering River' (Duma Manzi in Zulu) the two lodges – Fish Eagle and Sandstone - are a triumph of engineering as well as luxury. Antique rugs and local sculpture lead to a grand hall, full of African curios and dark wood furniture. All the rooms have floor-to-ceiling glass doors opening to balconies and the river. The only peeping toms here are fish eagles and over 300 other bird species. After taking a swim in my pool… and then my bath, I pirouetted round my room and dined like a king in the huge boma. Finally as I drifted to sleep I reminded myself that, exhausting though it might be, this job wasn't all bad!

Rooms: 10: 4 kings with bath and shower. 5 king/twin with bath and shower. 1 family unit with 2 bedrooms both king/twin with bath and shower and private garden.
Price: R1,700 - R2,100 pp sharing. Children under 12 half price.
Meals: All meals plus 3-course dinner included. Drinks excluded.
Directions: Directions emailed on booking.

Leadwood Lodge

Stuart Hilcove and Tina Roche

Tala Private Game Reserve, Cascades, Pietermaritzburg
Tel: 031-781-8000 Fax: 031-781-8022
Email: info@tala.co.za Web: www.tala.co.za/leadwood

'Tala' means 'Land of Plenty' in Zulu and surely an apter name could not have been found. Merrily skidding my way down the dirt tracks of this 7,000-acre reserve, I encountered a 'journey' of fifteen giraffe, a herd of temporarily docile buffalo and a male greater kudu so majestic Hemingway himself would've gasped in awe (… before shooting it). On arrival I was greeted and escorted to the lodge. From this point on, I too was gasping in awe. It began with the waterfall cascading into the pond at the entrance which flows underneath the house and out to the watering-hole below. Inside I was immediately drawn to the perfect blossoming orchids that adorned the George IV dining table and, hiding in the corner at the entrance to a cavernous wine cellar, a rare 1900 timekeeper softly ticking away. Leadwood brings great opulence to the bush; that much was already clear. But if further proof was required, my sleeping quarters provided it. A five-minute stroll took me to my very own palatial bush-marooned lodge. Trying not to laugh at my good fortune, I disrobed, ignored a bath big enough for three and headed straight for the outside shower. This shower is indeed so 'outside' that both the head and taps are built into a tree! From there to supper - rare blue wildebeest and a rich '01 shiraz - before returning to the lodge and slipping under the covers of my king-size four-poster bed. I fell into a deep slumber, with nothing but the rustly, chirrupy night sounds of the bush for company. *Quad biking, horse-riding and hot air ballooning are all now offered at Tala.*

Rooms: 6 lodges. All en-suite bath/shower and outside shower.
Price: R3,500 pp sharing. Single supplement +50%. Includes game drive/walk.
Meals: All included, including 5-course gourmet supper.
Directions: See website.

Penwarn Country Lodge

Peter and Barbara Dommett
Bushmen's Nek Road, Southern Drakensberg, Underberg
Tel: 033-701-1368 or 033-701-1651 Fax: 033-701-1341
Email: pdommett@mweb.co.za Web: www.penwarn.com
Cell: 082-773-9923

Late was the hour when I rumbled into the estate, negotiating my way past an inquisitive eland who blocked the path. From humble beginnings as an old dairy and fertilizer shed, the lodge was converted into darkly-beamed sitting rooms, a bar and bedrooms so large they make you want to run amok, before slumping into four-poster comfort. Reclining on a deep leather divan in 'Nimrod' (dedicated to a much-loved otter that previous guests may remember), I watched through vast windows the day's colours slowly fade from a lake caressed by willows and supervised by cranes. Dinner was a buffet extravaganza, but it was a wrench having to leave the uplifting company of the Dommetts and their staff (it is not easy to distinguish which is which). A fellow English couple confessed to being GG devotees and insisted that I visit them at the separate Mthini Lodge with its stellar position above the dam, looking out to foothills grazed by the naturally-occurring reedbuck and eland, springbok, wildebeest, zebra... and to the mountains beyond. The sense of space is liberating, with full-throttle activities rubbing shoulders with the gentler pursuits of fishing, horse-riding, flower walks in season and excellent bird-watching at the 'Vulture Restaurant'. Trace too the bushman cave figures painted a millennium ago. A magical place. *Penwarn is now part of the Waterford Estate which means they have access to 3500ha, 50 fishing dams, a World Heritage site and horse tours around the draft horse stud are on offer. They hope to do horse-back game tours and mountain treks soon too.*

Rooms: 11: 7 suites at Indabushe Lodge, 4 suites at Mthini lodge. All have en-suite bath and/or shower. (No cave dwelling anymore – sorry!).
Price: Full board R1,050 pp sharing. Singles +50%. Certain activities extra (from R150 - R400 pp). Ask about reduced winter rates for locals.
Meals: Full breakfast, lunch, 4-course dinner and all snacks incl'. Wine is not. Canoeing is free.
Directions: Exit 99 off N3 marked Underberg, Howick South, 110km west to Underberg, thro Boston & Bulwer. R617 thro Underberg towards Kokstad/Swartberg for 5km, R onto Bushmansnek Rd (dirt track). 16km L to Penwarn (drive 4km dirt track.)

Free State & Lesotho

Oaklands Polo & Country Club

Jamie and Caroline Bruce
Van Reenen
Tel: 058-671-0067 Fax: 058-671-0077
Email: info@oaklands.co.za Web: www.oaklands.co.za

No sooner had I stepped from my car than Caroline was helping me into her polo boots… and hey presto I was up on Geronimo (where was Dobbin? Where was Eeyore?!)… and playing polo! 'Bravo, bravo!' came the kindly call as I thrashed around uselessly. These words of encouragement came from Jamie, ex-British army officer, raconteur, lover of the outdoors and proud owner of the newly-refurbished and expanded Oaklands. It is typical of the Bruces to create this wonderfully daring country retreat, social hub and boutique hotel; but even more typical of them to make it such a roaring success. With tennis, hiking and trampoline-ing, as well as squidgy chairs for weary bodies and views for tired minds, Oaklands caters for all. Having survived Geronimo (who was a kindly lad after all) I sat and contemplated the spectacular Drakensberg one last time before retiring to my suite, itself big enough for a chukka or two. Each room is individual, but there are consistent themes with protea-patterned wallpaper complementing modern patterns on the luxurious silk cushions and bedspreads. Heading into the bar where a pool battle was under way, I marvelled at the Bruce family talent for bringing people together in the easy, laughing manner of old friends. Passing through the lounge, where a wall is covered in portraits of African women ("all ex-girlfriends" joked Jamie) the bonhomie and story-telling continued through three fantastic courses… and quite a few bottles if I'm honest. A greatly lively, fun, outdoorsy place that has been a favourite with this guide since the very start.

Rooms: 10: 4 suites with 1 double and 2 day beds and kitchen. 5 standard doubles. All with showor in bath. Self-catering house sleeps 6: 1 queen en-suite bath, 2 twins with shwr, full kitchen.
Price: Suites R1,200 - R1,400. Standard R500. Singles on request. 'Ukhubona' self-catering lodge is R1,500 per night.
Meals: Full breakfast and dinner a la carte. Lunch is also available. All meals can be provided for those staying in the self-catering lodge.
Directions: Take the N3 to Van Reenen, R at Caltex garage. 7km down dirt track - Oaklands signed to R.

The View

Ryk and Bea and Sasha Becker

20 Bell Street, Harrismith
Tel: 058-623-0961 Fax: 058-623-0961
Email: rmbecker@internext.co.za Web: www.harrismithaccommodation.co.za
Cell: 082-775-7381 (Bea); 082-921-3624 (Ryk)

How better to while away a sticky afternoon than by nesting in a rocking chair behind teak pillars on a shady verandah, overlooking a lush garden, slowly draining a pot of tea? Bea and Ryk have found a magic formula simply by being themselves at home! The actual view of the title is now interrupted by an abundance of verdure, but I for one was glad of the green shade and the peaceful sounds of twittering birds hidden among the branches. Inside, a portrait of Bea's big-bearded great-grandfather, President of the Free State (deceased, of course), overlooks the social epicentre of this family home. The lounge, complete with creaking wooden floorboards, vibrant rugs and daringly bright sofas, sweeps through folded-back doors into the dining room where the heavy table awaits those staying in for dinner. And I thoroughly recommend you are among them. You would travel a long way to find a better meal and you'll miss out on Ryk spilling the beans on what to do in this area where he grew up. Before heading up to my goose-feathered bed for my best night's sleep in years, no visit to The View would be complete without being introduced to the rest of the family: four springer and two cocker spaniels. *Son-in-law Simon can arrange star-gazing visits to his farm and other local activities.*

Rooms: 2: both doubles with en-suite bath and shower.
Price: R400 pp sharing. Singles R460.
Meals: Full breakfast included. Dinners on request from R165 pp.
Directions: From Jo'burg side into Warden Street (main street) go around church. 7 blocks from church turn R into Bell Street. From Durban & Bloem, on entering Harrismith turn away from Spur/Engen garage into King Street. Turn L into Warden Street at 1st stop-street. Bell Street is about 10 blocks from here on L.

Franshoek Mountain Lodge

Roz Evans

Franshoek Farm, Ficksburg
Tel: 051-933-2828 Fax: 051-933-2828
Email: lodge@franshoek.co.za Web: www.franshoek.co.za
Cell: 072-128-7356

Franshoek is a magical place where mad things happen. As I arrived, Roz emerged, beaming and welly-clad, having located her missing keys among the flowerbeds. Meanwhile the goose was trying to eat the laundry. The old, stonewalled exterior resembles a hobbit house, but through the wooden gates it's more like Aladdin's cave. Gilt mirrors, glass bowls of floating flowers, a gramophone and a tiny pet tortoise wiggling across the bar all came into view. Music played while guests, thoroughly enjoying themselves, reclined on elephant sofas. "It's a bit like one long house party," Roz reflected, loading up a roaring log fire. A storm was descending outside, but after the sky had ceased groaning and a yellow haze had descended over the mountains, we nipped out for a look around. The original farmhouse rooms are cosy and varied, many with adjoining kids' rooms. There's much to do with the polo farm next door, a home-made African steam hut, horses, a beautiful round pool and nearby rock art sites (if someone can remember exactly where they are). The new self-catering cottage looks out onto a marvellous mountain view and Roz is considering naming it after Orna, the wonderful, multi-tasking, green-fingered, pig-loving Thai woman for whom no job was too much. She has sadly returned to her native land. When I stayed, one couple went horse-riding to the top of the mountain and came back engaged! It's that kind of place and after champagne in the garden and much excitement, I reluctantly bid my farewells.

Rooms: 11: family units all sleep 4 with en-s shower; Honeymoon suite with bath & adjoining room with bunk beds with separate en-s shower; doubles come with en-suite showers. New self-catering cottage.
Price: R540 pp sharing. Singles on request. Includes full breakfast and 3-course Thai or European dinner.
Meals: Breakfast & dinner included. Light lunches on request.
Directions: Signed off R26 betw' Fouriesburg & Ficksburg. 23km south of Fouriesburg on R26, take S385 on R (10km of dirt rd) or 8km north of Ficksburg on R26 take S384 on L (12km on dirt rd).

Die Ou Stal

Piet and Zenobia Labuchagné

38 George Street, Zastron
Tel: 051-673-1268 Fax: 051-673-1268
Email: dieoustal@tiscali.co.za
Cell: 082-416-7832

In a place like Zastron, it's vital to find yourself a guide to show you the unknown gems that lurk around every corner and to recount the astonishing tales of yesteryear. Look no further than Piet. His enthusiasm for the geology and pre-history of Africa is infectious. After the whistle-stop tour of intriguing local rock formations, spiced up with ancient bushman legends, I'll never look at a cliff face in the same way again. Had I stayed longer, I'd have been begging him to take me on a day trip to nearby Lesotho, but alas I had to leave even before one of Zen's delicious suppers of bobotie or chicken pie. At least I had time to sit on the stoep outside the converted stables that are now the guest rooms and watch a lightning storm hammer away at the Lesotho mountains – a majestic sight indeed. The bedrooms are simple, cosy affairs with whitewashed walls and doors that open into a small kitchen. Breakfast, however, is served at the large dining table in the main house, atop wooden floorboards and next to a fridge surely dating from before fridges were invented (also wood): this intriguing feature is now a drinks cabinet. In a town that's won awards for its friendliness (driving around with Piet, the whole town and his uncle Joe came out to give us a wave), Zen is champion of champions.

Rooms: 2: 1 double with en-suite bath and shower; 1 twin with en-suite shower.
Price: R275 - R385 pp sharing.
Meals: Full breakfast included. Dinner on request: R65 pp.
Directions: From N6 turn onto R26 and follow signs to Zastron. In town, turn right opposite the corner of the church into Mathee Street, then take third left into Berg Strat and see signs.

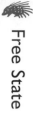

Artists' Colony Karoo Guest House

Robert and Susan Jewell
3 Church Street, Smithfield
Tel: 051-683-1138 Fax: 051-683-1138
Email: colony@global.co.za Web: www.artistscolony.co.za

For service to weary travellers like me, Robert and Susan deserve knighthoods. After a long trip through the Free State countryside, I reached the 'oasis' of Smithfield and it was with relief that I saw the yellow-and-white front door of the Artists' Colony heralding the end of my day's journey. Along with the cup of tea Susan pushed into my hand, the high yellowwood ceilings of the house were as soothing balms to my hotness and bother. The original settlers knew exactly what they were doing when it comes to keeping a Karoo-style house cool. Three of the rooms are across the road and behind a rich display of roses, lilies and irises in a building declared a national monument. Each has its own little quirk, whether it be the maroons and greens of the Birdcage Room, or the East African hair salon advert for all sorts of (slightly outdated) haircuts in the Barber Shop room. The original Oregon floorboards creak as you walk on them and the door frames have their own shape! But don't worry – tie rods hold the sun-baked bricks firmly together - true 1848 heritage accommodation. All this is part of the delightful charm of Artists' Colony and made me fall instantly in love with it. Being almost exactly in the centre of South Africa, close to the N1 and on the Friendly N6, you will undoubtedly have passed by on some trip or another. Next time don't pass by, drop in. This is a special place to stay.

Rooms: 5: 3 queens, with en-suite bath and shower; 2 twins, 1 with en-suite bath and shower, 1 with en-suite shower. All rooms have aircon, fridges, fans and tea and coffee.
Price: R275 - R300 per person sharing. Singles on application.
Meals: Full breakfast included. Local restaurants nearby.
Directions: Traveling south on N1, take exit 177 at Bloemfontein onto the Friendly N6 and it is approx. 120km to Smithfield. Traveling north on N1, take exit 8 to Gariep Dam and then onto the R701 and it is approx. 115km to Smithfield. In Smithfield, turn into Church Street opposite the church.

Springfontein House

Graeme Wedgwood
32 van Riebeeck Street, Springfontein
Tel: 051 783 0076 Fax: 051-783-0425
Email: wedgie@icon.co.za Web: www.springfontein-guest-house.com
Cell: 082-450-6779

Graeme used to run Smithfield House, which he brought to life with cultivated, Epicurean zeal. Well, the same applies here at his new home. Those with a taste for fine living will find a kindred spirit in Graeme, a man whose love of house and garden, countryside, good company, food and wine now sets the tone at Springfontein House. He was once a gallery owner in Johannesburg – a far cry from his first, 26-year career as a London stockbroker – and his personal art collection includes a rather racy Battiss, and other originals by South African artists, both established and emerging. African rugs, powdery sofas, bowls of dried rose petals and side tables proffering porcelain complete the sandy-coloured sitting room. Through glass doors is a slate-floored, frond-filled sunroom and an incarnadine dining room, with Georgian tables and silver candelabras. In the bedrooms the curtains are silk, the towels soft and the comfy beds have crisp linen, plump pillows and mohair throws. Outside, white walls dazzle and creepers climb above the stoep; there's a bricked patio and colourful flower-beds, a pool and a series of fishponds. But the reason you come here is to be looked after, and arriving from the biscuity veld, you'll feel lucky indeed. *Graeme will explain about biking, hunting, rare bird-watching, and hiking. He regrets that the house is not suitable for children under 12.*

Rooms: 5: 3 queens, 1 with en-suite bath/shower, 1 with en-suite shower and 1 with full bathroom en-suite; 2 twins, 1 with en-suite bath/shower and 1 with full bathroom en-suite.
Price: R350 - R400 pp sharing. Singles on request. Booking advised.
Meals: Full breakfast included. 3-course dinner available on request from R120, excluding wine (the guest house is fully" licensed).
Directions: Heading north on N1 turn off at Springfontein South sign. Follow rd, becoming Settler St. Van Riebeeck St is on L, & Springfontein House is at end on R. For those travelling south on N1 come off at Springfontein North exit & follow signs.

Map Number: 12   Entry Number: 286

Malealea Lodge and Pony Trek Centre

Mick and Di Jones
Malealea, Lesotho
Tel: 082-552-4215 Fax: 0866-481-815
Email: malealea@mweb.co.za Web: www.malealea.com
Cell: 082-552-4215

"Where are you heading?" asked the border official. "Malealea," I replied nervously. She smiled, "You'll enjoy it there." Here in the heartland of mountainous Lesotho where blanket-clad shepherds watch over their flocks, the Jones family have created a fascinating environment through a combination of their own personal warmth, native knowledge and a wealth of natural and cultural attractions. Malealea thrives on its genuine interaction with the neighbouring village and I arrived just as the choir was starting up, followed by a band playing home-made instruments with wonderful exuberance. The pony trekking centre is run entirely by the locals, who will take you on treks for up to six days (you stay in the villages you visit), and children lead you to waterfalls and rock art. Communal suppers are served canteen style - backpackers and ambassadors rub comradely shoulders – before the pub and Glen's singing around the fire lure you away. When the generator stops, your torch guides you back to thatched rondavel or farmhouse-style accommodation. I woke to the unmistakable cries of peacocks ringing out of the early-morning mist lying low in the valleys. I loved this place. For the adventurous, the family have recently opened chalets in the south of the country dramatically positioned beneath the sheer flanks of Mt Mooroosi, the scene of a fierce siege of the Maphuti by the British. As you make your way up the mountain, still strewn everywhere are cartridges, mortar and graffiti from 1879. Suddenly your trip just got longer.

Rooms: 39 Basotho rondavels and farmhouse rooms: 8 doubles and 31 twins all with en-suite shower.
Price: Rondavels R200 - R220 pp sharing, farmhouses R150 - R170 pp sharing. Single supplement 50%. Overnight horse treks R260 - R285 pp per day. Village accommodation R50 - R55 pp. Day rides from R120 pp.
Meals: Breakfast R45 - R50 pp. Lunch R50 - R60 pp. Dinner R75 - R80 pp. 4 communal kitchens available.
Directions: Faxed or emailed on booking.

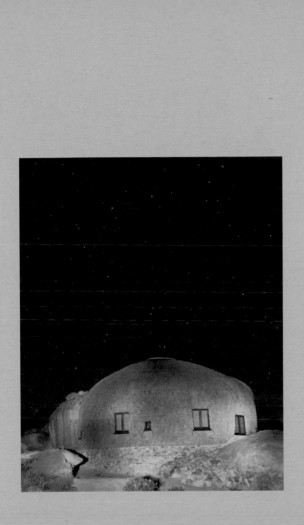

Northern Cape

Kuilfontein Stable Cottages

Penny and Leigh Southey
Kuilfontein Farm, Route N1, Colesberg
Tel: 051-753-1364 Fax: 051-753-0200
Email: kuil@mweb.co.za Web: www.kuilfontein.co.za
Cell: 082-552-2488

A drink is always welcome in the middle of the blazing Karoo and I was gasping when Penny poured mine in the chilled-out guest lounge. Kuilfontein has been in Leigh's family for five generations and is still a busy dairy and sheep farm. Surrounded by a vast hinterland of arid fields it's hard to believe it's only 1.2 kilometres from the N1. The white-washed Stable bedrooms are all named after racehorses, the theme continuing inside with newspaper clippings and framed shots of 'Danny Boy' or 'Equilateral' (among others) in action. French doors lead from your own verandah onto gleaming screed floors sporting locally-made furniture, as well as the odd family heirloom, while brightly-coloured walls and fine-quality linen create a homely feeling. The 'Feed Room' has been appropriately converted into a dining/breakfast room where resident chef, Maryke, produces tantalising meals from the organic produce on the farm. 'Home-grown' Karoo lamb, venison and fresh cream from the dairy are used in conjunction with cactus fruit and other Karoo specialities. Pre-dinner drinks are taken in the bar with its upside-down trough counter and a great selection of wines are available in an old feed bin. A tall wicker stool is the perfect spot to park yourself for cheerful banter, beverages and hilarity. Coffee and liqueurs are served under the spectacular starry skies. For the more energetic there is a spring-water swimming pool, boules and bird-watching. A popular stop-over point, but this farmstead is worth staying a lot longer for. *Children over 6 are welcome.*

Rooms: 8: 5 standard double bedrooms, 2 luxury double rooms and 1 family suite, all with en-suite showers.
Price: R360 - R490 pp sharing. Singles R60 supplement. Children 6+ on request.
Meals: Full 'health' breakfast included. 3-course dinner R115 - R145.
Directions: 12km south or Colesberg, 60km north of Hanover on N1.

Papkuilsfontein Farmhouse

Willem and Mariëtte van Wyk

Nieuwoudtville
Tel: 027-218-1246 Fax: 027-218-1246
Email: info@papkuilsfontein.com Web: www.papkuilsfontein.com

I'm going to stick my neck out and say that this is my favourite place to stay in South Africa! And here are my reasons.... You stay in an old stone cottage, surrounded by rock, gum tree and wildlife, not another human in sight. The quality of peace and stillness defeats description. Gas-fired plumbing for baths, hurricane lamps for light - many guests have refused to come back if Willem installs electricity. Then there's the small matter of the gorge and waterfall, which I would have kept secret if I wasn't insistent on your visiting the farm. Your jaw will drop 180 metres into the canyon. Take a picnic to the deep rock pools for swimming (all year round) above the waterfall (which runs in winter only) and you can climb down into the gorge in an hour and a half. There is also swimming in a pool next to the cottages. The wild flowers in season are sensational even by Namaqualand standards; the plantlife, divided between Cape fynbos and Karoo succulent, a botanist's dream; steenbok, klipspringer, porcupine and dassie love the terrain and have NOT been specially introduced. Alrie is an excellent cook (breakfast a string of surprises). It's a magical place that not many know about and the van Wyks are all lovely, friendly people who seem unable to put a proper price on what they have to offer! You should stay at least two nights. There's also a restored corrugated-iron cottage for those who need their electricity. *Bikes are available for guests to use.*

Rooms: 3 stone cottages: Rondekraal sleeps 2 (1 double) with bath and outside shower; De Hoop sleeps 4 with bath and outside shower; and Gert Boom sleeps 4 (although there are 2 more beds for children if needed), with 2 bathrooms, each with shower only.

Price: R250 - R300 pp sharing. Single rates + 50%. Minimum cost per cottage per night in flower season (without meals): Gert Boom R990, De Hoop and Rondekraal R680.
Meals: Full breakfast included. 3-course dinners R145 - R165 (from Aug 1st) pp. Simpler dinners R105 - R115 (from Aug 1st).
Directions: From CT take N1 then N7 to Vanrhynsdorp. Turn off onto R27 to Nieuwoudtville. Turn right into town, and straight through onto dirt road for 22km. The farm is signed to the right.

Map Number: 1

Entry Number: 289

Naries Namakwa Retreat

Julene Hamman

27km from Springbok (N7), on the way to Kleinzee (on R355),
Namakwaland; Tel: 027-712-2462 (reception) or 021-930-4564
(reservations) Fax: 021-930-4574
Email: reservations@naries.co.za Web: www.naries.co.za

Naries has several nice surprises in store for its regulars. Firstly, the road from Springbok, 27km away, has been tarred, making for quick access to the Goegap Nature Reserve, its beautiful plains scenery, its arid mountains and kopies, and its magical seasonal flower display – 600 species. Then there are the three fabulous cottages, the Namakwa Mountain Suites, which have been constructed on the edge of a high escarpment with an extraordinary eagle's eye view of the dramatic and barren mountains that march off to the sea 70km away at Kleinzee. The architecture is in the form of a domed cottage, which echoes the style of local Nama dwellings, and is perfectly integrated with the round granite kopies of the area. Their exterior simplicity, however, is deceptive, for the interiors are vast and luxurious, while retaining some very natural features: the almost woven texture of the walls of the cottage, for example, and the bare rocks which erupt into the space as bed-heads or in the sublime bathrooms. The old Cape Dutch manor, where dinners are served, also houses some fine bedrooms. The house has recently been refurnished and redecorated and the walls, painted in plain colours, offset the 1930s furniture perfectly. *Naries recommends various day excursions to explore the beauty of Namakwaland: De Beers Diamond Mines, 4x4 Shipwreck Experience, Goegap Nature Reserve, Namakwa and Richtersveld National Parks. Also, make sure you book well in advance for the desert flower season!*

Rooms: 11: 3 Namakwa Mountain Suites with en-s bathroom; 5 Manor H'se rooms with en-s bathroom; 2 Power House standard rooms; 1 family self-catering unit with en-s bath & shower, sleeps max 4.
Price: Namakwa Mountain Suites (DBB): from R1,150 pp sharing & R1,265 single; Manor Hse (DBB): R850 pp sh & R935 single. Standard (DBB): R470 & R520 single. Self-catering: R250 pp & kids (4-12) R125 pp. Ask for low-season specials +2010 rates.
Meals: Dinner & breakfast incl' in rates of Namakwa Mountain Suites, Manor House & Standard Rooms.
Directions: 27km from Springbok (N7), on your way to Kleinzee on tarred road (R355).

La Boheme Guest House

Evelyne Meier
172 Groenpunt Rd, Upington
Tel: 054-338-0660 Fax: 054-338-0661
Email: laboheme@mweb.co.za Web: www.laboheme.co.za
Cell: 083-383-8288

La Boheme claims its rightful place in this book on many counts: its fantastic view from a green, green lawn over the Orange River flood plain; its cool-blue pool; its palm trees that rustle in the hot breeze; and the delightful breakfasts served on the verandah at a communal table or near the cosy fireplace in winter. But all of these things play second fiddle to Evelyne herself, who is hugely friendly and energetic and a wholly exceptional host. A cultural blend herself, half-Hungarian and half-Swiss, her guest house also melds various ethnic styles that mix elegant finishes with artistic touches. There are only three rooms here, guaranteeing the personal touch and each offering something different. I had a trendy-Africa room with a huge bed of sculpted 'decocrete' and its own patch of outside with iron chairs. Next door has a private verandah, but more of a tropical island feel and for those wanting a little more space and a touch of Asia, there is a cottage with its own kitchenette and private patio surrounded by lush plants and mature trees. I highly recommend you find your way to Upington, which is an Orange River oasis in the middle of the Kalahari Desert. Not many do. The Kgalagadi Transfrontier Park (Kalahari-Gemsbok Park) is just a couple of hours away, Augrabies Falls less than that, and local vineyards and river cruises closer still. *French, German, Italian, English and Hungarian spoken. Restaurants within 3 to 10 minute drive.*

Rooms: 3: 1 king en/s bath & shower, 1 twin single sep' bath & sh'r (both have microwaves, basic cutlery & crockery); 1 cottage with kitchenette, queen & en-s sh'r (main bedroom) & twin single with en/s shower over bath (adjacent to bedroom).
Price: From R460 pp sharing. Singles from R1,100. Off-season rates (15 May – 30 June) on request.
Meals: Full breakfast (brunch-style) from R130 pp. Breakfast picnic & other options on request. Delivery of take-away meals available. BBQ areas in garden.
Directions: In Upington, take Schröder St towards Olifantshoek, N14 past Gordonia hospital. 1.7km past hospital, R at Engen Garage. Turn L (Groenpunt Rd), 2.5km to giant palm tree. Map on website.

Riviera Garden B&B

Anneke Malan
16 Budler Street, Upington
Tel: 054-332-6554 Fax: 054-332-6554
Email: ariviera@upington.co.za Web: www.upington.co.za/ariviera
Cell: 072-447-6750

Riviera is a true patch of paradise on the banks of the impressive Orange River, a patch that has given Anneke and her guests a lifetime of pleasure. Considering its position in Upington's city centre, its riverside setting is particularly special. It was the garden, though, that I loved above all, a lush parade of palm trees, roses and agapanthus and racing-green grass that cools even the most overheated of travellers (as I certainly was when I visited). The lawn flows like a tributary past the pool, right to the water's edge and a secluded, white bench at the end of the garden, the perfect spot to sit and contemplate the river's flowing depths. It's from here that guests hop onto a cruise boat at six o'clock for evening river trips, bobbing downstream, washing down the sunset with a G&T before ambling into town for some dinner. The evenings can be as hot as the days in this part of the world and you'll be glad to find the two cool garden rooms hidden among the greenery with their hefty beds and bags of cupboard space for longer stays. Another major draw at Riviera are the scrumptious and beautifully-presented breakfasts. From national parks (Upington is a gateway to the Kalahari Desert and Namibia) to vineyards there's plenty to keep you busy here and it's a must-do stop on any tour of the unspoiled Northern Cape.

Rooms: 2: 1 twin with bath and shower, 1 double with extra single and bath.
Price: R325 pp sharing. Singles on request.
Meals: Full English breakfast R55. Dinner on request.
Directions: Follow main roads right into the centre of Upington. From Schröder St turn onto River St towards the river. This leads into Budler St and Riviera is number 16 on the right about halfway down the street.

A La Fugue

Jacqueline Castella

40 Janggroentjieweg, Upington
Tel: 054-338-0424 Fax: 054-338-0084
Email: a-la-fugue@mweb.co.za Web: www.lafugue-guesthouse.com
Cell: 082-789-9324

Chaud, hot, heiss! Upington was knocking on almost 40°C when I visited, so Jacqueline definitely had the right idea, meeting me at the car in a pink swimming costume and sarong. Positively melting after hours on the road I was invited to flump myself down on a plant-shaded pillow by the pool and was fed a glass of iced tea. What initially struck me about A La Fugue, as I was led along a rose-lined and plant-dotted path, was the tropical garden, absolutely dazzling in the intense sunshine. Named after great composers, each of La Fugue's bungalows has their own unique identity. Rossini and Rusticana, two quaint wooden chalets, seem to originate from the Swiss element of your host, while studio bungalow Mozart and family unit Vivaldi perhaps embody the classic French side. The two B&B rooms in the house (Chopin and Bach), soothing in golds and creams, are found along a short landing where Jacqueline's stunning model daughter beams warmly from the wall. Jacqui's gourmet dinners and breakfasts, touched with a little foreign pizazz, are served outside on one of the bright mosaic tables (your hostess has a distinct flair for mosaics and you will find examples in many unexpected places). It's a good thing that each room has its own outdoor seating area as with such a garden you won't want to sit inside. Personally I would rarely be found far from the thatched African-themed poolside lapa and loungers. *Jacqueline is fluent in French, English and German, by the way.*

Rooms: 5: 2 self-catering studios, 1 self-catering family unit and 2 B&B double rooms. All with en-suite shower and own separate entrances.
Price: R195 to R285 B&B pp sharing. Ask about singles and self-catering prices.
Meals: Full breakfast included in B&B rate. For self-caterers breakfast-brunch additional R70 pp. Gourmet dinners on request (preferably with 24 hrs notice), R240 pp inclusive of all wine and drinks.
Directions: In Upington take Schröder St towards Olifantshoek, N14, under rail bridge past Gordonia hospital. 1.7 km after hospital, turn R at Engen garage. Turn L (Groenpunt Rd). From Bi-Lo (left), count 4 streets on R till Jangtroentjieweg.

Map Number: 10

Gauteng

Gauteng Side Dishes

A handful of highly-recommended things to do and places to eat in the Gauteng area...

Bamboo Lifestyle Centre

Art, jewellery, decor, fashion and seriously good food and drink make Bamboo a uniquely SA shopping experience. Leave the kids at a glass-blowing workshop while you enjoy a rejuvenating hot-stone massage or get to grips with some of SA's finest vintages... and plenty more all under one roof. Bamboo is a byword for contemporary, well-designed South Africana.

*Contact: Alison Green, 53 Rustenburg Road (cnr 9th Street), Melville, North-west of Johannesburg Centre; **Prices:** Breakfast and lunch around R60, tinsel bracelets from R495, dresses designed by Jacques van der Watt around R950... and many more well-made goods; **Tel:** 028-284-9827; **Web:** www.bamboo-online.co.za*

The Ant Café

The Ant Café is the longest-running restaurant in 7th Street and maintains the magical charm of 'old' Melville. An intimate venue with a rustic interior where you enjoy Italian classics, wine by the glass and coffee made with the best locally-produced beans available. What makes The Ant so special is its loving staff, unpretentious service and the fact that for thirteen years neither the coffee-machine nor the music has ever been turned off.

*Contact: Theuns Botha, Shop 11, 7th Street, Melville, Johannesburg; **Prices:** Breakfast R15 - R50. Mains R35 - R100. Cash only; **Tel:** 011-726-2614; 011-726-2614; **Email:** barranderos@gmail.com*

Asendulo Safaris

If you are concerned about getting around in Joburg, don't be. Just let Lionel and his team ferry you to your dinner reservation, airport or day trip on time and, most importantly, safely.

*Contact: Lionel Strick, Asendulo Safaris; **Prices:** Dependent on destination naturally. **Email:** asendulo@telkomsa.net*

Spear of the Nation

Experience an extraordinary look into South Africa's tumultuous political history through the eyes of engaging raconteur Robin Binckes. Take lunch in Alexandra and allow Robin to walk you in "the steps of Mandela" from Lielieslief Farm - HQ of the armed wing of the ANC - to Sophiatown and the Rivonia Trial. His tours are simply essential for those seeking an in-depth knowledge of South Africa's road to freedom. If you only have two days in Joburg, spend them both with Robin.

*Contact: Robin Binckes, Spear of the Nation; **Prices:** Between R1,500 - R1,800 per person per day. Includes lunch all entrances and disbursements; **Tel:** 011-463-9905; 086-631-7293; **Email:** rob@spearofthenation.co.za; **Web:** www.spearofthenation.co.za*

Melrose Place Guest Lodge

Sue Truter
12a North St, Melrose/Johannesburg
Tel: 011-442-5231 Fax: 011-880-2371
Email: melroseplace@global.co.za Web: www.melroseplace.co.za
Cell: 083-457-4021

Once ensconced behind the electric gates at Melrose you have entered an Eden-in-the-city. The verandah overlooks a large flower garden and enormous swimming pool, all shaded by trees. Eight new rooms don't crowd it at all. It is such a pleasant environment that you may find yourself shelving projected tasks for a day's lounging about. My room was a suite attached to the main house, with mounted TV, huge bed (built up with cushions and pillows), a big bathroom and double doors onto the garden. The high levels of luxury in all the rooms are not reflected in the rates. Sue is the sweetest of hostesses, quick to smiles and reacting sensitively to the mood and wishes of each guest. On the night I stayed we had a braai with an amazing array of meat dishes and salads which appeared from nowhere, and Sue's team will cook dinner for anyone who wants it every evening. Her aim is to maximise the number of happy campers staying. This is her home after all, complete with dachshund and a talking parrot in its 50s. While guest contentment is running at 100 per cent, it's difficult to see what else she can do. *Laundry provided on request and internet available. Nearby: Wanderers cricket ground, Rosebank and Sandton shopping precincts and many restaurants. Airport transfers arranged by Sue.*

Rooms: 14: all en-suite (1 bath only, 4 bath and shower, 9 shower only); includes two cottages.
Price: R800 - R1,000 pp sharing. Singles R1,150 - R1,450.
Meals: Full breakfast included. Lunches and dinners by arrangement.
Directions: Ask for a map when booking. Or a map is on the web site.

Liz at Lancaster

Liz Delmont
79 Lancaster Ave, Craighall Park, Johannesburg
Tel: 011-442-8083 Fax: 011-880-5969
Email: lizdel@megaweb.co.za Web: www.lizatlancaster.co.za
Cell: 083-229-4223

Liz's place on its own is our idea of a B&B (more on that later), but throw in Liz as well and you get something special. In my limited experience she is an anomaly among South Africans, having no great interest in rugby, football or cricket, and this despite being surrounded by a sports-mad family. Liz taught art history and post-graduate tourism development at Witwatersrand University for over 20 years, and is a fascinating person to speak to about South Africa both past and future… and about Jo'burg. She will point you in all the right directions for a genuine, heartfelt and hard-to-come-by insight into her home city. But guests at Liz's also have plenty of space in which to do their own thing. The big, comfy rooms are either side of the main house, with their own entrances and parking spaces and now come kitted-out with internet access and satellite TV. Two more have been added since our last book; that is to say, Liz has given over even more of her home to her guests. Two separate cottages have their own kitchen and sitting room. They all open up onto their own private patios, where breakfast is generally served, with potted plants climbing up the walls and plenty of shade. Between them is a rose-filled garden, while at the front of the house is yet more green space around the pool. Finally, a mention for the friendly staff, who have a stake in the venture.

Rooms: 5: 3 doubles (2 with kitchens) with en/s bath and shower, plus 2 cottages with kitchen and sitting room.
Price: R325 - R400 pp sharing. Singles R550 - R700.
Meals: Full breakfast included. Dinners on request but very close to Rosebank and Parkhurst and many restaurants.
Directions: Jan Smuts Ave runs down the middle of the city and Lancaster Ave is off it. Directions on website.

Random Harvest Country Cottages

Linda De Luca and David Valoyi

College Rd, Off Beyers Naude Drive, Muldersdrift, Mogale City
Tel: 082-553-0598 Fax: 086-644-9558
Email: linda@rhn.co.za or cottages@rhn.co.za Web: www.rhn.co.za
Cell: 072-562-3396

"I would make an ideal dictator…," Linda worryingly confessed shortly after I had crept through the gates and into this Narnia of saplings and shoots, "…of the environment that is." There's clearly no room for democracy in Linda's world when it comes to saving the nation's plants. This self-confessed nature addict set up the Random Harvest indigenous nursery, the first of its kind, 17 years ago. Back then everyone said she was mad, but now people flock from miles around to pick up their fashionable fynbos. "I think I preferred it when I was mad," chuckles Linda. This 50-acre site is a world away from the city it sits in. Paths battle with plants over rights of way and, key in hand, I navigated my way through a sea of green, winding past rondavels of chickens before tasting Yellowwood, my cottage for the night. It's a cosy little thatched affair with everything you could possibly want (huge bed, snug living room, secluded patio) and more besides, including a bottle of the freshest farm milk - the cows that produced it munch in a field around the corner. Sitting on my lawn surrounded by plants (indigenous only, of course), staring at the stars and listening to the frogs, it was hard to believe that I was in Africa's largest city.

Rooms: 8 cottages: 5 with showers & baths; 2 with baths only; 1 with shower only; 6 with self-catering option.
Price: R340 - R375 pp sharing or single.
Meals: Full breakfast included. Dinners and braai packs on request from R50 - R100. Many restaurants nearby.
Directions: Directions can be faxed or emailed on booking.

Maison Bordeaux

Cathy and Ron Veenis
26 Main Street, Bordeaux, Johannesburg
Tel: 082-601-6419
Email: info@maisonbordeaux.co.za Web: www.maisonbordeaux.co.za
Cell: 082-601-6419

Zen in the city. I sat by the pond and fountain, required only to listen to the sound of trickling water that somehow belonged to a land on the other side of the spray. Simply talking to Cathy and Ron is a relaxing experience in its own right. And relaxed was just how I felt after I had polished off an enormous chicken pie, courtesy of the lady next door who runs a catering company, and served by the helpful Les from Malawi. Flopping into bed came close to enjoying a second dessert, where one is rolled in a sumptuous duvet of meringue and whipped cream. Soothing neutral colours and solid wood floors go easy on the digestion and little nods to French elegance appear in the *fleur de lys* motif on the doors of the four rooms that face each other across the intimate plunge pool-courtyard and stoep. In the morning, Margaret (Cathy's mum) serves a wholesome breakfast at your choice of several petite blue tables. Cathy has done a tremendous job of renovating the house since taking over, creating an ambience of effortless ease here in the city. The only hardship was deciding where to put myself: sunning beneath the huge lavender tree, idling in a private rock garden, dipping toes into the pond, or simply sitting in my room with the shutters thrown wide open, picking from the fruit basket and listening to the birds singing. Formidable!

Rooms: 4 rooms: 2 kings with full en-suite and 2 twins with shower en-suite.
Price: R400 - R550 pp sharing. Singles R600 - R800.
Meals: Full breakfast included. Lunch and dinner on request.
Directions: Take William Nichol Drive exit from N1, eventually turning right onto Republic Road. Drive for 0.5km and then turn left into Main Street. Maison Bordeaux is 400m on the left.

Idwala Guest House

Judith Friese

13 Garrick Road, Darrenwood, Johannesburg
Tel: 011-888-1437 Fax: 011-888-1402
Email: stay@idwala.com Web: www.idwala.com
Cell: 082-865-0327

Johannesburg has one of the highest concentrations of trees of any city in the world. Certainly the fabulous purple blossom of the jacaranda blessed the drive to this miniature village in the heart of the city. The main house was built a hundred years ago when Jo'burg looked very different, but I was still astonished by views of green hills as I climbed through layers of garden, up to a tranquil lawn fringed by exuberant beds of roses, daisies, chives (for the eggs) and rosemary (for the pillows). Stepping into the first circle of the central lodge, I could see how breakfast and meals are served, drenched in sunlight when the windows disappear and serenaded by water trickling into the plunge-pool. The inner sanctum is a lounge big enough for family gatherings and backed by a fireplace inlaid with myriad cut stones. During the day the scent of fresh flowers wafts through, while at night the candles smoke and flicker in their glass bulbs. A circular passage connects all the rondavel rooms, whose proportions, beds and leather couches are universally large and luxurious. Bonus features include an elephant-framed mirror, under-floor heating, tall African lampshades, flat-screen TVs and bathrooms chiselled from the native Idwala rock itself. Judith knows what travellers want. "It's easy to make people happy if you just listen to them," she says as she shows me around the two neatly self-contained cottages, Protea and Olive, ideal for longer stays. Twenty-five percent return guests is her favourite compliment.

Rooms: 7 units: 3 rooms in the main house, 2 garden cottages, 2 garden rooms all variously king or king/twin with full en-suite or shower bathrooms. Cottages have sleeper couches too.
Price: R680 - R880 pp sharing. Singles R980 - R1,280.
Meals: Full breakfast included. Lunch and dinner on request. (3 courses from R190 pp).
Directions: Turn right off Republic Road into Blanche Road and Idwala is on the intersection with Garrick Road.

Nice By Nature

Charl Blom and Shelley Kerrigan

145 Indaba Lane, Honeydew, Johannesburg
Tel: 083-529 2588
Email: info@nicebynature.co.za Web: www.nicebynature.co.za
Cell: 083-389-1154

I was having a moment the evening I met Charl and Shelley. Hungry and weary, red mist had replaced all rational thought so that a major change in circumstances was needed to avoid an ugly travel tantrum. As I smacked the last digit into the entry gate, an ostrich swung two huge round eyes at me. They blinked twice with inch-long lashes and, inspection complete, vanished behind the fence. "User-friendly security", explained Shelley as she helped me dump my things. Less able to take myself seriously, I met the rest of the guards: a gaggle of geese, ducks, dogs, donkeys, hens, springbok, two skittish pot-bellied piglets, a couple of tortoises and their babies, and the leader of the force, Cherokee, who is a soppy cross between a boerboel and a mastiff. This may sound like pandemonium, but everybody quietly gets along. At this point I was thrown a towel, shown the pool, asked if I liked Oriental cuisine and told to do my own thing before drinks and dinner to unwind. How perfect was this! As a one-off, Shelley had given up her entire (beautiful) kitchen to a former Chinese guest to cook five courses for a dozen of us; my grin was shared across the table. Charl is equally relaxed, running breakfast as well as his garden maintenance business, from which three smiley staff (William, Alex and Kennedy) are fully employed to keep this 42-acre plot as trim as it is. Nice by Nature by name, nice by nature by nature!

Rooms: 12: 5 garden suites with en/s showers; 3 cottages with outside showers; 1 family room with bunkbed & shared en/s; 2 twins with bath & shower; 1 honeymoon king with en/s bath & shower & outside shower.
Price: R350 - R400 pp sharing. Singles R400 - R500.
Meals: Full breakfast included. Charl delights in specialities such as grilled haloumi cheese thick French toast. Restaurants nearby for other meals.
Directions: Call for directions.

Cotswold Gardens

Janine and Mike Hobbs
46 Cotswold Drive, Saxonwold, Johannesburg
Tel: 011-442-7553 Fax: 011-880-6285
Email: info@cotswoldgardens.co.za Web: www.cotswoldgardens.co.za
Cell: 082-829-3336

Aptly named, this villa-like property is offset by a varied palette of blossom dependent on the timing of your visit. A carpet of mauve, lining the avenues of Saxonwold's towering jacarandas, blessed my approach long before I reached the gates. The triangular pitched roof, pillars and cool open spaces of the entrance verandah project an aura of Mediterranean living, so it'll be a struggle to remember that you're in a city on balmy evenings out here. Having left the "monstrously egocentric world of advertising" (he says with a mischievous glint in his eye), Mike finds life here rewardingly tangible and has rediscovered connecting mind and soul via line drawing. A collection of prints, sculptures and paintings on display affirms this artistic bent extends across the family. It includes more than one Hundertwasser, glittering with metallic highlights; an ultra-crisp, poster-size shot of a building-in-a-building in nearby Millpark, by son Stephen; and flamingos (standing and in flight) sculpted in bronze by wife Janine's mum. Janine herself (aka 'the book-keeper') is curator of the gardens and currently exhibits strelitzias, dianthuses, roses, philodendrons and fuchsias – the exotic and indigenous mix being framed by undulating flowerbeds. Don't miss the courtyard installation, with leopard trees tucked between the main building and its conversion. If you're smart you'll reserve the corner suite on the garden side to enjoy a cute little balcony, almost within the jacaranda tree.

Rooms: 6: 4 B&B rooms (3 queens, 1 king/twin) with en/s baths and showers; 2 self-catering units (1 king/twin, 1 queen) with separate baths and showers.
Price: B&B: R375 - R475 pp sharing; singles R750 - R950. Self-catering: R450 - R575 pp sharing; singles R900 - R1,150.
Meals: Full cooked breakfast or continental breakfast included. Plenty of restaurants nearby, plus there's always Mr Delivery...
Directions: 30 mins from airport. See website for detailed directions.

Guesthouse The Views

Tako Seelemann

22 Grove Road, Mountain View, Johannesburg
Tel: 011-483-2568
Email: takosoulman@gmail.com Web: www.guesthousetheviews.co.za
Cell: 072-551-8197

Tako's an unusual guesthouse owner. If you want, he'll take you downtown and show you the very places most visitors to Jo'burg skirt around. Originally from Holland, he's rapidly integrated into the fabric of life here – mainly from a fascination with everything around him, which he's never too tired to share. He's therefore able to recommend little gems, such as the Sunday market in Rosebank or the antique fairs in Sandton-Mall or the Wanderers Club. When I pitched up, he'd just got back from taking an Aussie traveller round the landmarks and markets of Soweto. For variety, that evening we hit the strip of restaurants in Melville. Once you've had your fill from the city, the guesthouse is a little chill zone. Built on different levels of a hillside, the views stretch north to the foliage-rich suburbs of northern Johannesburg. A lower stoep bestows plumped cushions, beanbags, low tables and wicker chairs around a salt-water pool, with more of the same on an upper, larger breakfast terrace. Inside, every wall, shelf or lintel harbours a treasure of some guise – a Sangoma costume (traditional healer), African and Aboriginal masks, sculpted caricatures, taxidermies, framed manuscripts, jars of shells and baskets of ostrich eggs. Pastor Ricus, Tako's partner, works on a mission in Bronkhorstspruit, but is also a dealer in Russian icons and Dutch 18th-century antiques. Most artefacts are also for sale.

Rooms: 2: 1 king/twin with kitchenette and en/s bath & shower; 1 queen with kitchenette and en/s bath and shower.
Price: R250 - R350 pp sharing. Singles R450.
Meals: Continental breakfast included.
Directions: 15km from Tambo airport. See Tako's website for detailed directions.

Kiasoma Retreat & Bush Spa

Darlene Smith
D16 De Tweedespruit Conservancy, Near Cullinan
Tel: 012-734-2650 Fax: 012-734-2650
Email: kiasoma@telkomsa.net Web: www.kiasoma.co.za

The term 'retreat' doesn't go far enough. Come and surrender yourself physically and spiritually to a course that begins with aromatherapy, manicures and pedicures, continues onto reiki treatments and sweat lodges with firestone keepers, and culminates in a 'vision quest' with only water and the spirit world for company. Of course you may wish to splurge more than purge on lunch by the pool, followed by a massage in the tower and finally dinner in the lodge or boma, courtesy of the in-house chef. There are strong Native American accents to this ranch-style setting that spreads over an area supplied by a huge vegetable garden, bristling with tightly-canopied corkbush trees and hemmed in by clay cliffs as red as the dust I drove on to get here. Accommodation ranges from the rustic comfort of the stone cottage where wood-smoke-smelling Persian rugs have been unravelled over weathered tiled floors, to the low reed ceilings of the converted horse stables, to thick canvas teepees where everyone sleeps amazingly well. Everything has been designed to blend in with nature, but my favourite were the outdoor therapy 'rounders', circular stone structures open to the sky, one with a huge Moroccan-style bath and candle alcoves chiselled into the walls. Incredibly, Darlene, creator of this alternative paradise, is also a Johannesburg businesswoman. Such conundrums I considered as I shuffled around the meditation labyrinth towards the statue of a woman dressed in moons and stars, her arms outstretched to the heavens. Come at full moon.

Rooms: 6 units: 2 cottages sleeping 2 and 3, 4 stable rooms sleeping 2 each. All have en-suite showers.
Price: Cottages: R600 pp sharing; stable rooms: R385 pp sharing B&B; teepees R275 pp sharing. Singles on request.
Meals: Breakfast included with the stable rooms. Cottages and boma are self-catering. Lunch and dinner on request.
Directions: 20 minutes from Cullinan, east of Pretoria on the R513. Call or see website for detailed directions.

Soweto

Introduction

"Lots of tourists come for the day, but more should stay the night." If you really want to get under Soweto's skin, then staying over is a must. Soweto is a labyrinthine 50 square miles, crammed with an unofficial total of four million people, so getting lost is a distinct possibility. Your tour guide can drop you off at the guest-house and arrange transport to one of the funky local restaurants where extensive wine lists sit comfortably alongside samp n'beans, mutton curry and other Sowetan favourites. I went with Vhupo Tours' David Luthaga, a friendly bear of a man with a laugh that could shake Soweto's infamous power station. "You will see all of Soweto. The good, the bad and the very ugly, nothing will be hidden," was his opening gambit. And, true to his word, David showed us Diepkloof Extension, the millionaire's row also known as Diepkloof Expensive. He then handed us over to Reginald who walked with us around the squatter camp Motsoaldi, a patchwork of corrugated iron and wooden planks that he calls home. David emphasised that wherever we were, especially in the squatter camps, the inhabitants expected us to take photos so that people worldwide could witness their living conditions. This attitude stems from pre-apartheid days, when images from the Sowetan uprising of 1976 galvanised worldwide outcry, and it put paid to any concerns that I had over voyeurism.

Vhupo Tours
David Luthaga,
www.vhupo-tours.com
info@vhupo-tours.com
011-936-0411

For more information look out for the Soweto Township Complete Guide, published by Soweto Spaza and sold in the shop outside Nelson Mandela's former house on Vilakazi St.

Vhavenda Hills B&B

Kate Luthaga
11749 Mampuru St, Orlando West.
Tel: 011-936-4275 Fax: 086-503-0469
Email: vhavendahills@iburst.co.za
Web: www.sowetobnb.co.za
Cell: 082-213-1630

Soweto born and bred, Kate lives down the road from Nelson Mandela's old house. The great man himself popped round for tea after his release from Robben Island. This is very much a family home with pictures of Kate's children around the TV and friends of various offspring popping in and out. The bedrooms are comfortable with magnolia walls and multi-coloured coverlets. Ask for the palatial double room with its bath on a plinth and king-size bed where I fell asleep to the sound of cicadas and the buzz of Jo'burg traffic in the far distance, before waking to the smell of sizzling bacon.

Rooms: 4: 1 twin with en/s bath and seperate loo, 1 twin with en/s bath, 1 king size double with en/s bath and shower, 1 double with en/s shower and seperate loo.
Price: R285 - R385 pp sharing.
Meals: Cooked breakfast, plus yoghurt and cereal. Dinner on request R80 pp.
Directions: Arrange a pick-up from Johannesburg, though directions are available on website.

Dakalo B&B

Dolly Hlophe
6963 Inhlwathi St, Orlando West.
Tel: 011-936-9328 Fax: 086-661-7282.
Email: info@dakalobedandbreakfast.co.za.
Web: www.dakalobedandbreakfast.co.za
Cell: 082-723-0585

The term 'township chic' was invented for Dolly's B&B. I loved the bathroom tiled with blue-spotted mosaics and the rooms with their red quilts, mini-Zulu shields, strawberry tablecloths and zebra print curtains, hand-made by Dolly. Not only is she a wizard on the sewing-machine, but she is also heavily involved with local tourism. With opera playing in the background and freshly-cut arum lilies on the front table, the house exudes calm. Outside guests can sit under the lapa or admire Dolly's garden, where geraniums sprout from potjie cooking pots and pink bougainvillaea crawls up the walls. You are right in the heart of where history was made in Soweto and Dolly can count two Nobel Peace Prize winners amongst her neighbours. She has some astonishing stories herself of 'the struggle' and a short walk away is the fascinating Hector Pieterson Memorial & museum.

Rooms: 3: 2 twins & 1 double all en/s shower.
Price: R285 - R300 pp sh. R385 - R400 singles.
Meals: Full English breakfast. Evening meals on request for R85.
Directions: Arrange pick-up in Joburg.

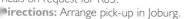

Entry Number: 304

Nthateng's B&B

Nthateng Motaung
6991 Inhlwathi St, Orlando West.
Tel: 011-936-2676 Fax: 086-600-5141
Email: info@nthateng.co.za
Web: www.nthateng.co.za
Cell: 082-335-7956

Nthateng seems far too glamorous to be an ex-driving instructor. Snappily dressed in tight jeans and gold jewellery, she happily took the time to talk to me about the history of Soweto. She then insisted that I accompany her to the wedding down the road between a Zulu man and a Swazi woman. "Everyone's invited," she said. Between the tribal colours and shaking dancers, Nthateng sat me down with some fried chicken and samp, washed down with a glass of sparkling ginger (apparently it wouldn't be a proper wedding without it!). Then it was back for a tour of her own place. Optical lighting illuminates the up-to-the-minute sandy-coloured rooms that boast carved wooden bedheads inlaid with red and gold mosaics. One double room also houses a vast Louis XIV-style dressing table. Insist that she takes you back stage on Soweto TV. It's a hub of creativity and the crew are really friendly.

Rooms: 5: 2 twins, 3 queens all full en/s.
Price: R285 pp sharing. R385 for singles.
Meals: Full cooked breakfast is included. Evening meals available on request for R55.
Directions: Arrange pick-up from Joburg.

Entry Number: 305

Mosetlha Bush Camp

Chris, June and Caroline Lucas

Madikwe Game Reserve
Tel: 011-444-9345
Fax: 011-444-9345
Email: info@thebushcamp.com
Web: www.thebushcamp.com
Cell: 083-653-9869

Mosetlha puts the wild into wilderness; no doors or glass here as they would hinder the feel and dust of Africa permeating your very core; no worries either as you leave them at the gate. Facilities are basic but real; guests draw their own hot water from a donkey-boiler before proceeding to the shower. Recently the kitchen was extended and a new thatch and stone lapa has been added for guests to read, relax and compare sightings, but the authenticity remains untainted. The wooden cabins are comfortable, but used only for sleeping - you are here for the wilderness experience of the outdoors. Chris's passion for conservation and his environment shines through and is contagious (which reminds me to say that the area is malaria-free). His guests depart much the wiser, not only because of the game drives, but also (conditions permitting) because of the superb guided wilderness walks. Yes, the Madikwe Game Reserve (70,000 hectares) has the so-called 'Big Five', but a game lodge worth its salt (such as this) will fire your imagination about the whole food chain. Even the camp itself is an education   all sorts of birds, small mammals and antelopes venture in. Come for a genuine and memorable bush experience. *Children welcome from 8 years old up.*

Rooms: 8 twins sharing 3 shower/toilet complexes.
Price: All-inclusive from R1,485 per person. Park levies and drinks from the bar extra.
Meals: All meals and refreshments (tea, coffee, fruit juice) included.
Directions: Detailed written directions supplied on request or see website.

The Bush House

Sue and Gordon Morrison

Madikwe Game Reserve
Tel: 083-379-6912 Fax: 086-678-6077
Email: camp@bushhouse.co.za Web: www.bushhouse.co.za
Cell: 083-379-6912

Sue and her husband Gordon stayed here as guests in 2006 and decided they didn't want to leave… so they bought the place, along with its history. The Bush House dates back to 1940, when this otherwise barren bushveld afforded no more than cattle farming and citrus fruit orchids. In 1987 it was bought out by the government, in anticipation of the largest translocation of animals on record (10,000) and the creation of one of the finest conservation areas in Africa, where rare species occur naturally and over 340 species of birds have been recorded. No one is better placed to guide you here than André, a walking, talking, driving encyclopedia of the bush. He bears an extraordinary (and tireless) ability to spot animals, no matter the time of day or night, is a passionate photographer and can withstand extreme cold in shorts (when the rest of the Landcruiser's trebling up blankets!). The lodge retains its structure as a farm building but has been revamped on the inside. The bedrooms come replete with birdseed, so you can feed the birds from your private patio. Dining is a relaxed affair, with everyone eating together, and in downtime guests can explore the grounds' nature trails on foot, leaf through one of the many David Attenborough books in the lounge, indulge in some savoury or sweet nibbles for high tea, or head to the beauty salon. One massage, manicure and pedicure later and you'll be ready for an evening game drive – never before having felt so glamorous out in the bush.

Rooms: 6: 2 double, 4 twins all with en-suite bath and shower.
Price: From R1,925 pp sharing.
Meals: All meals included plus two game drives a day.
Directions: From Pretoria take N4 to Zeerust, then R49/47 towards Madikwe. At Madikwe turn right at the Wonderboom Gate, The Bush House is signposted 1 km from entrance. Federal Air Flight also flies to the reserve daily.

Buffalo Ridge

Kate Naughton
Madikwe Game Reserve
Tel: 011-805-9995 Fax: 011-805-0687
Email: reservations@madikwecollection.com
Web: www.buffaloridgesafari.com

At the entrance I negotiated my way past a nervy-looking wildebeest and soon found myself up on the elevated lounge area at Buffalo Ridge Lodge, enjoying tea and biscuits. Whilst I got my bearings and chatted to the charming Priscilla, I could hear the chuntering of a band of baboons somewhere in the near vicinity… which added a bit of tone to my arrival. Up here the peace is more peaceful and the quiet is quieter (apart from such things as baboons, of course) and guests will soon find themselves synchronising their metabolic rate to that of the surrounding bush. The lodge has been built on the Tweedepoort Ridge overlooking the plains of the Madikwe Game Reserve and is perfectly placed for game-viewing. Wooden flooring, soft sofas, stacks of wildlife books and rock figs adorn the lower deck area, while there's an infinity pool on the upper deck which looks regally out over the mountains. And it's not just the setting that is so special. Buffalo Ridge is the first lodge in Madikwe wholly owned by a local rural community and black-and-white photos of the chief (who is involved in the project) hang on bedroom walls. Each suite - in natural colours, soft textures and with huge sliding glass doors - is sunrise-facing. At night, if you don't feel like walking to the dining area or boma, you can order up a private four-course dinner on your deck with the distant lights from Botswana as backdrop. I could hear the sound of singing as I left and I swore to return whenever I could.

Rooms: 8 doubles, all with en-suite shower.
Price: From R2,450 pp sharing.
Meals: All meals and safari activities included.
Directions: Map provided on booking.

Map Number: 19

Entry Number: 308

Thakadu River Lodge

Kate Naughton
Madikwe Game Reserve
Tel: 011-805-9995 Fax: 011-805-0687
Email: reservations@madikwecollection.com
Web: www.thakadurivercamp.com

Surrounded by forest and built on high ground in the fork between the Marico River and one of its tributaries, Thakadu has the perfect vantage from which to look down on the many animals that make use of the water below. This is a natural paradise and all effort has been made for the lodge to jar as little as possible with its surroundings. To this end: wooden floors, rattan furniture, bare stone walls, bamboo lights and lanterns decorating the boma, poles supporting lofty thatched roofs, carved wooden doors... natural fibres and construction materials at every turn. The lodge also makes much of its high position and wonderful views by leaving a huge open wall in the lounge area and by perching its pool and bar on the edge of the gully with fab views down river. Thakadu is also fenced and so particularly child-friendly. Kids can learn bush craft and take a course in 'spoor-ology' and they even run special game drives for the under 6s. When you are done bumping around in game vehicles, head to the infinity pool and soak up the views, book a massage or simply relax under the tented canopy of your own gorgeous private suite. Each has its own deck overlooking the river below. Decision-making was never such a pleasure. The lodge, by the way, is owned by the local community and there are framed pictures of the Molatedi people hanging everywhere.

Rooms: 12 tents: 8 doubles and 4 family units with doubles and extra sleeper couch. All with en-suite bath and shower.
Price: From R2,450 pp sharing.
Meals: Breakfast, dinner, high tea and game activities included.
Directions: See website for detailed directions.

North West Province

Tuningi Safari Lodge

Kate Naughton
Madikwe Game Reserve
Tel: 011-315-6194 Fax: 011-805-0687
Email: res@tuningi.co.za Web: www.tuningi.co.za

The plan was to track a pack of wild dogs that had been dead-ending impala on the southeast boundary fence. But, like the earlier idea of a languid, post-brunch foot safari, which culminated in the ranger and a couple of French businessmen standing thirty metres from a lion pride, our plan was to be turned on its head as the bush dictated the afternoon proceedings. This 75,000-hectare reserve is still a little-known secret within South Africa, and yet the game viewing is arguably second to none. Back at the lodge, the look and vibe is "Colonial African chic": there are porcupine quills on lamps, deep wicker-chairs in an open-plan lounge and a lantern-edged, fire-centred boma at the end of a sweep of wooden decking overlooking a well frequented waterhole. Each suite revolves around a huge bed (with miniature bottles of amarula waiting at its foot) and a two-way fireplace, enjoyable from bath to bed. Molton Brown toiletries, a huge tub, ceiling fans, air-con and an enormous outdoor rock shower are added luxuries; and as evening falls, should there be rain before dinner there'll be someone at the door proffering an umbrella. And what a dinner! Smoked fish, boerewors, lamb chops, the selection seemed endless... while long tables make for an involving and convivial party. Finally I was drawn, along with the other guests, to the adjoining wooden bar for a nightcap, until I could resist the lure of my wonderful bed no longer. Tuningi prides itself on its ability to make guests feel part of the family... and the hospitality really does feel unconditional here.

Rooms: 8: 4 double rooms with en-suite bath and outdoor shower; 2 family units each with 2 double rooms, kitchen, dining room, en-suite bath and shower. One unit has a private pool.
Price: From R3,695 pp sharing.
Meals: Includes all meals and game drives.
Directions: See website for detailed directions.

Jaci's Lodges

Jan and Jaci van Heteren

Molatedi, Madikwe Game Reserve
Tel: 014-778-9900 Fax: 014-778-9901
Email: jaci@madikwe.com Web: www.madikwe.com
Cell: 083-447-7929, reservations 083-700-2071

What a game drive! Lions on the hunt scattered by a charging elephant right in front of our vehicle! We're still abuzz when we return to our already-run baths and chat animatedly around the boma fire at dinner. Jaci's has this effect on you. Wonderfully indulgent, this is one of Tatler's favourites. Beyond the foyer's tree-pierced, blonde-thatch roof lies an expansive restaurant overlooking riverine forest and separated from the chic bar by a four-sided open fire, which together keep you in long cocktails and gourmet food. Relax the excess off in a hammock; alternatively there's a pool and gym. Save your gasps of delight for the treehouses. Sitting six metres above ground and linked by a rosewood walkway, their glass doors concertina open onto private decks. Vibrant colours form a backdrop for a bed festooned with silk cushions, burnt-orange suede beanbag and swollen stone bath with hand-made copper pipes. But Jaci's trump card is the rangers, whose enthusiasm creates a wonderful, wild adventure. What a job they have - daily taking breath away. Further along the river bank you'll find Jaci's Safari Lodge, opulent canvas and stone suites. The Safari Lodge is ideal for romantic safaris and children of all ages are welcome and specially catered for. Jaci's is owned and managed by Jaci and Jan and all staff members share a 25% stakeholding in the company, both of which facts make for fantastically caring service from all concerned.

Rooms: 8 tree-houses, each with king-size bed and bath and outdoor "jungle" shower.
Price: R2,895 – R4,795 pp sharing. Game drives, walking safaris, sundowner drink and meals included.
Meals: All meals and game drives included.
Directions: Only 1.5 hours' drive from Sun City or a 3.5 to 4-hour drive from Johannesburg. Daily road and air transfers from JHB and Sun City. Ask for details when booking.

Mpumalanga

Paperbark Bush Retreat

Will and Carol Fox
Lydenburg
Tel: 079-354-8538
Email: info@paperbarkretreat.com Web: www.paperbarkretreat.com
Cell: 079-354-8538

Will Fox is obsessed with leopards. "They're just such fascinating creatures," he tells me as I sip tea out on the stoep. His wife Carol is also an avid wildlife conservationist and both worked on Leopard Research with the Mpumalanga Parks Board before taking over the helm at Paperbark Bush Retreat. And a royal retreat it is too. Hidden among the indigenous forest at the foothill of the Leutla Mountain, Paperbark is chic, comfortable and, best of all, eco-friendly with electricity generated by solar power and river water re-routed for irrigation. There are also free-roaming leopards on the estate plus other resident game, waterfalls, mountain streams and pools. Rooms are wonderfully fashioned with African artefacts, locally-made furniture, soft fabrics and warm tones made even warmer by the open fires; sweet-smelling hand-made soap is also a welcome touch in the gleaming bathrooms. All cottages face onto a neat lawn, at the centre of which stands the retreat's namesake, quietly attracting a wonderful variety of colourful birds. Bushwalks, night drives and river bathing are just some of the activities on offer, and guests are also encouraged to become involved with the Ingwe Leopard Project (ever collared a leopard or set a camera trap?). However, the natural, unspoilt beauty of the place and stylish, luxurious comfort also allow for some serious R&R. Will and Carol also ensure your comfort serving up sumptuous three-course dinners using only the freshest ingredients and presenting them either in the dining room or out on the lapa under the African stars as you wish. Delicious. *On site activities included.*

Rooms: 4: 3 cottages, one with 1 double and 1 twin; 2 with twins with en-suite bath and shower. Main house: 2 twins with shared shower.
Price: R995 - R1,110 pp sharing.
Meals: Full breakfast, light lunch, 3-course dinner and soft drinks included.
Directions: Transfers available from Johannesburg or Nelspruit Airports. Also see website. Detailed directions issued on booking.

Numbela Exclusive Riverside Accommodation

Paul and Tracy Nepgen

White River
Tel: 084-491-2708 Fax: 0866-196-796
Email: relax@numbela.co.za Web: www.numbela.co.za

Numbela is found on 200 acres of bird-rich woodland next to the White Waters River, which bounds in spectacular waterfalls through the surrounding forests. Guests are welcome to go exploring at their will. The two guest cottages are separated by the owners' own converted Mill House. Yellowwood Cottage has a large raised verandah with a swing seat piled high with cushions while the interior is all about relaxation: candles, music and an open fireplace all play their part. The main bedroom is enlivened by earthy red-and-orange paintwork, the bedroom is dressed in blushing fabrics and the washed-blue bathroom comes with an outdoor shower. Smaller River Cottage is close to the river, as you might expect, with chalky walls, thatched roof, claret-coloured floor, high ceilings, an Oregon pine kitchen, stable doors and an open fire. The main bedroom is luxuriously furnished in white and blue. Both cottages are fully equipped for self-catering, although delicious breakfasts can be served (with prior arrangement) on your cottage patio. There is also the Tin House, a Pilgrim's Rest-style, fully-equipped self-catering house with a boma and four uniquely-decorated, luxurious twin bedrooms. Paul and Tracy, your hosts, are there to make you feel very welcome and have constructed a network of technical single-track mountain-bike trails and trail-running routes on their next-door farm. *Close to Casterbridge Farm shops and restaurants, golf courses and the Kruger Park gates. Children are welcome, though under 12s by arrangement.*

Rooms: 3: 2 self-catering/B&B cottages, 1 double with en-suite shower plus mezzanine single, 1 double & twin with en-suite bath and outdoor shower; 1 self-catering cottage with 4 twin bedrooms with en-suite showers, 1 private bath.
Price: Self-catering: R800 for 2 people; B&B R450 pp sharing; R1,500 - R2,400 in Tin House.
Meals: Full English or health breakfast by arrangement for cottages only.
Directions: 20km north of White River on R40 Hazyview rd. White oval sign on L. Turn L at 2nd oval sign, follow signs down 1km dirt farm rd to gate.

Plumbago Guest House

Ilara and Robbie Robertson

R40 between White River and Hazyview
Tel: 013-737-8806 Fax: 086-607-5222
Email: plumbagoguesthouse@mweb.co.za
Web: www.plumbagoguesthouse.co.za Cell: 082-954-0467

Through wrought-iron gates at the end of a bougainvillaea-lined drive I found Plumbago, as pretty as the flower that shares its name. Set on an avocado and banana farm, it sits above the plantation watching over it and out to Kruger Park in the distance. When I arrived, 1940s jazz was swinging out from the radio, just the right aural accompaniment to the nostalgic, colonial-inspired setting. In the drawing room and bar, an eclectic collection of antiques, paintings and rugs are interspersed with vases filled with exotic flowers and extravagant palm-leaf fans that stretch up to the ceiling. The rooms have the same casual gracefulness about them with their subtle, natural tones, Jacobean print curtains, mahogany beds and abundance of vased and water-coloured flowers. With a large lived-in verandah, elegant pool and sauna in the beautifully tended garden there's plenty of opportunity to relax and mull over days gone by, particularly in Robbie's history-reading section in the tennis court's viewing lapa. But what really makes this place stand apart are the Robertsons themselves. On my visit, Ilara (who honed her culinary skills cooking for diplomats) was deciding on that evening's dinner menu while Robbie was itching to go flying before being back for waitering duty later on. A young and active bunch, they are often busying about doing their own thing but are more than happy to share their passions with you. 20 mins to Kruger and close to Panorama Route and God's Window. Babysitting available. *Activities, game drives, beauty treatments can be arranged with help from Ilara. Small weddings can be arranged in the garden.*

Rooms: 3 garden chalets: 1 king/twin with en-s shower; 1 king with en-s shower; 1 king extra-length sleigh-bed en-s bath. All rooms air-con heating & cooling.
Price: R580 - R690 pp sharing. Singles +R150. Extra beds available on request. Pets & kids by arrangement.
Meals: Full breakfast incl'. Lunch & dinner on request.
Directions: From Jo'burg, take N4 to Nelspruit & then to White River. Go on R40 to Hazyview, Plumbago signed on R 34km out of White River & 10km before Hazyview. A comfortable 4hrs from Jo'burg.

Blue Jay Lodge

Philip and Margi Nichols

645 - 647 Blue Jay Lane, Hazyview
Tel: 013-737-7546
Email: phil@bluejaylodge.co.za Web: www.bluejaylodge.co.za
Cell: 082-575-1798

I would have been happy enough plonked in a hippo wallow on such a hot and humid day, but Blue Jay Lodge, a cool oasis hidden among lush, indigenous forest, was so much better! And when I say hidden, I really mean it. The neighbours are completely blocked out by the undergrowth and among all the sycamore figs and fever trees I could have been in dense rainforest. I had found my very own tropical oasis. Sensing my heat fatigue Phil showed me to my huge room (past blossoming orchids), switched on the air-con and invited me to take a chilled drink from the mini-fridge. A new calmness prevailed as I lay back on the giant bed and gazed up at the high thatched roof. A short walk across the screed floor was my balcony, where the braai area and swimming pool are visible beyond the leaves of an old kiaat tree whose branches reached out to me from under the balustrades. The Nichols are wonderful hosts and I managed to wangle myself an invite to join Phil and his family for lamb chops and boerewors. I slept particularly well that night and was only dragged back to consciousness by the irresistible smells of a cooked breakfast with my name on it. Sitting on the verandah, lingering over a second cup of coffee, I watched an African paradise fly-catcher ducking and diving between the leaves. With more than 80 bird species on offer you could easily forget the day's activity and just sit and bird-watch at the lodge. Like I did! *No children under 14. Blue Jay Lodge is 10 minutes from Kruger Park gates. Microflights and quad bike trails also available.*

Rooms: 5: 4 king/twins with en-suite bath and shower. 1 self-catering unit with king, kitchenette and en-suite bath and shower.
Price: From R590 - R690 pp sharing. R495 for self-catering.
Meals: Full breakfast included.
Directions: See website for detailed directions.

Buckler's Africa

Robert Buckler

Komatipoort
Tel: 013-793-7818 Fax: 086-524-7107
Email: info@bucklersafrica.co.za Web: www.bucklersafrica.co.za
Cell: 084-400-0703

Not many seconds after arriving, I found myself enjoying a sundowner with Robert on his expansive balcony, chatting about my day in the Kruger Park, while lightning crackled in the distant sky. The joy was that I hadn't really left the Kruger at all! There it was, just across the Crocodile River that meanders along the bottom of the garden. It is quite a sight, that expanse of nurtured green lawn, the river and then the wilderness stretching away. Elephants (and the odd lion) have been known to wander across, possibly to steal a drink from the swimming pool – evidence that Robert's hospitality really is infectious. Most of the accommodation, found in one long wing of the sand-yellow house, is self-catering. Bush style abounds here. The furniture and stairs are made of a heavy wood whose innate beauty has been left untarnished and exposed thatch towers above it all. African prints adorn the walls and back in the house wooden sculptures from Mozambique peer out from behind overflowing plants in the sitting room. My B&B room was in the main house with a solid iron bed and furniture, while my two bathrooms – I won't go unless I have two bathrooms! – housed an oceanic bath in one and a shower in the other. Outdoor showers in the self-catering units add to the adventure. I watched Robert cook my breakfast in his open-plan kitchen and ate it sitting out in the garden with the other guests as the sun warmed our backs. Buckler's offers a rare opportunity to feel part of the Kruger without paying a high price to be inside it.

Rooms: 6: 3 standard rooms with queens, twins or singles with en/s or private bathrooms with bath/shower; 3 self-catering units: 1, 2 or 3 bedroom queens, twins or singles with en-suite bathrooms, some with outside showers, all bedrooms air-conditioned.
Price: R375 pp sharing for B&B in standard room and for self-catering units (serviced daily). Exclusive property use from R6,000 per night 16 persons.
Meals: Full breakfast included for standard rooms.
Directions: 11.5km outside Komatipoort. Detailed directions on website.

Lukimbi Safari Lodge

Sally Kernick
Kruger National Park
Tel: 011-431-1120 Fax: 011-431-3597
Email: info@lukimbi.com Web: www.lukimbi.com

The giraffes and elephants that sauntered across the road to Lukimbi Lodge were in no rush. Unfortunately I was, having missed the evening game drive already, but it is impossible (and unwise) to get irate with these wonderfully leisurely beasts. And it was just as difficult to feel any stress once I arrived at luxurious Lukimbi. While sipping a home-made lemonade that had been eased into my hand the only thing I could think to write was a deeply-felt "Wow." With the sun beating down as it was that day, I lounged around on the huge deck, keeping an eye out for any game down by the river and watching the monkeys fool around on the stilts supporting us. The rooms, found down a wooden walkway past the boma, are mini-lodges themselves. They all have their own viewing decks, and even in my case a private plunge pool. Geckos scarpered as I jumped in, and while I wallowed, something about my stomach must have brought to mind the hippos doing the same thing so close by. One scrumptious supper later, during which the fellow guests gloatingly filled me in on what I'd missed that afternoon, we retired to beds covered by opulent mosquito nets in order to rise in time for the morning drive. To have our tea-stop interrupted by the growl of a territorial leopard is a thrill I'll never forget. It was only on return to the lodge, though, that the guests spotted the biggest baddest beast of them all: me, as I guzzled the breakfast laid out for us before my sad, but inevitable, departure. *There is a crèche, and activities for children are organised.*

Rooms: 16: all with king-size beds and en-suite bathrooms with indoor and outdoor showers.
Price: R2,890 – R4,150 per person sharing. Singles available on request.
Meals: All meals included (breakfast, lunch/high tea and 3-course dinner).
Directions: Directions available on website.

Trees Too

Sue and Martyn Steele

Komatipoort
Tel: 013-793-8262 Fax: 0866-880-177
Email: info@treestoo.com Web: www.treestoo.com
Cell: 083-654-1778

Sue and Martyn are perfectly suited to this B&B malarkey. Originally from old Blighty, they clearly love their new life in Komatipoort. The "wildlife mad" couple wanted to be near animals, and you'd be hard pressed to get much closer than this. A short drive from the Kruger National Park, Trees Too is ideal for less-exalted budgets that don't quite stretch to the top-end lodges in the park itself. With its kidney-shaped pool, draped with lush palms and crawling bougainvillaea, Trees Too's atmosphere is more tropical beach than arid savannah. It's unsurprising really, when you consider that Maputo - Mozambique's steaming capital - is only a couple of hours away. After a sticky day's game drive, grab a cool sundowner from the bar and submerge yourself in the pool before sitting down at the friendly poolside restaurant. It wasn't long before I found myself happily swapping stories with the other diners while tucking into a succulent fillet steak followed by delicious cheesecake pudding. With a storm brewing it was only a short skip to bed - terracotta flooring, a soaring thatched roof and comfortable, air-conditioning thankfully keep things cool in the forty degree heat of summer. The family room is my favourite with its gramophone shipped from the UK, plus piles of wildlife magazines and board games. If you manage to tear yourself from the pool and badminton court and tire of SA's biggest game park, then Sue and Martyn have plenty of ideas up their sleeves: elephant-back safaris anyone, or perhaps even a trip to a Mozambique beach?

Rooms: 8: 3 doubles, with en/s shower; 2 triple rooms with a double plus 1 single, with en/s bath and shower; 1 twin, with en/s bath/shower; 2 family rooms (one sleeping 4 and one sleeping 6, 1 with 4-poster bed), 1 with shower and 1 with bath/shower.
Price: R300 - R370 pp sharing.
Meals: Breakfast is a cold buffet with cheeses and cereals, plus a full English. Dinner available from small but interesting menu at restaurant.
Directions: Take the N4 from Jo'Burg. On reaching Komatipoort, turn left at the R571 into Rissik St, go 4km through 2 stop signs then right into Gilfillan St. Take first right into Furley St. Trees Too No.11 on L.

Idube Private Game Reserve

Sally Kernick
Sabi Sand Game Reserve
Tel: 011-431-1120 Fax: 011-431-3597
Email: info@idube.com Web: www.idube.com
Cell: 013-735-5459 (weekends)

There are few establishments where the staff seem to have as much fun working together as at Idube. Be they guides, trackers, managers or chefs, the Idube crew exude a delightful sense of goodwill to each other and to all mankind. And it's not difficult to see why. Warthog roam through the camp, elephants pass nearby; there is space and greenery, beauty and beast. The land was bought in 1983 by Louis and Marilyn Marais and Louis sensibly built the swimming pool before designing and constructing the rest of the camp himself. Guests sleep in chalets dotted around the sloping grounds, while the thatched seating and dining areas look out over the Sabi Sand Game Reserve. A rope bridge over the river bed takes you to a hide where you can admire the Shadulu dam and its regulars without being admired yourself. Two game drives per day plus guided walks give you the chance to see what's happening elsewhere in the reserve and tracker Titus amazed us with his ability to read bent grasses and droppings. We took time out for sundowners by a dam, accompanied by a bull elephant and a bull hippo. There was much posturing and manliness, not least from me, before a return to camp for dinner (which was excellent!) and conviviality under the stars. *A vast range of activities available - riding with wild horses, hot-air balooning, microlighting to name a few - please ask lodge for details.*

Rooms: 10: 2 kings and 8 doubles all with en/s bathrooms and both indoor and outdoor shower.
Price: Winter (May to end August) R2,500 pp sharing. Summer (September to end April) R3,500. Single supplement +35%.
Meals: All 3 meals plus morning and evening drives and a guided walk included. Drinks and transfers extra.
Directions: 34.4km from Hazyview along R536 towards Kruger Gate. Follow signs off to the left. 19.5km along a dirt road.

Rhino Walking Safaris - Plains Camp

Nikki and Gerrit Meyer (Managers)
Rhino Walking Safaris, Kruger National Park, Skukuza
Tel: 011-467-1886 Fax: 011-467-4758
Email: info@rws.co.za Web: www.isibindiafrica.co.za or www.rws.co.za
Cell: 083-631-4956

This is where I fell for Africa: sitting outside my tent in the Kruger, sipping G&T (for the quinine, you understand) and watching game serenely traverse the Timbitene Plain. This is the only private lodge where you can walk in pristine wilderness - nothing short of a privilege. Here the refined, pioneer tents have dark wood furniture with brass hinges and leather straps, bathrooms with copper taps protruding from tree stumps and the largest, softest towels. During the day, you can doze on the chocolate-leather sofa or sip highball cocktails in the plunge pool. Pith helmets, surveying tools, maps and a gramophone add to the bygone feel. Walking on rhino footpaths, the trails let you soak up both the scale and detail of the bush. No mad rush to tick off half-glimpsed Big Five, this – it's all about the quality of the sightings. That said, we encountered glowering buffalo, rampant rhino, lionesses on a hunt and had a pulse-quickening showdown with a bull elephant that I'll dine out on for ages. Afterwards we sent the sun down the sky and, wrapped in rugs, headed toward gas-lamp beacons for a never-ending feast. A safari fantasy come true.

Rooms: 4: all twin-bed African-explorer style tents, each with en-suite loo, shower and overhead fan. Tree house sleep-out option also available.
Price: R2,365 pp - R2,720 pp. Ask about 3-, 4- or 5-night packages and single supplement.
Meals: All meals, soft drinks, house wines and beer, safari activities (primarily walking) and optional sleep-outs included.
Directions: From the Paul Kruger Gate follow signs to Skukuza Rest Camp & Rhino Walking Safaris. Drive past Skukuza on H1-2 towards Tshokwane and Satara. Cross Sabie and Sand rivers and after second turning to Maroela Loop, turn left signed Rhino Walking Safaris. Meet at Rhino Post Safari Lodge.

Rhino Post Safari Lodge

Nikki and Gerrit Meyer (Managers)

Kruger National Park, Skukuza
Tel: 011 467-1006 Fax: 011-467-4758
Email: info@rws.co.za Web: www.isibindiafrica.co.za or www.rws.co.za
Cell: 083 631-4956

After 6 hours' drive from Jo'burg it was with a mixture of relief and anticipation that we rolled the last few kilometres through the Kruger Park to Rhino Post Safari Lodge. On arrival our bags were magically transferred to our lovely, luxurious, wood-framed chalet with its big glass windows and deck overlooking a dry river bed (or should I say animal motorway?). Although the chalets have phones and electricity, it still feels as rustic and as open to nature as is safely possible. The camp is not fenced so animals are able to walk through the lodge area (you will be escorted back and forth along the boardwalks after dark). So... first an outdoor shower, then tea up at the lodge, on a deck overlooking a frequently-used waterhole; and then straight out in search of game and adventure. Our thanks to Bernard, our guide and driver, for some wonderful experiences. I don't know if we were lucky or not, but 16 rhino on our first night didn't seem bad! We also saw two prides of lion fighting over a giraffe carcass, with scores of vultures in the trees and a large pack of hyenas watching the action for scavenging opportunities. This sunlit tableau is etched on my memory and it was a sighting to brag about that evening over fireside drinks. All the meals at Rhino Post are exceptional and it does not take long to get into the new schedule of early starts, late breakfasts, siestas, late-afternoon game drives... and finally dinner. It was a proper wrench to leave when the time came.

Rooms: 16: 2 double & 6 twin chalets. All en-s bathrooms, deep free-standing baths, outside showers, overhead fans, mini bar, telephone, safe & hairdryer.
Price: R2,190 - R2,590 pp sharing. Ask about 3-, 4- or 5-night packages and single supplement.
Meals: All meals and safari activities included.
Directions: From Paul Kruger Gate follow signs to Skukuza Rest Camp & Rhino Walking Safaris. Drive past Skukuza on H1-2 towards Tshokwane & Satara. Cross Sabie & Sand rivers & after 2nd turning to Maroela Loop, turn L signed Rhino Walking Safaris.

Iketla Lodge

Albert and Hennielene Botha

off R555, Ohrigstad
Tel: 013-238-8900 Fax: 013-238-8900
Email: relax@iketla.com Web: www.iketla.com

'Be relaxed... be peaceful' is Iketla's poetic English translation from the local Sotho dialect. Appropriately named, as it turns out. Surrounded on all sides by hills and rocky outcrops, Albert and Hennielene greeted me in the shebeen, where the late afternoon sun was gushing through the open sides, flooding the thatched, tiled dining area. For those that don't know, a shebeen is a drinking den and it's to this magnet that guests began to flock as they returned, brimming with exhilaration, from the day's adventures. Some had been exploring the Panorama Route, others had been walking guided trails through Iketla's 540 hectares of wilderness, inspecting all creatures great and small, and learning about the impressive range of birdlife and traditional uses of indigenous plants. They regaled us with their new-found knowledge and enthusiasm, with Albert, a bushman at heart, chipping in with many jewels of profounder expertise. A faint drumbeat interrupted the banter to signal supper, though my acute senses had already picked up the aroma of something sensational in the air... ostrich strips in a sherry sauce as it turned out. At daybreak I inspected my chalet, similar in style to the main lodge with rugged stone walls, a thatched roof and a verandah outside sliding glass doors. There I read my book and rested my bones, listening to the morning wildlife bring this African wilderness alive.

Rooms: 8 chalets: 3 doubles and 4 twins, 1 honeymoon suite, all with en-suite showers and outside showers.
Price: R865 - R950 pp sharing. Singles R1,120 - R1,240.
Meals: Full breakfast and dinner included.
Directions: From N4 turn off at Belfast and follow R540 through Dullstroom to Lydenburg. Follow R36 through Lydenburg (also known as Mashishing) to Ohrigstad. 4km past Ohrigstad turn left onto R555. Sign to Iketla 6km further on right.

Umlani Bushcamp

Marco Schiess
Timbavati Nature Reserve
Tel: 021 785-5547 Fax: 086-696-8518
Email: info@umlani.com Web: www.umlani.com
Cell: 083-468-2041

Rhino-tracking on foot; a rather exciting experience with a couple of bull elephants; sun-downers as the bush settles for the night... this is what safaris are supposed to be about. Umlani is set on a gentle slope above a dry river course (wet in spring) and only a high elephant fence separates guests from the Big 5. You do not, for example, leave your rondavel at night to investigate snuffling noises, and elephants regularly swing around the camp perimeter for a drink at the pool. You sleep in delightful reed-walled rondavels with thatched roofs (no bricks here), hurricane lamps (no electricity either), and you shower *au naturel,* but in complete privacy. Marco and his wife Marie ran the camp by themselves for a decade until the demands of a young family compelled them to find like-minded managers. After the evening game drive everyone sits out on the deck by the bar, or in the boma round the fire, mulling over what's just been seen, before sitting down to an excellent and often buzzy dinner at tables of 8. Thoughtful hosts and knowledgeable rangers provide the charming, human face of a full-on bush experience. I had many laughs during my stay, while another guest was in tears when she had to leave! Umlani is exceptionally personal and genuine and you live as close to nature as they dare let you. For the more adventurous a night in the treehouse 2km away is a must! Umlani Bushcamp is the 14th Establishment to receive the prestigious Fair Trade in Tourism South Africa Certification.

Rooms: 8 huts (3 sleeping 4, 1 sleeping 3 and 4 sleeping 2), all with en-suite outside showers.
Price: R2,475 pp sharing, singles R3,245. Children under 12: R1,238. 3-night special: R6,325 pp sharing, R8,316 singles, R3,163 kids under 12. 7-night special also on offer.
Meals: All meals, drinks and 2 - 3 game activities included.
Directions: You will get a map when you book.

Swaziland

Phophonyane Falls Lodge

Rod and Lungile de Vletter

Pigg's Peak
Tel: +268-437-1429 Fax: +268 437 1319
Email: lungile@phophonyane.co.sz Web: www.phophonyane.co.sz
Cell: +268-604-2802

Grab your passport, pop over the border into the Kingdom of Swaziland and immerse yourself in 500 hectares of pristine nature. Phophonyane Lodge is perched high on a valleyside in thick indigenous forest, with the constant background music of a thousand birds (230 species) and the rushing white water of the Phophonyane River cascading down the kloof below (waterfall-viewing walks are a must). You move between the main lodge and the various tents, cottages and beehives on cobbles and wooden walkways, past murals and rough wood sculptures, natural materials blending easily into the landscape. Some of the cottages have sitting rooms, private gardens, narrow wooden staircases up to bedrooms and balconies, big showers, kitchens et al. The safari tents with their private decks are simpler but more romantic. You are lost in the trees and I stayed in one of the two right down by the rushing water's edge, the best sleeping draught imaginable. The reserve is criss-crossed with hiking paths leading to natural rock pools for swimming, although there is the alternative of the recently-built saltwater pool. Phophonyane prides itself on its links with the local community, some of whom now entertain in the evenings with traditional Swazi dancing. An invigorating experience and a two-night stay is recommended. *4x4 drives to mountains and bushman paintings available along with a new chalet on the Crocodile River that overlooks the Kruger Park for Phophonyane guests.*

Rooms: 11: 3 cottages, 2 with shower, 1 with bath; 2 beehive huts, en-s with shower and king-size beds; 6 tents: 2 have en-s bathrooms: 1 with bath & shower & 1 shower only; 4 tents have private bathrooms with showers separate but close to tent.
Price: Safari tents, R420 - R460 pp sharing, singles R590 - R680. Beehives, R630 pp sh, singles R890. Cottages, R550 - R590 pp sh. Singles R780 - R860.
Meals: All cottages & 2 tents self-catering. A la carte restaurant on site & picnic lunches can be prepared.
Directions: 7km north of Pigg's Peak Town or 35km south from Jeppe's Reef/Matsamo border post to signposts, then c. 4km of dirt rd following signs to lodge.

Map Number: 21

Entry Number: 324

Limpopo

Limpopo Side Dishes

A handful of highly-recommended things to do and places to eat in the Limpopo area...

Kurisa Moya Village Home Stays

This is a truly unique experience - a Sotho village homestay. You not only stay the night with 'your' family, but you can also help with the daily chores of collecting wood and water, herding cows and goats etc. These villages still follow the cultural traditions of old. As you enjoy your traditional Sotho dinner you will hear of myths and legends and of the role of the chief and sangoma. You will gain a fascinating insight into the life of a South African village.
Contact: Lisa Martus, Kurisa Moya Nature Lodge; Prices: R350 for a tour and lunch, R950 for all-inclusive stay; Tel: 015-276-1131; Email: info@krm.co.za; Web: www.krm.co.za

Kaross

Kaross creates tableware, homeware, art pieces, wall-hangings and bed linen, every plate, stitch, weave and brush-stroke 100% hand-done. After 19 years these authentic Shangaan gifts have become highly sought after, due to the excellent quality and signature design. The job-creation and upliftment aspects are the driving force behind the project, as well as allowing mainly rural Shangaan women the opportunity to be creative within the realm of their own traditional background.
Contact: Irma Van Rooyen, Middelplaas, Giyani Road, Letsitele; Tel: 015-345-1458; 015-345-1155; Email: info@kaross.co.za; Web: www.kaross.co.za

Halkett Safaris

Mansel Jackson and Melissa Mansfield have started a safari company affiliated to Halkett House (see their accommodation entry number 332), doing guided tours for small groups of people. They stay off the beaten track and offer highly personal guiding. Given Mansel's background in wildlife management and a number of years doing guiding and walking safaris in the greater Kruger Park, he knows the park like the back of his hand and can offer people a great wildlife experience staying away from the crowds of tourists. They can also gain access to little known gems such as Makapane Caves where tourists never go. Tailor-made, off-the-beaten-track journeys from Limpopo Province to Kruger Park and beyond!
Contact: Halkett Safaris; Tel: 014-743-2525; Email: info@halkett.co.za

Pezulu Tree House Lodge

Claude and Lydia Huberty
Guernsey, Hoedspruit
Tel: 015-793-2724 Fax: 015-793-2253
Email: pezlodge@mweb.co.za Web: www.pezulu.co.za
Cell: 083-294-7831

The sorry victim of a treehouse-free childhood, I was intrigued by the concept of Pezulu - five different reed-and-thatch constructions spread among the trees surrounding the central building, which is itself entwined around a large amarula. They are all hidden from view behind branch and leaf, and many have bits of tree growing up through the floor to provide the most natural of towel rails, stools and loo paper holders. The 'houses' are named after the trees in which they sit: 'False Thorn' has a magnificent shower with views over the Thornybush Reserve – be prepared for inquisitive giraffe; while 'Huilboerboom' is a honeymoon suite set eight metres above ground (privacy even from the giraffe). Pezulu is situated in the Guernsey Conservancy on the edge of the Kruger Park. There are no predators in this area, only plains game, so you and the buck can wander around the property in perfect safety. Activities on offer include the usual two game drives a day. They can also arrange microlight flights and visits to rehabilitation centres... assuming they can persuade you down from the trees. *Children over 6 are welcome.*

Rooms: 5: 2 family units (1 double and 1 twin) and 3 doubles, variously with outside shower, and/or bath.
Price: R740 - R1,00 pp sharing, inclusive of all meals. Singles R890 - R1,100. Children under 12 40% discount. Game drives, microlight flights and other activities extra.
Meals: All meals included. Drinks and game activities extra.
Directions: Ask when booking.

Tshukudu Game Lodge

Ala Sussens

Tshukudu Reserve, Hoedspruit, R40 towards Phalaborwa, Hoedspruit
Tel: 015-793-2476 Fax: 015-793-2078
Email: tshukudugamelodge@radioactivewifi.co.za
Web: www.tshukudulodge.co.za Cell: 082-888-7199

I strolled onto the verandah on a hot dusty day at Tshukudu to find a cheetah sprawled out under one of the dining tables. After my initial panic subsided and it became clear she wasn't going to have me for lunch, I was properly introduced to Savannah. She was hand-raised here, along with other abandoned creatures, and released back into the wild… but she remains a frequent visitor. The other human guests were lounging round the pool watching the warthogs nibbling the lawn into shape and admiring the flying chillies (red-billed hornbills) dive-bombing the birdseed table. Kids will feel very at home here with animal duvets and paw-shaped soaps, while the rest of us can enjoy our private sitting areas, most of which look out onto the bush. After an animated lunch we met our two rangers, who looked after us for the duration of our stay – a great comfort with so many wild critters around! On our bush walk (and kids will LOVE this!), we were accompanied by Prince (a labrador), Smokey (a jackal), Savannah (the above-mentioned cheetah) and Chobe (a lion cub!). As a rehabilitation centre, the animals at Tshukudu are always changing so you could be walking with a serval cat, a squirrel or even an elephant! And after dinner all together in the boma, we managed to persuade our ever-attentive guide to take us to see the porcupines. These secretive and extraordinary creatures stole the show for me, spinning their quills round, as if in a dance, to scare away the approaching jackals.

Rooms: 13: doubles or twins with en-suite showers. 3 have wheelchair facilities. Family cottages available.
Price: R1,544 - R1,650 pp sharing. Singles R1,874 - R2,005. Includes all meals, 2 game drives and a bush walk. Children under 12 half price.
Meals: All-inclusive.
Directions: 4km north of Hoedspruit on R40 towards Phalaborwa, signed on the left.

Mohlabetsi Safari Lodge

Tony and Alma Williamson

Balule Nature Reserve, Hoedspruit
Tel: 015-793-2166 Fax: 015-793-9023
Email: safaris@mohlabetsi.co.za Web: www.mohlabetsi.co.za
Cell: 083-255-4956

Even the drive to the lodge was a game drive… with one hand on the wheel, and the other clutching my camera, dexterously snapping giraffe, waterbuck and warthog. Tony and Alma greeted me with a cleansing fruit cocktail before leading me to a happy table of Swedes sitting down to lunch under thatch. Ice cream topped with treacle-sweet papaya sauce stole the show. Guiltily indolent, I took up Veronica's offer of a pre-safari massage and draped myself over her forest altar, de-stressing to the click and chirrup of a thousand tiny insects. From one safe pair of hands to another, I then found myself up front in the Land Rover watching a leopard watching us. As well as getting close to the 'Big 5' the rangers here have a keen interest in the more secret delights of the bush. They'll point out dung beetles disposing of a mountain of rhino dung, or show you how to brush your teeth with nature's toothbrush and resin toothpaste. Swap tales later under the stars in the giant circular boma as Tony and Alma put on the dinner show, with a prelude of local women singing traditional songs, one of Mohlabetsi, a place of sweet water. Repair to your rondawel or family lodge, with cooling shade and outdoor showers, as well as tasteful authentic touches in the flagstone floors, tribal face-masks and intricate wall hangings. Outside a splendid lawn unfolds to the edge of acacia and amarula, through which the morning walk takes you back to breakfast, stopping first by the lake where the crocodile waits.

Rooms: 8 units: 6 rondawels (4 twin/king and 2 king with outdoor showers) and 2 family lodges (1 twin, 1 double with outdoor showers).
Price: R1,095 - R1,800 pp sharing. Single supplement plus R350. Price includes full board and 2 safari activities.
Meals: Full board.
Directions: 10km north of Hoedspruit along the R40.

Mfubu Lodge & Gallery

Olga Kühnel
Balule Nature Reserve, Phalaborwa
Tel: 015-769-6252 Fax: 015-769-6252
Email: olina@telkomsa.net Web: www.mfubu.com
Cell: 073-416-0451 (bad signal at lodge)

Olga is a wonderful, eccentric hostess and a long-standing GG favourite! Her home, Mfubu Lodge, is also long-standing, propped up as it is on tall stilts to protect against flooding from the Oliphants River which flows past the garden. I've been deeper into the bush, but rarely has it seemed so penetrating. There are no fences here, just the guarantee of hot water, cold beer and animals that come to you. At dinner we ate the best bobotie I can remember and awaited curtain-up. Silently, hippos trotted onto centre stage, a brilliant moon silhouetting them against the white canvas of an alluvial beach. With elephants strolling across the lawn and the proximity of the river I felt glad indeed for the tall stilts keeping us suspended above the action below. The river eases like oil, so in the morning we ran the gauntlet, wading through the water. Safely on the other side, we clambered aboard a Land Rover, mingled with rhino, buffalo and giraffe and watched birds from a hide. The lodge itself consists of a trio of thatched cabins with fans, electric lights and tented fronts, connected by a walkway which weaves amongst trees. Further off, there are two cottages with kitchens, game-viewing platform and art gallery. Olga collects local art and encourages guests to paint, pen or ponder. Early-morning coffee up by the gallery with Olga is a great start to the day. It's not so much "shamrackle" (one of Olga's spoonerisms) as delightfully unrushed. Our friend in the bush.

Rooms: 5: 3 twin cabins sharing two bathrooms; 1 twin timber cottage and 1 double stone cottage, both with own showers.
Price: R650 - R950 pp. Single supplement R100.
Meals: Full breakfast and 3-course dinner included. Drinks not included.
Directions: From Jo'burg N12, from Pretoria N4, through Witbank to Belfast. Left on R540 to Lydenburg, then R36 through Strijdom Tunnel following signs to Phalaborwa. Turn right onto R530 to Mica. 22km from Mica on R530 turn R on dirt road following Mfubu signs (about 9km).

Kurisa Moya Nature Lodge

Lisa Martus and David Letsoalo

Magoebaskloof, Near Polokwane
Tel: 015-276-1131
Email: info@krm.co.za Web: www.krm.co.za
Cell: 082-200-4596

Log cabins in an indigenous forest, a beautiful hand-crafted cottage overlooking mile upon mile of mountains and veld, or a rustic, thick-walled farmhouse? Kurisa Moya offers the lot and the hardest part of your stay will be choosing where to lay your head. I rested mine in the aged farmhouse, rescued by Lisa and her spouse Ben from near dereliction. All three destinations are self-cater-friendly, but home-spun "meals on 4x4 wheels" are on hand. They work tirelessly to tread as lightly as possible on their mountainside environment and that's what makes this such a tranquil place. The stilted cabins (my favourites) are so well hidden by a dense canopy of afro-montane forest that I was quite a surprised when the forest path led me to the wooden door. Bino-less birding is literally from your doorstep or you can go birding with the affable David, one of Africa's top two guides who'll introduce you to Knysna turacos, black-fronted bush shrikes and some 300 other species that are on show when they choose to be. At a candlelit table (guests are encouraged to conserve solar energy) in between mouthfuls of ostrich and the best-ever cabbage salad (trust me, I had five helpings), I learned about the Sotho village home-stays on offer. Guests spend 24 hours experiencing African culture by living it. I knew this was a special place as soon as I stepped onto the stoep and should the waterfall walks, massages, fly-fishing and Kruger expeditions not keep you coming back for more, I'll bet my bottom dollar that the deliciously peaceful atmosphere will.

Rooms: 4 venues: 2 forest cabins sleeping 4, sharing shower; 1 cottage sleeps 6, with outdoor shower; farmhouse with 2 doubles and 3 twins, 4 with en-suite shower and 1 with private bath and shower.
Price: Self-catering R450 - R600 pp. Kids under 12 half price.
Meals: Meals on request.
Directions: Directions emailed on booking.

Hill Top Country Lodge

Eleen and Charles Joubert

46 Lushof Estates, Tzaneen
Tel: 015-307 1590 Fax: 086-689-7259
Email: htclodge@mweb.co.za Web: www.hilltoplodge.co.za
Cell: 082-420-1868 or 076-914-2615

As I ascended past lush mango trees and up through the rainforest garden, I sensed that every green thing was craving rain. And when the clouds finally obliged you could almost hear the sighs of relief… and I, resting on my balcony, joined in this silent hallelujah. The hissing downpour presented me with the perfect excuse to luxuriate in this splendid place and not feel guilty about staying indoors. Over a glass of wine I plotted my evening and settled upon three simple spoily pleasures. Firstly, I wanted to explore this Aladdin's cave of a house that Eleen, a former art lecturer, had spent years creating. Treasures such as ancient pieces of heavy kuba cloths dress the walls and a beautiful hand-carved bench stands in the sitting room. I opted for the sofa (so high that my feet didn't touch the ground) and flicked through an antique copy of 'Unusual African Stories'. Padding across my suite's concrete floor - softened by a cowhide rug - I attended to number two on my list, viz plunging into a slipper-bath full of home-made potions while keeping the door to my outside shower open to the stars. Feeling spoilt - and loving it! - I ticked off number three and slipped into the white expanse of my enormous bed, beneath a plaster wall sculpture depicting ancient African figurines. I woke to a world as refreshed by rain as I had been by the pampering comforts of Hill Top Country Lodge… and the birds sang as I made delicious progress through breakfast. Alas, with no time to explore the walking trails, museums, art galleries and golf courses in the area, with the reappearance of the sun I bid my farewell.

Rooms: 4: all kings with separate bath and showers (3 with outside showers).
Price: R936 – R1,548 pp sharing. Singles R600 – R828.
Meals: Continental buffet and full cooked breakfast included. 4- or 5-course suppers available on request for groups of 8 or more.
Directions: N1 from Jo'burg to Polokwane take the R71 turn-off to Tzaneen. Continue on R71 over four-way stops through Haenertsburg. 30km after Haenertsburg at T-jct turn R R71/R36. After 3km turn left onto R71 off-ramp. Straight over four-way stop and after 4km Hill Top is on left. Map available on website.

Map Number: 20

Entry Number: 330

Mopane Bush Lodge

Paul and Rosemary Hatty, Andrew and Moira Rae

Mapungubwe, Off the R572, Musina
Tel: 083-633-0795 Fax: 015-534-7906 or 086-610-3410
Email: info@mopanebushlodge.co.za Web: www.mopanebushlodge.co.za
Cell: 083-679-8884

This is a fascinating, under-visited frontier of South Africa and both these facts make this a great destination. Hidden in 6,000 hectares of semi-desert mopane scrub, the lodge itself is an oasis where fine food (either taken in the huge, open-plan reception-dining area or outside in the boma round a fire), a swimming pool and intimate cottage-rooms provide all the trappings of sophistication and luxury you could wish for. The game reserve has plains game only, so walking about is safe and I recommend taking the track to a waterhole to birdwatch before dinner. But during the day I loved my two visits to the Mapungubwe National Park, five minutes' down the road. First an early-morning visit to the archeological site of South Africa's earlier version of Great Zimbabwe. This ancient civilisation took place on and around a gigantic rock in dramatic scenery interspersed with giant other-worldly baobab trees. And then a second visit took us to the lush confluence of the Limpopo and Shashi rivers and to a heavenly sundowner spot where you can look out onto Zimbabwe and Botswana. As for wildlife they have it all up here ('big five' etc), but the birdlife takes the palme d'or. You'll find some real rarities, including the broad-billed roller and the collared palm thrush. Another big draw at Mopane is the nearby wild dog breeding centre. I have been round and round South Africa, but this area was a real find and I heartily recommend both the lodge and its environment. *Mountain bikes are available for guests to use.*

Rooms: 8 rondavels: all can be double or twin, with en-suite indoor and outdoor showers.
Price: R1,130 - R1,400 pp. R250 - R450 for off-site tours.
Meals: All meals and all activities on Mopane's own private nature reserve are included.
Directions: Take the N1 from Johannesburg to Polokwane (Pietersberg). Follow signs through town for the R521 to Dendron. Travel 140km on this road to Alldays, then turn right to Pontdrif. Travel for 46km and turn right onto R572 to Musina & Mapungubwe. Mopane Bush Lodge is 29km along this road, just past the cell phone tower on right. Map on web.

Halkett House

Mansel Jackson and Melissa Mansfield
Koelemansrus Road, Naboomspruit
Tel: 014-743-2525 Fax: 014-743-2525
Email: info@halkett.co.za Web: www.halkett.co.za

As soon as my hands left the steering wheel, they were busy shaking other hands, stroking dogs and pouring Pimms down my dusty throat. The bestowers of this wonderful welcome were Mansel and Melissa, rare creatures in their ability to make one feel like a returning friend while effortlessly attending to your slightest whim. They have breathed new life into Halkett, which was bought in 1901 by Mansel's grandfather. Some rooms in some ways have changed little since: family medals from the Boer War are still on display, ancient copies of Shakespearian plays still sit on the book shelf and the walls have surely been privy to many a family story as Jackson generations succeeded one another. Feeling blessed, I took possession of my lovingly resurrected suite. Distressed walls, antique four-poster bed and dark wood wardrobes are made yet more romantic by plump duvets, mosquito nets and candles around a claw-footed bath. The bathroom with its courtyard shower is almost a suite in itself. Next stop, the dining room table, heavy with family silver, where Melissa revealed her secret identity as a master chef-magician. Each course was divine and unexpected and made use – by now I would have expected nothing less - of organic, locally-sourced ingredients. Waking to a cloudless day, Mansel met me with ponies (which he rescued) for a tour from the tennis court through to the old Shangaan village. A quick swim and breakfast (or should I say breakfeast?) later and I dragged myself back to reality. To summarize - gather up your loved ones and hurry to Halkett! *Exclusive hire only. See Limpopo Side Dishes for Halkett Safaris.*

Rooms: 4: 1 king with bath, shower and outside shower; 1 queen with bath and shower; 1 king/ twin with shower; 1 king/ twin in rondavel with shower.
Price: Exclusive hire only. R995 - R1,395 pp.
Meals: All meals included. Drinks excluded.
Directions: From N1 take Mookgophong (Naboomspruit) turn-off onto R101. Go through town, after 16km turn left at Mineral Baths sign. After 2km turn right at Koelemansrus sign. After 7km turn left & follow Halkett signs.

Kololo Game Reserve

Ton and Yvonne Jansen
Bakkerspas Road, Vaalwater
Tel: 014-721-0920 or 014-721-9910 Fax: 014-721-0922
Email: info@kololo.co.za Web: www.kololo.co.za

Don't ask me how, but Kololo manages to be private yet sociable, remote yet accessible… and allows guests to walk solo with zebra and buck one minute and then watch a lion devouring its lunch the next. The lodge is separated from the 20,000 hectares of the Welgevonden Private Game Reserve (to which Kololo guests are permitted unique access) by just an electric fence. The restaurant, which opens to the pool and then on to seemingly endless bushveld, is the beating heart of the lodge, and from here guests cross sweeping lawns, past bottle brush trees and swathes of florescent bougainvillea, to stone-and-thatch bush chalets. With their compact but complete kitchenettes the rustic and unfussy chalets are as private as it is possible to be; a revolutionary ecological air-conditioning system will keep you cool, while your private bush views stretch to the horizon. 'Oom Piet's' (Uncle Pete's), a traditional terracotta farmhouse, has changed little on the outside since its completion in 1916. Inside, Medusa-esque tribal masks and ancient maps adorn thick cooling walls, while an elderly sewing-machine and open fireplace survive from uncle Piet's day. Mounted buck and stuffed eagles on the walls of the luxurious king and queen rooms also doff the cap to a bygone era. With a private pool, boma, and huge dining and kitchen area and showers with infinite views it is an ideal family escape with adventure and relaxation, like everything at Kololo, in perfect equilibrium.

Rooms: 9 chalets: 6 with 1 king/twin all with shower. 1 with 2 king/twins with bath and shwr, 1 with 4 king/twins 3 baths and 1 outside shwr. 1 with 3 king/twins with 3 bathrooms all separate shower.
Price: R650 - R1,500 pp sharing.
Meals: Full breakfast included, other meals on request.
Directions: From Jo'Burg take N1 turn off onto R33 to Modimolle and pass Vaalwater. Turn left after 8km, following signs. Kololo is on right after 29km.

Namibia

Introduction

Namibia is a big country and knowing where to stay has always proved a problem for independent travellers there in the past. Until now, despite the wealth of information on accommodation available, there has never been any help in making the choice, i.e. while many brochures are distributed for free at the airport etc, there was no selective and evocative guide-book hand-picking places with charm and leaving out the rest. Which is were we come in.

I knew that the accommodation gems were there somewhere... but where? What I really needed was a resident expert to show us the way...

Just when I was pondering this very problem, Lily emerged out of my email inbox like the genie from the bottle, and our wishes were granted. She lived in Windhoek for several years and, although she has actually recently moved to the Gabon, is still very much in touch with Namibia and has spent a great deal of that time travelling to every out-of-the-way corner of the country staying at lodges and B&Bs. She is in fact on the road even as I write. She tells me that, with her husband at the wheel, they drove 60,000km in just two years! Her interest was not merely that of the holiday-maker, although her enthusiasm for the wonders of nature to be found across Namibia is certainly catching (see their new photographic book on the country 'Secret Namibia' published by Struik. To buy a copy go to www.amazon.com or contact Struik via www.struik.co.za). She had already written two books on accommodation in Thailand and The Phillipines. By the time we were in contact she already knew which places we wanted for the most part.

This Namibian section does not contain many entries, but we are providing you with really lovely places to stay in all the major areas that appeal to most travellers to the country, viz Windhoek, Swakopmund, Etosha, Sossusvlei, Caprivi, Aus, Namibrand, Naukluft. The photos (many of which were taken by Lily) and descriptions tell their own tale. Each place looks entirely enticing... edible almost!

As always the places to stay that Lily has chosen are all run by friendly enthusiastic people. This is the sine qua non of all GG selections. Our view is that a great guide-book will offer you all sorts of different excitements while never compromising on the essence of hospitality.

If you are about to make use of this part of our guide-book, well, frankly I am jealous!

Simon.

The next part of this introduction is by Lily.

DRIVING IN NAMIBIA
You can drive a saloon car on many roads in Namibia: the main tarmac roads from Windhoek to Swakopmund, to Etosha or to Rundu/Katima Mulilo/Kasane; and also

on the many excellent dirt roads of the country. But you will definitely feel more comfortable with a 4x4 on the dirt roads. If it rains a 4x4 is definitely the best plan. However, in some parts of Damaraland (for example), if the river is flooding (a rare occurrence), even with a 4x4 you might wait from a few hours to a few days for the water level to drop. That is Namibia for you! So it is always a good idea to check with the place you are going to visit to see if you're going to need a 4x4 and if, during the rainy season, the rivers can be crossed.

All the dirt roads are very well signposted, quite amazing in the middle of nowhere! In my experience, the best map – even if it is not always perfect - is "Map Studio Tourist Atlas - Namibia" published by Struik, and this can be bought in CNA. This map is also very useful as it indicates the fuel stations.

Take care to refill your tank every time you find a fuel station, as there are not that many in some parts of the country.

CAR HIRE
If you get enough time to visit and have a tight budget, it is much cheaper to rent a car in South Africa than in Namibia…but you will have to drive a long way. For example Cape Town to Windhoek is about 1400km. You can make interesting stops on the way, of course, but the distances generally in Namibia are huge.

PRICES IN NAMIBIA.
Accommodation is Namibia is more expensive than in South Africa, despite the fact that it is generally not as sophisticated. This is a pity, but you have to consider the fact that the guest farms or small lodges are often very remote, and that makes everything more logistically difficult and therefore expensive to run. For example in some places the owners have to drive 2 hours - or sometimes even 4 hours! - to do their shopping. So be prepared to spend a little more, but I never met anyone who felt that Namibia was bad value for money.

In Namibia there is a wonderful sense of wilderness. You can drive for hours without passing another car. The average size of a farm, for example, is 8,000 hectares! As you drive through most of the country you will see amazing landscapes of red sand dunes, fascinating rock formations and many animals and plants that don't exist anywhere else. The Caprivi Strip is very different – lush and green - and it is cheaper than Botswana and Zimbabwe although you will see the same kind of wetland terrain and wildlife.

MOBILE/CELL PHONES
In Namibia, many places have no coverage for cell phone. They work in the main towns (Windhoek, Swakopmund, Rundu, Katima Mulilo) but more whimsically in other parts. A word of advice: try calling from the highest point of the road or guest farm.

ADVANCE BOOKING
This is essential across the whole country except perhaps in the cities.

TELEPHONE NUMBERS
To call Namibia from the UK dial 00264, then drop the 0 from the local code. The numbers given in the Namibian chapter are all from within Namibia.

WILDLIFE

On the main roads you will see signboards with symbols of a kudu crossing, or a warthog crossing etc…This might seem quaint, but one day in a 100km stretch we counted 50 warthogs on the bend of the roads! Many accidents occur because of kudu or oryx crossing the road – this occurs mostly at dawn, but not only. Or on dirt roads. As they are often excellent, people forget that they are driving on a dirt road and go too fast. It is advisable to keep your maximum speed down to between 80km and 100km an hour on dirt roads.

TIPPING

In restaurants you give 10%, and if you pay by credit card, you write down the tip you want to give and add it to the bill.

TIME OF YEAR

All seasons are nice in Namibia, so there is no obvious best time to visit. It depends what you are looking for.

Winter in Namibia is approximately from June to end of August. During the day it is 20 to 25 degrees, very agreeable for hiking. At night, the temperature can drop to 4 degrees, or even to around zero.
Summer is approximately from November to March. It can be pretty hot during the day, 30 degrees or more in some desert areas.
In good years, there is a small rainy season in November. The main rainy season usually starts in January and ends in April, but in some regions, such as the south the rains come only every 2 years or even less frequently, and never last long. Except in the Caprivi, you will never have whole days of rain. The rain lasts for one or two hours a day. Namibia is beautiful after the rains, all green and blooming. It is hard to imagine that it's the same country that was so dry and yellow before!
But during the rains it is more difficult to see animals.
In the Caprivi, when the rain starts, the elephants go deep into the forest, but the hippo are still there and it is a good season for birding. It is very hot and humid during the rainy season in the Caprivi.
In Swakopmund, it is cool most of the time all year round (14 to 18 degrees during the day) and misty, except during summer where the temperature is very pleasant. Namibians love to go to Swakopmund to escape the heat. The sea is generally freezing (around 12 degrees) – that's what I think, anyway, but some people don't seem to mind! - because of the Benguela current. That explains the huge seal colony in Cape Cross. In summer the water can reach the dizzy heights of 20 degrees.

Lily.

The Hilltop Guesthouse

Angela Curtis and Allen Uys

12 Lessing Street,
Windhoek
Tel: 061-249-116
Fax: 061-247-818
Email:
hilltop@iafrica.com.na
Web:
www.thehilltophouse.com
Cell: 081-127-4936

Hilltop is a Bavarian-style building (1958) constructed, unsurprisingly, on a hill in a quiet cul-de-sac. The house is surrounded by a wooden balcony and guarded by a majestic araucaria that stands in the garden. Formerly a photographic studio, it was transformed by Angela and Allen into a guest-house full of character. They have retained the old-world look of the interior with its Oregon-pine floors, wood-lined semi-circular doors and dark, colonial furniture - these contrast strikingly with the ecru walls decorated with watercolours of animals. The Honeymoon suite is charming, with an antique fireplace remodelled in earthenware tiles. Antique charm, certainly, but you have every modern convenience as well. Meals are served in your room or on the garden terrace near the swimming pool looking out at the view over Klein Windhoek. Allen adores cooking and he also takes care of the service himself. His cuisine is light and creative: I feasted on an excellent spiced leek consommé followed by a tasty chicken curry with couscous and vegetables. Angela's specialities are the raising of white shepherd dogs - to whom she'll take great pleasure in introducing you - and making gourmet desserts (in that order). Both are absolutely charming hosts and very happy and able to advise you on your travel arrangements. And guess what? At Hilltop, you have both freshly-squeezed orange juice and great coffee for breakfast... details perhaps, but indicative of the approach here.

Rooms: 7: 1 single, 3 doubles and 2 family rooms; 1 single in a separate cottage.
Price: N$1,250 double, single N$700, triple N$1,700 and family room N$1,900.
Meals: Full breakfast included. Prices vary from N$25 to N$90 for other meals.
Directions: Take Nujoma Drive from international airport. Turn R at Nelson Mandela Ave, L at Robert Mugabe Ave, L again at Lilien Crohn St and L again at Langenhoven. Then take a R into Promenaden Rd and a final R into Lessing St.

Map Number: 16

Entry Number: 334

Vondelhof Guesthouse

Yvonne Schadee
2 Puccini Street, Windhoek
Tel: 061-248-320 Fax: 061-240-373
Email: vondelhof@mweb.com.na Web: www.vondelhof.com

As you approach Vondelhof your eye is first captured by the green turret of the old house in the middle of the garden. The atmosphere here, informal and convivial, is down to Yvonne who so effortlessly puts her guests at their ease with attention that is at once personal and relaxed. She looks after everything, from the booking to the cooking, and she is always ready to listen to you, to help with reservations or trips into town…. The outdoor patio is the focal point from which emanate the reception area, low buildings harbouring the bedrooms, the restaurant and the verandah. Guests come there to have a drink, write or simply to relax in one of the sun-loungers displayed around the swimming pool embedded in its wooden deck. The rooms are comfortable, each slightly different from the others with original crete-stone walls the colour of sand. They are simply, but tastefully furnished with tall wooden giraffes, basketwork and African fabrics. One of the rooms in the main building has a large wooden deck overlooking the gardens. Children will be delighted to find a jungle gym and a trampoline in the garden.

Rooms: 8: 7 double rooms and 1 triple room all with en-suite bathroom.
Price: Doubles N$405 pp sharing; singles N$560; triples N$320 pp sharing.
Meals: Continental breakfast buffet included. Light lunches from N$17.50.
Directions: Leaving the international airport, turn right onto the B6. When entering Windhoek after approximately 42km, turn right onto Sam Nujoma Drive and follow all the way through city centre. Go underneath the railway line, turn right onto Hosea Kutako Drive, then turn left into Puccini Street.

Bagatelle Kalahari Game Ranch

Fred and Onie Jacobs
On D1268, Mariental
Tel: 063-240-982 or 061-224-712 Fax: 063-241-252 or 061-224-217
Email: info@bagatelle-kalahari-gameranch.com
Web: www.bagatelle-kalahari-gameranch.com

On my arrival, the raucous cries of peacocks in the midst of the red parallel-running sand dunes of the Kalahari made me wonder if I had a touch of sunstroke! But it is just that Onie has a passion for animals: 38 peacocks, 7 cats who lounge at the entry in a wicker basket (taking turns in pairs!), 9 dogs, 4 cheetahs entrusted by the Cheetah Conservation Fund and several orphaned animals that Onie feeds by bottle… a delight for children. The lodge is the former home of Fred and Onie and with all their furniture and décor still in place, the atmosphere is warm, personal and relaxed. The library, near the fireplace, is filled with books about Namibia. You serve yourself from the fridge in the kitchen or from the bar, writing down what you take. Each of the different spaces of the lodge opens onto the next until you reach a shaded verandah overlooking the pool and the open air lapa. In the evenings, everyone gathers here to enjoy a good dinner in a convivial atmosphere, seated at candlelit tables that are arranged in a semi-circle facing the campfire. The air-conditioned chalets are all very comfortable, but it is the Dune chalets that command superb views over the Kalahari landscape of red dunes dotted with acacias. Each Dune chalet bathroom is equipped with a wonderful bathtub set in an alcove so that you can contemplate glorious sunsets whilst lying in your bath, sipping a chilled glass of wine!

Rooms: 10: 4 Dune chalets with en-suite bath and shower and 6 Strohbale chalets with en-suite shower.
Price: N$1,150 pp sharing for Dune chalet and N$1,050 pp sharing for strohbale chalet (additional adult possible in strohbale N$650). Single supplement N$350.
Meals: Full breakfast and afternoon tea included. N$95 light lunch. N$165 dinner (buffet style).
Directions: Accessible from Kalkrand and Mariental. On D1268, 25km from the intersection with the C20, and 40km from the intersection with the C21.

Klein Aus Vista

Piet, Willem and Francis Swiegers

2km west of Aus on the B4
Tel: 063-258-021 or 063-258-116 Fax: 063-258-021
Email: ausvista@namibhorses.com Web: www.namibhorses.com and
www.gondwana-desert-collection.com

Set against the Aus Mountains almost a mile above sea level, Klein Aus Vista overlooks the endless plains of the Southern Namib Desert. This is a proper family-run business managed by the friendly Swiegers brothers and sister, Piet, Willem and Francis. Near the reception and restaurant, the Desert Horse Inn offers tastefully-decorated rooms that are scattered on a small hillside each with a verandah facing the sunset. For those who seek solitude, the Eagles Nest chalets at the foot of an impressive chaos of granite boulders and just 7km from the lodge will be the right option. The rocks have been integrated into the buildings, hugging the chalets or emerging in the interiors in the most unexpected places. Each self-catering chalet is different: 'The Rock', my favourite, is perched on the side of a hill between two enormous boulders. The interiors are spacious, rustic and imaginative, each with a fireplace for cold winter nights. In the kitchen, the table is already set and the fridge is full of cold drinks. In the evening, the fiery rays of the setting sun touch the rocks and the chalets in dramatic fashion. The landscape around the Aus Mountains, not far from the red dunes of the Namib Desert, is spectacular and a paradise for hikers, with numerous trails on the 51,000 hectares of the private Sperrgebiet Rand Park. The flora is exceptionally rich after winter rains and boasts a stunning variety of succulent plants that paint the landscape in purples and yellows at times. You'd need a couple of days to fully explore Klein Aus Vista's own park and neighbouring Namib Naukluft Park. Most of the excursions offer the opportunity to visit the wild horses of Garub, 20km away in the Namib Naukluft Park.

Rooms: 6 self-catering chalets in 'Eagles Nest Lodge'; 24 rooms in 'Desert Horse Inn'.
Price: Eagles Nest Chalets: N$725 pp sharing B&B, N$890 single B&B; Desert Horse Inn: N$495 pp sharing B&B, N$620 single B&B. Rates only applicable till 31 Oct 2008.
Meals: N$66 breakfast, N$88 lunch, N$165 dinner.
Directions: Accessible from Aus (2km) and from Lüderitz (115km) on B4.

Büllsport Guestfarm

Johanna and Ernst Sauber
On C14, Naukluft Mountains
Tel: 063-693 371/63 Fax: 063-693-372
Email: info@buellsport.com Web: www.buellsport.com

In the heart of the Naukluft Mountains, Büllsport is the rallying point for hikers of all nationalities. Numerous excursions are detailed on their website. Don't miss the very scenic Naukluft Plateau Excursion and Quiver Tree Hike. After an early-morning breakfast, a game drive will take you to the top of the plateau – en route you will see moutain zebra, klipspringer, springbok, oryx and kudu. At the top you set off walking for 3 hours along a gorge with quiver trees growing up its steep slopes. The presence of water makes this a magical spot; the river is bordered with fig trees where birds and baboons live and in summer it is a treat to bathe in the crystalline water pools. And, at the end of the gorge there is a 4x4 patiently waiting with cold drinks! Then, in the evening, with everyone reunited at a big communal table, animated conversation takes place with Ernst and Johanna present too. Belonging to the third generation of Saubers living at Büllsport, Ernst is a mine of information on the history and the environment of his region. Johanna is passionate about horses which she rears. Beginners can go riding by the hour, while the more experienced can go on horse safaris lasting several days. The biggest draw here is the amazing natural environment which you can explore in an informal and unpretentious atmosphere with enthusiastic hosts.

Rooms: 6 double rooms, 1 triple room, and 1 family room (sleeping 4) with en-suite bathroom (shower).
Price: N$830 single room; N$1,460 double room; N$1,970 triple room. Naukluft Plateau & Quiver Tree Valley Hike: N$350; Rock Arch: $175; Scenic Farm & Game Drive (2 hrs): N$150. Sossusvlei excursions and horse-riding options (incl' overnight) on request.
Meals: Breakfast, Coffee and Cake, and dinner included. N$95 lunch.
Directions: Accessible from Maltahöhe, Walvis Bay or Windhoek. Büllsport is on the C14 at the junction with D1206 and D854.

Map Number: 15

Sossusvlei Desert Lodge

Tarryn Davidson
NamibRand Nature Reserve
Tel: +27-11-809-4300 Fax: +27-11-809-4400
Email: safaris@andbeyond.com Web: www.andbeyond.com

Cradled against ancient mountains in splendid isolation, Sossusvlei Desert Lodge combines extravagance, refinement, intimacy and wonderful local hospitality. Its location, the immense 180,000 hectare private reserve of the NamibRand, is absolutely fantastic! The futuristic architecture of the lodge, in curves of glass and stone, resonates strangely well with the barren and spectacular beauty of the surrounding countryside: vast red dune systems, punctuated with vegetation, golden plains that stretch to infinity and high sullen mountains in tortuous shapes. The immense 10 desert villas are on split levels; the sitting room leads out onto a private veranda and the bedroom has a huge bed beneath a star-gazing skylight. Naturally the villas are strong on creature comforts too: air-con, bar, CD system, fireplace, glass-walled bathroom, second outdoor shower and, if the mood takes you, the materials with which to draw your surroundings! The days pass too quickly here: wallowing in the luxury of your villa; savouring delicious meals; going for a morning walk; taking off on game drives into this striking reserve in search of oryx, springbok, zebra and ostrich; enjoying a romantic sundowner at the top of a petrified dune or comfortably seated on one of the decks back at the lodge. In the evenings you might be surprised to discover a very sophisticated observatory where an astronomer can point out the stars for you.

Rooms: 10 desert villas with split-level sitting area, en-s bathroom with shower & outdoor shower.
Price: $N2,650 pppn low season to $N5,000 pppn high season. No sing supp for 1st 2 rooms; 50% off full rate after that. Scheduled safari activities in NamibRand Nature Reserve, emergency evacuation insurance, transfers to/from airstrip & laundry incl'.
Meals: 3 meals, soft drinks, house wine, spirits, beers, tea, coffee, refreshments on game drives incl'.
Directions: About 130km south of Sesriem, accessible from Solitaire, Malthahöhe or Helmeringhausen, on C27. Access also by charter flight to Sossusvlei Desert Lodge's private airstrip which is 6 minutes from Lodge.

Zebra River Lodge

Rob and Marianne Field

on D850, Naukluft area
Tel: 063 693-265 Fax: 063-693-266
Email: marianne.rob@zebrariver.com Web: www.zebrariver.com

Some places, and Zebra River Lodge is one, seem to be blessed by the gods! From the road there is no hint of the dramatic beauty of this 13,000-hectare property in the heart of the Zaris Mountains. Having visited several times, I have still not explored all of the hiking trails there; the most spectacular of these crosses a canyon almost as deep as that of Fish River (just 60m less), at the end of which is a spring surrounded by centenary ficus. The limestone mountains are beautifully striated and form terraces where comiphora and moringa trees grow. Not only is this some of the most beautiful landscape in Namibia, but you will also be delighted by the warm and friendly welcome from Marianne and Rob. In the evening, everyone gathers in the living room, filled with a variety of objects, that give it great eclectic charm - antique pine furniture, dishes, old coffee-grinders, bouquets of dried flowers and Rob's own superb photographs of the dunes. You find the same atmosphere in the décor of the rooms. The new suite perched on the hill is particularly special! Marianne's cooking is excellent and it is a pleasure to stay on and chat beside the fire, enjoying the excellent wines chosen by Rob. He has a passion for the fascinating geology and palaeontology of the region. If you ask in advance, Rob will take you to the Sossusvlei dunes or into the Namib Naukluft National Park.

Rooms: 8 double rooms with en-suite shower and 1 honeymoon suite with en-suite bathroom.
Price: N$790 pp sharing in double room. Singles N$810.
Meals: Full breakfast, light lunch and 3-course dinner included.
Directions: Accessible from Maltahöhe, Duwisib, Sesriem, Büllsport. Zebra River Lodge is on the D850, 19km from the intersection with the D854 and 10km from the intersection with the D855. Access also by plane on the brand new airstrip.

Barchan Dunes Retreat

Hannetjie and Willem Van Rooyen
On D1275, Sesriem area
Tel: 062-682-031 Fax: 062-682-031
Email: barchan@iway.na Web: www.barchandunes.com and
www.natron.net/tour/barchan-dunes

Barchan Dunes is one of my favourite places in Namibia. Hannetjie, with her natural charm, and Willem, with his sense of humour, are truly great hosts. Their friendly welcome is reinforced by the enthusiasm of their dogs who rush to meet your car; and the dogs are followed in their turn by three cute pet meerkats! The generously-sized cottages, each decorated in a different theme, are built into the crescent-shaped hollow of the dunes that overlook a serene landscape of mountains and rocky outcrops in the distance. In the evening, dinner is served communally in the elegant dining room. This is a highlight, as much for the quality and quantity of Hannetjie's culinary skills (make sure you prepare for this by dieting beforehand!) as for the good conversation. Willem generously serves some excellent wines - you find your glass refilled as if by magic - and it is all included in the price. The retreat merits a stay of at least two nights to appreciate the beauty of the surrounding area and simply to pamper yourself. Don't miss walking in the canyon among the ghostly silver trunks of the moringa trees. Willem can organise excursions into the dunes of Sossusvlei, one hour away (book in advance). Late in the afternoon, Willem takes you on a game drive to see the 40 oryx on his farm or to contemplate the sunset, drink in hand, from a viewpoint on the rose-coloured dunes. "Another boring day ends in Africa!" he concludes with a laugh.

Rooms: 6: 2 rooms inside the main house, 3 cottages & 1 self-catering cottage. All en-suite shower.
Price: N$796 pp sharing full board. N$420 pp sharing breakfast included. Self-catering N$775 per unit. No single supplement. Farm drive also included.
Meals: Full board includes breakfast, coffee and cake in the afternoon, 3-course dinner, malt and soft drinks. In others cases, meals on request at www.kuangukuangu.com
Directions: On D1275. Accessible from Walvis Bay take C14, turn L on D1275 "Nauchas" for 15km; or from Rehoboth take C24, in Nauchas turn R to D1275 to Spreetshoogte Pass. After pass it is 20km.

Kobo Kobo Hills

Kirsten Behrens

Off D1985, halfway between Windhoek and the coast, Karibib District
Tel: 064-204-711 Fax: 064-204-297
Email: info@kobokobo.com.na Web: www.kobokobo.com.na
Cell: 081-127-1712 (main telephone!)

Kobo Kobo was born of the fertile imagination of Kirsten's father, Gert Behrens, who was a photographer. It is a secret and magical place, making an ideal retreat for a group of friends. The cottages, with their stone walls and thick thatched roofs, are built on a sharp, rocky outcrop, an islet dominating the rugged landscape of granite boulders. The rocks are incorporated into the interior design and determine the shape and form of the cottages, each of which is different. The whitewashed interiors are rustic and cosy and remain cool even at the height of summer. The views are all superb and, with the beds often set right at the level of the window overlooking the precipice, you can admire them while lying down in comfort. The rallying point is the lapa, where there is a swimming pool embedded in the rocks, a bar and an observation point sheltered by a thatched roof. From there, you have a view below of the dry riverbed and a waterhole, overlooked by a tree filled with green parrots, where the animals come to drink. Aided by her mother, Kirsten is the enchanting fairy of the realm. She will look after your well-being with the greatest attention, concoct wonderful breakfasts and barbeques full of flavour, and she can take you on a sundowner game drive to the summit of a hill.

Rooms: 5 thatched cottages (2 for families), all with indoor wash basin, some with outdoor shower, some indoor shower; and 3 North African-style cottages, each with en-suite shower.
Price: N$850 pp. No single supplements. Minimum group size of 4 people or minimum of 2 nights.
Meals: Full breakfast, lunch and dinner included.
Directions: From Walvis Bay or Swakopmund drive along C14 or C28 respectively, into Namib Naukluft Park for about 150km. Then turn onto D1985. Halfway along road, turn off onto farm road, passing through 3 gates (that are open) for 10km. Possible access also from Windhoek and Sossusvlei. Detailed map on the web site.

Sam's Giardino

Samuel Egger
89 Anton Lubowski Ave, Swakopmund
Tel: 064-403-210 Fax: 064-403-500
Email: reservation@giardinonamibia.com Web: www.giardinonamibia.com

"Hospitality with a touch of heart" is the slogan of Sam's Giardino. Holding a Swiss diploma in hotel management from Lausanne, Samuel Egger is no newcomer to the world of hospitality and this is immediately apparent. The guests are welcomed by an efficient and smiling team, all of whom are completely interchangeable: each member of staff takes it in turn in a very modern kitchen to cook the 5-course menu no less! A tasting of South African wines is offered in the impressive cellar and dinners are served with flair at individual tables near the new fireplace. Food and drink are an essential part of the experience here! The atmosphere throughout is convivial, the guests gathering in the living room to watch National Geographic CDs, or browsing in a very well-stocked library. There is a cosy lounge on the gallery upstairs with tourist info, where you can organize your visits while having a coffee. Sam will help you with advice on the main points of interest, and book activities and restaurants on your behalf. Sam's Giardino, a comfortable house built in Swiss style with a glass wall in front, is found in the midst of its own bijou garden with rose trees and a fish pond. The rooms are spread out over two floors and decorated in tones of red and green. Sam's passion, and this you will understand when you meet her, is his pedigree bernese hound, Ornella, whom Sam refers to as the Public Relations Manager. The guest house has this year undergone a complete refurb, new bar, new lounge, new showers....

Rooms: 10: 9 with en-suite shower.
Price: N$900 - N$1,150 double. N$700 - N$900 single. Dogs and cats also welcome if well-behaved! (by prior arrangement).
Meals: Swiss breakfast included. N$190 - N$220 for 5-course dinner. N$100 wine tasting at 6.30pm.
Directions: In Swakopmund, from Sam Nujoma turn left into Moses/Garoeb street, then left again into Anton Lubowski Ave. 15 minutes on foot from town centre.

The Stiltz B&B

Danie Holloway and Catharina Hofmeister

Strand Street South, Swakop River, Swakopmund
Tel: 064-400-771 Fax: 064-400-711 Email: info@thestiltz.in.na
Web: www.thestiltz.in.na Cell: 081-127-2111(Danie), 081-107-3525
(Catharina), 081-149-4979 (after hours)

You enter the Stiltz as if through a secret door to a well-guarded kingdom of sea, wind and surrounding dunes, and yet it is just a few minutes' walk to the centre of town. Built high up on stilts on the edge of the dry Swakop River's bed, the wooden, thatched chalets are linked together by walkways. If possible, ask for a chalet facing the sea. The architect, Danie Holloway - who is clearly partial to elevated structures having built The Raft at Walvis Bay, The Tug at Swakopmund and Erongo Wilderness Lodge - has created something magical here. At night, you are lulled to sleep by the sound of the waves and in the morning you wake to contemplate the wild tamarisk bushes as pink flamingos fly overhead. All the chalets are big and bright and are colourfully and stylishly decorated. Wood, sometimes collected from the riverbed, has been used throughout, from the light, twisted wood of the sofas to the large double bed. The bathrooms are made from rosewood, glass, stainless steel and coloured ceramic tiles and you have a wonderful shower with a large showerhead. Breakfasts, served in the honeycomb, polygonal structure of wood and glass, are superb. The new huge luxury Villa is extremely atttractive with an incredible view onto the sea.

Rooms: 10 chalets: 3 twins and 4 doubles, 1 honeymoon, 1 family (sleeps 4) and 1 Villa (sleeps 6). All with en-suite bathroom.
Price: From N$585 - N$700 pp sharing. Singles from N$880 - N$995. Family unit N$1,995 (4 pp). Villa: price on request (2, 4 or 6 persons).
Meals: Full breakfast included. Selection of restaurants, including 'The Tug' (good seafood), 5 mins away.
Directions: In Swakopmund, from Sam Nujoma, turn left into Strand Street (along ocean), pass "The Tug" restaurant and the aquarium, turn left at Gull's Cry, and The Stiltz is on your right.

Kunene River Lodge

Peter and Hillary Morgan
D3701
Tel: 065-274-300; For reservations call Reservation Destination on
061-224-712 Fax: 061-224-217
Email: reservations@resdes.com.na Web: www.kuneneriverlodge.com

Peter and Hillary, an English couple, came to stay at Kunene River Lodge on a visit to their daughter who was then working in Namibia as a volunteer... and fell in love with the place. In an admirable and dramatic display of free will, six months later they had sold up in the UK and become the owners. They have since infused the place with new energy. At Kunene River Lodge, there is no unnecessary luxury but you feel the serene atmosphere, the magic presence of the Kunene, bordered with magnificent jackalberries, wild jasmine, ficus, mopanes and bamboo. The area is well known to ornithologists because of the endemic species found here, one of which being the Cinderella waxbill. Peter is passionate about birds and has already counted over 230 species. He will take you to watch them by boat, preferably very early in the morning or late in the afternoon at sundowner time. The rooms have been built in a garden of flowers behind the camp sites by the river. So, it is the latter that have the best view, which is very democratic! You will have every opportunity to enjoy the view as well, on the footpaths along the river or on the huge wooden terrace, built on piles, where meals are served. Activities not to miss are birdwatching, rafting on the rapids in the Onduruso Gorge, canoeing, Cinderella birding trips, fishing or a visit to a Himba family.

Rooms: 7 bungalows (5 with 2 double beds and 2 with 3 single beds) and 4 A-frame chalets, all with en-suite shower.
Price: Chalet: N$520 pp sharing and N$704 single. De Luxe Roooms N$750pp sharing and N$1050 single.
Meals: Breakfast included. Lunch and dinner à la carte.
Directions: Via Ruacana towards Swaarbooisdrift or via Opuwo-Epembe (D3700 - D3701). Gravel roads.

Mushara Lodge

Mariza and Marc Pampe

8km from Namutoni gate of Etosha National Park
Tel: 067-229-106 Fax: 067 229-107
Email: reservations@mushara-lodge.com Web: www.mushara-lodge.com

I arrived at Mushara with the first rains, an unforgettable moment in Namibia as a heavy perfume of dry grasses and scorched earth fills the air. Mariza and Marc built the lodge ten years ago, naming the lodge after the purple pod terminalia trees, 'mushara' in the local Ovambo language. The immense interior room with its high ceiling, incorporating the reception, bar and lounge, reminds me of a scene from *Alice in Wonderland* with the play of mirrors reflecting the garden and the ostrich egg chandeliers like stars. The wooden screens allow for cosy seating arrangements; leather sofas, kilim carpets, cashmere throws, paintings and drawings collected by Marc's parents and black-and-white photographs of elephants all combine to give the area a refined atmosphere. Under Mariza's supervision, dinner is an elegant affair of candles and white cloths - a pleasure for the eye as well as for the taste buds. The air-conditioned chalets are large and very comfortable, decorated with the same mix of modern and traditional Africa. I couldn't imagine how the two newer 'Villa Musharas' could really surpass these already superb chalets, but an involuntary "Ah!" of admiration sprang to my lips as I walked in! A piece of advice: don't plan to do much else than bathe in all the luxury. My desire to hit the hiking trail was quickly subdued by the fact that a lion had been seen there some days before. The luxury of Mushara can make you forget that you are at the entrance of the Etosha Park!

Rooms: 10 doubles, 2 singles & 1 triple, all with en-suite showers. 2 luxury 'Villa Musharas' with living-room, bedroom, en-s bath & shower. Family House with living room, 2 bedrooms and 2 bathrooms.
Price: DB&B: N$2,200 per double room. N$1,100 per single room. N$3,300 per triple room. 'Villa Mushara' is fully inclusive: N$3,800 pp sharing first night, N$3,500 2nd night, N$3,000 all nights after that. Family House N$4,400.
Meals: Full breakfast & dinner included. N$80 lunch or packed lunch N$55. Full board included in Villa Mushara.
Directions: Accessible from Tsumeb, after 73km on B1 turn L direction Namutoni gate. Mushara 8km before gate of park.

Map Number: 24

Etosha Mountain Lodge

Sonderwater Farm, D2680, Etosha area
Tel: 067- 687 090/1 Fax: 067- 687 092
Email: etoshamountainlodge@iway.na
Web: www.etosha-mountainlodge.com

Etosha Mountain Lodge borders the southwestern part of the Etosha National Park. But with their own 48,000 hectares, populated by both black and white rhino, giraffe, eland, sable antelope, zebra, waterbuck, kudu and oryx, among many others, you may not need to leave this place… especially as you will feel so deliciously well! Here you have luxury and space. The architecture is such that all the rooms, including the bathrooms, open out onto natural vistas through numerous picture windows. Only the most beautiful, natural materials have been used: open-face stone walls, superb flame colours in schist floors, thatched roofs, polished wooden railway-sleeper furniture. Colourful cotton veil curtaining at the high windows adds a flamboyant touch. The principal building is a honeycomb of juxtaposed cells, built on wooden piles and linked by a circular exterior terrace. It overlooks an attractive grey-tinted turquoise swimming pool, stunningly set in a teak deck. The service is irreproachably professional yet very friendly too, with great attention to detail, such as in the mopane leaves which bind the table napkins and the scattering of pretty seeds on the tablecloths. As for the subtly-spiced meals, they are as much a delight to the eye as to the palate. For those who can't do without computers, there is even an impressive Internet corner at your disposal. *No kids under 8 I'm afraid.*

Rooms: 6 bedrooms in 3 duplex cottages and 1 suite with private plunge pool. All rooms have an en-suite bathroom with bath and shower.
Price: N$1,250 - N$2,850 pp sharing; singles N$1,600 - N$3,600. Game drives: N$170.
Meals: Full breakfast, afternoon tea, and dinner included. Suite rates are fully-inclusive (lunch and game drives included). Lunch N$65; dinner N$180.
Directions: Accessible from Kamanjab or from Outjo. From Kamanjab take C40, turn on 2671, then after 27km turn L on 2680 for further 23km. From Outjo, before Okuakuejo gate, turn L on D2695, then 2671 & 2680. Check direction with lodge.

Hobatere Lodge

Steve and Louise Braine
Next to Otjovasandu gate of Etosha west
Tel: 067-687-066 Fax: 067-687-067
Email: hobatere@mweb.com.na
Web: www.africa-adventure.org/h/hobatere/index.html

Hobatere, a concession area of 32,000 hectares bordering the Etosha National Park, is blessed with a beautiful undulating landscape of hills, trees and rocks. During day game drives you have a very good chance of seeing numerous elephants, lions, hyenas, zebras, elands, kudus and giraffes. When we visited, the elephants were right at the foot of the thatched deck at the swimming pool and, from the hide overlooking the waterhole, 300 metres from the lodge, we watched five lions hunting. Later that night we heard them roaring not far from the lodge. On a night game drive, quite rare in Namibia, we encountered the nocturnal wildlife: spring hares jumping from their holes, nightjars landing on the track; we even saw a cheetah and a wild cat. Steve and Louise, who have operated the concession for the past 19 years, are the soul of the place and their kind, informal but attentive welcome assures that, once found (Hobatere means 'find me'), it is a place to which you will want to return. Steve has a great sense of humour and is passionate about nature. No creature is too small or insignificant in his book and he shares his knowledge of birds, butterflies and insects, as well as the larger beasts, with infectious enthusiasm. He also organises birding trips in Namibia. The rallying point in the evenings is the stone terrace in front of reception, surrounded by a rock garden, where you dine well under Louise's discreet but watchful eye.

Rooms: 14: 6 chalets, 3 double, 3 twin and 2 single rooms with en-s shower. 1 rustic tree-house overlooking waterhole.
Price: Dec to Feb & June: N$635 pp sharing, singles N$705; Mar to May, July to Nov N$895 pp sharing, singles N$990. Children sadly can't go on guided walks or night drives due to lions. Game drive N$200 pp; night drive N$230 pp; morning guided walk: N$170 pp.
Meals: Full breakfast and dinner included. Lunch from N$45 - N$95; dinner N$145.
Directions: On C35, 64km north of Kamanjab towards Opuwo on tarmac. 1km past Otjovasandu entrance to Etosha Park L at entrance to Hobatere property. Follow dirt rd for 16km to lodge.

Map Number: 23   Entry Number: 348

Ndhovu Safari Lodge

Horst Kock

Divundu, Caprivi
Tel: 066-259-901 or 061-224-712 Fax: 066-259-153 or 061-224-217
Email: ndhovu@iway.na Web: www.ndhovu.com
Cell: 081-236-2542

On the banks of the River Okavango, opposite Bwawata National Park and only 4km from Mahango Park, you will find a tented camp secreted amidst tall trees, with a backing track of running water, the sporadic grunts of hippos and birdsong. The camp was bought and renovated in December 2004 by Horst who upped sticks from his farm near Windhoek and headed for the green Caprivi. This was a place where, personally, I felt unbelievably well! The lapa opens onto the river and is decorated with originality, the central living area made from rattan, littered with embroidered cushions from South Africa and framed by sculptured mirrors reflecting the water, which is omnipresent here. You dine in style at rustic rosewood tables, and off Zimbabwean ceramic dishes, hand-painted in naïve colours. Amateurs - and I am one - will be delighted to be able to buy these here. The tents all face the river, each one graced with a verandah and gaily decorated in pretty cottons. My night was punctuated by an atmospheric cacophony of animal calls, the croaking of frogs, the howls of hyenas and in the really wee hours the roar of a lion.... Horst, with unextinguishable enthusiasm, will take you out in his motor-boat to go fishing, or to bird-watch or just to be there, glass in hand, at the spectacular sunsets. Marango Park is particularly interesting as much for its fauna - rare roan antelope, lechwe, nyala, elephant, buffalo - as for its very varied landscapes which alternate between marsh, prairie, baobab groves and forest.

Rooms: 8 tents with en-suite shower, plus one floating tent on river. Tents 6, 7 and 8 are very private but farther from the lapa. 1 exclusive campsite.
Price: N$875 pp sharing. N$300 single supplement. 10% increase from the 1st November 2009.
Meals: Full breakfast & dinner included. N$85 lunch.
Directions: Coming from Victoria Falls (Katima Molilo) or from the Etosha National Park (Rundu) on the B8 turn south at Divundu onto D3403, towards Mohembo border post between Namibia & Botswana for 20km. At signpost turn L towards river through Kamotjonga Village, then follow black & white elephant signboards for 2km to lodge.

Index

Index by town name sorted under South Africa, then Namibia

For our rural properties, we have listed the nearest town

Index

Index by house name sorted under South Africa, then Namibia

Index of activities

Gardens
Places with lovely gardens and owners who are enthusiastic gardeners.
5, 6, 7, 8, 10, 12, 13, 14, 15, 17, 18, 19, 22, 24, 25, 27, 30, 31, 37, 40, 41, 42, 43, 44, 45, 46, 47, 48, 49, 50, 51, 52, 53, 54, 55, 56, 57, 61, 62, 63, 66, 67, 69, 71, 77, 78, 80, 81, 82, 83, 84, 85, 86, 87, 88, 89, 90, 91, 93, 94, 95, 97, 98, 100, 107, 108, 109, 110, 111, 112, 113, 114, 115, 116, 118, 121, 123, 124, 126, 127, 128, 129, 130, 134, 135, 136, 138, 139, 140, 142, 144, 146, 147, 148, 150, 151, 156, 157, 158, 160, 164, 165, 166, 168, 169, 172, 173, 174, 175, 178, 181, 182, 185, 186, 187, 188, 192, 193, 194, 195, 197, 198, 199, 200, 202, 203, 204, 205, 206, 207, 208, 209, 211, 220, 221, 224, 226, 232, 233, 234, 235, 236, 237, 238, 239, 240, 241, 242, 244, 245, 249, 250, 251, 253, 254, 255, 256, 257, 260, 265, 266, 267, 268, 269, 271, 272, 273, 275, 276, 279, 281, 282, 283, 285, 286, 287, 290, 291, 292, 293, 296, 298, 299, 300, 307, 312, 314, 315, 316, 322, 324, 328, 329, 330, 331, 333, 345

Rock art
Sites found either on the property or guests can be shown/guided to nearby sites.
6, 8, 66, 67, 68, 69, 70, 92, 138, 146, 147, 149, 176, 191, 196, 197, 210, 211, 229, 230, 233, 236, 238, 262, 264, 265, 266, 268, 269, 270, 271, 272, 273, 275, 280, 281, 282, 283, 284, 287, 289, 299, 312, 317, 324, 331

Culture
Township visits can be organized by owners or cultural experiences (e.g. Zulu dancing) available on site.
1, 4, 6, 8, 10, 11, 12, 14, 15, 16, 17, 23, 25, 27, 28, 29, 30, 31, 32, 33, 34, 35, 36, 37, 38, 40, 43, 45, 46, 48, 49, 51, 52, 53, 54, 56, 57, 76, 77, 79, 80, 81, 82, 84, 85, 89, 90, 91, 92, 95, 97, 101, 104, 105, 112, 113, 121, 125, 127, 137, 139, 148, 149, 152, 156, 171, 172, 173, 174, 175, 176, 177, 178, 179, 182, 185, 186, 187, 196, 199, 202, 203, 205, 206, 209, 210, 211, 213, 217, 218, 219, 220, 221, 223, 224, 228, 230, 233, 236, 242, 243, 244, 245, 246, 247, 248, 249, 250, 251, 252, 253, 254, 255, 256, 257, 258, 259, 260, 262, 263, 264, 267, 268, 269, 270, 271, 272, 273, 275, 278, 279, 280, 282, 283, 284, 287, 292, 295, 296, 297, 298, 299, 300, 301, 302, 303, 304, 305, 308, 309, 311, 312, 313, 315, 316, 317, 318, 319, 324, 325, 329, 330, 333, 345

Wine-maker
Wine made on the property.
76, 77, 78, 83, 84, 85, 88, 105, 106, 107, 113, 117, 118, 129, 184

Good and original cuisine
9, 10, 14, 18, 23, 43, 44, 61, 64, 65, 68, 72, 73, 75, 76, 77, 78, 81, 85, 86, 89, 105, 116, 121, 123, 124, 130, 133, 134, 135, 137, 146, 148, 149, 151, 154, 156, 160, 167, 173, 183, 186, 188, 189, 192, 193, 195, 197, 199, 201, 204, 206, 208, 209, 210, 212, 213, 214, 218, 232, 235, 237, 243, 251, 255, 256, 258, 261, 262, 264, 265, 267, 269, 271, 272, 278, 279, 281, 282, 283, 286, 288, 289, 290, 293, 298, 308, 309, 310, 311, 312, 314, 318, 319, 321, 322, 232, 325, 326, 330, 331, 332, 333, 334, 335, 337, 339, 340, 341, 342, 343, 346, 347, 348

Horse-riding
Available on site.
10, 16, 51, 61, 70, 76, 79, 83, 84, 86, 98, 117, 123, 129, 135, 138, 140, 146, 149, 164, 169, 178, 182, 191, 201, 205, 208, 212, 217, 218, 224, 228, 230, 231, 232, 236, 245, 248, 253, 255, 256, 259, 261, 264, 266, 269, 270, 272, 276, 277, 279, 280, 281, 283, 287, 315, 316, 332, 333

Whale-watching
Available from the property or from so nearby that it makes little difference.
1, 2, 3, 5, 6, 7, 8, 9, 10, 13, 14, 19, 20, 58, 59, 60, 62, 63, 64, 65, 112, 120, 122, 124, 125, 126, 127, 128, 129, 130, 131, 132, 133, 143, 148, 153, 155, 157, 159, 165, 167, 170, 173, 174, 175, 176, 179, 181, 183, 188, 200, 220, 225, 226, 227, 228, 241, 244, 246, 247, 248, 252, 254, 255, 258

Boat Charter
Property owns boats or can organise charters.
2, 4, 5, 6, 8, 9, 10, 11, 12, 14, 15, 16, 18, 19, 20, 22, 27, 29, 32, 33, 34, 35, 37, 40, 43, 48, 51, 52, 54, 58, 62, 63, 64, 65, 84, 98, 110, 112, 124, 126, 127, 128, 130, 131, 132, 133, 135, 139, 146, 148, 150, 151, 152, 153, 154, 155, 158, 160, 161, 162, 164, 167, 168, 169, 171, 172, 173, 174, 175, 176, 177, 178, 179, 182, 183, 185, 186, 198, 199, 200, 201, 202, 203, 213, 216, 217, 218, 219, 220, 221, 222, 223, 224, 228, 239, 240, 242, 244, 245, 246, 247, 248, 250, 252, 253, 254, 255, 256, 257, 258, 259, 260, 266, 273, 275, 279, 284, 292, 326, 343, 344, 345, 349

Canoeing
Canoes owned or organised by the property.
1, 4, 5, 6, 8, 9, 12, 14, 16, 18, 20, 27, 29, 32, 34, 35, 43, 46, 52, 60, 61, 62, 63, 64, 65, 66, 68, 69, 70, 75, 81, 84, 85, 86, 112, 120, 121, 123, 124, 125, 126, 127, 128, 129, 130, 131, 132, 133, 137, 138, 145, 146, 147, 148, 149, 150, 151, 152, 153, 154, 155, 156, 157, 158, 160, 161,

162, 165, 166, 169, 171, 172, 173, 174, 175, 176, 177, 178, 179, 182, 183, 185, 186, 190, 192, 198, 199, 200, 201, 203, 211, 213, 215, 216, 217, 218, 219, 220, 221, 222, 223, 224, 227, 228, 229, 230, 233, 239, 240, 242, 244, 245, 247, 248, 252, 253, 254, 255, 257, 258, 259, 266, 267, 268, 275, 280, 284, 291, 343, 344, 345

Historic house
These places are historic buildings
7, 8, 28, 30, 36, 40, 41, 42, 44, 57, 61, 72, 76, 79, 81, 82, 84, 85, 88, 89, 95, 105, 107, 112, 113, 117, 126, 130, 136, 137, 139, 140, 141, 142, 143, 146, 151, 153, 181, 189, 190, 193, 195, 196, 203, 208, 210, 230, 232, 233, 234, 235, 236, 238, 245, 266, 268, 269, 270, 275, 276, 278, 282, 284, 285, 288, 290, 298, 307, 332

Self-catering
option is available here.
3, 5, 6, 12, 14, 15, 16, 17, 18, 19, 20, 24, 26, 28, 29, 32, 34, 40, 41, 45, 48, 49, 51, 52, 53, 54, 55, 56, 58, 59, 60, 61, 66, 67, 69, 70, 71, 74, 75, 76, 78, 81, 82, 84, 85, 87, 88, 89, 92, 96, 98, 99, 100, 103, 106, 108, 109, 110, 112, 113, 115, 117, 118, 119, 120, 122, 126, 129, 130, 137, 138, 143, 145, 147, 148, 152, 153, 159, 163, 164, 166, 172, 173, 179, 180, 181, 183, 184, 188, 190, 191, 198, 200, 202, 203, 210, 219, 220, 221, 222, 226, 229, 230, 231, 233, 238, 239, 240, 241, 242, 244, 249, 257, 261, 263, 266, 267, 273, 274, 275, 276, 277, 281, 283, 284, 287, 289, 290, 293, 295, 296, 298, 300, 301, 302, 313, 315, 316, 324, 329, 333, 337, 340, 341

Bird-watching
Owners are enthusiasts.
2, 3, 5, 6, 8, 9, 10, 12, 13, 14, 17, 22, 46, 48, 51, 53, 55, 57, 58, 61, 62, 63, 64, 65, 66, 67, 68, 69, 70, 71, 74, 75, 76, 77, 78, 82, 84, 85, 86, 87, 88, 89, 91, 92, 94, 97, 100, 103, 106, 107, 113, 114, 116, 117, 118, 119, 121, 123, 124, 126, 127, 128, 129, 130, 131, 134, 135, 138, 139, 141, 142, 143, 144, 145, 146, 147, 148, 149, 150, 151, 153, 154, 156, 157, 158, 160, 161, 162, 163, 164, 166, 167, 168, 171, 172, 173, 174, 175, 176, 177, 178, 180, 181, 182, 185, 186, 187, 188, 189, 190, 191, 192, 193, 194, 196, 197, 198, 199, 200, 201, 203, 204, 205, 206, 208, 209, 211, 212, 213, 215, 217, 218, 219, 220, 224, 226, 227, 228, 229, 230, 232, 235, 236, 238, 239, 240, 244, 245, 246, 248, 249, 250, 251, 252, 253, 254, 255, 257, 258, 259, 260, 261, 262, 263, 264, 265, 266, 267, 268, 269, 270, 271, 272, 274, 275, 276, 277, 278, 279, 280, 281, 282, 283, 285, 286, 288, 289, 291, 292, 296, 298, 299, 302, 306, 307, 308, 309, 310, 311, 312, 313, 314, 315, 317, 319, 320, 322, 323, 324, 325,

326, 327, 328, 329, 330, 331, 332, 333, 339, 340, 343, 344, 345, 348, 349

Beach house
6, 10, 58, 60, 62, 64, 65, 112, 120, 122, 124, 126, 131, 132, 133, 143, 153, 159, 176, 179, 183, 198, 200, 220, 225, 226, 228, 241, 244, 258

White-water rafting
Can be arranged in-house.
6, 8, 38, 68, 139, 146, 185, 233, 267, 268, 270, 271, 275, 278, 280, 315, 325, 326, 345

Fully child-friendly
Places where children will be particularly well looked-after.
5, 10, 14, 15, 16, 18, 23, 31, 32, 46, 51, 54, 66, 77, 79, 86, 88, 101, 105, 106, 113, 115, 120, 121, 126, 127, 129, 130, 138, 141, 143, 148, 152, 163, 164, 166, 171, 181, 184, 186, 190, 191, 192, 196, 199, 203, 205, 208, 210, 216, 220, 221, 227, 228, 230, 239, 244, 245, 249, 252, 253, 254, 260, 261, 266, 268, 270, 271, 273, 277, 281, 282, 283, 284, 285, 287, 292, 293, 294, 296, 307, 309, 310, 311, 317, 326, 328, 331, 332, 333, 336, 341